SHAKESPEARE SURVEY

ADVISORY BOARD

1. Shakespeare and his Stage
2. Shakespearian Production
3. The Man and the Writer
4. Interpretation
5. Textual Criticism
6. The Histories
7. Style and Language
8. The Comedies
9. Hamlet
10. The Roman Plays
11. The Last Plays (with an index to *Surveys* 1–10)
12. The Elizabethan Theatre
13. King Lear
14. Shakespeare and his Contemporaries
15. The Poems and Music
16. Shakespeare in the Modern World
17. Shakespeare in His Own Age
18. Shakespeare Then Till Now
19. Macbeth
20. Shakespearian and Other Tragedy
21. Othello (with an index to *Surveys* 11–20)
22. Aspects of Shakespearian Comedy
23. Shakespeare's Language
24. Shakespeare: Theatre Poet
25. Shakespeare's Problem Plays
26. Shakespeare's Jacobean Tragedies
27. Shakespeare's Early Tragedies
28. Shakespeare and the Ideas of his Time
29. Shakespeare's Last Plays
30. Henry IV to Hamlet

SHAKESPEARE SURVEY

AN ANNUAL SURVEY OF SHAKESPEARIAN STUDY AND PRODUCTION

30

EDITED BY
KENNETH MUIR

CAMBRIDGE UNIVERSITY PRESS
CAMBRIDGE
LONDON · NEW YORK · MELBOURNE

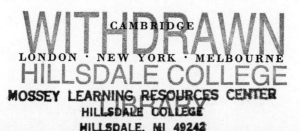

Published by the Syndics of the Cambridge University Press
The Pitt Building, Trumpington Street, Cambridge CB2 1RP
Bentley House, 200 Euston Road, London NW1 2DB
32 East 57th Street, New York, NY 10022, USA
296 Beaconsfield Parade, Middle Park, Melbourne 3206, Australia

ISBN: 0 521 21636 2

First published 1977

Shakespeare Survey was first published in 1948. For the first eighteen volumes it was edited by Allardyce Nicoll under the sponsorship of the University of Birmingham, the University of Manchester, the Royal Shakespeare Theatre and the Shakespeare Birthplace Trust

Printed in Great Britain
at the University Press, Cambridge

The Library of Congress originally catalogued Vol. I of this series as follows:
Shakespeare Survey; an annual survey of Shakespearian study & production. 1–
Cambridge [Eng.] University Press, 1948–
v. illus., facsims. 26 cm.
Editor: v. 1– Allardyce Nicoll.
'Issued under the sponsorship of the University of Birmingham, the Shakespeare Memorial Theatre, the Shakespeare Birthplace Trust.'
1. Shakespeare, William – Societies, periodicals, etc. 2. Shakespeare, William – Criticism and interpretation. 3. Shakespeare, William – Stage history. 1. Nicoll, Allardyce, 1894– ed.
PR2888.C3 822.33 49–1639

EDITOR'S NOTE

Many of the papers included in this volume were delivered at the International Shakespeare Conference at Stratford-upon-Avon in August 1976. The subject was '*Henry IV* to *Hamlet*'. As already announced, the theme of *Shakespeare Survey 31* will be 'Shakespeare and the Classical World'. It will include a retrospect of recent work on the subject by John W. Velz as well as a cumulative index for volumes 21 to 30. The theme of No. 32 will be the three comedies, *Much Ado About Nothing*, *As You Like It* and *Twelfth Night*. Contributions on this theme, or on other topics should reach the Editor (The University of Liverpool, P.O. Box 147, Liverpool L69 3BX) by 1st September 1978, and preferably earlier. Contributors are required to provide brief summaries of their articles and they should leave generous margins, use double spacing, and follow the style and lay-out of articles in the current issue. A style-sheet is available on request. Contributions should not normally exceed 5,000 words. Books for review should be sent to the Editor rather than to the publisher.

K. M.

CONTRIBUTORS

WILLIAM BABULA, *Professor of English and Chairman of the Department, University of Miami*

N. W. BAWCUTT, *Senior Lecturer in English Literature, University of Liverpool*

J. PHILIP BROCKBANK, *Professor of English, University of York*

NICHOLAS BROOKE, *Professor of English, University of East Anglia*

BARBARA EVERETT, *Fellow of Somerville College and Lecturer in English, University of Oxford*

INGA-STINA EWBANK, *Professor of English, Bedford College, University of London*

ANDREW GURR, *Professor of English, University of Reading*

G. R. HIBBARD, *Professor of English, University of Waterloo, Ontario*

R. F. HILL, *Senior Lecturer in English, King's College, University of London*

JOHN ORRELL, *Professor of English, University of Alberta, Edmonton*

RICHARD PROUDFOOT, *Lecturer in English, King's College, University of London*

NORMAN SANDERS, *Professor of English, University of Tennessee*

LEAH SCRAGG, *Lecturer in English, University of Manchester*

DANIEL SELTZER, *Professor of Drama, Princeton University*

CLIFFORD SISKIN, *Assistant Professor, Wayne State University*

J. A. B. SOMERSET, *Associate Professor of English, University of Western Ontario*

JOYCE VAN DYKE, *University of Virginia*

ROGER WARREN, *Lecturer in English, University of Leicester*

CONTENTS

PLATES

'HENRY IV' and 'HAMLET'

G. R. HIBBARD

The hazards inherent in a topic such as this have been unforgettably dramatized by Shakespeare himself. In *Henry V*, as the battle of Agincourt nears its end, Fluellen rashly sets about drawing a Plutarchan parallel between Harry of Monmouth and 'Alexander the Pig' of Macedon, for the edification of Captain Gower. Part of this laboured essay, all too anticipatory of the efforts of many a modern student of literature faced with the odious task of comparison, runs thus:

> I tell you, Captain, if you look in the maps of the 'orld, I warrant you sall find, in the comparisons between Macedon and Monmouth, that the situations, look you, is both alike. There is a river in Macedon; and there is also moreover a river at Monmouth; it is call'd Wye at Monmouth, but it is out of my prains what is the name of the other river; but 'tis all one, 'tis alike as my fingers is to my fingers, and there is salmons in both. (IV, vii, 21–7)[1]

I hope to avoid the more obvious 'salmon-falls'; but a somewhat speculative argument netted from 'the invention-crowded seas' of *Henry IV* and *Hamlet*, either of them an

> Ocean where each [m]ind
> Does streight its own resemblance find,

may legitimately, I think, with apologies to Yeats and Marvell, whose words I have already twisted, claim a touch of 'fishiness' as its right and natural prerogative.

To return to dry land and prose: *Henry IV* and *Hamlet* are both big plays; big not only in the scale of their achievement but also in the simple elementary sense that they are long. And here, to dispose of a much vexed question in summary fashion, let me say at once that I regard the two parts of *Henry IV* as one play in ten acts. I do not think Shakespeare planned it thus. I believe he set out originally to write a play about Hotspur's revolt, but then came to realize, long before that play was complete, that he must continue it because the rich vein of ore he had struck was far from exhausted. Accordingly, he took care to set up the necessary signposts in Part 1 to indicate that Part 2 was to follow; and, by the time he had reached the end of Part 2, Hotspur's revolt had been subsumed into an enormous panoramic view not only of the reign of Henry IV but also of the life of the English people in the days of Queen Elizabeth.

Henry IV and *Hamlet* are long because their author has so much to say, and also because, as I tried to suggest with that reference to the opening lines of W. B. Yeats's 'Sailing to Byzantium', each is impregnated and pervaded by a wonderful fertility, almost a prodigality, of invention. In them the dramatist is like an explorer who has found his way into a new territory that teems with life, and he transmits the excitement of the discovery to us. They abound with themes, with ideas, with actions, and with highly individualized characters, each endowed with his own specific idiom, that manner of thought and utterance which we soon come to recognize as peculiarly and distinctively his. This fertility of invention is evident in the large casts – twenty-seven parts

[1] The text used for all quotations from and references to Shakespeare's writings is that of *The Complete Works*, ed. Peter Alexander (1951).

in *Hamlet*, thirty-five in *1 Henry IV*, and forty-four in *2 Henry IV* – and, above all, in the readiness with which Shakespeare introduces important new characters at a late stage in the action. In *Henry IV*, Shallow and Silence do not appear at all until the second scene of act III in Part 2, nearly half-way through it, and Davy not until the first scene of act V. In *Hamlet*, the last act throws up no fewer than three brand-new figures: the two grave diggers, as earthy as the clay they work in and as dry as the old bones they handle with such familiarity, and the water-fly Osric. In both plays, moreover, there is a fertility and subtlety of design that affects their very texture, making the relationships between some of the leading figures especially intricate and dynamic. By their very co-existence in the same play these figures serve to define and illuminate one another, and, at the same time, to define and give substance to motives and ideas that are of central importance to the drama. Hotspur, Hal, and Falstaff do this for one another and for the idea of honour; Laertes, Hamlet, and Fortinbras do it for one another and for the motive of revenge. In this respect, each play is like a hall of mirrors, reflecting many different yet complementary images of its major concerns and preoccupations.

This wealth of characterization and this richness and complexity of texture, working together to give a potent sense of reality and immediacy to everything that is said and done, are, surely, one of the main reasons why the two plays always have been and still continue to be so popular with audiences and readers alike. But there is, of course, another: each contains a figure who exerts a special kind of fascination because of what he is in himself. Falstaff and Hamlet, dissimilar though they are in other ways, both live by virtue of saying so much and saying it so supremely well: the Monarch of Wit and the Prince of Paradox. Indeed, I should like to suggest that, within the context of Shakespeare's work as a whole, they live in a dialectical relationship to each other. Each is so fully imagined, so instinct with life, so complete and unique in himself, that he begins to take on symbolic overtones. For me, Falstaff ultimately becomes the flesh, not in any allegorical or religious sense, but quite simple as the body, free from all censorship from conscience, morals, or custom, using every resource of wit and intelligence to preserve itself and to gratify its appetites: the flesh, in all its splendour and all its frailty, made articulate as it is nowhere else in literature. And I have Falstaff's own word for this reading of him. Accused by Hal of blatant lying, he retorts:

> Dost thou hear, Hal? Thou knowest in the state of innocency Adam fell; and what should poor Jack Falstaff do in the days of villainy? Thou seest I have more flesh than another man, and therefore more frailty. (*1 Hen. IV*, III, iii, 164–7)

Hamlet – need I say it? – is the obverse of Falstaff: the spirit, subject to conscience, the censor, and using every resource of wit and intelligence, not to stay alive, but to find out the truth, to learn what is the right thing to do, and then to do it. His first words, when he is left alone by himself, are significantly:

> O, that this too too solid flesh would melt,
> Thaw, and resolve itself into a dew!
> (I, ii, 129–30)

They echo, with a striking shift of emphasis, Falstaff's description of himself in *The Merry Wives of Windsor*, as 'a man of continual dissolution and thaw' (III, v, 102–3). The one desires to be free from the flesh; to the other, the loss of even a few ounces of the precious stuff is a cause for complaint and regret.

The two characters have one further thing in common, which may well be a consequence of their proclivities for living in worlds which, though opposite, are both ideal: over the past two hundred years they have obstinately refused to stay within and be confined by the play world in which they began and to which they properly belong. Hamlet, assisted by Goethe and Coleridge, climbed out of it at the end of the eighteenth century and the beginning of the nineteenth. Falstaff, that skilled and unscrupulous recruiter, having enlisted the aid of Maurice Morgann, had made his escape from art into history somewhat earlier, in 1777, to be precise, some eighteen years before the publication of *Wilhelm Meisters Lehrjahre*. The more austere practitioners of the art of literary criticism, those who warn us against 'the intentional fallacy' and the like, may regret, reprobate, and even attempt to reverse such a development; but is it not thus that the truly great products of the creative imagination have made themselves constituent parts of the modern consciousness?

However that may be, it seems clear to me that it was Shakespeare himself who prepared the way out for each of them by providing him with a quite unusually full and interesting past for a character in an Elizabethan play. One who can say, as Falstaff does to the Lord Chief Justice, 'My lord, I was born about three of the clock in the afternoon, with a white head and something a round belly' (*2 Henry IV*, I, ii, 176–7), cries out for a biographer and stakes his claim to a real existence. What would not Boswell have given for such a piece of information about the birth of Dr Johnson? And then there are all the other details of Falstaff's wayward youth: how he lost his voice 'with hallooing and singing of anthems' (I, ii, 177–8); how he was 'page to Thomas Mowbray, Duke of Norfolk' (III, ii, 24–5); how he broke 'Scoggin's head ... when 'a was a crack not thus high' (III, ii, 27–8), and so forth. His fleeting reference to 'old Mistress Ursula, whom I have weekly sworn to marry since I perceiv'd the first white hair of my chin' (I, ii, 226–7) is an open and irresistible invitation to the fancy to indulge itself in the pleasures of conjecture. Who was she? Presumably some misguided and gullible woman with money, on whom the old rogue sponged for years. Among my fishier speculations is the possibility that Ben Jonson took pity on the poor deluded ghostly Mistress Ursula, clothed her generously with flesh, and made her the pig-woman of *Bartholomew Fair*, much the most perfect mate in the whole of Elizabethan drama for Doll Tearsheet's 'whoreson little tidy Bartholomew boar-pig' (II, iv, 221–2).

As for Hamlet, the apparently casual bits of information scattered about the tragedy, that fill in so much of his life up to the beginning of the action, are too well known to require rehearsal; but I cannot forbear from mentioning the curious occasion of his birth. It took place, we learn, on 'that day that our last King Hamlet overcame Fortinbras' (V, i, 140) and killed him, which also happened to be the day, 'thirty years' ago, when the First Clown, who acquaints us with these important facts, took up grave-digging as his life's occupation. In Hamlet's case, when he was born is what matters, not what he looked like when he was born, for there is a fateful concatenation of circumstances depending on that date. The Clown, as he says all this, is standing in the grave he is digging for Ophelia. The next grave he digs will, no doubt, be Hamlet's. Like the iceberg and the *Titanic* in Hardy's poem, he and the Prince have been gradually converging for thirty years, just as the young Fortinbras, without knowing it, has been moving nearer and nearer to the throne of Denmark. Seen in this long perspective of retributory history, Hamlet's tragedy begins, not with his father's murder, nor with his mother's marriage to Claudius, but with his own birth. The play has something of a tragic biography about it.

There are then, it seems to me, certain marked similarities between *Henry IV* and *Hamlet*; but I have not got to the root of the matter yet, for the features of the two plays that I have touched on so far are, I shall now contend, only the more obvious and readily identifiable manifestations of a more profound connection: their pivotal position in the intricate story of the development of Shakespeare's art as a poetic dramatist. At this point I find a text useful, and I take it from T. S. Eliot's essay on John Ford, first published in 1932, and then reprinted in his *Selected Essays*. Eliot writes:

> The standard set by Shakespeare is that of a continuous development from first to last, a development in which the choice both of theme and of dramatic and verse technique in each play seems to be determined increasingly by Shakespeare's state of feeling, by the particular stage of his emotional maturity at the time. What is 'the whole man' is not simply his greatest or maturest achievement, but the whole pattern formed by the sequence of plays; so that we may say confidently that the full meaning of any one of his plays is not in itself alone, but in that play in the order in which it was written, in its relation to all of Shakespeare's other plays, earlier and later: we must know all of Shakespeare's work in order to know any of it. No other dramatist of the time approaches anywhere near to this perfection of pattern, of pattern superficial and profound; but the measure in which dramatists and poets approximate to this unity in a lifetime's work, is one of the measures of major poetry and drama.[1]

We should all agree, I think, that there is a unity of some kind in the Shakespearian *oeuvre*, amazingly varied though that *oeuvre* is, and that this unity embraces the non-dramatic poetry, which Eliot leaves out of count, as well as the plays. But is there anything more to it than our intuitive sense of its presence, and, if there is, in what does it consist, and how is it to be defined? A partial answer to these questions is to say that the unity is there in the voice, in the style, which, while modulating into many tones and many accents as it puts itself at the disposal of a multitude of characters and of almost every form known to dramatic art, nevertheless contrives to retain a distinctive music which is not that made by the voice of Marlowe, or Ben Jonson, or whoever else. Voices are, however, tricky things to deal with; if they were not, there would be no argument over the authorship of *Henry VIII*, for example; and, more to the point, it is not the voice that Eliot writes about; the pattern he refers to is a pattern of meaning.

What he is really on to, though I do not think he puts the matter with the clarity it deserves, is what I take to be the most salient characteristic of Shakespeare's art: the fact that it is pre-eminently an art which is constantly building on itself through a sort of reciprocal process. On the one hand, it is an art that is very open to suggestion. As he writes one work, Shakespeare seems to see the possibility of another growing out of it. On the other hand, it is also extremely self-critical. The links between one play and another are, consequently, of many kinds: some simple and straightforward, others very subtle indeed. The more obvious kind of link is the one I began with: *1 Henry IV* leading to *2 Henry IV*, thence to *Henry V*, and, finally, as I think, to *The Merry Wives of Windsor*. The first sequence of the history plays would seem to have come into being after much the same fashion, and so, with some differences, would the Roman plays. But how did Shakespeare move from the writing of *Henry V* to the writing of *Julius Caesar*, composed in the same year, 1599? Here, incidentally, we can, for once, be reasonably sure about that matter of sequence which Eliot, all too lightly, assumes to be completely established. Much of the answer is, I would suggest, implicit in Fluellen's Plutarchan parallel, for in Plutarch the parallel life to that of Alexander is that of Julius Caesar. Shakespeare had Alexander in mind when writing *Henry V* because he had Caesar in mind, as the Prologue to act V so clearly demonstrates; and my guess is that he had

[1] T. S. Eliot, *Selected Essays* (1951), pp. 193–4.

Caesar in mind, had been reading or re-reading the life, and was already planning a play about him, because Caesar, the Roman conqueror of Gaul, was the classical parallel to Henry V, the English conqueror of France.

There are other connections between *Henry V* and *Julius Caesar* that I should like to touch on briefly for the light they throw on Shakespeare's manner of going to work. Oratory has a large role in both plays; but, while the eloquence of Henry V is an inspiring force binding men together, the eloquence of Antony is a disruptive force, the weapon of the dangerous demagogue. Furthermore, in *Julius Caesar* Henry V himself splits into two, as it were. Hal, the wild prince who shows his real quality at Shrewsbury, becomes Antony, the Roman playboy who shows his real quality as he faces the conspirators immediately after Caesar's assassination; while Henry V the efficient politician becomes Octavius Caesar. The most fascinating thing about *Julius Caesar* in relation to *Henry V* is, however, this: that it is not Caesar's triumphs that Shakespeare chooses to dramatize but his overthrow. It is here that one sees the workings of his creative self-criticism. As a result of writing *Henry V*, he had learnt that success is not so fertile a soil for dramatic cultivation as failure. *Julius Caesar* is about the defeated: Brutus and Cassius, as well as Caesar himself.

The same kind of development, springing from a perception of the other possibility, if I may so describe it, is evident in three other pairs of plays, if not more, in which Shakespeare, having written one play, seems to ask himself the question that Peter's grandfather puts at the end of Prokofiev's 'Peter and the Wolf': 'But what if Peter had not caught the wolf, what then?' In *As You Like It* disguise is a source of strength, enabling Rosalind to stage and control the *dénouement* exactly as she wishes; but in *Twelfth Night* disguise becomes a source of vulnerability, as Viola discovers increasingly as the play goes on, and nowhere more so than in the last scene. *King Lear* and *Macbeth* offer the most striking example of what a reversal in point of view can lead to. Stripped down to the barest essentials of plot, the two tragedies are remarkably alike. But in *King Lear* we see that action from the point of view of Lear/Duncan, whereas in *Macbeth* we see it from the point of view of Macbeth/Albany and Lady Macbeth/Goneril. Something not altogether dissimiliar links *Antony and Cleopatra* to *Coriolanus*. In the one we witness the end of the Roman republic and the beginning of the empire; in the other the infant republic is just emerging from the monarchy which had preceded it. In the one the hero is a middle-aged warrior, in the other a soldier who is little more than a boy. Both are undone by a woman; yet it would be hard to think of two women more unlike than 'the serpent of old Nile' and the Roman matron Volumnia.

I have one further class of connections to add to my list, but before dealing with it I should like to turn back for a moment to T. S. Eliot. He says, you may recall, that 'the choice both of theme and of dramatic and verse technique in each play seems to be determined increasingly by Shakespeare's state of feeling, by the particular stage of his emotional maturity at the time.' I do not think this, as it stands, is very helpful. To argue the degree, at any given time, of Shakespeare's 'emotional maturity' – a rather suspect term in any case in the light of Eliot's essay on *Hamlet* – from the evidence provided by what he was writing at that time is, I think, to engage in idle and pointless speculation. The maturity he seems to have had from a very early stage in his career is artistic maturity, the inner knowledge which either assures the artist that his technical resources are capable of meeting the challenge he is about to subject them to, or warns him against undertaking a task for which he is not yet properly equipped. I mention this artistic maturity here, because it helps to account for those many occasions in Shakespeare's work when he picks up and explores in much greater depth and detail something he has already handled before. The clearest example is, perhaps, his two treatments of the old story of Apollonius of Tyre, which he uses for the frame plot of *The Comedy of Errors* and then refashions, nearly twenty years later, into *Pericles*; but there are many more. *The Rape of Lucrece*, to go no further, already contains the germs of much that will re-appear, far more fully worked out and charged with new significance, in *Troilus and Cressida* and in *Macbeth*.

There is then, a unity about Shakespeare's work, and Eliot is right when he says that we must ideally see each play 'in its relation to all of Shakespeare's other plays'. More than that, however, as the author of 'Tradition and the Individual Talent' rather surprisingly fails to mention, it also needs to be seen in its relation to the whole body of English drama in existence at the time when it was written. The general notion set out in that essay about the way in which each truly new work of art modifies the existing order is peculiarly applicable to Shakespeare's plays, for he was, of all the dramatists of his time, the best informed about English drama of the past, the keenest and most discriminating student of it, and the most skilful in exploiting it for his own specific purposes. Instead of abjuring the 'jigging veins of riming mother wits', as Marlowe had done, he recognized their possibilities and set them to work in the Pageant of the Nine Worthies in *Love's Labour's Lost* and in the 'tedious brief scene of young Pyramus/And his love Thisby' in *A Midsummer Night's Dream*.

I have one final point to make about Eliot's comment, a point which will take me back to *Henry IV* and *Hamlet*. He writes of 'a continuous development' in Shakespeare's art. That is acceptable enough, provided that 'continuous' is not allowed to carry any connotation of 'steady' with it, for there are plays, quite a number of them, in which the dramatist seems to be more concerned with consolidating and exploiting advances already made than with doing anything radically new; and there are others – *Henry IV* and *Hamlet* are, I think, the supreme examples – in which his art makes a sudden leap forward, plays which the modern technological jargon would, no doubt, dub 'break-throughs', but which I prefer to think of, adhering to the kind of horticultural metaphor that Shakespeare himself was so given to, as 'growing points'.

This subjective impression of the newness of the two plays can gratifyingly be supported by evidence from a most unlikely source: statistics. Back in 1943, Alfred Hart published the results of what must have been a most arduous and painstaking piece of research in the form of two articles in *The Review of English Studies*: 'Vocabularies of Shakespeare's Plays' and 'The Growth of Shakespeare's Vocabulary'.[1] Adopting, with a few modifications, E. K. Chambers's dating of the plays, Hart took the vocabulary of *2 Henry VI* as his base, and then counted, among other things, the new words – new in the sense that Shakespeare had not used them before – that the writing of each play, and of the Poems and Sonnets which he treats as a single unit, had brought with it. The earliest entries in his Table IV, which sets out this 'Inflow of Fresh Words', do not, of course, tell one very much, because the first few plays are needed to establish the basic working vocabulary; but if one takes the total derived from the first tetralogy and a couple of the earliest comedies as a base, what follows is likely to be significant. Ignoring, as Hart does not, such important considerations as the varying lengths of the plays and the number of new words in

[1] *Review of English Studies*, XIX (1943), 128–40 and 242–54.

a play as a percentage of its total vocabulary, I shall now quote a few of the raw figures. *Hamlet*, it will surprise no one to learn, has the largest number of new words, 606. It is followed closely by *Love's Labour's Lost*, with 587. Next comes *1 Henry IV*, with 493; then *2 Henry IV*, with 445; and then, to go no farther, *Romeo and Juliet*, with 413.

Now a large influx of new words into a writer's vocabulary is surely an indication that he is doing something fresh: either handling new material or doing something original and unexpected with material that is not new in itself. It therefore follows that the five plays which head the list must all be growing points of some kind, which is exactly what I take them to be. But in the case of *Love's Labour's Lost* the figures do require to be treated with special caution, for, as we all know, one of the main themes of that play is language itself, its use and its abuse, the difference, to put the matter in a nutshell, between 'guerdon' and 'remuneration' – two words which make their first appearance in it, and which Shakespeare only employed once again in his later writing, 'guerdon' in *Much Ado About Nothing* (v, iii, 5) and 'remuneration' in *Troilus and Cressida* (III, iii, 170). Consequently, while I do see *Love's Labour's Lost* as a very important play in the process of development that I am trying to map out, I would place it after the two parts of *Henry IV* and *Romeo and Juliet*, in terms of its significance for this purpose, rather than before them.

There is one further point to be made about Hart's figures before I leave them: they give absolute support to Eliot's view that the development of Shakespeare's art was a continuous process, for they show that the dramatist went on enlarging his vocabulary right down to the end of his career. *King Lear* led him to use no fewer than 408 words that he had never used before; *Antony and Cleopatra* added 281; and *Coriolanus* a further 280. For *Cymbeline*, *The Winter's Tale*, and *The Tempest*, the totals are all in the two hundreds.

In one way, of course, *Henry IV* is the natural and expected sequel to *Richard II*, prepared for and almost promised in that play by such incidents as Richard's prophecy to Northumberland, in v, i, and Bolingbroke's questions about his 'unthrifty son' in v, iii. As Part I opens, the king emphasizes this quality of continuity by deliberately referring back in his first speech to his final words, concluding *Richard II*, in which he promised to 'make a voyage to the Holy Land'; and from this point onwards allusions to Richard II and the usurpation recur again and again until Henry IV is carried off to die in the Jerusalem chamber, the nearest he will ever come to the crusade of expiation that he planned. Moreover, these references to *Richard II* persist into *Henry V*, leading many to conclude that the four plays were planned as a tetralogy. So far we seem to have nothing new. But who in the original audience for *1 Henry IV*, having seen *Richard II* and, perhaps, Shakespeare's earlier histories as well, could possibly have imagined the kind of play that he was about to see? All six of the histories written prior to *Henry IV* are 'tragical histories', and, as befits the dignity of the muses of tragedy and history, they are verse plays. Four of them, *1* and *3 Henry VI*, *King John* and *Richard II* are entirely in verse, except for a five-line proclamation in prose in I, iii of *1 Henry VI*, the only plays in the canon that are wholly in verse. *Richard III* resorts to prose for the murderers of Clarence; and *2 Henry VI* has an unusually high proportion of it, first in the Petitioners' scene, I, iii, then in the Simpcox scene, II, i, and finally and most extensively in the scenes of act IV dealing with Cade's rebellion. Here the prose is, in its own manner, very good indeed, but its primary function is to distinguish the commons from the royalty and nobility.

A further characteristic of the six earlier

histories is that they depend, either immediately, or at second hand, through such intermediaries as the author of *The Troublesome Reign of King John* or Samuel Daniel, on the chronicles for their material. It is true that Shakespeare plays fast and loose with chronology, when it suits him to do so, and that he invents many scenes; but even the invented scenes, such as Richard of Gloucester's wooing of Anne Neville and the murder of Clarence, are at least logical dramatic developments out of historical fact as Shakespeare knew it. After all, Richard did marry Anne, which presumes a wooing of some sort, and, according to Holinshed, Clarence was drowned in a butt of malmsey.

Henry IV, on the other hand, though it is not without its tragical motives and moments, is predominantly 'comical history', for the comedy in it is not confined to the scenes in which Falstaff figures. Hotspur, in particular, makes his own contribution to it as he explodes like a fire-cracker in his scene with Worcester and Northumberland, I, iii, or baits Glendower in III, i. Furthermore, almost half of Part 1, and more than half of Part 2, are in prose, not verse; and most of what happens in these prose scenes has no basis whatever in the chronicles. It is essentially invented by the dramatist; and this observation still applies to the scenes that do bear some relationship to scenes in *The Famous Victories of Henry V*, for the material culled from that source has been so expanded and transmuted as to be almost unrecognizable; out of horse-play and buffoonery has sprung witty exuberant comedy. Paradoxically yet rightly, these invented scenes in *Henry IV* are, it is perhaps worth mentioning, the only scenes in Shakespeare's histories that are taken seriously as history by professional historians. The student of English life and society in the later sixteenth century flies to them like a homing pigeon. Indeed, I have a strong suspicion that Shakespeare, with his keen sense of how the theatre could re-create the past – one remembers Cassius's lines:

> How many ages hence
> Shall this our lofty scene be acted over
> In states unborn and accents yet unknown!
> (*Julius Caesar*, III, i, 112–14)

– knew, when he was writing these scenes, that he was playing his part in the making of a new kind of historical writing which was just coming into being at the time. William Harrison's *Description of Britain* and *Description of England* were only twenty years old when *Henry IV* was first staged, and, since they were part of Holinshed's Chronicle, it seems highly likely that he had read them.

It is, however, in its dramatic and verse techniques, to which I would add prose techniques as well, that the newness of *Henry IV* is most apparent. I spoke earlier about the depth and shadowing that Hotspur, the Prince, and Falstaff give to one another. A somewhat similar technique determines the relationship of scene to scene. It has often been observed how the play-acting in II, iv of Part 1 anticipates, in an ironical manner, the first reconciliation of the Prince with his father, III, ii, and the final scene of Part 2, the rejection of Falstaff. Less notice has, I think, been accorded to the very careful placing of the reconciliation scene. If it had followed immediately on II, iv, it would have been much affected by the scepticism about the sincerity of Hal's reformation which that scene engenders. But between the two scenes comes the rebel council of war. It begins in apparent harmony, but within a few lines of the opening that harmony is broken by Hotspur's contempt for Glendower's belief in omens. Soon they are quarrelling over the division of an England they have not yet conquered; and this quarrel leads, in its turn, to another quarrel about poetry. It is all gloriously funny, but it also has its more serious implications; before it is over, we have grave doubts as to whether a rebellion led by men as divided as these can possibly be successful. The reconciliation scene reverses the process. It begins with the king and the Prince very much at odds; but, by letting his father talk himself out, something Hotspur never lets anyone do, and then promising reformation, Hal eventually establishes harmony between them. Consequently, the king's assertion 'A hundred thousand rebels die in this' (l. 160) carries real weight with it.

But we have not done with III, ii yet. It closes with father and son making their exit together in unity. No sooner have they gone than we find ourselves in the Boar's Head with Falstaff and Bardolph; but the subject is still repentance and reform, with this crucial difference, that these things are now the target of a devastating mockery and disbelief. The scene opens thus:

> *Falstaff.* Bardolph, am I not fall'n away vilely since this last action? Do I not bate? Do I not dwindle? Why, my skin hangs about me like an old lady's loose gown; I am withered like an old apple-john. Well, I'll repent, and that suddenly, while I am in some liking; I shall be out of heart shortly, and then I shall have no strength to repent. An I have not forgotten what the inside of a church is made of, I am a peppercorn, a brewer's horse. The inside of a church! Company, villainous company, hath been the spoil of me.
>
> *Bardolf.* Sir John, you are so fretful you cannot live long.
>
> *Falstaff.* Why, there is it; come, sing me a bawdy song, make me merry.
>
> (*1 Hen. IV*, III, iii, 1–12)

Sic transit contemptus mundi; repentance is having a bad time, and it continues to have it, for when Hal arrives on the scene and eventually tells Falstaff of his reconciliation with the king, which will, he says, allow him to 'do anything', Falstaff's response is: 'Rob me the exchequer the first thing thou doest, and do it with unwash'd hands too' (ll. 181–3). Far from checking this outrageous suggestion, the Prince allows it to stand, and goes on to tell Falstaff that he has procured him 'a charge of foot'. This act of kindness ensures that Falstaff, like the rest, will make his way to Shrewsbury, but it does not lead us to exclaim 'A hundred thousand rebels die in this.' The ambiguities that III, ii seemed to have laid to rest have reared their heads once more. The four scenes, taken together, are like a series of shifting planes, corresponding to the way in which reality presents itself to us in the actual business of living.

Since I have written about them elsewhere,[1] I shall be brief in what I have to say on the new techniques of verse and prose that the writing of *Henry IV* brought with it. No one here will need to be reminded of such extraordinary *tours de force* as the characteristic idioms of Mistress Quickly and Master Justice Shallow, the one chock-a-block with the circumstantial detail of the born gossip, and the other rattling with the repetitions of the old man whose congenital inability to concentrate his mind on anything grows more pronounced with every year that passes. But the achievements that really matter for the future are the poetry of Hotspur and the prose of Falstaff, which stand, I think, in a complementary relationship to each other. Adumbrated to some extent in the relaxed rhythms of the Nurse in *Romeo and Juliet* and in the incorporation of colloquial diction into the verse of the Bastard in *King John*, Hotspur's verse is marked by its 'unpoetical' quality, its responsiveness to the tones of the speaking voice, and its predilection for imagery that is exact and down to earth – the courtier, for example, whose

> chin new-reap'd
> Show'd like a stubble-land at harvest-home.
>
> (*1 Hen. IV*, I, iii, 34–5)

It is verse that bespeaks the man, and, unless I

[1] G. R. Hibbard, '"The Forced Gait of a Shuffling Nag"', in *Shakespeare 1971*, ed. Clifford Leech and J. M. R. Margeson (Toronto, 1972), pp. 87–8.

am badly mistaken, it had an impact on poetry at large. When John Donne begins his poem 'The Triple Foole' with the lines:

I am two fooles, I know,
For loving, and for saying so
In whining Poetry...

I feel pretty well convinced that the 'great frequenter of Playes' in his youth[1] had seen a performance of *1 Henry IV* and listened with approval to Hotspur's tirade against 'mincing poetry' in III, i. Hotspur, I believe, anticipates Donne in his rejection of 'poetical' poetry. As for Falstaff, I will merely quote myself:

> His prose gathers its richness from the infusion into it of the qualities that are more often associated with poetry. It is, to use his own words, 'forgetive, full of nimble, fiery, and delectable shapes' (*2 Hen. IV*, IV, iii, 96–7). The sources from which he draws his images range from the Bible to the belly, but the images themselves are always wonderfully apt.[2]

Hamlet, 'the great amphibium', equally at home in verse and prose, and shifting with effortless ease from the one to the other, is, in this sense, a development out of Hotspur and Falstaff. The Hotspur note is there, for example, in his description of Claudius as

a vice of kings;
A cutpurse of the empire and the rule,
That from a shelf the precious diadem stole
And put it in his pocket.
(III, iv, 98–101)

But, unlike Hotspur, Hamlet does not avoid the poetical and the mythological. He resorts to both in order to express his admiration for his father:

See what a grace was seated on this brow;
Hyperion's curls; the front of Jove himself;
An eye like Mars, to threaten and command;
A station like the herald Mercury
New lighted on a heaven-kissing hill...
(III, iv, 55–9)

His verse has a range that Hotspur's cannot encompass, just as his prose takes in more than Falstaff's. The Falstaffian wit and fondness for unsavoury similes are present in his reply to Rosencrantz's question: 'Take you me for a sponge, my lord?' It runs:

> Ay, sir; that soaks up the King's countenance, his rewards, his authorities. But such officers do the King best service in the end: he keeps them, like an ape an apple in the corner of his jaw; first mouth'd, to be last swallowed; when he needs what you have glean'd, it is but squeezing you and, sponge, you shall be dry again. (IV, ii, 15–20)

But there is an aggressive contempt there which is quite out of Falstaff's reach.

In fact, what is entirely new about Hamlet's whole manner of speaking, whether in prose or verse, is the quite extraordinary intensity of which it is capable, and its power 'to shake our disposition/With thoughts beyond the reaches of our souls' (I, iv, 55–6). The words are his; they are addressed to the Ghost; and, since time is short, I now want to use the Ghost as an illustration of one new dramatic technique that is typical of the play. Our sense today of the Ghost's novelty is likely to be badly blunted by the fact that this ghost is probably the first stage ghost we ever saw. Not so the original audience for *Hamlet*; they were familiar with stage ghosts, whose normal behaviour is described for us by the author of *A Warning for Fair Women*:

a filthy whining ghost,
Lapt in some foul sheet or a leather pilch,
Comes screaming like a pig half-stickt,
And cries 'Vindicta! revenge, revenge!'[3]

What must have fascinated that original audience is that the Ghost says nothing whatever either in I, i or in I, iv, for the earlier stage ghosts of the time are extremely loquacious. Moreover, the thought processes of those

[1] Sir Richard Baker, *Chronicle of the Kings of England* (1643), Part II, p. 156.
[2] See note 4.
[3] Modernized from the facsimile edition by J. S. Farmer (1912), Ind., 48–51.

earlier ghosts, though obsessive in their concern with revenge, are, in other respects normal, disappointingly so. But the Ghost in *Hamlet*, having unfolded its terrible story, goes on to tell the hero: 'Taint not thy mind' (I, v, 85). As a piece of practical advice, that is positively lunatic. One feels that the Ghost must have taken leave of its senses; and then one realizes that to take leave of one's senses, or rather to be taken leave of by them, is the necessary first step to becoming a ghost. It is precisely its abnormal ways of thinking that make this ghost so ghostly.

In one sense, *Hamlet* seems to have sprung out of nowhere. By this, I mean that I can make no guess as to how it came into being or what shift of imaginative interest led Shakespeare to this subject, so unlike anything he had handled before. Was it a reaction from the deliberate restraint that he appears to have exercised in the composition of *Julius Caesar*? I do not know. The one thing I can, I think, say with confidence is that *Hamlet* would not be the play it is, had not Shakespeare come to the writing of it by way of the history play. In the other revenge plays of the time, both earlier and later, plotting, murder, adultery, fornication and, above all, revenge are not merely full-time occupations but the only occupations. As a result, even such a masterpiece in its own kind as *The Revengers Tragedy* tends, in the last analysis, to lose touch with reality; the world in which it takes place is too circumscribed a place for us to accept it as an adequate image of human life anywhere or at any time. But in *Hamlet* this is not the case. The Danish court is the place where the government of the country is carried on; ambassadors go from it to other countries; players come to it to provide entertainment for a king and his courtiers. The value of all this in anchoring down the strange business of ghosts and poisonings to the sea-bed of common experience is enormous.

I have one last point to make. In suggesting that *Henry IV* and *Hamlet* are revolutionary plays I have, I am relieved to say, the support of their author. Both are the work of a man who knows that he has altered the shape and scope of English drama and who expects his audience to be aware of the fact. Ancient Pistol is clearly an inveterate playgoer, with a pronounced taste for the heroic. Much addicted to the mighty line, and blessed with a memory that is both retentive and inaccurate, he is a master in the art of garbling. Audiences warmed to him because he had a double appeal for them. On the one hand, he reminded them of many a play that had given them pleasure in the past; on the other, he offered them the added and more refined pleasure of recognizing how absurd and ridiculous much in those old plays now appeared in the light of what Shakespeare was doing in *Henry IV*.

Similarly, he relies on his audience's knowledge of earlier English drama, in order to keep the two inset plays in *Hamlet* distinct both from the play proper and from one another. 'Aeneas' tale to Dido . . . where he speaks of Priam's slaughter' (II, ii, 440–2) is not – and here I find myself in complete agreement with Clifford Leech[1] – meant as burlesque, but it is intended to appear, and does appear, somewhat archaic and stiff by contrast with the flexible verse of the main play. There is much of Marlowe about it. The archaism of the second play-within-the-play is another matter. The poetic cheese with which 'The Mousetrap' is baited is decidedly mouldy. Its three marked features are: its almost unremitting use of closed couplets; its wrenching of normal syntax for the sake of rhyme; and its recourse to long-winded peripharases. The Player King requires no fewer than six lines in order to tell the Player Queen 'We have been married

[1] Clifford Leech, 'The Hesitation of Pyrrhus', in *The Morality of Art*, ed. D. W. Jefferson (1969), pp. 41–9.

thirty years', something she might have been expected to know as well as he.

The man who wrote these inset plays, created Ancient Pistol, and gave Falstaff that Euphuistic speech in the play-acting scene of *Henry IV* clearly knew the tradition inside out, and knew also what he, with his individual talent, had done to the tradition. But since I do not wish to emulate the Player King's prolixity, I conclude.

PRINCE HAL AND TRAGIC STYLE

DANIEL SELTZER

There is one stage direction in an interlude of 1567, called *Horestes, or an interlude of Vice*, probably by John Pickeryng, which is worth, I think, all the rest of the text. After Horestes's assault upon the castle of Clytemnestra and Aegisthus, and his battle (which, we are told, must be as long as possible),[1] the play becomes for some pages a moral debate between Nature and Horestes over the punishment of his mother. Once Horestes has captured Clytemnestra, and ordered Aegisthus killed, he has to decide what to do with her – and he must decide this by himself, for Electra doesn't appear in this little interlude. He gets counsel, however, from another source – the Vice, of course, who has been previously unnamed, but who soon identifies himself: his name is Revenge. Horestes is given very few lines at this point in the play, though the decision is one of some moment; and one can't help the feeling that John Pickeryng, whoever he was, suddenly found himself with a character on his hands who needed more words than he knew how to provide. Nature urges Horestes not to become a matricide, and offers all the right reasons in lumbering fourteeners; but the Vice approaches, tells Horestes that his name is, after all, Revenge, and offers to solve his problem for him; let *him* kill Clytemnestra. It is here, in the margin of the text, where the stage direction to which I have referred is printed: 'Here Horestes sigheth hard.'[2]

Poor John Pickeryng: he had brought himself, unwittingly, to one of the hardest problems which could confront a playwright. The Elizabethans had no jargon name for it, but they certainly knew about it as a phenomenon of character on stage. We do have a name, borrowed from the vocabulary of actor training: internalization. It is clear that if Pickeryng had had the words he would have written them – 'would they out', as Thersites says of Ajax – but his stage direction is the best he can muster, and for our purposes it tells us much.

It is the first evidence of which I am aware in the developing Tudor drama which reveals literally a playwright's concern for expression of inner feeling below the textual surface of a play. Now we might assume that it takes no ghost come from the grave to tell us *that*; that naturally a character's words – or stage action – would always express interior emotion and thought. Surely in about three decades Shakespeare's characters and others were doing just that, and surely that is what acting has always been about, whatever its style.

But after all it is not that simple, and the complexity arises not because such expression can be done well or badly, either by playwright or actor, but because we have, I suggest, no reason to assume that before Shakespeare any playwright had really considered, let alone solved, the problem of causing verbal expression to spring naturally from the inner life of the stage personality – nor, indeed, that the conception of a character as a 'personality', as we use the word, possessing a life below the level of the text, was really a dramaturgical issue. I am aware that I am getting dangerously close to discussing what Stanislavski called a

[1] Malone Society Reprints, ed. Daniel Seltzer (Oxford, 1962), ll. 861–8 (Sig. D.i).

[2] ll. 891–3 (Sig. D.i. verso).

'*sub*-text', and doing it in a scholarly paper, too; but I think discussion of the problem is enlightening, and even if it may be indecorous it will do none of us any harm.

Obviously there is no question that earlier dramatists had dealt with the issue of motivation producing results, of reaction and choice springing from an interior or exterior stimulus. When Tamburlaine has to decide whether or not to allow himself to love Zenocrate, Marlowe gives him a soliloquy[1] in which to set forth the pros and the cons, and then to make his choice: that adoration of Zenocrate's beauty, far from making his military persona effeminate, will actually enlarge his *virtù*, the majesty of his own worthiness, as would the acquisition of a new continent. Margaret of Fressingfield, in Greene's *Friar Bacon*, has to decide between becoming a nun or marrying Lacy, and as the late Alfred Harbage used to say, one can hear the cheers of the audience echoing down the centuries when she exclaims, after what must be assumed to have been an inner decision, 'The flesh is frail... Lacy for me, if he will be my lord!'[2] And of course there are many, many other examples of action which is meant to be caused by apparent or verbalized interior processes of choice-making. The point is that although in each case the choice is made and the action taken – whether it be weighty or trivial – never before a certain point in the development of western drama is the choice-making itself a subject, as it were, of the drama. A character may discuss how difficult a certain decision is; or, as is the case in *Horestes*, some external stage action will demonstrate that difficulty – but the felt existence of an inner life from which motivation and action both spring, one causing the other, was not, I think, a component of Elizabethan dramaturgy before a certain time in the development of Shakespeare himself.

I want to suggest that this time occurred in the late nineties, during the composition of the *Henry* plays; that although Shakespeare shows us earlier that he was aware of the need for such a technique (for a technique it is, after all), he did not render it fully in plays written before *1* and *2 Henry IV*; that the technique itself, while no doubt Shakespeare did not acquire it as a conscious exercise, was a pre-requisite for the creation of the central figures of those plays we call the major tragedies; and finally, therefore, that Hal himself becomes the stage character whose 'personality' is one of the most pivotal in the playwright's career, for in its composition he acquired the ability to make a character change internally.

Let me make it clear that I am not speaking – or speaking only – here about a character's 'expression' of the difficulty of expression. Some years ago, Anne Barton dealt with such matters,[3] and brilliantly developed related questions of stage personality and language, and she cited, for example, the lines of the sadly inadequate King of Persia, Mycetes – lines which indeed open Part I of *Tamburlaine*: 'Brother Cosroe, I find myself aggrieved, / Yet insufficient to express the same, / For it requires a great and thundering speech:...'

There are many examples of Elizabethan characters who comment on the inadequacy of language itself, or that it is itself, or other outward physicalizations of emotion, inappropriate, or that they themselves are incapable of it. Quintillian's advice to orators was well-known, that if one wished to articulate the greatest hyperbole then he should say simply that such articulation was impossible – that there were no adequate words. Hamlet tells his mother that wearing mourning is only one way to show sorrow, and an inadequate one at that, for he has that within which no outward form could

[1] v, i, 135–90.

[2] Sc. xiv, ll. 86, 92.

[3] Anne Barton, 'Shakespeare and the Limits of Language', *Shakespeare Survey*, *24* (Cambridge, 1971), pp. 19–30.

accurately demonstrate:

> 'Tis not alone my inky cloak, good mother,
> Nor customary suits of solemn black,
> Nor windy suspiration of forc'd breath,
> No, nor the fruitful river in the eye,
> Nor the dejected haviour of the visage,
> Together with all forms, moods, shapes of grief,
> That can denote me truly. These indeed seem,
> For they are actions that a man might play;
> But I have that within which passes show –
> These but the trappings and the suits of woe.
>
> (I, ii, 76–85)

The speech is of course familiar, but Hamlet's reference to acting has perhaps not received the sort of attention it merits in this context. Elizabethan acting styles are not specifically my subject here, and in any case I have dealt with them at length elsewhere;[1] but to pursue the present point one must at least summarize some opinions which are now so general that they need not be documented at length. The Elizabethans believed, as did citizens of any age, that the best performed arts of the stage were those which, quite simply, conjured up an impression of reality itself, and Hamlet, no doubt a good amateur actor, is only paraphrasing, though eloquently, a series of commonplaces which he elaborates later in the play in his Advice to the Players. He speaks of moderation and good taste as essential talents in holding a mirror up to Nature, and, appropriately, he has just praised Horatio – just as eloquently – only a moment or two earlier, for being such a reasonable, well-moderated human being. Hamlet does not include in his Advice to the Players any words about inner feeling, or the relation of such feeling to verbalized expression; but very soon one of his most anguished soliloquies is itself motivated by the fact that one of these professionals actually began to cry during a speech about Priam's death and Hecuba's reaction to it. Polonius, with the astonishment of many vulgar and unfeeling laymen, has noted the same thing: it is amazing to him that the actor can *feel*, that the words are connected with feelings, and that it is the *feelings* which are being acted – and indeed – though of course Polonius would not be interested – that the words are only part of a fabric of action, all of which exists in the first place because of feelings. The energy of the 'Rogue and peasant slave' soliloquy itself emerges from Hamlet's anguish not that he can't feel enough, but that for one reason or another he is not acting in a certain pattern of ways upon his feelings. And he does not say that the Player's tears were fraudulent; his anger grows out of his observation that in fact they were real – and Hamlet is a reliable and sophisticated playgoer, even if Polonius isn't.

Discussion about Elizabethan acting styles has taken several turns over the past two decades, and critics have held varying and sometimes conflicting viewpoints; but here the important observation to make is not whether these styles were, could we see them, 'formalized' or 'naturalistic',[2] or whether they were (as I think) what we would define as a curious combination of techniques – the point is rather that Shakespeare took it for granted that, whatever their style, good actors did indeed feel the emotions of the characters they were playing, that there was indeed some magical enjambment of the talented stage artist's interior person with the needs and feelings of the role. There is of course a strong tradition that Burbage in some way actually entered the roles which made him famous – that he seemed to observers (whatever his style) actually to 'become' the character.

We can take this point a little further. In his reply to Gertrude in the second scene, Hamlet lists a number of actions 'that a man might play', none of which, he says, would 'denote

[1] 'The Actors and Staging,' in Kenneth Muir and S. Schoenbaum, ed., *A New Companion to Shakespeare Studies* (Cambridge, 1971), pp. 35–54.

[2] See 'Reading List,' *ibid.*, p. 264.

me truly'. Hamlet is making a distinction between two modes of human behavior, both translated into a performance metaphor, which are applicable to the same two modes of stage activity, and the way people in the theatre describe them, today. One mode is very rare indeed: it is the one of which Hamlet observes the player to have been capable, that is, not simply an evocation of something 'like' life, but life itself – the phenomenon we observe all too rarely in the theatre, the fully inhabited performance, as one might say. The second mode is very common, and although we pay lip service to the other, we silently acknowledge that most of the time, we have to be satisfied with a collection of denotements, of actions (the same words would come up in modern rehearsals) 'a man might play', meaning that in 'playing' them he is only – another jargon word – *demonstrating*, rather than 'being'. Some actors are very good demonstrators, and most of the time we are so bored, or so preoccupied with unrelated matters, or simply so accustomed to common stage habits, vocal or physical, that they become our habits, our accepted signals of reality, as well as those of the lazy, or ill-rehearsed, or – as Hamlet would know – untruthful actor – that is, the actor whose personality is standing to one side of the one he is playing, and, however skillfully, only 'demonstrating' it.

Curiously, the word *demonstrate* is used by Shakespeare, the few times he uses it in this context, the same way a modern acting student or teacher would do: to 'demonstrate' is to 'play' without the truth of inner feeling, to act 'out', rather than to 'be'. Perhaps the most terrifying line in *Othello*, for example, is Iago's flat statement to Roderigo, 'I am not what I am' – and he elaborates, explaining the difference between being and seeming. 'The native act and figure of my heart' is Iago's phrase for what is really, innerly, true, and it is – as are many of Iago's phrases – as apt as any other could be in precision and directness; Iago speaks of the 'outward action' which might '*demonstrate*' this 'native act and figure of my heart / In complement extern', and then, leading up to the proof ('I am not what I am') he observes that following that 'demonstration', it will not be long before he '[wears his] heart upon his sleeve / For daws to peck at...' In other words, 'actions that a man might play' are not only such behavioral acts as Hamlet's list of the demonstrations of mourning, but are like Richard Gloucester's list of mimetic abilities in *3 Henry VI*, and Buckingham's, in *Richard III*, which prove that he 'can counterfeit the deep tragedian'. Among these techniques, Richard says, are 'artificial tears', but it's worth emphasizing that such tears and those of the actor whose color altered and whose tears welled up as he spoke of Hecuba are, while differently motivated, equally 'truthful' – for Richard is a consummate actor. We all have known in our own lives at least one person who could make the tears come when needed, whether or not such a person earned a living on stage; but the way it is done is first to conjure up the feeling which might produce the result – Stanislavski called it 'Sense Memory' – in other words, to 'denote truly'. For Richard Gloucester, the tears are a demonstration only from our moral viewpoint; artistically they might be as truly denoted as those of Hamlet's actor. For that matter, having brought Horestes to the emotional state in which he finds himself before Clytemnestra's judgement, there is no reason to assume that Pickeryng's stage direction requiring the actor to '[sigh] hard' could not be accomplished with true feeling. After all, when Macduff is too moved to speak, he can only pull his hat over his eyes. The moments are of course vastly different in degree of sophistication of writing and evocation of situation; but in kind they are the same theatrically.

I have dwelt long upon Shakespeare's – and his characters' – awareness of the distinction between felt and demonstrated action because if there were none, one could not postulate the capability to change inwardly which is a characteristic of heroes capable of tragedy. That change is not simply built into so many words – does not exist only on the verbal level of the texts – but is the criterion of a certain kind of human being's felt projection of an inwardly oriented life; and we perceive it exactly that way.

One of the things actors of the larger Shakespearian roles come to realize, and one of which I think scholars must be aware as well, is that characteristic of a role which allows it to grow in a time-scale commensurate with the experiential time of the play. The phenomenon of compressed time in Shakespeare, such as in *Othello*, with which we are all familiar, is exactly the opposite of this characteristic, which specifically exists in the sequentially expressed words and actions of one of the major figures, in most speeches lasting more than a few lines. It is a difficult but an important phenomenon to try to describe, and my documentation (if that is what it is) is here and there as much intuited as it is supported by explicit textual references.

We are all familiar with that sort of speech in Tudor playwriting – especially in earlier decades – which can be called explanatory in nature. Professor Beckerman has described[1] the various modes of solo speech found throughout the period, and we know that often they overlapped – what might be called soliloquies of introspection and explanation often merge with those apostrophic in nature. We also know, or think we can assume with some confidence, that there was perhaps more audience address in solo speech than scholars of the subject used to think. Especially in speeches by the Vice character and his descendants, even in the most sophisticated ones such as Iago's, the spectators would be included in the speaker's hopes and plans, and the tone of address would be often, though not always, direct and explanatory. Even in speeches composed of subject matter one might automatically categorize as 'introspective' or 'meditative', a tone is pervasive which one can only call explanatory – not, as in the Vice's, of actions about to be taken and why, but of feelings felt, or about to be felt. Sometimes, indeed, the playwright's decision is to have his character announce to the audience, in the tone of explanation, what it is he is about to meditate upon, such as in these lines from *Calisto and Melebea* (*c.* 1527), in which Calisto prays for Sempronio's good fortune, then says,

> To pass the time now will I walk
> Up and down within mine orchard,
> And to myself go [commune] and talk,
> And pray that fortune to me be not hard,
> Longing to hear whether made or marred....
> (306–10)

The speech is rather remarkable in that it does so clearly what seems to be the case so often in later plays, even well into the Shakespearian period: it is not sententious, but personal; but the character presents, in fact, the subject matter for a soliloquy which the playwright did not wish (or did not know how) to compose. Although the speech is, in its own terms, 'introspective', it rings of explanation. Calisto *announces* what his emotions are, but does not actually express them (on stage, anyway). Although granting that this is a very primitive example, it represents a mode of Tudor dramaturgy which pervaded the whole period – which became so sophisticated, of course, by the turn of the century, and especially later, in the plays of the better dramatists, as to be hard to detect; but it is vital that we do so, for it is exactly the sort of speech which denotes,

[1] Bernard Beckerman, *Shakespeare at the Globe, 1599–1609* (New York, 1962), pp. 183–6.

one might say, which is written in such a manner as to make it difficult for an actor to use as a channel toward inner feelings, and then use his art to show that the feelings have in fact conjured up the words. The mode to which I am referring may be called 'descriptive', or, perhaps, 'presentational'. Emotions are described, as it were, instead of seeming to spring into being with the words – and (this is important) at precisely the same time as the articulation of the words.

The plays of Shakespeare are full of such speeches, and not only at the beginning of his career; eventually (by which I mean around 1598–9) he simply writes, with incredible ease, it seems, exactly the sort of speech the actor 'needs' at that precise moment in the play. But speeches in the descriptive mode were the most common device of self-presentation of character which Shakespeare would have found in professional stage practice in the early 1590s, and naturally be began at once to use what he found – it was, after all, one of his greatest talents to do so, and eventually to transform what he found into something more apt for his purposes. As scholars and teachers we are perhaps too fond of pointing out what a traditionalist he was, how his conventions of playwriting were after all the conventions of his time; but while these things are true in many terms, it is also vital to recall that he was also in some ways a profound innovator, that many of his plays, or portions of them, would be regarded, were we able to detect them in works equivalently new today, as containing important new devices of stage practice.

The two plays called tragedies, written before the *Henry IV* plays, are *Titus Andronicus* and *Romeo and Juliet*, but I think it is unnecessary to discuss at length the reasons why we generally regard them, whatever their individual values, as experiments in modes of playwriting to which Shakespeare did not return – unless, in terms of *Romeo*, we remember that accident, mistaken identity, both literal and metaphysical, and error – in the full force of the word – were narrative devices to which he was indeed to return in his development of forms of comedy. Neither play anticipates the real resonance of later Shakespearian tragedy because neither contains any moment during which an interior growth occurs within the hero, or, for that matter, the heroine. I am not unaware of the ways in which Shakespeare demonstrates how great sorrow can make a central figure of drama in some ways a better poet – but this is, after all, exactly the point; Titus, Romeo, and Juliet may become more movingly adept at *describing* the emotional weight of what they feel, but there are no lines in either text which seem to spring, moment by moment, line by line, in precise counterpoint to real time, from inwardly felt change, from true human growth, except, perhaps, for Romeo's 'Oh I am Fortune's Fool', or 'then I defy you, stars'. The plays in which such moments occur, with lines to body them forth, are the two histories, *Richard III* and *Richard II*. Interestingly, it was in the histories that Shakespeare learned to focus upon the developing experience of a single character, that experience eventually projected in ways which elicit the emotional responses, both in the character and in an audience, implicit in the theatrical effect we call 'tragic'.

Both Richard III and Richard II are masters of improvisatory techniques. Their artistic talents of this sort are very similar, in fact, to those which a good acting teacher would be delighted to discover in one of his students: both can extract situational and verbal development from a given situation (which is what improvisation means), can build creatively upon the 'givens' of a particular situation – Richard III in the traditionally active ways of the Elizabethan villain, Richard II with that emotional fecundity which gives easy access to feelings, the incremental sequence of which reflects a special type of personality, and which have just as quick an access to verbal expression. If I may stay with the image of an acting-class for a moment, Richard III's instructor would find him especially adept at improvisations requiring immediate physicalization of intellectual activity, while Richard II's teacher, noting an equal lack of inhibition to physicalize emotional reactions, would see at once that this pupil's major energy expresses itself instead in an uninhibited flow of words, a supple talent to dramatize inner emotions poetically.

In both cases, their stage lives – the series of exposures to us of *their* experience of their lives – are full of examples of full theatrical correlation between the felt thought or need and the requisite words, but also of the mode I have been trying to describe in more detail: that in which the actor (in full fusion with the 'character') seems somehow to stand a little to one side of himself, and to describe what is going on inside him. Whenever Shakespeare chooses this mode, it is exactly what is wanted – Richard III's speeches of planning, for example, in which his self-irony actually comments upon and expands our sense of his relish in that planning; Richard II's extended images of himself as a martyr or religious recluse, or, more to the point, his presented images of himself as annointed king, full of a magisterial command of the right descriptive vocabulary.

Both roles contain as well, however, examples of the true denotement of the 'act and figure' of their hearts, the absolutely closed circuitry between impulse and action, verbal or physicalized; this is a kind of theatrical realism which I submit was new, in kind, in the period. One thinks of Richard III's inspired – and, I am certain, entirely improvised – wooing of Lady Anne, or, for that matter, the words that spring from his shocked surprise that his own physical self-image may not be after all as grotesque as he had supposed; or Richard II's impulse actually to kiss English ground as soon as he sets foot upon it, or his marvellously complex and self-confident use of those two vitally important stage properties in the so-called 'deposition' scene, the crown and the mirror. These are actions and words in which we feel the presence of interior life and outward manifestation entirely enmeshed, simultaneous – as I have suggested, a circuit of energies that makes them inseparable.

There are two other sections in the stage lives of each of these Richards, however, which do not seem to me so successfully rendered, though one may come closer to what the playwright was aiming for than the other. I mean those moments which come to represent, in the later tragedies, the central figure's newly developed ability to define himself, to identify not only what we might call his present emotional situation, but to understand, feelingly, how he has come to it: to perceive, to put it a little differently, the significance of his part in the narrative through which he has just passed. This juncture comes very close to what Aristotle must have meant by *anagnorisis*, a new 'in'-sight – a statement which has emotional meaning, but which also tends to define moral function – a function which the character's stage life has shown us to have been distorted, or obscured, perverted by misdefinition, by passion, or by a combination of these with a misuse of other human beings, or indeed by danger wrought by them as well. To paraphrase the oracle in *The Winter's Tale*, it is a moment, or series of moments, when that which has been lost is found – and, when found, articulately but also feelingly described by the character. These articulations will be a *felt* denotement of the 'native act and figure of the heart'. More, these moments come when they do – almost always at the end, or close to the end, of the total action – because they have a theatrical logic which could have placed them nowhere else, at no earlier time. Such a moment corresponds, then, exactly, to the development in the hero's life when he is emotionally and intellectually able to articulate the feelings it embodies, and not before. When successfully rendered by the playwright and the actor, it is always a supreme example of the phenomenon of dramaturgy I mentioned a little while ago: the precise chronological correspondence between a time in the character's life and our minute-for-minute perception of its passage. It is not 'compressed'; neither is it emblematic or symbolical: in every sense it is a conjuring up of felt reality.

Shakespeare clearly attempts to give both Richard III and Richard II speeches which represent the textual surfacing of this sort of self-knowledge. In the case of the former, it remains, however, almost entirely in the self-descriptive, 'presentational' mode, though there are moments of true closure with an active inner reality: 'I am a villain! Yet I lie, I am not. / Fool, of thyself speak well...' – and a bit later, 'There is no creature loves me; / And if I die, no soul will pity me...' (v, iii, 192–3; 201–2). Yet most of the speech following Richard's dream retains the tonality of a character somehow standing to one side, describing emotions rather than believing them. We are really only further along the path of the same dramaturgy in which Cambises, staggering on stage with his own sword in his side, simply announces that his own misdeeds have been just reason for the accident which takes his life; Richard, almost in the mode of a Brechtian scene description flashed on a screen before or after an episode, describes not only what we have just seen, but what is going on internally: 'Methought the souls of all that I had murdered / Came to my tent, and every one did threat / Tomorrow's vengeance on the head of Richard' (205–7).

At the corresponding moment toward the end of *Richard II*, the hero again tries to articulate interior thought and emotion. The tone is self-descriptive and explanatory almost throughout:

> I have been studying how I may compare
> This prison where I live unto the world;
> And for because the world is populous,
> And here is not a creature but myself,
> I cannot do it....
>
> (v, v, 1–5)

There is a moment of anguished immediacy, of present-time union between the inner wish and the words: 'Yet I'll hammer it out!' In its energy and immediacy, the moment is very similar to Hamlet's 'About my brain!' – both characters seem to say, in effect, here and now I'll solve it. But then, for about thirty lines Richard hovers between explanatory description of the process and a feeling projection of the process itself; until his fantasy of regained kingship thrusts both the playwright, the character, and the actor simultaneously into the mode which makes us aware that moment for moment, we are experiencing *his* experience:

> Thus play I in one person many people
> And none contented; sometimes am I king,
> Then treasons make me wish myself a beggar.
> And so I am. Then crushing penury
> Persuades me I was better when a king.
> Then am I kinged again, and, by and by,
> Think that I an unkinged by Bolingbroke,
> And straight am nothing. But whate'er I be
> Nor I, nor any man that but man is,
> With nothing shall be pleased, till he be eased
> With being nothing. (ll. 31–41)

Here – I believe for the first time in Shakespeare, and, therefore, for the first time in English drama, our focus in the theatre is forced upon the central character's acceptance and identification of what might be called the responsibility of the self; and the focus is achieved by dramaturgical means which allow us to believe in the immediate reality of the situation, which is at once objectively moral and subjectively and emotionally oriented.

'Allow us', I say, because we would have no choice even if we wanted one: the phenomenon of living theatre is precisely to conjure up new life, not simply to 'mirror' it as though it were off in another room somewhere, as if an imitation – that word we have been taught to use – were all that appears before us. This is the thing itself, not an 'action that a man might play'; though the 'playing' (the ritual magic that an actor contributes, infused by the opportunity given by a text) is the medium that effects the energy of the moment. Richard II achieves what he knows and feels exactly at the moment we understand, feelingly, that he knows and feels it; there is no descriptive element, no after-the-fact analysis.

This moment in the sequential action of a certain kind of play is essential to the effect we call 'tragedy', and to the sense of gift we experience, of human and humane generosity, when great actions end – and perhaps the whole phenomenon is really why tragedy, at least Shakespearian tragedy, is more life-affirming than it can ever be made nihilistic, even by the most massive stage talents such as Peter Brook's or Paul Scofield's. Our own inner concentration remains where the character's has found its greatest and deepest point of self-realization.

Now this was a most important device of dramaturgy for Shakespeare to have found, or developed (I would never suggest, let me repeat, that he came upon it as a planned exercise); but so far in his career it had existed in such depth once only, or at least very rarely, except during moments of stage life when it was not so necessary, so elementary to the final effect of the play. I want to suggest that the range and depth with which it exists in *Hamlet*, *Othello*, *Macbeth*, and *Lear* could not have been found by the playwright had he not first utilized this mode with such experimental variety in the role of Hal in *1* and *2 Henry IV*. Hal of course is no *tragic* hero, but the depths of the character correspond in interesting ways to depths which the center of tragic focus must achieve. There is no question that Shakespeare wanted him to hold the human and moral center in both plays – even though he is only on stage for five episodes in Part Two – and to project more than the persona of a prince educating himself in some curiously modern socio-economic laboratory of human relations; and certainly more than a young, manipulative conservative pretending to be hail-fellow-well-met. Surely we have had enough complex, deep, and ranging performances of the role in our own times to tell us there is great potential and inner conflict in the part – and that if these emerge in performance, they do not appear to be there only because such deep, varied, and (perhaps) conflicted actors have projected such qualities of their own, or their directors', invention. I think of Kenneth Tynan's review of the young Richard Burton, making his Stratford debut in 1951:

> Burton is a still, brimming pool, running disturbingly deep. At 25, he commands repose and can make silence garrulous. His Prince Hal is never a roaring boy; he sits, hunched or sprawled, with dark unwinking eyes; he hopes to be amused by his bully companions, but the eyes constantly muse beyond them into the time when he must steady himself for the crown. 'He brings his cathedral on with him', said one dazed member of the company. . . . Fluent of gesture, compact . . . of build, Burton smiles where other Hals have guffawed; relaxes where they have strained; and Falstaff . . . must work hard to divert him. In battle, Burton's voice cuts urgent and keen – [he is] always likeable, always inaccessible. If he can sustain and vary this performance through the end of *Henry V*, we can safely send him along to swell the thin company of living actors who have shown us the mystery and the power of which heroes are capable.[1]

I wish I could have seen this Hal; I suspect that some sense of the remoteness of personality

[1] *A View of the English Stage, 1944–63* (London, 1975), p. 112.

which comes through in Tynan's review must have been similar to that which I felt in Ian Holm's projection of the part in more recent years. Obviously, it was a remoteness – an inaccessibility, to use Tynan's word – which simultaneously prevented, or precluded, intimacy but was capable of projecting warmth. This prince was clearly an attractive human being, yet one who suggested, as did Mr Holm's, a complex interior life – one full of conflicting needs, and, therefore, vulnerable: which probably accounts for that strange ability to attract which some young people have who are themselves human beings of few words, whose inhibitions socially are themselves reasons to like them, or to feel as though one could like them if allowed to do so. I realize that I am extrapolating; but Tynan's review has that characteristic of good dramatic criticism which does really conjure up what it must have been like at the performance itself; and, more important, the texts of the plays themselves seem to articulate, often by what is left unsaid, the same invitation, the same challenge. There is no need to rehearse here the spectrum of criticism, pro and con, of Hal's 'character', nor to observe what have become the commonplaces of our understanding of these plays in historical context – except that it is interesting, on the one hand, that what one might call the 'personal' assessments of Hal have always been just that, both in the nineteenth century and today: 'personal'. He evokes, as do the larger characters still to come, the assumption, even among very sophisticated critics, of a life beyond the words, of a personality upon which one can pass judgement, and productive of behavior which *can* be said to be 'good' or 'unattractive'. Secondly, it is interesting that nothing historical criticism has taught us over the past three or four decades has made it any easier either to perform these plays with Hal holding the center, or to teach them in a way which convinces students – really good students – that he *should* do so. In other words, the conventional descriptions are not sufficient either to a pedagogical or a theatrical desideratum.

As I have implied, I think part of our problem is that Shakespeare has created a character who is typically impure, who contains – as do all the important creations of good playwrights – an inwardly oriented *raison d'etre* for existence, and that this confuses him as often as it may confuse us. Note that one could not speak this way about a stage character who did not seem to contain within him the pulse of life; and I suggest that this pulse may be understood better if we see that the playwriting which bodies forth the personality is adjusted to that mode of simultaneous circuitry I have been trying to describe: a mode which is 'descriptive' only when the character is, and not because Shakespeare is using the wrong technique, but which most of the time springs from a real time-scheme of development – all the more appropriate because these two plays are about the development of a personality, and the choices made in the course of that development. The character is that of a man in flux, and we should attach more importance to that sense of changing, of continual process, than is implied in our more or less common academic understanding that this is a prince 'educating' himself. If we understand that a fundamental element of the action is that a constantly changing Hal is its focus (an emphasis an actor would understand, perhaps intuitively), many of the play's problems – I am speaking of both Parts – become not simpler, but more approachable, more capable of inclusion in the same personality; indeed, if anything, these problems, when considered as acting problems, as they might be called in rehearsal, become if anything more complex, more interesting, when seen to spring from a character who is represented – in the writing – as constantly in touch with his own conflicted needs, whose acted expressiveness is in terms of those conflicts – as the life of the play develops. That is important, for as a qualification it asks of the scholar and student of the play to consider the prince as knowing and feeling neither more nor less at any given moment in time than *his* experience of the play, so to speak, allows him to have at that moment. So considered, his words evoke a reality which is mainly not 'self-descriptive' (except, in an interesting way, for his soliloquy early in Part 1), but which is carried forward by a technique uniquely Shakespearian: that of expression, moment by moment, of an inner state and an immediate present time.

The first soliloquy, considered in this way, is indeed in the long tradition of self-descriptive speeches in Tudor drama, and very conventionally so – but with a difference which I think removes it from the opprobium so often attached to it. A long critical tradition, which is I am sure still very active – not to mention the responses of undergraduates – holds that the speech proves Hal's priggishness, his conscious intention to manipulate his attractively naive comrades at the Boar's Head, and, worse, because by appearing to enjoy an eternal 'holiday', he will appear all the more glorious when he assumes the crown. The most teachers and critics who feel, perhaps in spite of themselves, a sympathy for the prince often say in response to this is, 'Yes, but it is a conventional speech; Elizabethan characters often describe themselves in a way which sounds almost authorial, as though they knew the end of the plot of the play in which they were acting.' Now there is truth in this, but I think we should trust Shakespeare's dramaturgy in a more complex way. He knew what he was doing. A good actor, no matter whether his training occurred on one side of the Atlantic or the other, would want to ask first, and demand to have answered, the question: *why* does the prince speak now at all? That is, in response to what stimulus do these words occur? It is not such an outrageous question after all; asked in terms of any of the important soliloquies in the major tragedies, the answers are apparent – and the query of an actor could be satisfied in perfectly conventional terms.

Hal's soliloquy is spoken in direct reaction to the scene at the end of which it occurs; it is spoken, one might say, because of what has occurred during the scene, and in response to it. We have all been teaching for years how the verbally dense episode with Falstaff, before Poins's entrance, is in fact not simple badinage but a battle, and not always a purely friendly one, between the old man's needs for a reign of license and the young man's rather clear and sometimes double-edged refusals to answer those needs. The explicit proposal to participate in a robbery produces, in these circumstances, a response that is ambiguous only to the extent that Hal can accept the potentially comic results when Poins explains them. The prince is, as Tynan described Burton, 'inaccessible' to both Falstaff and Poins, and his pact with the latter to 'make one' is already colored with analytical thought about to be expressed: 'I know you all, and will awhile uphold / The unyoked humor of your idleness'. The present thought springs from the present stimulus, and so does all that follows it, necessarily self-descriptive, but necessarily describing a plan, if we can call it that, which projects Hal's self-experience only as far as this part of his journey through the play can have carried it. The soliloquy *is* to some extent manipulative, though hardly condescending or cruel; it also contains some platitudes – 'If all the year were playing holidays, / To sport would be as tedious as to work' – which are to some extent alibis. The description of his plan, so far as he is experiencing it at this moment in the play, points toward a time when two things, Hal feels, will happen: first, he will 'pay the debt [he] never promisèd', which, for the character and the actor, is full of repressed resentment (who chooses to be his father's son?) and, secondly, to '[Redeem] time' itself – when others least expect him to. There is relish in the whole speech, as well as a shoring up of personal defenses, in proving to himself – and, therefore, to us – that he does 'know you all'. As self-description, it seems exactly the mode which would be logically elicited by what has just happened, and it is in this context, it seems, that the playwright wrote it, that the character and actor can perceive it, and that we can make of it what we can. Surely it is not the only moment in the major plays when Shakespeare chooses to place the actor and those who perceive him in an ambivalent situation within a continuous flux of human action and experience.

We need not examine Shakespeare's exposures of Hal's experience, episode by episode, through both plays; but each would reveal, on such examination, a response by the stage personality to present time, in words which are capable of verbalizing the thoughts and feelings of the moment.

Examples of a few such exposures will serve the purpose. The first is Hal's response to Poins after the episode with Francis, whose automatic, unthoughtful, unanalytical response to life, and to the possible choice of a new style, makes the prince, in a moment, in what is only an apparent *non sequitur*, think of Hotspur. Poins, no deep observer himself, asks Hal, '... what cunning match have you made with this jest of the drawer? Come, what's the issue?' – to which Hal replies only obliquely: 'I am now of all humors that have showed themselves humors since the old days of goodman Adam to the pupil age of this present twelve o'clock at midnight' (II, iv, 91–7). Hal, perhaps a little freer of speech because of drink is not a whit more accessible: if sack makes him more easily verbal, it certainly opens up no more inner recesses – at least not for Poins's benefit; but it does for him and for us. To be able to come tangent to all types of human beings – all humors – made manifest in mankind from the moment of creation to the very present moment is a trait typical of a man who, while he can talk with any tinker in his lifetime, has not yet come to terms with himself – though he may not be entirely aware of this. Hal knows he will have to pay the debt he never promised, and that when he does, somehow he will redeem time itself, through which he is now passing; but what brings great poignancy and depth to the role is that he himself does not yet know what those experiences of debt-paying and redemption will be *like*: they are not yet part of the experience of the play. At this point, almost manic with the relish of it, he can observe, watch, and imitate; and he can draw his own moral – for his mind jumps from Francis's intransigence, his inability to put free thought into words beyond a formula of 'anon, anon', to: 'I am not yet of Percy's mind, the Hotspur of the North: he that kills me some six or seven dozen of Scots at a breakfast, washes his hands, and says to his wife, "Fie upon this quiet life! I want work"' (103–7). From this charade it is an easy leap to the conception of a play – which, while it won't be the one Hal suggests to Poins, will be acted out shortly. This is a type of playwriting in which the immediate thought is not only transformed at once into words; it is a way of playwriting which gives the character the potential for inner change. Hal changes internally every time we see him, such as in the role-playing with Falstaff, as each assigns to himself, and to the other, parts which mesh with a range of relationships between the two men, from a kind of wish fulfillment on Falstaff's side to a gritty realism on Hal's, with all degrees of 'identified' or 'descriptive' acting in the spectrum between. Both begin with acting styles in which verbal mannerism is chosen as a way to convey content which neither man chooses, at first, to project 'feelingly'; Falstaff's is not necessarily, then, the less sophisticated of the two, for his 'vein' – which refers not to his words but to his acting style – requires emblematic properties and a held 'countenance', and may not be so far from the prince's first style as he 'plays at' being his father. The genius of the episode, however, is that it carries us from this mode, which holds reality at a safe distance, to the very mode which I have been trying to discuss, one that is very deeply internalized, which carries, not to put too fine a point on it, a *sub*-text:

> No, my good lord: banish Peto, banish Bardolph, banish Poins; but for sweet Jack Falstaff, kind Jack Falstaff, true Jack Falstaff, valiant Jack Falstaff, and therefore more valiant being, as he is, old Jack Falstaff, banish not him thy Harry's company, banish plump Jack, and banish all the world! . . . I do, I will.
>
> (II, iv, 479–86)

Here the characters' internal experience surfaces verbally; the core of each's intention is put precisely into so many words. But Shakespeare's achievement here is to have given these intentions, by this time in the episode, a great deal more emotional ballast than *can* be verbalized – or verbalized in exactly these, or any other, terms. This richness and resonance beyond actual statement is an implicit part of internalized technique – the technique required if one is to present a stage personality with the capability of inner change.

At each juncture in Hal's stage life, a new internal level is disclosed, or suggested – through use of either mode of writing (which of course requires varying modes of acting) or combinations of them. The great richness of the mode which Shakespeare himself developed for the English stage is nowhere better illustrated than during this magnificent exchange in Part Two:

> *Prince.* Before God, I am exceeding weary.
>
> *Poins.* Is't come to that? I had thought weariness durst not have attacked one of so high blood.
>
> *Prince.* Faith, it does me, though it discolors the complexion of my greatness to acknowledge it. Doth it not show vilely in me to desire small beer?
>
> *Poins.* Why, a Prince should not be so loosely studied as to remember so weak a companion.
>
> *Prince.* Belike, then, my appetite was not princely got, for, by my troth, I do now remember the poor creature, small beer. But indeed these humble considerations make me out of love with my greatness. What a disgrace is it to me to remember thy name! Or to know thy face tomorrow! Or to take note how many silk stockings thou hast, [as] these, or those that were thy peach-coloured ones! Or, to bear the inventory of thy shirts, as: one for superfluity and another for use! . . .
>
> *Poins.* How ill it follows, after you have labored so hard, you should talk so idly! Tell me, how many good young princes would do so, their fathers being so sick as yours at this time is?
>
> *Prince.* Shall I tell thee one thing, Poins?
>
> *Poins.* Yes, faith, and let it be an excellent good thing.
>
> *Prince.* It shall serve among wits of no higher breeding than thine.
>
> *Poins.* Go to. I stand the push of your one thing that you will tell.
>
> *Prince.* Marry, I tell thee, it is not meet that I should be sad, now my father is sick. Albeit I could tell to thee, as to one it pleases me, for fault of a better, to call my friend, I could be sad, and sad indeed, too.
>
> *Poins.* Very hardly, upon such a subject.
>
> *Prince.* By this hand, thou thinkest me as far in the devil's book as thou and Falstaff for obduracy and persistency. Let the end try the man. But I tell thee, my heart bleeds inwardly that my father is so sick. And keeping such vile company as thou art hath in reason taken from me all ostentation of sorrow.
>
> *Poins.* The reason?
>
> *Prince.* What wouldst thou think of me if I should weep?
>
> *Poins.* I would think thee a most princely hypocrite.
>
> *Prince.* It would be every man's thought, and thou art a blessed fellow to think as every man thinks. Never a man's thought in the world keeps the roadway better than thine. Every man would think me an hypocrite indeed. . . .
>
> (II, ii, 1–18, 28–57)

Hal minces fewer words with Poins to his face than he does even with Falstaff, where, in II, iv of Part I, their role-playing had served at first, at least, as a kind of shield against personal hurt. But in the course of this scene, it is obvious that the weight of inner emotional content grows as the direct speech on the textual level goes forward. The words of the text, in this mode of playwriting, themselves become referential; they demand, for their full effectiveness, an understanding of, or at least our assumption that the character possesses, an interior life which is developing its own energies sub-textually.

When he concluded the little play scene in Part I with a direct statement of inner intention to banish Falstaff, Shakespeare lets Hal do so through both modes of acting, by writing the line in two tenses: 'I do, I will.' 'I do', as the persona of king whom I am now denoting truly; and, he might have added, in the 'native act and figure of [his] heart,' 'I will' in actuality, when I am no longer performing only a role. The vital aspect of the dramaturgy of Hal's part is precisely that he does not yet know how it will feel actually to banish Falstaff – and his projection of this feeling when it comes is perhaps as much a cause of our poignant response to the scene at the end of Part 2 as is the fact of the banishment itself and our feelings for Falstaff, whatever they may be.

> I know thee not, old man. Fall to thy prayers.
> How ill white hairs becomes a fool and jester!
> I have long dreamt of such a kind of man,
> So surfeit-swelled, so old, and so profane,
> But, being awaked, I do despise my dream....
> (V, V, 47–51)

Surely, we have now lived with this moment long enough – in our studies, our classrooms, on the stage – to admit that it needs no simple defense or apology; to try to explain why it 'is not cruel' is to do it vast injustice. The *rigor* of what Hal has known from the beginning he will eventually have to do has been all along part of the deep pain within his role, his life: to 'steady himself for the crown', in Tynan's excellent phrase, is precisely what an actor might take as a fundamental 'intention', in Stanislavskian terms, for study for performance of both Parts. Now, when, finally, the act must be done, the character already carries with him in our perception of his experience the full complement of an inner life, no small part of which is awareness of loneliness, of the great pain of knowing all others' humors while struggling to identify one's own, and then, finally, all alone, to assume a debt never promised, an act of redemption for which it is perfectly legitimate for us to feel he may not yet be quite certain he is capable of performing.

A full study of Shakespeare's development of the mode of internalized writing for the stage would show further experiment in his projection of Brutus, but full fruition in the four major tragic heroes. But without his delving into Hal, in whom all known modes of playwriting and this new one as well are used to project the character's experience of himself, he could never have carried Hamlet, Othello, Macbeth, or Lear to their ultimate moments of inner perception – moments without which we could not experience them as embodiments of tragic understanding:

> Not a whit, we defy augury. There is special providence in the fall of a sparrow. If it be now, 'tis not to come; if it be not to come, it will be now; if it be not now, yet it will come. The readiness is all. Since no man knows aught of what he leaves, what is't to leave betimes. Let be. (*Hamlet*, V, ii, 221–6)

> No, no, no, no! Come, let's away to prison:
> We two alone will sing like birds i'th'cage;
> When thou dost ask me blessing, I'll kneel down
> And ask of thee forgiveness: so we'll live,
> And pray, and sing, and tell old tales, and laugh
> At gilded butterflies, and hear poor rogues
> Talk of court news; and we'll talk with them too,
> Who loses and who wins, who's in, who's out;
> And take upon's the mystery of things,
> As if we were God's spies; and we'll wear out

In a walled prison packs and sects of great ones
That ebb and flow by th' moon . . .

(*King Lear*, v, i, 8–19)

We often speak of the great gift offered by Shakespearian tragic heroes. One of the reasons they are able to be so magnanimous resides in their ability to communicate experientially, to convey the inwardly oriented knowledge which they come, in the course of their stage lives, to possess. This ability is potentially implicit in the forms of playwriting I have tried to describe as 'internalized'. Throughout the rest of his career, of course Shakespeare varied his methods, and the presence of one technique never excluded the other; almost all of Leontes's role, for example, in *The Winter's Tale*, is written in a very internalized mode, though Prospero's, perhaps because of the great compression of action and the making of choices in *The Tempest*, includes much that is self-descriptive ('Though with their high wrongs I am struck to th' quick, / Yet with my nobler reason 'gainst my fury / Do I take part. The rarer action is / In virtue than in vengeance . . .' ([v, i, 25–8]). In any case there seems to me little question that it was in the *Henry IV* plays, and specifically in those episodes in which our experience of the prince's thoughts and reactions is deepest, that Shakespeare brought the internalizing technique to perfection, and through it denotes truly the silent, wordless motion of the mind and heart.

THE TRUE PRINCE AND THE FALSE THIEF: PRINCE HAL AND THE SHIFT OF IDENTITY

NORMAN SANDERS

Much of Shakespeare's drama is centrally concerned with men's need to make choices in life and the necessity for taking full responsibility for the actions which result from these choices. One of the dramatic techniques he often uses to explore this aspect of the human condition is an interchange of roles between characters who are in some way parallel, owing to a similarity in situation, personality, action, or attitude. Thus Edgar can 'represent' Cordelia during the storm scenes in *King Lear*, so that she becomes, in a sense, the philosopher on the heath from whom her father learns life's awful lessons. In a similar way, the lines of action open to Hamlet, but not followed by him, can be explored with their consequences in the persons of the other revenging sons, Laertes and Fortinbras. And the same device lies behind the handling of such different characters as Portia and Jessica, Viola and Sebastian, the twin Antipholi, Perdita and Hermione, and the pairs of lovers in *As You Like It*.

However, in no play does Shakespeare use this technique quite so deliberately in both verbal and dramatic forms as in the *Henry IV* plays. Further, the almost self-conscious consistency shown in its employment is clearly related to the conception of the character of Prince Hal; and consequently may throw light on the divergent attitudes that critics have taken to him.

Throughout the two plays, Shakespeare frequently lifts Hal out of his own person or transfers to another character some aspect of his identity. The most obvious verbal example of this is King Henry's desire, in the opening scene of Part I, to have Hotspur for a son instead of Hal:

> O that it could be prov'd
> That some night-tripping fairy had exchang'd
> In cradle-clothes our children where they lay,
> And call'd mine Percy, his Plantagenet!
> Then would I have his Harry, and he mine.
> (*1 Hen. IV*, I, i, 85–9)[1]

The implications of these lines are clear. The king is seen as choosing for himself a more symbolically appropriate son than the one he has; for Hotspur, who is soon to be a rebel against the crown, is a proper heir to the man who sneaked home like a poor unminded outlaw and

> In short time after he depos'd the King,
> Soon after that depriv'd him of his life,
> And in the neck of that task'd the whole state.
> (*1 Hen. IV*, IV, iii, 90–2)

It is, of course, ironical that the act that provokes such a longing as this in the king is Hal's abandonment of court and family, which constitutes in practice exactly the severing of paternity that Henry so desires.

Another verbal transference of identity, rather more complex because it is a double one, takes place in the interview between father and son in III, ii of the first play. Here the king uses words which effectively detach Hal from

[1] Quotations are from the new Arden edition of the plays edited by A. R. Humphreys (1960, 1966).

his lineage:

> Yet let me wonder, Harry,
> At thy affections, which do hold a wing
> Quite from the flight of all thy ancestors.
> (*1 Hen. IV*, III, ii, 29–31)

He then reinforces this observation by vividly placing Hal in parallel with Richard II. First, he depicts himself as the model of retiring success:

> Had I so lavish of my presence been,
> So common-hackney'd in the eyes of men,
> So stale and cheap to vulgar company,
> Opinion, that did help me to the crown,
> Had still kept loyal to possession,
> And left me in reputeless banishment,
> A fellow of no mark nor likelihood.
> By being seldom seen, I could not stir
> But like a comet I was wonder'd at,
> That men would tell their children, 'This is he!'
> Others would say, 'Where, which is Bolingbroke?'
> And then I stole all courtesy from heaven,
> And dress'd myself in such humility
> That I did pluck allegiance from men's hearts,
> Loud shouts and salutations from their mouths,
> Even in the presence of the crownéd King.
> (ll. 39–54)

This is the ideal that the father-usurper-king sets up for his erring son: one which, by his own testimony, is at odds with loyal possession of the crown. It is a picture of a man who 'stole courtesy from heaven', who 'plucks allegiance from men's hearts'. Against this tarnished figure is offered an equally vivid portrait of the legitimate monarch:

> The skipping King, he ambled up and down,
> With shallow jesters, and rash bavin wits,
> Soon kindled and soon burnt, carded his state,
> Mingled his royalty with cap'ring fools,
> Had his great name profanéd with their scorns,
> And gave his countenance against his name
> To laugh at gibing boys, and stand the push
> Of every beardless vain comparative.
> (ll. 60–7)

Both Henry and Shakespeare place Hal 'in that very line' – that is as heir to Richard; while the king is transformed into an earlier Hotspur:

> For all the world
> As thou art to this hour was Richard then
> When I from France set foot at Ravenspurgh,
> And even as I was then is Percy now.
> (ll. 93–6)

While Hal, the legal heir, is 'the shadow of succession', Hotspur 'hath more worthy interest to the state' that Henry stole. With such alternatives open to him, Hal can promise to fight Percy; but personally he can only vow

> I shall hereafter, my thrice gracious lord,
> Be more myself. (ll. 92–3)

It is in dramatic rather than poetic terms that an even more complex and significant transference takes place in the tavern's comic counterpart of the serious court interview. In answer to Falstaff's plea to Hal to rehearse his excuses to his father, two playlets are arranged. In the first of them, Falstaff (the King of Misrule with no moral right to reprimand personal disorder) will play King Henry (also a king of misrule, by virtue of his act of usurpation, who has no moral right to lament national disorder). Hal will play himself in his twin roles as legitimate son to his father and apparent spiritual son to his surrogate tavern father, Falstaff.

Falstaff's admonishment, as it winds its euphuistic way, actually makes in comic form some of the points repeated by the king to his son two scenes later. First, it questions the reality of the father–son relationship:

> That thou art my son I have partly thy mother's word, partly my own opinion, but chiefly a villainous trick of thine eye, and a foolish hanging of thy nether lip, that doth warrant me. If then thou be son to me, here lies the point . . . why, being son to me, art thou so pointed at?
> (*1 Hen. IV*, II, iv, 397–402)

Then Hal's truancy from court is questioned: 'Shall the blessed sun of heaven prove micher, and eat blackberries?' (ll. 402–4). Third, the question is raised as to whether Hal can associate with criminals without becoming criminal himself:

> There is a thing, Harry, which thou hast often heard of, and it is known to many in our land by the name of pitch. This pitch (as ancient writers do report) doth defile, so doth the company thou keepest.
>
> (ll. 406–10)

And finally, there is the extended praise of Falstaff himself.

It is at this point that Hal sets up the second playlet, in which the roles played are very different. The prince takes the part of his own father, and in that role castigates himself and his weaknesses in the person of Falstaff, who can aptly personate those associations to which Hal is committed by his conscious decision to separate himself from the illegality of his father's reign. As this second play proceeds, Hal 'deposes' his father, Falstaff; and then casts out his devil by turning away that element in his necessary truancy represented by the old Vice. Nowhere are Hal's position of aloneness and the isolation he feels in the England of the plays made more clear than when he utters his banishment of Jack Falstaff and 'all the world'.

Both in this scene and that with his father, it is plain that the prince conceives himself to be solely responsible for making his way to the crown in an environment that has nothing of the normal security and aids which an heir might expect to be available to prepare himself for future kingship. His society is sick; established authority is riddled with guilt; the opposition to this authority is doubly guilty; and the only condition which will effectively dissociate him from both parties entails engagement with the usual enemies of social order – idlers, rogues, and thieves. Hal can indeed only promise to be more himself, and accept the charges of coldness and machiavellian calculation that have been levelled at him.

As it has often been noted, the second part of the play, despite the brilliant realism of the scenes in Gloucestershire, moves very close at certain points to the manner of the old morality drama. And whatever one believes about the relationship between the two parts, it is demonstrable that some episodes in the second play do repeat, or make more explicit, or expand effects and events which the first part deals with more suggestively and (in my opinion) more subtly.

It is not surprising, therefore, that we find in two crucial episodes of Part 2 the same technique being used in the management of Hal's character. In the scene between the newly proclaimed Henry V and the Lord Chief Justice (v, ii), Hal once again juggles with his identities; only in this case he does so in a way that is complexly linked to the basic issues of kingship and its position in the social structure of the nation.

The Lord Chief Justice places Hal in the position of being his own father, even as Hal had himself in the tavern play scene:

> Question your royal thoughts, make the case yours,
> Be now the father, and propose a son,
> Hear your own dignity so much profan'd,
> See your most dreadful laws so loosely slighted,
> Behold yourself so by a son disdain'd:
> And then imagine me taking your part,
> And in your power soft silencing your son.
> After this cold considerance sentence me;
> And, as you are a king, speak in your state.
>
> (*2 Hen. IV*, v, ii, 91–9)

Hal accepts the role and passes judgement on himself:

> You are right, Justice, and you weigh this well.
> Therefore still bear the balance and the sword;
> And I do wish your honours may increase
> Till you do live to see a son of mine
> Offend you and obey you, as I did.
> So shall I live to speak my father's words:
> 'Happy am I, that have a man so bold
> That dares do justice on my proper son;

And not less happy, having such a son
That would deliver up his greatness so
Into the hands of justice.' (ll. 102–12)

But he goes further than ever his own father could; by abstracting the concept of Justice from its particular human representative, he places himself beneath the law in a classic formulation of the Tudor principle concerning the position of royal magistrates:

I do commit into your hand
Th'unstained sword that you have us'd to bear,
With this rememberance – that you use the same
With the like bold, just, and impartial spirit
As you have done 'gainst me. There is my hand.
You shall be as a father to my youth,
My voice shall sound as you do prompt mine ear,
And I will stoop and humble my intents
To your well-practis'd wise directions.
(ll. 113–21)

Justice is thus dissociated from the reign of Henry IV and the wildness of Hal's youth and his father's illegal reign are firmly linked in the words used:

believe me, I beseech you,
My father is gone wild into his grave,
For in his tomb lie my affections;
And with his spirits sadly I survive
To mock the expectation of the world,
To frustrate prophecies, and to raze out
Rotten opinion, who hath writ me down
After my seeming. (ll. 122–9)

In richly associative terms, Hal sees his blood, which had flowed in consciously adopted 'vanity' and was deflected from its true path of nobility by the decision forced upon him by his father's guilt, as reassuming its right channel:

The tide of blood in me
Hath proudly flow'd in vanity till now.
Now doth it turn, and ebb back to the sea,
Where it shall mingle with the state of floods,
And flow henceforth in formal majesty.
(ll. 129–33)

However one may react to the emotional and human impact of Henry V's final rejection of Falstaff in the last scene of Part 2, its terminology is perfectly consistent with the pattern of dissociation of identity I have tried to trace. Hal's experience has indeed been unreal and like a dream: one in which seeming has been taken for truth, where actual criminality has been necessary to achieve true legality, when the self has had to be split in two and one part of it turned away:

I have long dreamt of such a kind of man, ...
But being awak'd I do despise my dream. ...
For God doth know, so shall the world perceive,
That I have turn'd away my former self; ...
When thou dost hear I am as I have been,
Approach me, and thou shalt be as thou wast.
(*2 Hen. IV*, v, v, 49, 51, 57–8, 60–1)

If Shakespeare worked so deliberately and consistently to connect Hal with this pattern of dislocation from self and society, it follows that this means of dramatic portrayal must be connected with the way we are intended to view the prince and his unique difficulties in the situation in which he finds himself. And many other aspects of these plays seem to provide evidence that Shakespeare carefully constructed a world which forced upon Hal self-definition via apparent criminality as the only choice open to him.

First, both plays are loaded with reminders of the immediacy of Henry IV's ever-present guilt about what he did to get the crown, and with vivid recollections of the past by such characters as Hotspur, the Archbishop, and Worcester. These allusions are further reinforced by the cumulative effect of the imagery of sickness, weariness, and sleeplessness associated with Henry's reign, and also by the long shadow that Richard II's deposition and death throws over the plays. The rebels against this diseased rule are similarly devalued; for throughout both parts they are characterised by division, bickering, distrust, and weakness. In fact, despite the variety offered by such features as the violent and colourful animosity of Hotspur, the calculating illness of Northumberland, the pseudo-mysticism of Glendower, and the crafty manoeuvrings of Worcester, there is basically little to choose between the moral stances of the two sides. We find at various points in the plays definite interrelationships indicated between the moral deficiencies of both. In Part 2, the Archbishop accurately depicts the dilemma facing the usurper-king:

> the King is weary
> Of dainty and such picking grievances;
> For he hath found, to end one doubt by death
> Revives two greater in the heirs of life:
> And therefore will he wipe his tables clean,
> And keep no tell-tale to his memory
> That may repeat and history his loss
> To new remembrance. For full well he knows
> He cannot so precisely weed this land
> As his misdoubts present occasion.
> His foes are so enrooted with his friends
> That plucking to unfix an enemy
> He doth unfasten so and shake a friend.
> So that this land, like an offensive wife
> That hath enrag'd him on to offer strokes,
> As he is striking, holds his infant up,
> And hangs resolv'd correction in the arm
> That was uprear'd to execution.
>
> (*2 Hen. IV*, IV, i, 197–214)

The final image of family strife in the last five lines here is a telling one, for Hal's position between opposing forces is similar to that of the infant pictured between father and mother. In the first part of the play, Worcester describes the equally impossible situation in which the rebels find themselves:

> It is not possible, it cannot be,
> The King should keep his word in loving us;
> He will suspect us still, and find a time
> To punish this offence in other faults:
> Supposition all our lives shall be stuck full of eyes,
> For treason is but trusted like the fox,
> Who, never so tame, so cherish'd and lock'd up,
> Will have a wild trick of his ancestors.
> Look how we can, or sad or merrily,
> Interpretation will misquote our looks,
> And we shall feed like oxen at a stall,
> The better cherish'd still the nearer death.
>
> (*1 Hen. IV*, V, ii, 4–15)

It is this process of rebellion–repentance–recrimination–new rebellion–revenge set in train by Richard II's deposition and murder that Hal must put an end to. He must redeem that temporal pattern which decrees that

> heir from heir shall hold this quarrel up
> Whiles England shall have generation.
>
> (*2 Hen. IV*, IV, ii, 48–9)

Given these conditions, how else is Hal to create single-handedly a totally new royal milieu except by complete and apparently criminal dissociation from all the norms that a sick nation offers him? Shakespeare's dramatic solution is to make Hal's defection real to both the court and tavern worlds, while assuring the audience that the prince so offends to make offence a skill. His being, yet not being, a part of Falstaff's corrupt realm is typified by his role in the Gadshill robbery, in which the justice he creates is of his own rather than his society's making. He is for the same reason verbally detached from his father's lineage; even as he can strike his father's Justice, yet submit himself to the same Justice when it is the main prop of his own reign.

Because Hal's possession of the crown must be seen to be 'plain and right', Shakespeare devises a scene, which, although explicable in human terms, also shows Hal symbolically stealing the crown of England from his father rather than receiving it at his hands. In this scene (*2 Henry IV*, IV, v), Hal draws a careful distinction between the debt he owes his father as a loving son:

> Thy due from me
> Is tears and heavy sorrows of the blood,
> Which nature, love, and filial tenderness
> Shall, O dear father, pay thee plenteously,
>
> (ll. 36–9)

and the right he possesses by virtue of what he has made of himself:

> My due from thee is this imperial crown,
> Which, as immediate from thy place and blood,
> Derives itself to me. [*Putting it on his head*]
>
> (ll. 40–2)

As Henry says, more truly than he knows, 'God put it in thy mind to take it thence.... Thou wilt needs invest thee with my honours'; for no one else in his England can rightfully perform the ritual.

The Prince of Wales, in these two plays, faces alone the task of finding, while laden with an awesome duty, a *modus operandi* in an impossible world; just as the later Prince of Denmark was to undertake a not completely dissimilar task and meet it in a similar way. For Hamlet, the ultimate objective is the discovery of self and true being; whereas for Hal, it is the discovery of public role and right doing – which is to say that one is a tragic hero and the other a political one. As it is necessary for the greater prince to play the fool for wisdom's sake; so, for the lesser, a true prince may and does, for re-creation's sake, prove a false thief.

FALSTAFF, THE PRINCE, AND THE PATTERN OF '2 HENRY IV'

J. A. B. SOMERSET

A chief – perhaps *the* chief – fascination of the *Henry IV* plays is the rejection of Falstaff and the succession of Hal: this puzzle, as one observer has written, 'divides the critics into Ephesians and Precise Brethren'.[1] The sympathetic views of Morgann and Bradley have in this century been opposed by sterner stuff, so that those who cannot forgive Hal are now answered by those who find it hard to forgive Falstaff. Another area of lively discussion is the relationship of the two plays (or, perhaps, two parts of one play): here also the house divides without consensus. Generally, those who see *2 Henry IV* as an inferior pot-boiler are those who regard it as a sequel, and vice versa.[2] (There is some evidence that the Elizabethans were less enamoured of it than Part 1).[3] On the other hand, some who argue that *Henry IV* is a ten-act play are attempting to link the three plays dealing with Hal, the whole tetralogy, or even both tetralogies: continuing lines of development, and continuing thematic interests like 'kingship' are stressed. But whichever view is espoused, the similarities between the plays tend to receive attention at the expense of their differences, as Professor G. K. Hunter points out: he suggests that we need to accept 'the self-sufficiency of the separate play'.[4] Whatever may be their formal relationship in the development of Shakespeare's art, the two *Henry IV* plays are quite distinct in tone, imagery, and structure. I shall later propose some new ways of seeing their relationship. Both of these problems, especially the rejection of Falstaff, have been explained previously by pointing to Shakespeare's use of morality play elements. I suggest, however, that this 'key' to the plays has really obscured the uniqueness of *2 Henry IV*, and its relationship to *1 Henry IV*.

Since Professor J. W. Spargo's essay appeared in 1922, the morality plays have been investigated for the light they shed on characters, plot structure, and Shakespeare's intentions in these *Henry IV* plays.[5] Though not always clearly distinguished by writers on the subject, Shakespeare's borrowings seem to be of two types, the first being simple verbal allusions. As everyone knows, Falstaff is characterized by Hal as 'that reverend vice, that grey iniquity, that father ruffian, that vanity in years ... that villainous abominable misleader of youth, Falstaff, that old white-bearded Satan' (*1 Henry IV*, II, iv, 440–9). The attack is jocular – Hal is play-acting his father, and presumably is suggesting something about Bolingbroke's taste for morality

[1] Alice Lyle Scoufos, 'The Martyrdom of Falstaff', *Shakespeare Studies*, 2 (1966), 175.

[2] William Shakespeare, *Henry IV, Part II*, ed. A. R. Humphreys, New Arden Shakespeare (1966), introduction, p. xliii. (In quoting from the plays I have used the one-volume edition by Peter Alexander.)

[3] H. E. Cain, 'Further Light on the Relation of *1* and *2 Henry IV*', *Shakespeare Quarterly*, III (1952), 25.

[4] G. K. Hunter, 'Shakespeare's Politics and the Rejection of Falstaff', *Critical Quarterly*, I (1959), 235.

[5] 'An Interpretation of Falstaff', *Washington University Studies*, 9 (1922).

plays as well as giving a clue about Falstaff. In *2 Henry IV*, Falstaff alludes to Justice Shallow as a 'vice's dagger' (III, ii, 310). The frequent references to Falstaff's gluttony have led one critic to suggest a debt to Gluttony in Henry Medwall's *Nature* (printed *c.* 1525).[1] While the resemblances are striking, Medwall drew his allegorical character from tradition, and hence Shakespeare need not have drawn directly from the earlier play. These and other verbal allusions indicate some knowledge of the morality plays by Shakespeare and his audience. However, such allusions are nebulous in origin and unimportant: they might stem from tradition or Shakespeare's reading, and could arise relatively unconsciously. We need not detect them in the theatre – they don't affect our response importantly, and we cannot deduce from scattered allusions that Shakespeare composed with the morality plays continuously in mind. They are such stuff as commentaries are made of, and their little life is rounded with a footnote.

Critics have suggested a second type of dependence upon the morality play. The chance allusions, it is held, are evidence that the early plays supplied Shakespeare with a model which he used consciously. Hence, it is argued, our response must be conditioned by a knowledge of the morality plot-structure, and early audiences must have been familiar with such plays. Further, the sentimentalities of Morgann and others have arisen because of ignorance of Shakespeare's morality play model. In my view, it is dangerous to suggest that Shakespeare's art depends upon extrinsic factors, or that a 'right' interpretation can be discerned. Since J. Dover Wilson's *The Fortunes of Falstaff* (1943), however, critics have generally seen the link between *1* and *2 Henry IV* and the morality plays as one of formal dependence, if a debt is admitted at all.

The resultant reading of the plays centres upon Hal's allegedly educative progression to kingship, of which his coronation is the triumphal *rite de passage*. Perhaps too little attention is paid to other aspects of the action, particularly the dubious means of Bolingbroke's rise to power and his stratagems of maintaining it. This reading seems to assume that Hal will eventually wield power as does his father, rather than prompt us to question the nature of power. Falstaff becomes cast firmly in the Vice-role, and so we are provided with guidance about our proper attitude to his activities and his eventual rejection. Since, we are told, the plays are rooted in homiletic allegory, 'an old moral convention survives in him [Falstaff] and controls his fate', as Professor Spivack writes.[2] Generally this reading is espoused by those who argue against sympathy for Falstaff, while it is questioned by the knight's defenders. This morality analogy has also led to reading the plays as two parts of one play, closely linked thematically and forming two celebrations of Hal's education, in the complementary spheres of military and civil virtues. While there is a reformation at Shrewsbury, Hal's education is held to be incomplete. Hal's profligacy in *2 Henry IV* causes some difficulty, to which we shall return; however, both parts are seen as concerned with 'the traditional story of the Wild Prince reformed'.[3] As a morality, then, *Henry IV* is closely unified, and unquestioningly royalist: the triumphant accession of Hal crowns all.

This morality analogy has not lacked objectors, of course. Other analogies have been suggested – Hal has been seen in terms of a folk-hero, for example, whose course is one of vanquishing successive opponents and absorb-

[1] J. W. Shirley, 'Falstaff, an Elizabethan Glutton', *Philological Quarterly*, 17 (1938), 271–87.

[2] 'Falstaff and the Psychomachia', *Shakespeare Quarterly*, VIII (1957), 459.

[3] Humphreys, ed. *Henry IV, Part II*, p. xxvii.

ing their best qualities.[1] Perhaps an analogue is not required at all. William Empson, who opined that to know Falstaff was a liberal education, voiced an objection shared by many, that Falstaff's humanity and humour are slighted if we see him simply as a Vice.[2] Another problem is that the morality pattern is not quite applicable. Hal makes clear in his first soliloquy, 'I know you all...' (*1 Henry IV*, I, ii, 219 ff.), that he is never really seduced into evil, and hence his success is never in doubt. But at least Falstaff has hopes that 'this pitch, as ancient writers do report, doth defile; so doth the company thou keepest' (II, iv, 400), and his presumption that Hal resembles him is jarred only later, upon the battlefield. Other characters share Falstaff's opinion, so we may agree that Hal is an errant prodigal at least in their misapprehensions. The notion of 'misleading' is also presented through Falstaff's paradoxical accusations that the prince has corrupted *him*!

2 Henry IV is far less susceptible of a reading in terms of the morality, since its plot structure seems totally unlike the familiar morality pattern. The 'misleader' and his supposedly 'misled' subject meet only once, very briefly and coolly, in the Boar's Head tavern. This has caused some critical unease over morality influences. Professor Humphreys, for example, isolates little motifs, rather than a pattern or structure, from the earlier plays: 'the morality substratum gives the elements of guilt oppressed by anxiety, hubris riding for a fall, youth choosing codes of conduct'.[3] Professor Leech refers generally to the play's 'overt morality intention'.[4] Such caution is proper. Further, the traditional '*humanum genus*' morality pattern (in which a central *humanum genus*, or mankind, figure is persuaded by vices and virtues), is inapplicable to *2 Henry IV*, and to think of the play in its terms is misleading.

We have no way of knowing about the planning of the two parts of *Henry IV*, but at some time Shakespeare presumably decided on a second part and considered (one assumes) both plays as wholes in his mind. *1 Henry IV* ends with a reconciliation of Hal and his father, in deeds as well as promises and words: it seems complete and triumphant, and will shortly issue into further military campaigns since the play closes (as a history play must) with a sense that history carries on. What could Shakespeare do for a part two? Avail himself of the same plot structure, and write a sequel along the same lines as *1 Henry IV*? Or perhaps write a different sort of play? In his excellent essay, Professor Leech rightly begins by assuming that *2 Henry IV* need not be simply 'more of the same' because it is a sequel. He points out the distinctive tone – grave and sombre, rather than dashing and gay – of Part 2, the new relationships of the characters, the concern with time and age, and the inclusiveness of social types and geographical settings in the play. Hal becomes more and more kingly, but at the same time the play raises grave doubts about basic political assumptions and activities. But we are carried toward the new order, of *Henry V*, and near the end of the play a new note of sobriety and sternness is introduced, 'in an attempt to silence the basic questions that so often in the play demand to be put'.[5] One might say that we are there ordered to wonder at kingship, having previously been invited to wonder about it: *2 Henry IV* is a more deeply questioning play, and we may find our questions unanswered in logical terms. It seems, then, un-

[1] Philip Williams, 'The Birth and Death of Falstaff Reconsidered', *Shakespeare Quarterly*, VIII (1957), 359–65.

[2] 'Falstaff and Mr. Dover Wilson', *Kenyon Review*, 15 (1953), 256.

[3] p. liv.

[4] 'The Unity of *2 Henry IV*', *Shakespeare Survey 6* (Cambridge, 1953), p. 23.

[5] *Ibid*, p. 20.

necessary to posit a repeated structure for the second play, or to assert that two such different dramas are interdependent and cannot stand alone.[1]

The traditional *humanum genus* morality was doubtless recognized in the 1590s, and Shakespeare may well have had it in mind while writing *1 Henry IV*. However, this was not the only type of morality play then current, and if Shakespeare wished to recall homiletic drama in *2 Henry IV* (and allusions in both plays suggest it), he need not have repeated himself. Ignorance of this has led some investigators into seeing 'two princely reformations', and to speaking of the wild prince as a prodigal, because such are the ingredients of the *humanum genus* pattern detected in *1 Henry IV*. But if we may safely assume that at least the more literary Elizabethans could recognize the traditional morality plot-structure, may we not assume an acquaintance with its successor? *Humanum genus* plots had ceased to be written about 1550, and by 1580 (so far as surviving texts show) they had been outnumbered by moralities and vice-interludes which experimented with social types and themes, Biblical history, and so on. The period in question is often ignored as an era of 'degeneration', but most of the extant moralities were written during it, and it deserves to be better known as a period of vigorous experimentation and thriving theatre.

Professor Alan C. Dessen has isolated one result of developments in this period, the 'estates play' of the 1580s and 1590s – examples are Robert Wilson's *Three Ladies of London* (1581), Greene and Lodge's *A Looking-glass for London and England* (1590), and *A Knack to Know a Knave* (1592). These plays adopt a social (often urban) scene, and show social evils permeating various classes, professions, or 'estates'.[2] A group of morality plays which preceded and influenced these, written between about 1565 and 1580, deserve attention. Surviving examples include *Like Will to Like* (1568), *All for Money* (1576), *The Tide Tarrieth No Man* (1576), *Enough is as Good as a Feast* (1560–70), and *The Trial of Treasure* (1567). These are the last moralities to preserve the 'Vice' character, here fully developed into prominence. They are professional plays of Shakespeare's youth, and are the surviving relics of a vigorous troupe theatre. Later allusions recalled them, and a performance of *Like Will to Like* occurred at the Rose in 1600, so presumably they were as familiar then as they are now forgotten.[3] One cannot propose these plays, or any one of them, as a 'source' for *2 Henry IV* – the evidence does not admit of 'ocular proof'. But what a source is, as Humphreys points out, is elusive:

> Literary sources are, rightly speaking, the whole relevant contents of the writer's mind as he composes, and no account of them can be complete. To specify the *Henry IV* plays' 'sources' is to run the risk of seeming too narrow, of circumscribing works that so generously embrace Elizabethan life and thought as to be an individual's expression of a whole nationhood.[4]

I think that these late moralities exhibit striking similarities to *2 Henry IV*, which suggest that Shakespeare may well have used them as a structural model. Consequently, I think, the earlier *humanum genus* pattern, never happily applied to *2 Henry IV*, can be dispensed with. The change in Falstaff and Hal's relationship from Part 1 to Part 2 receives illumination, and we also may more clearly see why the ending of *2 Henry IV* seems to be

[1] Cf. J. Dover Wilson, *The Fortunes of Falstaff* (1943): 'Part I possesses, indeed, a kind of unity, lacking in Part II . . . but is no less incomplete without it than Part II is itself unintelligible without Part I' (p. 4).

[2] *Jonson's Moral Comedy* (Evanston, Illinois, 1971), chap. I.

[3] E. K. Chambers, *The Elizabethan Stage* (1923), III, 317.

[4] p. xxix.

imposed by events and simply passed off as a restoration of kingly order, as Professor Leech noted.

These late moralities' messages are social and moral (often summed up in the proverbs of the play-titles), and their truths are enacted repeatedly, in the lives of various characters. Their plot-structure replaces the earlier single mankind hero with a varied array of social type-figures. Casting limitations, as Professor Bevington has shown, produced a structure in which two separated casts of virtuous and unregenerate types appear alternately with their attendants (allegorical, or what have you).[1] Repentance and reformation is rare, and Calvinism pervades – the elect are shown with their separate dispensation of grace, while the unregenerate are subject to the law of nature (in which 'the young dace be a bait for the old pike' to snap at him).

The variety of vice-types in a given play gives a sense of inclusiveness – we feel we are seeing a whole commonwealth, city, or whatever, as many occupations and groups are represented.[2] Universality is gained through this variety of particular vignettes in these 'morality variety shows' (as they might aptly be named). The Vice is no longer primarily a seducer, but becomes symbolic or 'public' in Professor Dessen's phrase.[3] He consorts with his typical confederates, symbolizing an evil everywhere at work: he need not have a special relationship to any one type-figure, nor be the instigator of every venality. Although more like 'one of the boys', the Vice remains dramatically central because of his comic verve, symbolic importance, and size of part (usually not doubled extensively). The Vice leads an amazingly varied existence as he appears in turn with various groups of type-figures: his actions with them vary between deceits, encouragements, tricks, promises, jests, warnings, and so on. When the unregenerate end badly, we feel some sense of justice because their earlier espousal of vice was stupid and unthinking. As part of the social emphasis of these plays, we note that the punishments delivered are this-worldly – prison, sickness, penury, and the like. Justice and law are often included in the plays' concern with this world's evils. In *All for Money*, for example, various evil social types appear in a long court scene, and manage through bribes to buy off the law though they are arrant knaves all (like William Visor of Woncot, appearing before Justice Shallow). Evil can have some success, and is not easily eradicable; the Vice-actions present a stark, honest, and lively picture of it.

Unregenerate activity is contrasted with virtuous living, which succeeds at last, after some form of trial which reveals the grace of the virtuous. This aspect of the plays receives far less emphasis. As one would expect, the virtuous and vicious meet only rarely (doubling patterns make this inevitable anyway). The virtuous rejoice in this moral *apartheid*, but the vicious at times pretend to a friendly relationship which doesn't exist. The mask of virtue will not serve, however, and such attempts suffer the reproof of the virtuous. The trials of the virtuous are imposed by the unregenerate disorders of vice, towards which the virtuous display aloof intolerance or downright hostility, perhaps mingled with a reforming zeal. Virtuous Living, for example, thus recognizes and rejects the Vice, Nichol Newfangle:

> My friend? Marry, I do thee defy,
> And all such company I do deny;
> For thou art a companion for roisters and ruffians,
> And not fit for any virtuous companions.
>
> (*Like Will to Like*, 701–4)

After this, Virtuous Living is rewarded with a crown and sword (representing victory and

[1] D. M. Bevington, *From 'Mankind' to Marlowe* (Cambridge, Mass., 1962), *passim*.

[2] Dessen, *Jonson's Moral Comedy*, pp. 13–15.

[3] *Ibid.*, p. 15.

kingship). In these plays, the suggestion of virtue strengthened by trial, or revealed as strong through action, gives a sense of finality – unregeneracy reigns for a while, but finally is controlled and justly rewarded.

My account of these morality variety shows has tried to suggest some features similar to *2 Henry IV* – certainly closer, at any rate, than the *humanum genus* morality plot. These late moralities, like *2 Henry IV*, lack a single virtuous hero seduced into evil, and they share with Shakespeare's play a pervading sense of the time's disorders (especially in laws and justice). In *2 Henry IV*, Falstaff and his fellows are *separated* from the court and from Hal, and the quality of contacts between the two parties seems analogous to the abovementioned relationship (or more exactly, lack of relationship) of upright and unregenerate. The fat knight leads a virtually separate existence, and on the few occasions when Falstaff is in contact with the court we see him evading reproofs, attempting to gain a hearing, or presuming a familiarity. When brought to book over his companions and conduct (by the Lord Chief Justice in II, i, and Hal in II, iv), Falstaff calumniates his female friends of Eastcheap to set himself apart from them. Mistress Quickly is 'a poor mad soul, and she says up and down the town that her eldest son is like you' (II, i, 100), while Doll Tearsheet 'is in hell already, and burns poor souls' (II, iv, 325). Falstaff is reproved early in the play for his manner of living by the Lord Chief Justice, and there the divorce between the fat knight and Hal is signalled directly:

Falstaff. God send the companion a better prince! I cannot rid my hands of him!
Chief Justice. Well, the king hath severed you...

(II, ii, 187–8)

Falstaff presumes upon his military valour in being thrust upon dangerous actions, just as later he pretends to intimacy with court affairs, interrupting the Lord Chief Justice and Gower:

Falstaff. Comes the king back from Wales, my noble lord?
Chief Justice. You shall have letters of me presently. Come, go along with me, good master Gower.
Falstaff. My lord!
Chief Justice. What's the matter?
Falstaff. Master Gower, shall I entreat you with me to dinner?

(II, i, 170–6)

The pretence seems both empty and a little pathetic: Falstaff has no place in this world of high affairs. The same holds for his relationship with Hal. Leaving aside for a moment the position of Hal at court and with his father, the prince's meeting with Falstaff in Eastcheap is similar to Falstaff's other encounters with the court. The tone is cold, and while the jokes may amuse us they don't rouse Hal to laughter – he is on his guard against merriment. Militarily, as well, Falstaff is redundant in the eyes of his betters. At Gaultree forest he receives scant thanks (for an exploit which, while richly comic, is also honourable and merciful, at least until Prince John arrives to deal with Coleville):

Falstaff. My lord, I beseech you, give me leave to go through Gloucestershire; and, when you come to court, stand my good lord, pray, in your good report.
Prince John. Fare you well, Falstaff. I, in my condition, Shall better speak of you than you deserve.

(IV, iii, 80–4)

His detour to Gloucestershire epitomizes Falstaff's separability – it may be for this reason that Shakespeare altered the locale of Justice Shallow from the main London route to a remote corner of England.[1] In *2 Henry IV*, as in the late moralities, the casts work out their

[1] A. R. Humphreys, 'Justice Shallow and Gloucestershire', *Notes and Queries* n.s. XI (1964), 134–5, points out that Shakespeare apparently first associated Shallow with Stamford, near Lincoln, and later shifted his location to Gloucestershire.

fortunes separately, and it is only Falstaff, Pistol, and perhaps Bardolph who cherish any illusions of influence and success.

Falstaff, his confederates, and his victims recall aspects of the vice-group of the late morality variety shows, rather than the earlier seducer-vice. The fat knight combines aspects of rapacious debtor, friend, and setter-on, in a varied action moving through the length of England. The greater freedom and variety of this play, as opposed to *1 Henry IV*, have been remarked by many. It is created around the 'honeyseed rogue' for whom every encounter is an opportunity, a main chance. He is no threat to Hal, but just generally to peace and order, his creditors, and our funnybones. He is among his natural companions, and his pretensions are more ludicrous when seen against the lowness and vapidity of his company (albeit comic), and his distance from court. His actions are part of the pattern of false surmises and absurd hopes which run through the play. Falstaff's hopes of preferment, his pretences to power, are denied like most other expectations in the play. The loans he wheedles from Mistress Quickly and Justice Shallow have as little hope of repayment – their trust in Falstaff is as absurd as that of, say, Cutbert Cutpurse and Pierce Pickpurse in *Like Will to Like*, who trust that the Vice will bring them prosperity through the 'land of the two-legged mare' (the gallows).

2 Henry IV has another anarchic group, the rebels, with their own interests as pretenders to power. Comparisons between the rebels and Falstaff are continually invited; among such, the echo of Lady Percy's tender eulogy of Hotspur in Mistress Quickly's thoughts of the 'honester and truer-hearted man' going to the wars, and the reflection of Northumberland's treachery in Falstaff's gulling of Mistress Quickly, are examples. While the two groups are more than just mutually illuminative, and the rebels' cause gives rise to many of the serious political reflections in *2 Henry IV*, the rebels and Falstaff are alike in their presumptions of power and the sterility of their visions of success. The death of order, on another level, is the stealing of any man's horses: hence the rebels' idealism is cut down to its true size, self-interest, while Falstaff's hedonism and moral escapism are seen as anarchical.

Before we pass on to look at the other side of the question – the Lancastrians and the succession – the most remarkable similarity of all between the Vice and Falstaff, their comedy, should be looked at. Without appreciating the scope and extent of Vice-comedy one cannot comprehend the late morality variety shows' flavour, but the place of comedy in homiletic drama has caused surprise. The lessons of the morality variety shows concern the ultimate futility of evil and its punishment, and the contrasting sure success of those who espouse the values sanctioned by the plays. The Vice-scenes are, therefore, examples of degenerate activity, but the dramatic impact of the morality plot runs a chance of back-firing on the author, since another main aim of these scenes is comic entertainment. The characters are often (if speciously) appealing and funny, and Vice-scenes are good 'big' scenes full of conventional business, songs, dances, jokes, horseplay, comic soliloquies, tricks played on the audience, and so on. Space forbids examples – and in any case the life of these things consists in action and is lost in extraction and comment. But it is true to say that these scenes were a company's 'get-penny'. Moral disapproval often seems far off – and some types of degeneracy, such as drunkenness, have been from that day to this stage-conventions and opportunities for extravagant comic action. To hold that the Vices (or Falstaff) are evil *because* they are funny is, I think, too simplistically moral and assumes that laughter must always be derisive.[1]

[1] Bernard Spivack, *Shakespeare and the Allegory of Evil* (New York, 1958), p. 218.

It is probably truer to see these Vice-actions as representative of 'the way of the world', which might well lead to, or mask, evil. At times this way is one we are tempted to follow, vicariously, through our relaxed enjoyment of Vice-comedy. On the other hand, the righteous always strike us as upright, dull, and severe, although they finally triumph. We are asked to follow their virtuous codes at the plays' ends, and we see we must, but as one critic writes in another context, 'so strict a rejection of what has pleased us may be the tribute duty owes to responsibility; yet it impoverishes our sense of life'.[1] His context is, of course, *2 Henry IV*, and his subject Falstaff. Shakespeare is like the writers of these late moralities in sailing close to the wind, allowing the comedy to give us a vision of life which, in some respects at least, we must lament losing. Shakespeare's is the riskier attempt, perhaps, because the morality writers can and do impress upon us that their final vision, their values, are theological and eschatological. To reject them is to reject the truths of revealed religion.

What are the positive values which, in *2 Henry IV*, are set against the moral holiday of Falstaff by the world of statecraft and politics? We should first consider together the whole group of courtiers, as Shakespeare invites by making no one prominent. The Lancastrians are concerned with the imminence of change in the order of things – worried glances are cast forward as the king's death is expected and feared, and the court is weak and disordered. Though rebellions can be quelled, rebellion cannot: Hastings's prophecy has cogency, and is not so shallow as Prince John thinks. Political stability is rather hoped for, than celebrated or enjoyed. One normally terms those who espouse the values of a morality play 'the virtues', but one hesitates to call Henry IV and his courtiers by that name, since it begs the question. A royalist reading of the play would agree with it, but others would object, laying stress upon Bolingbroke's usurpation, his Machiavellian policies, and such stratagems as the Gaultree Forest betrayal. But, at least, the Lancastrians are concerned with order and the succession which are secured at the end of the play, particularly by Hal.

What is Hal's place in that world, and his attitude to Lancastrian values? It seems to me that the most acute distortions occur if Hal is considered as a *humanum genus* type of character, an erring prodigal, subject in this play (as in Part I) to temptations and in need of recall – even if the temptations are second-hand, via the Lord Chief Justice who encounters Falstaff far more directly. Hal does not, I think, return from 'prodigality' to his true role only at the end of the play. As I have suggested, his coolness towards Falstaff is everywhere marked. Virtually no relationship exists between them, except in memory. Hal must even enquire 'does the old boar feed in the old frank' (II, ii, 140), in ignorance of Falstaff's habits. In Eastcheap the memories are epitomized by Mistress Quickly's reminder of 'when the Prince broke thy head for liking his father to a singing-man of Windsor' (II, i, 85). Other facets of Hal are created by his relationships with Poins and his father, and by Bolingbroke's opinion of Hal. With Poins, a younger brother employed as a waiting-gentleman, we must carefully distinguish between others' reports and what we ourselves see. Although his company calls forth anguish from Bolingbroke (who considers Poins a 'weed' choking Hal's promise), we see nothing in Poins's relationship to Hal which should cause a moment's disturbance to the most precise of Brethren. Poins simply vanishes after II, iv, as Shakespeare apparently didn't think enough of his alleged 'vileness' to consider him worth rejecting. Dover Wilson's reading of II, ii, as an interview in which Poins

[1] Dipak Nandy, quoted by Humphreys, (ed.) *Henry IV, Part II*, introduction, p. lx.

fails Hal, seems to me an unconvincing gloss which tries to paint Poins in the opprobrious terms used by Hal's father about his son's 'continual followers'. Hal's relationship with his father (or rather lack of one) and Henry's opinion of his son are most important because 'Henry's anguish . . . centres mostly on Hal's wildness'.[1] Certainly the king's fears are strong, and are centred upon Hal's companions:

> Harry the Fifth is crowned. Up, Vanity,
> Down, royal state. All you sage counsellors, hence.
> And to the English court assemble now,
> From every region, apes of idleness.
> Now, neighbour confines, purge you of your scum.
> Have you a ruffian that will swear, drink, dance,
> Revel the night, rob, murder, and commit
> The oldest sins the newest kinds of ways?
> Be happy, he will trouble you no more.
> England shall double gild his treble guilt.
>
> (IV, V, 120–9)

But are not such fears baseless? We only accept Hal's wildness if we accept them, but as Bolingbroke's views lack any corroboration we may question them and see them rather as misprisions on Bolingbroke's part. These mistaken forebodings give rise to a personal anguish which humanizes Henry even as it kills him by inches, and they are the antithesis of Falstaff's presumptions about Hal. The prince, it seems, will belie all expectations.

Hal seems to make himself a man of mystery. He is not among the solicitous relatives and courtiers who cluster around Henry's council table and sick-bed: Hal has separated himself from court and this is presumably one reason for Bolingbroke's dark thoughts about him. The hero of the hour at Shrewsbury has deserted the ship of state. An important insight into Hal is gained if we contrast this aloofness and his actions here with Part 1, without assuming (as many do) that Shakespeare merely repeated the character in the two plays. The famous soliloquy, 'I know you all . . .', in Part 1 has often been taken as *the* key to Hal, and applied to all his actions, even Agincourt in *Henry V*. The plans revealed in that soliloquy do not seem reprehensible in *1 Henry IV*, since cold-blooded use of his boon companions does not occur in that play.[2] We rather see Hal as aware of what eventually must occur (with emphasis on 'eventually'), and his playful side predominates until crisis intervenes and he must 'redeem the time'. In *2 Henry IV* Hal's actions would seem far more questionable if related to that soliloquy. Indeed, it is by reading the soliloquy in relation to the rejection scene that critics have condemned Hal, in Masefield's famous phrase, as 'a prig of a rake'. But perhaps this process, of searching both plays for every evidence for the defence or prosecution, is itself questionable. Perhaps the rejection proceeds out of the different structure and tone of Part 2 alone. Shakespeare has provided a counterpart in *2 Henry IV* to that famous soliloquy – the weary troubled interchanges with Poins, 'now my father is sick' (II, ii). Considerations of position – his own greatness, and the 'vile company' he keeps with Poins – occupy Hal's mind, along with a significant preoccupation with what 'every man would think' (l. 56). This may provide a clue as to why he does not return to court. Hal's one visit to Eastcheap is in disguise. It is purposeful folly to 'see Falstaff bestow himself tonight in his true colours' (l. 163), far from the humour of the joke in *1 Henry IV*:

> The virtue of this jest will be the incomprehensible lies that this same fat rogue will tell us when we meet at supper: how thirty, at least, he fought with; what wards, what blows, what extremities he endured; and in the reproof of this lies the jest.
>
> (I, ii, 178–83)

Hal's new purpose is akin to that of the disguised king of folktales, and of such plays as *Measure for Measure* and *Henry V*.

[1] Humphreys, ed., *Henry IV*, *Part II*, p. xlv.

[2] I assume we don't take Hal's interchange with Francis too seriously – or the joke on Falstaff at Gadshill.

2 Henry IV, with its different structure, is a second study of Prince Hal facing the more immediate prospect of succession. He should presumably appear older, in keeping with the other characters taken over from the earlier play. He is more self-conscious, and he affects a wildness he no longer inwardly enjoys; significantly, this profligacy goes no farther than 'the poor creature, small beer' – a far cry from the addiction to sack proposed by Falstaff! Hal allows suppositions about himself to multiply, and remains aloof from court, and this allows, in time, his magnificent *coup-de-théâtre* transformation into a king, which belies all expectations:

> And with his spirits sadly I survive,
> To mock the expectation of the world,
> To frustrate prophecies, and to raze out
> Rotten opinion, who hath writ me down
> After my seeming.
>
> (v, ii, 125–9)

Professor Edgar Schell has recently shown that this involves not a reformation, but a closing of the gap between what Hal is and what Bolingbroke (and others) take him to be.[1] Hal is probably playing on the meanings of 'seeming' above: his course has been one of conscious self-revelation, not choosing. His aloofness is creditable, however, in that he stands apart from the unquiet court and the cold-blooded stratagems used against opponents. We may agree that Hal is cold and imperious at the rejection; however, I think we could not accept it at all were Hal also, say, formerly involved with Prince John at Gaultree. It is often said that the Lancastrians are all alike – that Prince John parallels Prince Hal – but this ignores the distance Shakespeare puts between them, and his pains to make Hal a man of mystery, not of disorder or excessive rigour.

We may briefly look at the play's conclusion, and its aforementioned mood of sobriety and sternness. The morality variety plays showed the easy doom of unregeneracy and the contrasting success, after trial, of upright virtue: in *2 Henry IV* the state and the succession are finally assured, and order prevails over anarchy, but perhaps these are only Lancastrian values. Can we say that Hal is justified because he will be strong, or on the other hand that we reject his sober command? Shakespeare subjects kingship and state to a deep questioning through the action, wherein ruthless means put down ruthless men. But throughout the political action we are also asked if the end is worth the candle after all. 'Uneasy lies the head that wears the crown' we are told, and it will continue to be so in the 'after times' which Hastings tries to fathom. Continual references to time past, present, and future involve us in a perspective of lifetimes, generations, and ultimately the relationship between the play's time and our own. We see a vision of life in time which makes us see that all political life is greatly involved with time.[2] In the long term, it all looks so futile, and Falstaff's life-style is infinitely more attractive. But we also see that political activity is necessary at a given time because its opposite (for example, Northumberland's anarchy) is unthinkable. Stability may seem dehumanizing, especially after the Rabelaisian variety of the play with its strong contrasts of tone. The move from this to a 'necessary' resolution which cuts off energy and life is, I think, the conscious result of a carefully controlled structure. It is analogous to that of the later morality plays which create contrasted modes of action, and then force a resolution, but it differs in an important respect. While events bring a revelation and a resolution in *2 Henry IV*, Shakespeare has not intruded and told us how we must react, but

[1] 'Prince Hal's Second Reformation', *Shakespeare Quarterly*, XXI (1970), 19.

[2] L. C. Knights, 'Time's Subjects: The Sonnets and *King Henry IV, Part II*', in his *Some Shakespearian Themes* (Harmondsworth, 1970), pp. 40–57.

has left us wondering about the exercise of political power in all its manifestations. Prince John, who ends the play gloating over Hal's 'fair proceeding' and hoping for action in France, is a final disturbance.[1] It is also a final irony, because the 'after times' would ultimately see John's life wasted in trying to hold the France he eagerly expects his brother to win, and over which he was regent during Henry VI's reign, 'which oft our stage hath shown'. Rather than a *humanum genus* pattern leading to a triumph like Shrewsbury, *2 Henry IV* presents a pattern of variety and inclusiveness resulting in this final ordering, which leaves us to ponder its disturbing implications.

[1] J. S. Pettigrew, 'The Mood of *Henry IV*, *Part II*', *Stratford Papers on Shakespeare 1965* (Toronto, 1965), p. 166.

WHATEVER HAPPENED TO PRINCE HAL? AN ESSAY ON 'HENRY V'

WILLIAM BABULA

E. M. W. Tillyard is right in his assertion that Shakespeare in *Henry V* was 'jettisoning the character he had created' in the *Henry IV* plays.[1] The Hal that developed out of those earlier histories is not present at the opening of *Henry V*. This does not mean that Shakespeare has now accepted a Henry 'who knew exactly what he wanted and went for it with utter singleness of heart...'[2] Nor has he, as Mark Van Doren would have us believe, stretched a hero 'until he struts on tiptoe and is still strutting at the last insignificant exit.'[3] Nor, on the other extreme, is Henry the ideal humanistic hero, 'conceived of as beyond the limitations of nature, able to impose the order of philosophy on the protean world of history.'[4] Rather, as H. M. Richmond notes, Henry in this play begins as a 'clever young hero masquerading as the ideal king', and ends as 'a mature man'.[5] Thus the process of growth that Henry undergoes in the play is crucial.[6] While this process may render the second tetralogy inconsistent, it gives a marked consistency to the play *Henry V* as it stands alone. For in it Shakespeare has decided to dramatize again the maturation of a ruler. He is repeating, for the purposes of effective drama – the play is meant to be presented by itself – the pattern of the education of a prince shown in the previous *Henry IV* histories.[7] Critical confusion arises when this Henry is expected to be identical to the Henry who rejects Falstaff in *Henry IV*. Rather, the king is a character very much like Hotspur as the play begins. The main difference, however, is that Henry can learn moderation. He can do so because he is dealing with the realities and limitations of territorial acquisition; he should do so because he is a king. Hotspur cannot because he covets the limitless abstraction honor; he would not because he is a rebel.

The play opens with a Chorus that provides part of the context in which the audience sees Henry. In typical epic fashion the poet through his Chorus presents the invocation: 'O for a Muse of fire, that would ascend / The brightest heaven of invention...' (Prologue, 1–2).[8] It

[1] *Shakespeare's History Plays* (New York, 1946), p. 306.

[2] *Ibid.*, p. 313.

[3] *Shakespeare* (New York, 1939), p. 170.

[4] Ronald Berman, Introduction to *Twentieth Century Interpretations of 'Henry V'* (Englewood Cliffs, N.J., 1968), p. 10.

[5] *Shakespeare's Political Plays* (New York, 1967), p. 200.

[6] Tillyard ignores the process. He argues that Shakespeare is creating an inconsistent character to satisfy 'the requirements both of the chronicles and of popular tradition' (*Shakespeare's History Plays*, p. 306). The result is not development but a 'patchwork character' (*ibid.*, p. 308).

[7] In his introduction to the Arden edition (1954), p. xxx, J. H. Walter comments upon Henry's character: 'At the outset of the play his virtue after his conversion, complete though it may be, is yet cloistered...' For Walter, Hal has been baptized before the play begins (pp. xvii–xxi). This is quite the opposite of maturation and education.

[8] All citations in my text are to *Shakespeare, The Complete Works*, ed. Hardin Craig, revised David Bevington (Glenview, Ill., 1973).

sounds as if we are going to see the epic hero many have seen in Henry V. And there is no reason to doubt this notion as the Chorus turns apologetic:

> But pardon, gentles all,
> The flat unraised spirits that have dared
> On this unworthy scaffold to bring forth
> So great an object: can this cockpit hold
> The vasty fields of France? or may we cram
> Within this wooden O the very casques
> That did affright the air at Agincourt?
> (Prologue, 8–14)

The theme is presented as epic but the audience is also reminded that they are seeing an illusion created by art. The Globe, the 'scaffold', this 'cockpit', this 'wooden O' are to be transformed into the vastness of France. A perfect apology for the limitations of the Elizabethan stage? If so, every play would require it to some degree.[1] Or perhaps Shakespeare is introducing the audience to one of his major concerns: the distance between art and reality. In this case it applies to the theatre. It will come to apply, however, to the distance between the art, the words, the rhetoric of Henry and the reality of his actions. There is an art that covers reality in the political world as well as in the playhouse.

As the play proper opens the audience hears of what it is going to see and hear of so much in *Henry V*: the quarrel. In this case the Parliament is contemplating a bill that will strip the Church of its wealth. As Canterbury comments, 'If it pass against us, / We lose the better half of our possession' (I, i, 7–8). The pivot upon which this question rests is the king. Canterbury then begins to heap praise upon this king – a character we have not yet seen in this play. Henry, no longer the riotous prince, is now like a 'paradise'. He can 'reason in divinity', 'debate of commonwealth affairs', and cut 'the Gordian knot' of policy – a reference to Alexander the Great that will rebound ironically later in the play. Yet all of this idealized language can be explained rather cynically. When the Bishop of Ely asks which side is Henry on, Canterbury replies that the king is 'rather swaying more upon our part...' (I, i, 73). And certainly it is difficult to miss the suggestion of a bribe when Canterbury explains the king's favor – note the 'for' in particular:

> For I have made an offer to his majesty,
> Upon our spiritual convocation
> ... to give a greater sum
> Than ever at one time the clergy yet
> Did to his predecessors part withal.
> (I, i, 75–6, 79–81)

Could Henry make an unbiased choice?[2] All of the grand-sounding language by which Canterbury describes the king sounds like the epic and idealizing language of the Prologue. In fact it sounds as if the bishop would cover the limitations of the king just as Shakespeare would disguise the limitations of his playhouse. But beneath the language there is an inescapable reality of person and platform.

In the second scene Henry appears for the first time. He sends for Canterbury and requires of him:

> My learned lord, we pray you to proceed
> And justly and religiously unfold
> Why the law Salique that they have in France
> Or should, or should not, bar us in our claim:
> And God forbid, my dear and faithful lord,
> That you should fashion, wrest or bow your
> reading... (I, ii, 9–14)

One critic has commented: 'To consult his spiritual advisers on a matter of this gravity

[1] Michael Goldman in *Shakespeare and the Energies of Drama* (Princeton, 1972), p. 59, comments on the Chorus: 'Nowhere else does he use it to call attention to the inadequacies of his stage, which is of course no more inadequate to this story than to the material of the other histories.'

[2] Walter (pp. xxiii–xxviii) and the New Cambridge editor J. Dover Wilson (pp. xix–xxiv) argue against this view. For them the French war was justified by feudal law.

was the correct thing for a king to do...'[1] Yet the audience knows that the bishop, to protect Church property, must have the war in France; it is hard to imagine that this politic king does not know the same thing. What he seems to want are the words that will legalize aggression. He also wants to abdicate his responsibility for any of the slaughter to follow.

> For God doth know how many now in health
> Shall drop their blood in approbation
> Of what your reverence shall incite us to.
>
> (I, ii, 18–20)

Verbally Henry pretends to have little to do with what will happen; the active verb 'incite' is given to the bishop – whatever happens will be his fault. It is not a very pleasant situation for Canterbury. This is indeed a politic king but not necessarily an epic hero.

Canterbury then launches upon a 62-line defense of Henry's right to the French throne. No audience simply hearing this complicated and twisting explanation could have much idea what it means. In terms of stage action the king himself seems confused. After he has been told in Canterbury's involved speech that he is the proper heir, he still has to ask: 'May I with right and conscience make this claim?' (I, ii, 96). He does not really understand the basis of his claim and neither could the audience.[2] The bishop assures him, however, by reference to 'the book of Numbers'. The search for authority seems rather desperate. One would hardly think of the book of Numbers as providing 'unhidden passages' through which an English king could claim a French throne.

When Henry resolves to claim the throne, before the French ambassadors enter, he states: 'France being ours, we'll bend it to our awe, / Or break it all to pieces...' (I, ii, 224–5). It is the absolute demand of the immature man, the kind of demand we would expect from Hotspur. But when the ambassadors come in and tell Henry the Dauphin rejects all of his claims and has sent over some 'tennis-balls' instead, Henry projects himself as an epic hero – but note how his self-glorification reminds us of Richard II, another sun-king:

> ...I will rise there with so full a glory
> That I will dazzle all the eyes of France.
> Yea, strike the Dauphin blind to look on us.
>
> (I, ii, 278–80)

It sounds impressive, but Richard II sounded impressive, too. Henry pretends this insult has resolved him when he had already made up his mind to claim France.[3] Also, Henry does to the Dauphin what he did to Canterbury; he takes responsibility from himself and puts it on another. It is the Dauphin who 'hath turn'd his [tennis] balls to gun-stones' (I, ii, 282). It is the Dauphin whose soul 'shall stand sore charged for the wasteful vengeance / That shall fly with them...' (I, ii, 283–4). If the audience has put aside the Hal of the *Henry IV* plays, it is seeing a clever, but not necessarily attractive, immature man.

Act II begins with a Prologue that verbally presents an idealized English army as the opening Chorus had presented an idealized Henry who was the equal of Mars:

> Now all the youth of England are on fire,
> And silken dalliance in the wardrobe lies:
> Now thrive the armourers, and honour's thought
> Reigns solely in the breast of every man...
>
> (II, Prologue, 1–4)

Yet there is ambiguity in this Chorus as well. The young men are compared to 'English Mercuries' as Henry was compared to Mars. Obviously the reference is in part to the speed

[1] M. M. Reese, *The Cease of Majesty* (New York, 1961), p. 323.

[2] The same point is made in Harold C. Goddard, *The Meaning of Shakespeare* (Chicago, 1951), p. 211.

[3] Walter points out the change that Shakespeare has made from his sources in Hall and Holinshed where the tennis balls arrive before Henry has decided upon war. But oddly Walter argues: 'It makes no difference to the issue. Shakespeare uses it to show Henry's Christian self-control' (p. xxiii).

with which they will move to France, but Mercury is also the god of thieves. All may not be so honest in this attack upon France. Also among the nobility, three sold out to France and plot to kill Henry.

Thus the reality of these heroes is quite different from the description the Chorus provides. What we heard from the Chorus does not match what we see on the stage. In II, i, we have the third quarrel of the play, this one between two of these 'English Mercuries', Nym and Pistol. While Henry and the Dauphin quarrel over who shall possess France, these two quarrel over who shall possess Nell Quickly – once engaged to Nym but now the wife of Pistol and previously accused of running a 'bawdy house'. The two men meet and almost begin to duel. They also employ a rhetoric that parodies that of the angry king. Pistol, for example, warns as Henry warned the Dauphin:

> O braggart vile and damned furious wight!
> The grave doth gape, and doting death is near;
> Therefore exhale. (II, i, 63–5)

The entire argument takes a turn downward when Pistol states to Nym:

> O hound of Crete, think'st thou my spouse to get?
> No; to the spital go,
> And from the powdering-tub of infamy
> Fetch forth the lazar kite of Cressid's kind . . .
> (II, i, 77–80)

Pistol tells him to marry a prostitute suffering from venereal disease. The parallel between this argument and the argument over France is not lost on the audience. Once more Henry's quarrel seems a bit tainted, or what even may be worse, useless. This argument, however, is settled by Pistol's paying a 'noble' to Nym. The idea of prostitution is reinforced by the suggestion of sale, and the passing of money reminds us how the first quarrel of the play – that between Church and Parliament – was settled: by a 'mighty sum' from Church to Henry.

The next scene picks up the further degeneration among the 'English Mercuries' noted by the Chorus. Henry sets a trap for Cambridge, Scroop, and Grey when he asks them whether he should free a man 'who rail'd against our person'. They argue against mercy and thus when their treachery is revealed Henry can respond to their pleas of mercy: 'The mercy that was quick in us but late, / By your own counsel is suppress'd and kill'd . . .' (II, ii, 79–80). Their own words condemn them, but the same sort of self-condemnation will return to haunt Henry later in the play. He too will be sorry for what he said earlier. There is also irony in that at least one of the conspirators, Cambridge, was out to do what Henry seems to be doing, to place a man, Edmund Mortimer, on the throne because of his descent through the female line.

Yet, in terms of stage action, the idea of deposing this monarch is shocking both to Henry himself and the audience. And as he condemns the three he comments on the fall of these 'English monsters':

> Such and so finely bolted didst thou seem:
> And thus thy fall hath left a kind of blot,
> To mark the full-fraught man and best indued
> With some suspicion. (II, ii, 137–40)

The king's advice should be heeded by the audience as well. For Henry is the 'best indued' man of this play and yet it would be wise to watch him and his quarrel 'with some suspicion'. Indeed, a suspicious eye should be cast on the words of patriotic exhortation with which Henry closes the scene: 'Cheerly to sea; the signs of war advance: / No king of England, if not king of France' (II, ii, 192–3). The words and attitude seem to belong to the discredited Hotspur of *1 Henry IV* who commented as he prepared to challenge the army of Henry IV: 'Doomsday is near; die all, die merrily'.

Henry V is not the ideal monarch that he seemed to be in the words of the Chorus: 'the mirror of all Christian kings'.

In the following scene Pistol gives his wife advice in words that parallel Henry's:

> Trust none;
> For oaths are straws, men's faiths are wafer-cakes,
> And hold-fast is the only dog, my duck . . .
>
> (II, iii, 52–4)

His comment reiterates Henry's statement that all must be watched 'with some suspicion'. Pistol's words certainly apply to the three traitors of the previous scene, but they also seem to apply to Henry. It is in this scene that Falstaff's death is announced, and earlier Nell had said of Jack: 'The king has killed his heart' (II, i, 92). While Falstaff may have no place in the new order of things, yet it is hard to imagine that Shakespeare is trying to cast a favorable light upon Henry by such references to his former friend. Indeed, as Goddard has argued, we may feel that the words Henry applies to Scroop: 'Ingrateful, savage and inhuman creature' (II, ii, 95), reflect upon Henry and Falstaff.[1] And the next few lines that Pistol adds to his speech above, also parody Henry's comments to his lords: 'Now, lords, for France; the enterprise whereof / Shall be to you, as us, like glorious' (II, ii, 182–3). Pistol urges his cohorts: 'Let us to France; like horse-leeches, my boys, / To suck, to suck, the very blood to suck' (II, iii, 58–9). Henry's glorious enterprise may not be much better.

Yet as Shakespeare carries his audience to France once more, Henry is created verbally as the hero. The Constable informs the doubting Dauphin that Henry only covered 'discretion with a coat of folly' (II, iv, 38). The French king himself says they must fear 'the native mightiness' of Henry. Certainly such language used by the enemy creates a favorable impression of Henry upon the audience. Yet it seems difficult not to see the demand he makes through Exeter as anything less than absurd and blood-sucking:

> . . . when you find him evenly derived
> From his most famed of famous ancestors,
> Edward the Third, he bids you then resign
> Your crown and kingdom, indirectly held
> From him the native and true challenger.
>
> (II, iv, 91–5)

In fact, every reference to 'ancestors' reminds the audience of the weakness of Henry's claim to the English throne. Also, as the threats follow, we hear another example of Henry avoiding responsibility. Exeter says that if you do not deliver up the crown, Henry is

> . . . on your head
> Turning the widow's tears, the orphans' cries,
> The dead men's blood . . . (II, iv, 105–7)

So it is the French king's fault; so the bishop was the incitor of this war. No audience, heeding Henry's own warning to be suspicious of everyone, can take very much of this verbal chicanery.

The Chorus then returns to tell the audience to imagine the 'well-appointed king' sailing in epic splendor to France. And quite properly to the epic tone Henry will not accept a compromise with the French; he is not satisfied with the king's daughter Katharine and 'some petty and unprofitable dukedoms'. Instead, the cannon will fire and the siege of Harfleur will continue. Yet even in this epic-sounding Chorus there are certain ambiguities. Is it a positive act for Henry to have left England, 'Guarded with grandsires, babies, and old women' (III, Prologue, 20)? The reference to the cannon by the Chorus seems clearly ironical: 'And down goes all before them' (III, Prologue, 34). It is just not true. Harfleur is not coming down. Once more words are found quite distant from the reality of the situation.

[1] Goddard, *The Meaning of Shakespeare*, p. 230.

As the scene shifts to before Harfleur the audience hears the rhetorical Henry exhorting his men: 'Once more unto the breach, dear friends, once more; / Or close the wall up with our English dead' (III, i, 1–2). It may be a compelling statement, but as Richmond notes the attacks repeatedly fail.[1] Also, Henry's own language suggests the distortion of human nature required to carry on these brutal acts:

> Then *imitate* the action of the tiger;
> *Stiffen* the sinews; summon up the blood,
> *Disguise* fair nature with hard-favour'd rage;
> Then *lend* the eye terrible aspect...
>
> (III, i, 6–9)

The words in italics all suggest an unnatural making-over of man for war.[2] Yet Henry sees in these men, these 'English dead' a 'noble lustre'. What such a lustre comes to is quite apparent in the scene that follows.

Once more Nym, Bardolph, and Pistol represent the English army. The cowardly Bardolph immediately parodies Henry's exhortation: 'On, on, on, on, on! to the breach, to the breach' (III, ii 1). But these soldiers, these 'noblest English' are not interested in any of it. For Nym 'the knocks are too hot' and the Boy wishes he 'were in an alehouse in London'. The result is that no one moves until Fluellen enters and repeats Henry's resounding but ineffectual phrase: 'Up to the breach, you dogs! avaunt, you cullions' (III, ii, 21). They must be forced just as Henry's language of 'imitate', 'stiffen', 'disguise' suggested they would have to be. While Henry termed his men the heirs of 'so many Alexanders' (III, i, 19), what we see on the stage is, as Fluellen calls them, a collection of dogs and rascals.

While these characters are driven up to the breach the Boy manages to stay behind and describe his companions: Pistol 'hath a killing tongue'. So we might feel do Henry and the Chorus. According to the Boy: 'They will steal any thing, and call it a purchase'. They can use words to call a crime by a better name. Once more we may think of the bishop, the Chorus, and Henry himself. Then the Boy comments that they would corrupt him as well, but he would rather find a 'better service' for:

> ...if I should take from another's pocket to put into mine...it is plain pocketing up of wrongs. I must leave them...
>
> (III, ii, 53–5)

It is hard not to see in this moral criticism of these thieves – now operating in France – a moral criticism of Henry as well.

Absurd quarrels begin to reappear. As the Boy exits, Fluellen, Gower, Macmorris and Jamy come on stage. In rather confusing Welsh, Irish, and Scotch dialects an argument breaks out concerning 'the disciplines of the Roman wars'. The subject itself certainly seems unrelated to the present action. At the same time the confusing language affects the audience just as Canterbury's description of the Salic laws: the audience is not sure what the quarrel is about. Indeed, it seems to be over nothing. Yet, in this case, it leads to such things as Macmorris' threat to Fluellen: 'I will cut off your head.' Meanwhile, in a situation that parallels Henry's, Fluellen is defending the 'derivation of my birth'. Yet on stage the whole scene looks and sounds like a senseless quarrel. With such a context, it is quite easy to examine the quarrel that Henry has raised with France with 'suspicion'.

The scene then shifts back to the central quarrel. Incredibly, Henry, as he speaks to the Governor of Harfleur, is denying responsibility for what will happen in the city. He describes in detail the terrors that will befall Harfleur if it does not surrender, then warns the Governor: '...you yourselves are cause...' (III, iii, 19).

[1] Richmond, *Shakespeare's Political Plays'*, pp. 182–3.

[2] The italics are mine but my reading is indebted to that of Derek A. Traversi in *An Approach to Shakespeare* (New York, 1956), p. 39.

He also terms the Governor 'guilty in defense'. This is just too much from Henry.[1] Shakespeare makes his own attitude clear when he compares through Henry the war the king is ready to unleash 'to the prince of fiends'. It is a devil that Henry brings. Even more pointed is the irony in Henry's calling his soldiers 'Herod's bloody-hunting slaughtermen' (III, iii, 41). It is impossible to take the allusion as a compliment. More and more the doubts about the validity of Henry's quarrel are growing. Yet, for the first time something seems to be changing. Harfleur surrenders because the Dauphin cannot aid it. But as Henry accepts his prize – consider the rhetoric he employed a moment ago – he seems somewhat deflated and his language reflects this change: 'The winter coming on and sickness growing / Upon our soldiers, we will retire to Calais' (III, iii, 55–6). For the first time Henry stops sounding like an epic hero and starts sounding like an honest man. Rhetoric is put aside. Henry trapped in a discredited war is beginning to mature.

As Henry exits, Katharine, already mentioned in the Prologue to act III as a possible wife for the king, comes on stage with her maid and attempts to learn some English. Perhaps indicative of her interests, she first wishes to learn the English words for parts of the body. Her introduction at this point, and the puns that develop from English words that sound like French obscenities, relate this scene to the earlier argument between Nym and Pistol over Nell Quickly. The audience, presented with something they can see on the stage, may begin to consider her as the prize. Indeed, the theme of the battle over women was suggested by Henry's reference to the threatened virgins of Harfleur: '... pure maidens [who will] fall into the hand / Of hot and forcing violation' (III, iii, 20–1). This idea is reinforced by the Dauphin's comments in the next scene about Frenchwomen:

> Our madams mock at us, and plainly say
> Our mettle is bred out and they will give
> Their bodies to the lust of English youth
> To new-store France with bastard warriors.
>
> (III, iv, 28–31)

All of these arguments recall the foolish quarrel over Nell that was finally settled with money.

The parallels that Shakespeare set up early in the play between Henry and the low characters do, however, begin to break down. Bardolph, the English soldier, has been condemned as Pistol relates: 'For he hath stolen a pax, and hanged must a' be' (III, vi, 42). In Holinshed the stolen object is said to be a *pyx*, the vessel that contained the sacred host. The reason for the change to the *pax*, a plate, is not to make the crime less shocking but to parallel Bardolph's crime with Henry's, which was to steal the *pax* or peace.[2] But even while the audience may be associating the two crimes, it begins to see a Henry who is becoming a man of peace rather than of war. When he is told Bardolph has been condemned for his crime, he agrees, but for apparently commendable reasons:

> We would have all such offenders so cut off: and we give express charge, that in our marches through the country, there be nothing compelled from the villages, nothing taken but paid for... for when lenity and cruelty play for a kingdom, the gentler gamester is the soonest winner.
>
> (III, vi, 113–20)

There was no 'gentler gamester' before Harfleur.

When the French ambassador enters in the same scene it is he who fills the air with the rhetoric of war: 'Our voice is imperial: England shall repent his folly...' (III, vi, 31–2).

[1] Walter comments, however: 'Henry's threats to Harfleur sound horrible enough, but he was... following the rules of warfare' (p. xxv).

[2] See Richmond, *Shakespeare's Political Plays*, p. 184 and C. H. Hobday, 'Imagery and Irony in *Henry V*,' in *Shakespeare Survey 21*, (Cambridge, 1968), p. 111.

Instead of reacting in kind, as he did when he received the tennis balls, Henry simply asks him to leave the country:

> Turn thee back,
> And tell thy king I do not seek him now;
> But could be willing to march on to Calais
> Without impeachment . . . (III, vi, 148–51)

Henry is asking for peace. But almost more important is his rejection of the epic art associated with the opening prologues. It is, as Henry notes, foolish to admit your weakness to your enemy. But Shakespeare seems to want to make it clear that Henry is no longer covering reality with words. So while the statement may be illogical from a strategical point of view, it is dramatically logical as it shows Henry's maturation. Thus in honesty, without artifice, he comments:

> . . . to say the sooth,
> Though 'tis no wisdom to confess so much
> Unto an enemy of craft and vantage,
> My people are with sickness much enfeebled,
> My numbers lessen'd . . . (III, vi, 151–5)

This is not the Henry who reminded the audience of Hotspur in the opening scene.

In fact all of the disagreeable elements that Shakespeare associated with the English earlier now begin to pass over to the French. At the moment it is Henry who is seeking peace. Also the petty quarrels are now French petty quarrels. In III, vii, the Constable of France, Orleans, and the Dauphin argue about their armor and their horses. Going the furthest, the Dauphin says of his horse:

> It is the prince of palfreys; his neigh is like the bidding of a monarch and his countenance enforces homage. (III, vii, 29–31)

This is too much for Orleans but the Dauphin will not be stopped. He declared: 'I once writ a sonnet in his praise and began thus: "Wonder of nature"' (III, vii, 42–3). In fact the Dauphin states: 'My horse is my mistress' (III, vii, 46). The argument begins to parallel that of Nym and Pistol over Nell; only now the question is far more absurd. The mistress in question now becomes a horse. It is the French who are being presented as absurd.

Instead of Henry's rhetoric, the audience hears the bragging of the French who are all impatient for the day when 'by ten / We shall have each a hundred Englishmen' (III, vii, 168–9). Yet it will be the English who will be out on the field of battle first. And now instead of Henry it is the Dauphin who is looked at with suspicion. When he exits the Constable of France calls the Dauphin a braggart who can never do harm. When Orleans says that the Dauphin is valiant, the Constable ironically agrees, for 'he told me so himself' (III, vii, 117). If the audience is watching for parallels it can see one between Pistol and the Dauphin. Gradually Henry is moving away from the unattractive elements in the play. Shakespeare is shifting them to the French.

Yet, petty quarrels continue to plague the English camp. Henry disguises himself with a cloak as a 'gentleman of a company'. Soon he runs into Pistol and though the king shows restraint he does provoke an argument with him when he tells Pistol he is Fluellen's kinsman. It all ends with Pistol's 'The figo for thee, then!' (IV, i, 60). As Henry continues through the camp he meets the positive parallels to Nym, Bardolph, and Pistol in Bates, Court, and Williams. When Henry says, however, the king's cause is 'just and his quarrel honourable' (IV, i, 133), Williams replies, 'That's more than we know' (IV, i, 134). In fact he then goes on to hold the king responsible if the cause is not just:

> But if the cause be not good, the king himself hath a heavy reckoning to make, when all those legs and arms and heads, chopped off in a battle, shall join together at the latter day and cry all 'We died at such a place . . .' (IV, i, 140–5)

Once more a raw nerve is struck in Henry and in a speech that covers 42 prose lines (IV, i,

154–6), the audience hears him denying responsibility again. He avoids the central issue of the just cause and presents such statements as: 'Every subject's duty is the king's; but every subject's soul is his own.' On stage, though Williams and Bates agree, the speech is hard to follow – recall Canterbury's treatment of the Salic laws. And it just does not answer the question of responsibility that Williams posed. Henry is not yet free of his rhetoric.

In fact, the soldiers continue cynical when Henry tells them the King has said he would not be ransomed. As Williams says:

> Ay, he said so, to make us fight cheerfully: but when our throats are cut, he may be ransomed, and we ne'er the wiser. (IV, i, 204–6)

This exchange leads to another foolish quarrel and Henry and Williams exchange favors so that they can recognize each other and fight at a more appropriate time. Oddly, it is not Henry, but Bates who stops the quarrel: 'Be friends, you English fools, be friends...' (IV, i, 239). As the soldiers exit, Henry in soliloquy, upset by Williams' remarks about the king's responsibility, comments:

> Upon the king! let us our lives, our souls
> Our debts, our careful wives,
> Our children and our sins lay on the king!
> (IV, i, 247–9)

Yet the war is his responsibility. It is hard to miss Shakespeare's irony when Henry laments: '... in gross brain little wots / What watch the king keeps to maintain the peace...' (IV, i, 299–300). It was Henry who, like Bardolph, stole the *pax* or peace. While Henry is still confined by his rhetoric, he is growing more honest. He is ready to admit that not only is there some doubt about his claim to the French throne, but there is doubt about his right to the English crown. As the scene ends, referring to the murder of Richard II, he prays:

> Not to-day, O Lord,
> O, not to-day, think not upon the fault
> My father made in compassing the crown!
> (IV, i, 309–11)

The process may be taking a long time, but Henry is maturing.[1]

I spoke above of the parallel between the Chorus's admission that it was covering a limited stage with devices of art and our sense that Henry may have been doing the same thing in his role as epic king. In the Prologue to Act IV, the Chorus now apologizes for the battle scene:

> ... O for pity! – we shall much disgrace
> With four or five most vile and ragged foils,
> Right ill-disposed in brawl ridiculous,
> The name of Agincourt. (IV, Prologue, 49–52)

But this apology does not nearly come up to the apology required. In the Prologue to the play, the Chorus asked the audience 'into a thousand parts divide one man' (l. 24) and thus imagine the large battle. Another apology for technical limitations? Hardly. None of this prepares us for what we are going to see in the only actual battle scene where French and English meet: IV, iv. What Shakespeare has asked us to do is to divide Pistol the coward and a more cowardly Frenchman into a thousand parts to represent the monumental English victory at Agincourt. Pistol takes him prisoner and says he will cut his throat. The Boy translates the French soldier's reply:

> He prays you save his life: he is a gentleman of a good house; and for his ransom he will give you two hundred crowns. (IV, iv, 47–9)

The offer satisfies Pistol, who states: 'As I suck blood, I will some mercy show' (IV, iv, 68). His words recall his earlier intentions as he left for France: 'To suck, to suck, the very blood to suck' (II, iii, 58). Shakespeare is not

[1] In contrast Una Ellis-Fermor argues that Henry's prayers are an attempt to 'bargain with his God like a pedlar', in *The Frontiers of Drama* (1948), p. 47.

limited by his theatre, he has chosen to present Agincourt in the worst way possible. The only hero we see on stage is one whom, as the Boy comments, 'Bardolph and Nym had ten times more valour than . . .' (IV, iv, 74).

As the French begin to sense defeat, Bourbon urges them on in terms that recall the argument over Nell, the reference to Frenchwomen giving 'their bodies to the lust of English youth . . .' (III, v, 30) and Henry's references to the rape of virgins as he stood outside Harfleur. Orleans says he who will not follow him into battle is

> Like a base pandar, [who will] hold the chamber-door
> Whilst by a slave, no gentler than my dog,
> His fairest daughter is contaminated.
>
> (IV, v, 14–16)

Then the battle, if possible, becomes even less attractive. Exeter describes in pathetic terms the deaths of York and Suffolk. Henry is moved almost to tears. But at this very moment Henry learns the French are regrouping and he commands: 'Then every soldier kill his prisoners: / Give the word through' (IV, vi, 37–8). Immediately juxtaposed to this act is the French act of brutality: they have slaughtered the boys who were with the luggage. For this, Fluellen explains, 'The king, most worthily, hath caused every soldier to cut his prisoner's throat. O, 'tis a gallant king!' (IV, vii, 10–11). The irony seems inescapable. Just as Henry decided to attack France before the insult of the tennis balls, Henry now ordered his massacre before the French carried out theirs. Pistol and the French soldier are not bad 'ciphers to this great accompt'. Once more the reality of the battle has been quite different from the promises of the early Choruses. If we are going to admire the Henry that was maturing before the battle, Shakespeare must extricate him from this degrading turmoil.

But it is not time yet. Fluellen and Gower compare Henry who could 'cut the Gordian knot' and Alexander the Great who comes out in Fluellen's Welsh distortion of big as Alexander the Pig. Both epic heroes are being trimmed down to size. The audience may imagine, however, that Shakespeare is going to compare Henry's victory with Alexander's conquests. But this is hardly the case. There is a comparison, however, as Fluellen states:

> If you mark Alexander's life well, Harry of Monmouth's life is come after it indifferent well . . . Alexander . . . did, in his ales and his angers, look you, kill his best friend, Cleitus.
>
> (IV, vii, 34–6, 39–41)

When Gower objects that Henry never killed any of his friends, Fluellen responds with Falstaff:

> Harry Monmouth, being in his right wits and his good judgments, turned away the fat knight . . .
>
> (IV, vii, 49–51)

The comparison with Henry presented as cold-blooded, can hardly be to his advantage.[1]

In fact, as he enters immediately after this passage he threatens the French prisoners once more: 'We'll cut the throats of those we have . . .' (IV, vii, 66). Yet when the French surrender Henry can take a new tone: 'Praised be God, and not our strength, for it!' (IV, vii, 90). In contrast to his earlier bragging, in contrast to the French bragging, his tone and attitude seem refreshing. But another quarrel, much less important, must be settled as well. Williams and Henry are to meet after the battle. But to avoid insult to the royal person, Henry gives the favor that marks him as Williams' enemy to Fluellen. He is careful, however, that nothing serious should pass and

[1] Walter (p. xxi) finds great praise for Henry in the comparison to Alexander. Reese (*The Cease of Majesty*, p. 328) similarly finds it to be an 'enchanting comparison'. But see Robert P. Merrix, 'The Alexandrian Allusion in Shakespeare's *Henry V*,' *English Literary Renaissance*, 2 (Autumn 1972), 321–33 for an extensive treatment of the satiric implications of the reference.

he sends certain lords to 'follow, and see there be no harm between them' (IV, vii, 190). Yet we see on stage another quarrel as Williams recognizes the favor and strikes Fluellen. The audience must by now desire peace on stage. Henry enters to settle the quarrel and tells Williams that he had insulted the king the night before the battle. Williams defends himself, however, by saying it was Henry's fault:

> ... what your highness suffered under that shape, I beseech you take it for your own fault and not mine ... (IV, viii, 56–8).

And as Henry rewards this fellow the audience feels he is finally beginning to take responsibility. It was his fault. Yet Fluellen's advice to Williams at this point can apply to Henry as well:

> I pray you to serve God, and keep you out of prawls, and prabbles, and quarrels, and dissensions ...
> (IV, viii, 69–70)

The Prologue to act V presents the conqueror Henry in rather unheroic terms. That is, Henry is no longer a braggart. What follows is his reaction to a triumphal procession:

> ... he forbids it,
> Being free from vainness and self-glorious pride;
> Giving full trophy, signal and ostent
> Quite from himself to God.
> (V, Prologue, 19–22)

It is easy to be cynical about this pose, yet it does present us with a Henry who is more humble than the character we experienced at the beginning of the drama. He also becomes more attractive to us when the Chorus, ignoring real time, now carries Henry back to France – only now he is there for peace and not for war. His new role is juxtaposed to the roles his soldiers still play. The audience watches while the English soldiers continue to argue among themselves. Fluellen, in terms of stage action, had just condemned 'quarrels and dissensions' but now he is ready for another meaningless argument with Pistol about the Welsh and the symbol of their pride, the leek (V, i). Once more there is confusion and dissension on stage when the audience is weary of this kind of thing. We have been overwhelmed with quarrels, debates, and wars; everything should be over. No wonder Henry looks so good in the final act when he brings peace to a play that is itself in turmoil.

Indeed, Henry is removed from the conflicts that take place on stage. Fluellen beats Pistol on the stage for mocking the Welsh, a punishment well earned. In fact, Pistol has been driven out of the army as the worst aspects of Henry's character seem to have been driven out of him. Now Pistol, whom we will hear of no more, comments:

> Old do I wax; and from my weary limbs
> Honour is cudgelled. Well, bawd I'll turn,
> And something lean to cutpurse of quick hand.
> To England will I steal, and there I'll steal:
> And patches will I get unto these cudgell'd scars,
> And swear I got them in the Gallia wars.
> (V, i, 89–94)

He will continue to be a thief, an occupation that Henry has now apparently disavowed. Also throughout the play Pistol's boasting served to parody the epic language of the king and the Chorus. Pistol is going to continue to boast and swagger like a 'turkey-cock' – he is going to present himself as a soldier wounded in the wars – while the audience will see in the next scene a Henry who has put off such swaggering language. Thus Pistol who served in the play as a parallel to Henry, reminding us of the king's limitations, now serves as a contrast to a matured king. Having shown us what Henry is not going to be, he departs forever from Shakespeare's stage. It is the perfect moment to dismiss him.

This time Henry has come not to suck the blood of France but for peace. Yet even this late in the play we are reminded of an earlier

Henry. The king tells Burgundy that peace is the French King's responsibility: 'Well then the peace, / Which you before so urged, lies in his answer' (v, ii, 75–6). Will the king accept Henry's 'just demands?' Once again he is avoiding responsibility. But there is a difference. He is now ready to compromise, something a Hotspur could never do. He tells his negotiators:

> . . . take with you free power to ratify,
> Augment, or alter, as your wisdoms best
> Shall see advantageable for our dignity,
> Anything in or out of our demands
> And we'll consign thereto.
>
> (v, ii, 86–90)

He is much more concerned with wooing Katharine.

Indeed it is in this action, as they are left alone on stage (except for Alice), that the audience really sees a new Henry.[1] The change in Henry is particularly signified by the change in his language. He once spoke in epic rhetoric concerning war, he now speaks in simple prose as he pleads his love. In fact he insists upon an honesty of style; he is not covering anything with art. This is certainly different from the Henry we saw before and from the Chorus who admitted covering reality with art. Now Henry woos:

> But, before God, Kate, I cannot look greenly nor gasp out my eloquence, nor I have no cunning in protestation; only downright oaths . . .
>
> (v, ii, 146–9)

Though love is certainly different from war, the audience does see and hear a Henry who seems to have rejected the deceptive arts of rhetoric. For the first time we may be having a fully positive reaction to him. There is no longer a distance between words and reality, a distance we felt so keenly between the words of the Chorus and the realities of the action. No longer does he need the confusing legal language of the bishop; no false claims are being covered up by words. Also all of the imagery of the rape of Frenchwomen, which certainly reflected upon Henry's purposes in attacking France, now only serves as a contrast to his honorable proposal of marriage.

Thus the quarrel is finally resolved with the marriage of Henry and Katharine – the ending reminds one of the conclusions of various comedies. Peace is the value stressed. Yet there is one final irony that obviously affected the Elizabethan audience. If more and more the audience felt as it watched this play the futility of all 'dissensions', what more support could it require than the Epilogue?[2] Henry dies and leaves both France and England to his son. But the Chorus – now like Henry in the last scene, speaking without art or rhetoric – tells us honestly that:

> Henry the Sixth, in infant bands crown'd King
> Of France and England, did this king succeed;
> Whose state so many had the managing,
> That they lost France and made his England bleed.
>
> (Epilogue, 9–12)

Thus, with no cover of art, the audience is

[1] This scene, and indeed, all of act v has often been criticized. Dr Johnson, whom Van Doren cites (*Shakespeare*, p. 175) wrote: 'The truth is that the poet's matter failed him in the fifth act . . .' Van Doren (*ibid.*, p. 176) elaborates: 'The figure . . . collapses here into a mere good fellow, a hearty undergraduate with enormous initials on his chest.' The scene, however, has had its recent defenders. Walter (p. xxviii) argues from Renaissance conceptions of the ideal king that the Christian prince to complete his virtues must be married. Reese (*The Cease of Majesty*, p. 331) comments: 'Henry's wooing, so often criticized as heavy-handed and hypocritical, was in the accepted manner of the light-hearted gallant.' In contrast, though he defends the scene, Robert Ornstein in *A Kingdom for a Stage* (Cambridge, Mass., 1972), p. 198, finds 'Harry less attractive as a lover than as a soldier . . . because the conqueror of Agincourt cannot, even in his "passion", forget his royal self . . .'

[2] Robert B. Pierce, however, in *Shakespeare's History Plays, The Family and the State* (Columbus, Ohio, 1971), p. 234, argues that the Epilogue only gives us a 'vague consciousness' of the coming collapse.

reminded of the uselessness of the entire glorious action. The reality of war is no longer disguised; the Chorus presents it as accomplishing nothing.

Thus the play presents several positive elements in its conclusion. If it began in war, it suggests the value of peace at the end. If it begins with a foolish king, it seems to end with a mature one. If it begins with an artificial language, it ends with an honest one. Thus process and development must be recognized if the play is to be understood. It is as if Shakespeare had decided to redo the education of a prince presented in *1* and *2 Henry IV*. Any inconsistency that Shakespeare may be charged with is historical. That is, he begins in *Henry V* to write about a monarch who resembles the earlier character Hotspur. This is a new play in which a rash, rhetorical, young and foolish king will learn a lesson in moderation. The audience can follow his development as it responds to his language and the language of the Chorus. At the end of the play both king and Chorus eschew the rhetorical language with which they disguised facts. Art has been stripped off and the reality remains. At the close of the play Henry is honest and peaceseeking; he has matured as monarch and man. Thus in *Henry V* we simply do not have Hal. Shakespeare repeats the theme concerned with the education of a prince, but it is a different prince. Overlooking this fact has led many a critic astray who could not locate the Hal of the earlier plays in this one. He is not there. Thus the unity of *Henry V* is internal and does not depend upon a tetralogy for justification. *Henry V* must stand alone if its dramatic unity is to be appreciated.

'HENRY V' AND THE BEES' COMMONWEALTH

ANDREW GURR

Henry V, whatever one's view of its king as hero or prig, owes a debt to the mirror for princes tradition of Augustine, Erasmus and Sackville in one way or another. The Chorus to act II, in calling Henry 'the mirror of all Christian kings', conflates Erasmus's *Institutio principis Christiani* with the *Mirror for Magistrates*. The list of instances in which Henry's conduct fits the requirements of Erasmus's prince is a long one.[1] Consequently it is the more striking when we find Shakespeare using an incident which occurs in Erasmus but in a way which differs radically from his version. The incident which Shakespeare altered in what I take to be a significant way is the fable of the bees, which Henry's Archbishop offers to him in a lengthy speech as a pattern for the organisation of his commonwealth in time of war (I, ii, 187–204).[2]

The first known use of the parallel between human society and the beehive was in Virgil's *Georgics IV*, where of course it was readily available to Shakespeare.[3] Its first use as a lesson for a young prince was by Seneca in his *De Clementia*, written for his pupil Nero. Thomas Elyot also used it for the young Edward VI, and it appears in a similar context in Erasmus's *Institutio*.[4] There was no particular reason why Shakespeare should visit Erasmus for this detail when it enjoyed such general currency, of course, although Erasmus made much more pointed use of it than anyone else. What I find striking is that Shakespeare's version ends up pointing in precisely the opposite direction from Erasmus. It makes an intriguing coincidence.

Erasmus begins

> Who has not heard with interest of the government of the bees and ants? When temptations begin to descend into the youthful heart of the prince, then his tutor should point out such of these stories as belong in his education.

So far, it would seem, though Henry is perhaps rather old for this kind of thing, the Archbishop is tutoring the young prince as Erasmus suggested. But, continues Erasmus,

> He should tell him that the king never flies far away, has wings smaller in proportion to the size of its body than the others, and that he alone has no sting.

This is hardly the point to make when a foreign war, one moreover greatly to the Archbishop's advantage, has been decided on. Worse still from the Archbishop's point of view is what Erasmus goes on to say:

> From this the tutor should point out that it is the part of a good prince always to remain within the limits of his realm; his reputation for clemency should be his special form of praise.

The Archbishop is evidently less perfect in modelling his conduct on Erasmus than his pupil.

[1] See for instance J. H. Walter, ed., *Henry V*, New Arden Shakespeare (1954), pp. xvii–xviii.

[2] Quotations and line references are to the edition of Peter Alexander, *The Tudor Shakespeare* (1963).

[3] T. W. Baldwin, *Small Latine and Lesse Greeke*, 2 vols, (Urbana, Ill., 1944), II, 472–8 examines the passage in relation to the commentary by Willichius which Shakespeare probably knew.

[4] See *The Education of a Christian Prince* trans. Lester K. Born (New York, 1936), p. 147.

Speculation that Shakespeare was playing with his sources in this reversal of Erasmus might stop there if it were not for the occurrence in the passage last quoted of a word resonant with associations in the play, and one which opens to question the whole pattern of Henry's conduct as a Christian prince. This is the word which Erasmus fastens on at the end of his instruction that the prince should stay at home, implying elliptically that he should strive for it rather than military glory: clemency. Erasmus's Latin (*clementia*) is an echo of the title of Seneca's original mirror for princes, which also made the point that the queen bee has no sting, and was very largely concerned with the prince's exercise of justice and mercy. Clemency turns up in *Henry V* in a curious aside of the king's at III, vi, 108–9. After pronouncing sentence on the drone Bardolph for looting, and ordering his soldiers to treat the French civilians fairly, he justifies his order, saying

> for when lenity and cruelty play for a kingdom the gentler gamester is the soonest winner.

Lenity, or clemency, it appears is the best policy abroad as well as at home. Henry is adjusting Erasmus's point to fit his own different circumstances. Personifying the two terms like this makes them almost proleptic of the game played at Bosworth between lenitive Richmond and cruel Richard when the gentler gamester wins with support from the subjects alienated by Richard's cruelty. But here there is no adversary following the other policy. Henry is balancing alternative courses of policy open to himself as invader and putative ruler of France. It is this deliberate choice of an Erasmian Christian policy which marks Henry's conduct here and throughout the play.

Policy, however, the art of the possible, is all too likely to run into circumstances which hinder its enforcement. The Archbishop's use of the bee fable shows how circumstances alter cases. Henry's character, and with it Shakespeare's picture of his glorious commonwealth in which all men like the bees work 'contrariously' to the one end, is conditioned first by his concern to conduct himself like a Christian prince, and secondly by his management of the war.

The two aspects interlock, because the most conspicuous test for any prince who professed to be Christian was the Just War. Hotspur put it at its most elementary level before he died at Shrewsbury:

> Now, for our consciences, the arms are fair
> When the intent of bearing them is just.
> (*1 Henry IV*, v, ii, 88–9)

Hotspur though was a notorious over-simplifier, not inclined to chase the question past the thickets of private motivation. A monarch has more than his private conscience to satisfy in deciding what is a just war, and he puts at risk far more bodies than his own. Both Augustine who invented the concept and Erasmus who was the most famous Renaissance authority on it were pacifist and anti-imperialist. It is not difficult to find in Augustine polemics declaring, for instance, that 'to make war on one's neighbours and from them to move on against the rest, crushing and subduing peoples who have given no offence, out of mere lust for dominion – what else can this be called except brigandage on a grand scale?'[1] Erasmus was known as a pacifist, and said so in almost all his writings. His *Dulce Bellum inexpertis* appeared in England in 1533 as *Erasmus against War*.

When we look at the list of parallels between Shakespeare's Christian prince and Erasmus's in the *Institutio principis Christiani*, we should not forget to match up the contrasts as well.

[1] *The City of God against the Pagans* trans. George E. McCracken and others, 7 vols (Cambridge, Mass., 1957–72) IV, 25 (Book IV, 6).

Erasmus criticised warlike rulers in all his writings in sweeping language which allowed little room for exceptions. A characteristic statement is in the opening to the *Utilissima consultatio de bello Turcis inferendo*. He wrote this essay for and dedicated it to Charles V, who was trying to guard his Italian interests by making war on the Turks, a crusade against the infidel which fell within Augustine's definition of a Just War. Not that it was meant only for Charles V. Erasmus also sent a copy to Henry VIII in 1517. It begins 'All monarchs are cut from the same cloth. Some busy themselves with collecting the sinews of war; some, with generals and machines; but hardly any plan for the betterment of human life, which is the basis for everything else and which applies with equal importance to everybody.' Erasmus did not record any opinion on Henry V, but if he had his approval would not have been unqualified.

Lily Campbell in calling *Henry V* a 'model dramatisation of the treatises on war'[1] took a fairly short perspective on the war industry which flourished in England under Elizabeth. The characteristic tone of the apologists for war was that of Matthew Sutcliffe, the bellicose Dean of Exeter, who began his tract *The Practice, Proceedings, and Lawes of Armes* (1593) with the claim that it was quite unnecessary to argue 'whether it be lawfull, either for Christian Princes to make warres, or for christians to serve in warres', because the only people who fail to wave the question aside are 'both heretical, and phrenetical persons'.[2] Cornwallis reckoned that blood-letting in war, like purgation of the human body, was good for the health of the body politic. 'Warre is the remedy', he wrote in 1601, 'for a State surfeited with peace, it is a medicine for Commonwealths sick of too much ease and tranquillitie.'[3] Shakespeare gave the same medicinal image to the rebel Archbishop of York in *2 Henry IV*, iv, i, 63, who speaks of ' fearful war / To diet rank minds', and to Coriolanus who urges war, again medicinally, to 'vent / Our musty superfluity' (I, i, 223–4). Cornwallis was patriotic, not bothered about either the opponents in such a war or about any moral issues. The Dean of Exeter to some extent did have a moral stance, and it is worth noting how far he thought the limits of a just war extended. Wars are justified, he said, 'in defence of our country, true religion, our goodes or liberty'. And he stretched it a little to cover a kind of police role: 'It is likewise lawful to represse pirats, and publique robbers by force of armes.' Wars of defence were much more easily justifiable than wars of offence, or wars undertaken to back up a claim to another country's throne. That question hung in the balance.

There is no doubt that Shakespeare knew where he was in the debate over the Just War. A crusade to the Holy Land, like the one which Henry IV hopes to undertake and urges on his son as a means of keeping the nobles busy, and which Henry V in his turn promises to his own son, that was exactly Augustine's idea of a justifiable campaign. Henry V chooses to pursue his claim to France instead and leave the crusade to his son. Whether or not he takes his politic father's point about distracting

[1] Lily B. Campbell, *Shakespeare's Histories: Mirrors of Elizabethan Policy* (San Marino, 1947), p. 271.

[2] Sig. D1r.

[3] *Discourses upon Seneca the Tragedian* 1601, sig. H1r. The Just War was not a dead issue among sixteenth-century theologians. I am grateful to Martin Jarrett-Kerr, CR, for the interesting observation that while the Latin version of the Thirty-Nine Articles refers in Article XXXVII to 'justa bella' ('Christianis licet, ex mandata magistratus, arma portare, et justa bella administrare'), the English version speaks only of 'the wars' ('It is lawful for Christian men, at the commandment of the Magistrate, to wear weapons, and serve in the wars'). Latin for the scrupulous; the less contentious English form for the uninitiated?

giddy minds with foreign war he certainly ignores the implication that the only safe war is an unquestionably just one. His promise to his son (*Henry V*, v, ii, 221) suggests that he took the point. A crusade, moreover, would not only have been just but would have removed the temptation from the French of financing further rebellion, as they do with Cambridge, Scroop and Grey. Shakespeare of course had history on his side here as everywhere else. But he chose to highlight the war question above all, and the alternative possibility of a crusade, raised before and after the French war, is part of his chiaroscuro.

In contemporary accounts the balance of opinion over the French war went in Henry's favour. Gentili, whom Sutcliffe and the other militants took as their prime authority, said that Henry's claim to the French throne 'was not an empty one'.[1] Even the more individualistic writers like Fulke Greville held that war to enforce a legal claim was justifiable.[2] The real difficulty was the extra weight which a war laid on the already heavy responsibility a king had for the welfare of his subjects.

War, like all foreign policy, was a royal prerogative. Any decision over the justice of a cause lay specifically with the monarch and confronted him with his responsibility in its most acute form. In extreme cases of just or unjust war there was no difficulty. Then the subject had only himself to blame if he got himself into a bad situation. 'If the warres be notoriously unjust,' wrote Sutcliffe, 'let every man take heed howe hee embrewe his handes in innocent blood.' The monarch carried the greatest weight when the cause was doubtful. 'If the unjustice of the warres be not notorious, the subject is bound to pay and serve, and the guilt shall be laide to his charge that commandeth him to serve'.[3] This responsibility the Dean affirmed by reference to Augustine.

Erasmus put it more ominously still in his chapter 'On Beginning War' in the *Christian Prince*. I shall quote two sections, one with a specific and one with a general application. The first relates to the 'small time' of Henry's conquest, and the manner in which the Roses struggle grew out of the shambles of France. 'The prince will understand some day', writes Erasmus, 'that it was useless to extend the territory of the kingdom and what in the beginning seemed a gain was (in reality) tremendous loss, but in the meantime a great many thousands of men have been killed or impoverished.' His more general point goes beyond Augustine's just and holy war to point out that the first Christian teachers were against war of any kind. The passage has all Erasmus's power behind it, and is worth quoting at some length.

> Plato calls it sedition, not war, when Greeks war with Greeks; and if this should happen, he bids them fight with every restraint. What term should we apply, then, when Christians engage in battle with Christians, since they are united by so many bonds to each other? What shall we say when on account of a mere title, on account of a personal grievance, on account of a stupid and youthful ambition, a war is waged with every cruelty and carried on during many years?
>
> Some princes deceive themselves that any war is certainly a just one and that they have a just cause for going to war. We will not attempt to discuss whether war is ever just; but who does not think his own cause just? Among such great and changing vicissitudes of human events, among so many treaties and agreements which are now entered into, now rescinded, who can lack a pretext – if there is any real excuse – for going to war? But the pontifical laws do not disapprove all war. Augustine approves of it in some instances, and St Bernard praises some soldiers. But Christ himself and Peter and Paul everywhere

[1] Quoted by Walter, ed., *Henry V*, p. xxv.

[2] *A Treatise of Monarchy*, lines 522–6, in *Remains* ed. G. A. Wilkes (Oxford, 1965).

[3] Quoted by Paul E. Jorgensen, *Shakespeare's Military World* (Berkeley and Los Angeles, 1956), p. 164.

teach the opposite. Why is their authority less with us than that of Augustine or Bernard?[1]

Henry's debate with Bates and Williams in *Henry V*, IV, i needs the light of this thoroughgoing disapproval of war and its effects on the dutiful subjects involved in it – from the book which has been taken as the model for Henry's conduct – before we can pass any sort of judgement.

The most straightforward way of looking at the debate is to see it as each side putting down the most favourable account of its position, and minimising personal responsibility as far as possible. But the arguments are asked to carry far more weight than that. Henry's sophistries are the best rationalisation of his position he can offer, and they show up his insecurity, psychological and philosophical.

Curiously enough his arguments have not called out the efforts of Henrician loyalists as much as we might expect. Campbell only notes the question of the king's responsibility for his subjects in battle as the most acute aspect of the larger question. Jorgensen claims openly that Henry puts an unsatisfactory case. His answer to Williams, Jorgensen suggests, is far from complete. 'One may suspect a baffled, tentative quality in Williams' acquiescence. The truth of the matter – whether Shakespeare intended it or not – is that the King has explained away only a fraction of what is troubling Williams.'[2] Ornstein, by no means a Henrician, sees it as one instance among many, starting with the 'I know you all' speech in *1 Henry IV*, I, ii, of Henry's need to justify himself and to seek reassurance that his role is a kingly one.[3]

The Chorus which starts act IV, and the whole of the first scene, including the debate, are an integral section of which the debate is a climax, the last lap of a circuit of the army and its morale. What we see is Henry labouring to shore up and strengthen his soldiers' morale for the coming battle. From *Richard II* onwards in the plays on English history morale has been a factor in every transfer of power; low in the Welsh who deserted Richard in Gloucestershire, high in Blunt and the others who died for Henry IV at Shrewsbury by wearing his armour, low in the rebels Northumberland and Mortimer who avoided Shrewsbury, and low in the rebel army after Hotspur's death (*2 Henry IV*, I, i, 112–18). At Agincourt Shakespeare makes it the key to the English victory. He omits any mention of tactics such as the stakes which protected the English archers from the French cavalry. All the chroniclers attributed the victory to Henry's tactics, but not one gets a mention in the play apart from the killing of the prisoners,

[1] *The Education of a Christian Prince*, pp. 250–1. It is a pity that there is no sign of Shakespeare knowing Hoccleve, whose poem *De regimine principum* (1411–12) was dedicated to Henry V. It argues that war is only justified when it is waged to convert unbelievers, and ends with a plea for peace addressed to the kings of England and France as the chief agents of peace and concord. That was three years before Agincourt.

[2] Jorgensen, *Shakespeare's Military World*, pp. 166–7.

[3] Robert Ornstein, *A Kingdom for a Stage* (Cambridge, Mass., 1972), pp. 183–5. Ornstein's view of the play concentrates on Henry's cold-blooded acting on the stage of his kingdom. This is what he has to say about Henry's posture over the argument with Bates and Williams (pp. 194–5): 'Although he has learned the language of common men in the tavern, Harry cannot sympathise with the lowly born. He is not really moved by the prospect of his soldiers' fates, nor does he grieve for the lonely impoverished widows and orphaned children they will leave behind. What agonises him is the thought that he will be accountable for all this suffering. He joins the men about the campfire partly to confess the anxieties he dare not reveal as King and partly to be absolved by them of guilt for the impending disaster . . . When they reject his facile arguments, he complains, as so often before, that he is misunderstood. Perhaps he is right, because his soldiers are at least as obtuse as he is. Just as he would shrug off responsibility for their deaths, they would place the burden of their immortal souls on him. He would forget that he led them to the edge of a catastrophe; they would forget their eagerness to be led.'

which has a special non-military importance. The work of raising morale is, in Shakespeare's presentation, Henry's essential contribution to the victory.

The Chorus begins act IV by picturing the English army as 'this ruin'd band' ready for defeat, saved only by the little touch of Harry in the night which the scene goes on to display. Henry begins his work with his brother-commanders, offering them only the macabre joke that there is good in the situation because it makes them all early risers, 'Which is both healthful and good husbandry'. To old Sir Thomas Erpingham he is more solemn and orotund, conscious of his responsibility. His own worry comes into the open when he thanks Sir Thomas for speaking cheerfully. So of course does Pistol who follows him, but with Pistol the now disguised king gets nowhere. The sight of Gower and Fluellen going about their business cheers him up a little too before he joins the soldiers. So far his little touch has not made a deep impression.

The first part of his discussion with the soldiers is largely a striking of poses, the soldiers openly gloomy, the king rather aggressively looking forward to the battle as an opportunity for honour and glory – 'methinks I would not die anywhere so contented as in the king's company, his cause being just and his quarrel honourable' (IV, i, 125–7). Bates disclaims his responsibility by arguing that it is not for him to judge the cause, and that if it is unjust the fault is all the king's. Williams enlarges on the gruesome consequences of many deaths laid on the king's conscience if the cause is unjust. It is then that Henry launches into his forty-line catalogue of justifications, which boil down to three arguments against loading everything on the king. Good intentions are one let-out; private conduct, the independent sins of the individual soldier are another; and God of course finds war useful: 'war is His beadle, war is His vengeance; so that here men are punish'd for before-breach of the King's laws in now the King's quarrel.' The exchange of views ends there, with Williams admitting dubiously that a bad death is not the king's responsibility. Neither party takes the issue any further. What they have conspicuously left untouched in the light of contemporary discussions is the key question of the king's responsibility for the deaths of good men in an unjust quarrel. After the soldiers have gone Henry picks up only the original attempt to lay responsibility for everything on the king. He goes into a lengthy display of self-pity, amounting in effect to the view that the only pay-off for the burden of conscience the king carries is ceremony, and that

> The slave, a member of the country's peace,
> Enjoys it; but in gross brain little wots
> What watch the king keeps to maintain the peace
> Whose hours the peasant best advantages.
>
> (ll. 277–80)

The extreme language (strictly, slaves were not members of any body politic) reflects the hurt Henry feels that his soldiers don't acknowledge their share of the burden.

On past evidence he had no reason to expect that they would. Even in act I when the decision over the justice of the French war was being publicly weighed, Henry himself was the only one to point out the moral issue, and to picture clearly all the deaths and destruction which go with war.[1] His speech in I, ii, 281–96 about the ferocity of war gives point to his consciousness before Agincourt of what he has set in train. Moreover his own morale is in a fragile state. He is no Tamburlaine. The Chorus talks eagerly, foreknowing the result of the battle, of Henry's 'cheerful semblance', the artistic touch with which he works on morale. But a semblance it is, an act of generalship to cover his own fears. The moment when

[1] Cf. *ibid.*, p. 181.

he parts from Bates and Williams is the low point, when his insecurity throws him further off balance than we ever see him. His morale-boosting labours, despite what the Chorus says, end by throwing him into a torment of resentful and unreasonable gloom.

It is from this posture of near-desperation that Henry turns to prayer – a plea for that high morale in his soldiers which he had failed to create by himself at the beginning of the scene. Morale he links in his prayer, revealingly, with title, his own claim to authority which his father's deposition of Richard still makes dubious. This is the prime source of his insecurity. Agincourt thus becomes a test of his title as a mark, for Henry himself, of God's willingness to forgive his father's usurpation. His worthiness then appears in the Crispin's Day speech which ends this section on morale. It gives us the measure of Henry's character in adversity, the determination which in the end overrides his fear and misery and brings victory.

Ironically perhaps, Henry does not need Agincourt to strengthen his authority. The ease with which he puts down the rebellion of Cambridge, Scroop and Grey confirms that. Cambridge, after all, was the rival claimant to the throne through the line of Richard II, and should have been a serious threat. But in spite of his easy control of that situation, Henry's intense fury at the rebels' disloyalty shows that he has more than a touch of his father's insecurity. There is no safety where there is room for a challenge. It is this fear for his safety which makes Agincourt, to Henry, the ultimate trial of his strength, his title, his authority. In act v he is a different man. Before Agincourt insecurity is the base on which all his actions are mounted, and his chief motive for the war in France. An insecure title makes an insecure king. An insecure king is likely to fight for his title before he fights or works for the commonwealth. So much for Erasmus.

If we grant Henry this one motive more than the justice of his claim to the title of France, we open the door to others. Glory is the bait he offers to his commanders in his speech before Agincourt, and he seems not entirely free from lust for it himself. He talks like Hotspur in that speech, claiming that the less English there are to gain the victory the greater the share of glory for them all. Like Hotspur too his presence lifts morale. 'All things are ready, if our minds be so'. Glory is one of Henry's primary targets in France, as he tells the Ambassador in act I. Using the rising sun image of the 'I know you all' speech he declares

> I will rise there with so full a glory
> That I will dazzle all the eyes of France.
> (I, ii, 278–9)

From this perspective Agincourt is the climax of the plan announced so long before, whereby the sun-king will shine more brightly for the contrast of the 'base contagious clouds' which hid it, and

> My reformation, glitt'ring o'er my fault,
> Shall show more goodly and attract more eyes
> Than that which hath no foil to set it off.
> (*I Henry IV*, I, ii, 206–8)

Henry knows all along what he is doing. The glory he looks for in France he wants partly in order to fulfill his own prophecy of a glorious career, partly to cure the insecurity of his title and his psyche. And the two motives interlock. An inglorious title can be made secure by glorious deeds – 'No king of England,' he declares, 'if not king of France'.

Henry's sense of insecurity shows in all the steps he takes to strengthen his authority. He conducts himself almost throughout his reign with a studied care for the right way to behave in every situation. Long after Hotspur and Falstaff have left the stage he remains sensitive to the clouds of riot and dishonour. When he receives the crown his first act, like Trajan's, is to return the sword of justice back into the hands of the law, a gesture which calms the most immediate fears of his subjects as Trajan's act did before him.[1] The next step is to call his parliament and the third is to pursue glory with a just war in France. But for all his correctness and all his theory reality is a tough business, and the journey through France shows that text-book correctness is not enough.

Correct behaviour in a king is good for the morale of his subjects and a comfort to him in his insecurity. But in a war, just or not, lenity and the other constraints on rule are not the easiest of courses to follow. At Harfleur Shakespeare left his sources and gave Henry a speech like Tamburlaine's before Damascus, threatening the citizens that he would shut off all mercy if they did not surrender. As Ornstein says, kindness is a theme in *Henry V*,[2] but it is kindness (in royal terms lenity) under pressure. Henry refuses mercy to the rebels at Southampton, whether out of insecurity or policy; he threatens to deny it to the citizens at Harfleur; and most tellingly of all he denies it absolutely to the prisoners at Agincourt. Lenity stops near the frontier.

It seems reasonable to assume that Henry's policy in war as well as in peace is to act in conformity with the precepts of his time. The text-books for military commanders stood alongside the guidebooks for Christian princes on his bookshelf. Jorgensen goes so far as to say that in this play 'the dramatist made a careful study of military theory, and sketched character with the theory constantly in mind ... Shakespeare derived most of Henry's conduct and speech as a general from the precepts of military books'.[3] The one act which might challenge Jorgensen's claim is Henry's order to kill the prisoners in IV, vi. It is a complicated incident in act and motivation, and it shows up as well as anything does the complex shadings Shakespeare put into the primary colours of his picture of the commonwealth.

In IV, vii Gower and Fluellen get into a muddle over what it was that led up to Henry's order. They react to it with the same wrong-headed goodwill which they show all through the play. Their misleading reactions, the only direct comment we hear, are part of the shading process. Immediately after Henry has given the order Fluellen explodes on to the stage with his moral outrage against the French slaughter of the 'poys and the luggage' as a breach of the laws of war (IV, vii, 2). Gower follows him in mistakenly assuming that Henry ordered the French prisoners' throats cut as an act of revenge for the attack on the baggage train. What we have actually witnessed just before this confusion is Henry giving the order when he hears the trumpets signalling what he takes to be a new attack by the French. Whatever his reason for giving the order, Gower's assumption that the motive was revenge is wrong. The anger we hear in Henry over the slaughter of the boys when he returns to the scene is divorced from his order to kill the prisoners. He gives the order neither in revenge nor, since he claims never to have lost his temper in France until the baggage train incident, in anger.

Elizabethan verdicts on the historical slaughter of the prisoners were divided. Gentili in *De Jure Belli* laid it down that prisoners of war are not to be killed except in extreme circumstances, for self-preservation. The Agincourt slaughter he singled out for condemnation. 'I cannot praise the English', he wrote,

> who, in that famous battle in which they overthrew the power of France, having taken more prisoners

1 Trajan handed the sword of justice to the Prefect of Rome at his coronation, saying 'Use it for me or against me as I shall deserve.' Buchanan used it on the medallion struck for the coronation of James VI of Scotland in 1567.

2 Ornstein, *A Kingdom for a Stage*, p. 187.

3 Jorgensen, *Shakespeare's Military World*, p. 186.

than the number of their victorious army, and fearing danger from them by night, set aside those of high rank and slew the rest.[1]

On the other hand Gentili's fellow-lawyer Crompton, in the year that Shakespeare wrote *Henry V*, excused it in an account marginally closer to what Shakespeare pictured:

The French, as they are men of great courage and valure, so they assembled themselves againe in battell array, meaning to have given a new battell to king Henry, which king Henry perceiving, gave speciall commaundement by proclamation, that every man should kill his prisoners: whereupon many were presently slaine, whereof the French king having intelligence, dispersed his army, and so departed.[2]

Shakespeare made less of the French bravery and more of Henry's perhaps overhasty resolution. As Geoffrey Bullough notes,[3] he could have used several other contemporary versions of the incident, all of which glossed it favourably. There were as many sources open to Shakespeare for this play as he ever had. But he chose for this incident the least favourable version and underlined his choice with the uncomprehending muddle of Gower's interpretation of it.

The place of this incident along the path of lenity makes lenity itself less of a goal, and more like a tactic to be discarded when necessary. The king, under supreme pressure, takes personal responsibility for the monstrosities of war which he is so keenly aware of. For the sake of victory he sets aside lenity and takes so many deaths on his conscience. In victory he is an Alexander, at least to Fluellen, and in victory we should perhaps overlook the fact that Augustine condemned Alexander as an unjust warrior. Lenity stops at the national boundary. Its upholder will bear the responsibility for foreign slaughter if slaughter can secure it the goodwill of homebred spirits.

There is a further point about the incident of killing the prisoners which leads to another pattern of motives, this one in the commonwealth at large. It is a complication of the picture, like Gower's misunderstanding, but it is one which has reverberations through the whole play, and through the story of rule in the English history plays as a whole. Exeter in act I contributes one of the play's many uses of a musical metaphor to describe state policy:

For government, though high, and low, and lower,
Put into parts, doth keep in one consent,
Congreeing in a full and natural close,
Like music. (I, ii, 180–3)

Technically this is an argument for delegating executive authority, by a counterpoint of activities. It is to this musical simile that the Archbishop adds his gracious account of the whole society in terms of a beehive. The Archbishop's conclusion, however, is a little

[1] *De Jure Belli* trans. John C. Rolfe, 2 vols. (Oxford, 1933), II, 212.

[2] Quoted in G. Bullough, *Narrative and Dramatic Sources of Shakespeare's Plays*, 8 vols., (1957–75), IV, 365.

[3] *Ibid.*, p. 364. There was, for instance, Stow's verson in his *Annals*, pp. 571–2 (1592 edition): 'At the last, the victory obtayned, and the great hoste of the Frenchmen overcome, slaine, wounded, taken and vanquished, forthwith an other hoste of Frenchmen, no lesse than the first, supposing the Englishmen to be wearied by their long travell and fight, disposed them to beginne againe the battell anew. When the Englishmen (which had many moe prisoners than they were of themselves in number) saw this newe field assembled to give them battell againe, fearing in this new field, lest they should fight both against their prisoners, and their other enemies, they put to death many of their said prisoners, both noble & rich men among whom the Duke of Brabant, who at that field was taken prisoner, was one.

The prudent king of England seeing the resemble of his adversaries sent his heraults unto them, commanding them, either forthwith to come to battell, or else immediately to depart the field, and if they delayde to depart, or to come to battell, both those of their company alreadie taken prisoners, and also all they that should thereafter be taken, without mercie or redemption should be put to death.'

more ambiguous than Exeter's:

> I this infer,
> That many things, having full reference
> To one consent, may work contrariously.
> (ll. 204–6)

He intends this merely as an orotund way of supporting Exeter's argument for the disposition of the national defences while Henry is in France. But like the ladies who protest too much, the noble's and the priest's elaborate metaphors tell us more than they think. They are eager for the war. Many things and many men may work with one consent to the war in France, but as the Archbishop's revealing word has it, they work contrariously. The one consent incorporates a wide variety of motives.

Considering all the trumpeting and morale-raising which goes into the battle at Agincourt, it is remarkable that the only actual combat on stage is Pistol's in IV, iv. Moreover that incident involves not fighting but bargaining for a ransom, 'egregious ransom' as Pistol calls it. A flourish of comic threats to 'cuppele gorge' gets him the promise of two hundred crowns, the French crowns which Henry has offered as the bait for victory. That comic flourishing is the sum total of the battle scenes in this most warlike play. Not that it is a battle scene at all, of course. It is Pistol dieting his rank mind with his own menu for the feasts of war, working contrariously within the general consent to war. Private interests are served as liberally as the general interest in this feast.

But Pistol's private interest feeds less well than most. His threats to 'cuppele gorge' are translated into reality by the king's order to cut the prisoners' throats, and with the order off goes his hope of ransom. The last we see of Pistol is when, cudgelled by Fluellen and deprived of his wife the hostess (by 'malady of France'), he returns penniless to England and a life of thievery and cony-catching.

Henry's order to kill the prisoners puts the comedy of Pistol's scene with his French prisoner in a grimmer light, in retrospect. The scene exists largely to undercut the Chorus's heroics, since it is the only part of the battle where antagonists confront each other with drawn swords, but it also adds a human dimension to the subsequent cutting of the prisoners' gorges. In consequence of the order Pistol is left as one of the few English who has not fed his private interest in the war.

The starvation of Pistol is only one conclusion to the series of private motives which work contrariously through the play. Self interest is a more pervasive theme than the king's lenity or his insecurity. When the Chorus of act II solemnly declares that 'honour's thought / Reigns solely in the breast of every man', he goes on in the next lines to give himself the lie by describing the 'nest of hollow bosoms' in which the rebels are hatching their French crowns. After the Chorus there follows on stage the 'nest of ruffians', the drones of the commonwealth, from the Boar's Head. They proudly address one another by their military titles while rubbing their hands at the prospect of pickings in France. 'I shall sutler be / Unto the camp', says Pistol, 'and profits will accrue.'

The 'traitors,' as the patriotic Chorus now calls the rebels, have greed for their prime motive. Cambridge's claim to the throne is not mentioned at all; only his price in French gold. But of course before the rebels appear at Southampton we have already seen a far more weighty display of self interest in the opening scene of the play. Here too the grandeur of the Chorus is brought sadly down as the Archbishop explains to the Bishop of Ely why they must turn the king's attention away from his threat to seize the Church's property. Shakespeare always broaches his major themes at the start of his plays. Here the contrast of trumpeting Prologue and politic Archbishop makes the point that self interest is one motive underlying the glories of war.

Henry's threat is the bill introduced in the Commons to sequester Church property, 'the better half of our possession'. Ely asks how this can be prevented, and the Archbishop explains at length, with breaks for unctuous praise of wild Harry's reformation, that he is offering a huge grant to the king to finance a war against France. So far as the bill is concerned, the king

> seems indifferent;
> Or rather swaying more upon our part
> Than cherishing th'exhibiters against us.

Evidently a lot of political manoeuvring has already taken place. The Archbishop is in no doubt as to why the king is likely to favour the Church, 'for', he says, 'I have made an offer to his Majesty'. The offer is in cash, and is

> ... in regard of causes [lawsuits] now in hand,
> Which I have open'd to his Grace at large,
> As touching France. (ll. 77–9)

The visit of the French Ambassador has interrupted the negotiations over this offer, and now at the beginning of the play the Archbishop is waiting to continue his explanation of the case for Henry's title to France. In scene ii he resumes his explanation. When Henry finally decides at the end of the act to wage war in support of this 'cause' the Archbishop's manoeuvres have gained their purpose.

A lot depends on one's reading of this opening. Some critics, notably Dover Wilson, have been reluctant to see the Archbishop as a wily politician because it diminishes his honesty as the expounder of Henry's title to France and therefore puts clay feet under Henry's image as the just warrior. Instead they have preferred to stress his praise of the reformed Henry or the extent to which Shakespeare moderated Hall's and Holinshed's attacks on the prelacy. J. H. Walter prefers to stress I, i, 25–34, where the Archbishop describes Henry's reformation in terms of the baptismal service, and points out that 'to portray Henry as the dupe of two scheming prelates, or as a crafty politician skilfully concealing his aims with the aid of an unscrupulous archbishop, is not consistent with claiming at the same time that he is the ideal king'.[1] The Archbishop's use of the baptismal metaphor and the bee fable do not make Henry an infant either.

Such readings of act I are limited in several ways. First, they narrow down the critic's task to a judgement of Henry: is he in Shakespeare's picture an ideal king or a hypocrite? Henry is a fiction of course, a dream of reason, and speculation over whether he should now be in heaven or hell is idle. Secondly, such readings narrow their perspective from the whole commonwealth to its head. Henry is not England, though he can call himself so. England has its prelates who want to keep their property; it has its rank-minded nobles who want glory; it has its rogues who want loot. Worker bees and drones alike want a foreign war out of self interest, and unite with the head in that one consent. His of course is the supreme self interest: personal glory and a secure title for his two kingdoms. There is something to be said for the view of Shakespeare which takes commodity to be the mainspring of action in his commonwealth. Only the innocents like Bates and Williams seem to be without this motivation.

The only members of the commonwealth who act out of loyalty rather than self interest are the common soldiers. Fluellen and the other captains are professionals, who enjoy their work as craftsmen do. They stand midway in motivation between the nobles with their hope of glory and the common soldiers with their nearly dumb obedience. Bates and

[1] Walter, ed., *Henry V*, p. xxiv.

Williams have the least to gain. Their minds are closed to the prospect of loot which brought Bardolph and Pistol to France. Both of them end with only the honour of fighting in their king's company, to which Williams can add fortuitously a glove-full of gold dropped from Henry's sunny image, cash for being feed to a comic turn. These are the men whose deaths in his service Henry refuses to take responsibility for.

It should be said that to see *Henry V* only as a display of self interest at work is to fall for one of the more insidious temptations that criticism is heir to, the temptation to see the play schematically. Self interest, as Henry probably knows, is a motive which can be harnessed in the service of the king. The play studies kingship under pressure, utilising a collection of self-interested wills in a war whose cause is doubtful only in the moral sense. Societies work contrariously. As Mandeville put it much later, all bees are out for themselves. Foreign war has the advantage of drawing all interests into one consent, and of strengthening lenity to friends through harshness to enemies. Henry is in his more complex and secretive way following his father's advice to busy giddy minds with foreign quarrels. That is the way he chooses to release his title from the pressure put on it by his father's doubtful purchase.

When Henry struts through the final act, selling France peace in return for the promise that he will inherit it all, and claiming Katherine as a guarantee for that promise, his manner is different because his throne is secure. His personality, knowing, just and glorious, has brought peace in his time. His calculating nature muffles the counterpointing of glory in the choric summaries and the more dubious realities of the scenes themselves. But the peaceful olives he plants, unlike those celebrated in the sonnet, are not of endless age, as the final Chorus reminds us. 'This star of England', the 'mirror of all Christian kings', can hold to his policy of lenity inside his own kingdom and for the duration of his own lifetime, but his legacy is more war. Busying giddy minds with a just crusade was not a course open to Henry VI. His father had committed him to France, and his policy had to follow the art of the possible.

'ALL'S WELL THAT ENDS WELL'

NICHOLAS BROOKE

All's Well exercises a recurrent fascination for criticism, because so many things about it are of striking, and contemporary, interest. Yet despite that fact (or possibly partly because of it, because it can be difficult to correlate 'contemporary' with supposedly 'Elizabethan' interests) the play never quite takes, never quite seems to work. The problem – it's always called a 'problem' play in one sense or another – is just what 'working' should, for this play, consist of. This paper has no more specific title because its aim is simply the play itself, not any single aspect of it; but if it is to have a well-ending, it must respond to G. K. Hunter's challenge that 'criticism of *All's Well* has failed, for it has failed to provide a context within which the genuine virtues of the play can be appreciated'.[1] That is an ambitious aim, and the ambition in my love (of the play) thus plagues itself and must take refuge in the obvious scepticism of Shakespeare's title; a perfectly satisfactory conclusion is hardly probable, however much I believe it to be possible.

Scepticism, at least, will be generally granted to the play (unless 'cynicism' is preferred). Scepticism about *what* is more difficult. Presumably about romance, since in one sense or another it certainly enacts a romance plot. Not merely does girl get boy, but she also achieves a social rise of a kind usually thought of as rags to riches, or servant to princess, on the way; and she uses a pretty potent magic (of obscure kind) to do it – curing the King. But it has to do with the nature of this play that my terms have already become inappropriate. Helena is socially inferior, but she is a gentlewoman and certainly not in rags. Bertram is a count and a ward of the King, but he is not a prince. The social distinctions are stressed and yet reduced in scale: a folk tale which usually thrives on extremes of contrast is modified into perception of social niceties; and it is when made nice that such distinctions are apt to be most offensive.

The modified social pitch is given at once in the opening prose dialogue between the Countess and Lafew:

> In delivering my son from me, I bury a second husband. (I, i, 1–2)

'Son' and 'husband' mark a domestic pitch, still more remarkable when they discuss the King:

> *Countess.* What hope is there of his majesty's amendment?
>
> *Lafew.* He hath abandon'd his physicians, madam; under whose practices he hath persecuted time with hope, and finds no other advantage in the process but only the losing of hope by time. (ll. 11–15)

This King is a sick *man*, with incompetent doctors. There is respect but no hint of royal glamour in the dialogue, and none ever arises in the play. The plain language does have a suggestion of courtliness in the balanced clauses, but that is its only elevation. It contains at once a touch of sententiousness, of riddling, and of the kind of elegance that

[1] ed. G. K. Hunter: *All's Well That Ends Well*, The Arden Shakespeare (1959), introduction, p. xxix. All quotations are from this edition.

restricts emotion:

Countess. . . . No more of this, Helena; go to, no more; lest it be rather thought you affect a sorrow than to have –
Helena. I do affect a sorrow indeed, but I have it too.
Lafew. Moderate lamentation is the right of the dead; excessive grief the enemy to the living.
(ll. 47–52)

Lafew is courtly; Bertram imitates the manner but misses the tone in his farewells:

The best wishes that can be forg'd in your thoughts be servants to you! [*and then, to Helena*] Be comfortable to my mother, your mistress, and make much of her. (ll. 71–4)

That is not only cold, it also contrives to stress the social inferiority – or, Bertram's consciousness of it. Lafew's old man's petting is only less insulting:

Farewell, pretty lady; you must hold the credit of your father. (ll. 75–6)

Both speeches, of course, anticipate the play's development. Helena's soliloquy immediately brings out emotional, sexual, and social undercurrents from this reticent opening:

O, were that all! I think not on my father,
And these great tears grace his remembrance more
Than those I shed for him. What was he like?
I have forgot him; my imagination
Carries no favour in't but Bertram's.
I am undone; there is no living, none,
If Bertram be away . . . (ll. 77–83)

That is verse, and strikingly so. But of a kind that develops naturally as an intensification of prose speech: it is not romance eloquence; indeed, the opposite. The speech rhythm cuts across the verse, typically creating half-lines of short, singularly bare phrases: 'I think not on my father' – 'What was he like? / I have forgot him' – 'I am undone' – 'There is no living, none, / If Bertram be away'. The terseness is remarkable, and so also is it that in seven lines there is not a single image of any kind. The one which follows is all the more conspicuous, and it does have a limited eloquence:

'twere all one
That I should love a bright particular star
And think to wed it, he is so above me.
In his bright radiance and collateral light
Must I be comforted, not in his sphere.
(ll. 83–7)

The 'bright particular star' offers a richer possibility, but that is limited by the precision of its reference: Bertram is a star only because she is in love with him, and because he thinks himself one, not (as we have just seen him) in fact; and that is stressed in the neat ambiguity of 'he is so above me' – socially far more than astrally. Further, stars are proverbially cold, and that is emphasized in the expansion '. . . Must I be comforted, not in his sphere' which hints at the warmth of physical embrace. Those last two lines are the largest rhythmic unit the speech allows.

Behind the love there is an implicit recognition of sexuality which gets nearer to direct utterance on Parolles's entry:

I love him for his sake,
And yet I know him a notorious liar,
Think him a great way fool, solely a coward;
Yet these fix'd evils sit so fit in him
That they take place when virtue's steely bones
Looks bleak i'th'cold wind . . . (ll. 97–102)

She turns with relief from virtue's steely bones to bawdy chatter with Parolles. The old objection to this was, of course, merely silly prudery; but more recent explanations that this was all taken for granted in Elizabethan circles are equally false to the play. The Countess's complacent assurance of conventional values has already been jolted by the revelation of Helena's ambitious love. Her stress on 'modesty' is adjusted here in another way: Helena is a great deal more real (and therefore more attractive) than a merely conventional use of the word would allow:

Parolles. Are you meditating on virginity?
Helena. Ay.

(ll. 108–9)

So she is, but she encourages a routine line of banter before at last bringing it round towards her private thoughts:

How might one do, sir, to lose it to her own liking?
(l. 147)

He answers at length, but little to the point, and when he concludes 'Will you anything with it?' it is obvious that her mind has been wandering, in her distrait response

Not my virginity yet:
(l. 161, F punctuation)

and her speech transposes into a meditation on Bertram at court which ends characteristically:

Now shall he –
I know not what he shall. God send him well!
The court's a learning-place, and he is one –
Parolles. What one, i'faith?
Helena. That I wish well. 'Tis pity –
Parolles. What's pity?
Helena. That wishing well had not a body in't
Which might be felt . . . (ll. 171–8)

The reluctant, and movingly sharp, revelation of feeling repeats the form of utterance which has by now become established as a characteristic of the play. So far I have shown it only in Helena's language, but it is by no means confined to her. Parolles answered her first question – 'Man is enemy to virginity; how may we barricado it against him?' – with rare bluntness:

Keep him out. (ll. 110–12)

In the next scene, the King responds to a courtier's flattery:

I fill a place, I know't. (I, ii, 69)

That defines admirably the play's pitch: no more, and no less. None of Richard II's glamorous royalty, for instance, in this unromantic king. The language of the play never strays very far from this pitch, and its most impressive moments share this striking bareness. Lavatch makes even more explicit than Helena what drives her on:

My poor body, madam, requires it; I am driven on by the flesh . . . (I, iii, 26–7)

Parolles, after he has been exposed in act IV, is equally terse:

If my heart were great
'Twould burst at this. Captain I'll be no more,
But I will eat and drink and sleep as soft
As captain shall. Simply the thing I am
Shall make me live. (IV, iii, 319–23)

What he is – as he knows – is a braggart and a fool.

Hunter – echoing several others – complains that 'There is a general failure in *All's Well* to establish a medium in verse which will convey effectively the whole tone of the play . . .' (p. lix) That, I think, is wrong. What Hunter had in mind emerges in his admission that 'one cannot pretend that every speech is a failure or that there is no great Shakespearian poetry in the play'. The speeches I have quoted are certainly not failures, and some of them seem to me very impressive poetry; but they are not great in the sense Hunter's phrase implies – that is, they are not eloquent, they do not sprout garlands of imagery. On the contrary, the play's characteristic medium is precisely this uniquely bare language which excludes decoration and so makes all imagery, or any romantic valuation of experience, evidently superfluous. 'Simply the thing I am' is me plain, not dressed up in delusory clothings of romance, magic, or religion.

In that I find it very impressive. Its effect, evidently, is to stress the 'natural' at the expense of the romance, and it therefore governs the unromantic tone in which the romance plot is developed. 'Naturalism' is notoriously an insecure term, or at least a relative one; it is necessary here because the language so insistently relates romance conventions to a more immediate form of experience. It continually delivers the shock of actuality into the context of anticipated fiction. But the naturalism of such speech is not merely bluntness. It has the quality too of the reticence of natural speech. Without eloquence, not much can be said, and not much *is* said (except by implication). Helena's hesitant and limited comment to Parolles is characteristic: he does not understand her (though we do); and he is not meant to. Even her soliloquy, revealing as it is, does not reveal all; Lavatch's 'driven on by the flesh' is the obvious comment which Helena herself does not quite arrive at.

It follows that reticence is as characteristic of the play as bareness of language; is, indeed, a function of it, and equally a condition of naturalism. Helena's soliloquy in I, i is virtually the only such utterance that allows self-revelation. She does have other soliloquies, but they announce the action, not the emotional resources of it. In one sense this is not remarkable: heroines in Shakespearian comedy are not in the habit of profound self-examination; the expectation of more here is generated out of the particular tone I have analysed. It is generated by it, and it is also frustrated by it. To tell the whole truth about ourselves is impossible (because words always falsify); it is also dangerous, and we instinctively avoid it. The point is made very sharply when it emerges that Helena's last speech in I, i (on her plans to get to Paris and to get Bertram) is not protected by the conventions of stage soliloquy, but has been overheard by the Countess's steward. He reports to his mistress, and she proceeds to extract the information from Helena without revealing her sources; first by pressing on Helena's evasion of the term 'mother', and then more directly:

Helena. Good madam, pardon me.
Countess.
Do you love my son?
Helena. Your pardon, noble mistress.
Countess. Love you my son?
Helena. Do not you love him, madam?
Countess.
Go not about; my love hath in't a bond
Whereof the world takes note. Come, come, disclose
The state of your affection, for your passions
Have to the full appeach'd.
Helena. Then I confess,
Here on my knee, before high heaven and you,
That before you, and next unto high heaven,
I love your son. (I, iii, 180–9)

The confession has to be forced, and it is forced. The Countess has the perception to force it only because she has the eavesdropper's report. She is sharp, but never very perceptive; as she is affectionate but slightly sentimental. Helena, forced to confess her love, still masks her ambition:

I follow him not
By any token of presumptuous suit,
Nor would I have him till I do deserve him;
Yet never know how that desert should be.
(ll. 192–5)

The first statement is simply untrue; the second is quibbling if not meaningless. With that reservation, she goes on to make an eloquent and moving declaration of her feelings:

Yet in this captious and inteemable sieve
I still pour in the waters of my love
And lack not to lose still. Thus, Indian-like,
Religious in mine error, I adore
The sun that looks upon his worshipper
But knows of him no more....
but if yourself,
Whose aged honour cites a virtuous youth,
Did ever, in so true a flame of liking,
Wish chastely and love dearly, that your Dian
Was both herself and love – O then, give pity...
(ll. 197–208)

This is fine; but it does rest on deception – and Helena does not know that the Countess knows that:

> Had you not lately an intent – speak truly –
> To go to Paris?
> *Helena.* Madam, I had.
> *Countess.* Wherefore? tell true.
> (ll. 213–14)

So a bit more is squeezed out of her. She can and does easily tell true about her hope to cure the King, but she does not tell the whole truth – that she plans to use that to trap Bertram. And that, the Countess does not extract.

The scene is brilliant in its gradual exposure of reticence; and brilliant too in the final incompleteness of the exposure (it subsequently emerges that the Countess assumes the catching of Bertram; but not here). It establishes a dramatic strategy as distinctive of the play as its characteristic language: of trap, and forced exposure. Bertram is trapped into marriage with Helena and exposes his vulgarity in the unguarded snobbery of his resentment (not in the fact of it). He is trapped by Diana into giving her his ring; she, like the Countess, has information she does not reveal:

> *Diana.* Give me that ring.
> *Bertram.*
> I'll lend it thee, my dear, but have no power
> To give it from me.
> *Diana.* Will you not, my lord?
> *Bertram.*
> It is an honour 'longing to our house,
> Bequeathed down from many ancestors,
> Which were the greatest obloquy i'th'world
> In me to lose.
> *Diana.* Mine honour's such a ring;
> My chastity's the jewel of our house,
> Bequeathed down from many ancestors,
> Which were the greatest obloquy i'th'world
> In me to lose. Thus your own proper wisdom
> Brings in the champion Honour on my part
> Against your vain assault.
> *Bertram.* Here, take my ring...
> *Diana.*
> When midnight comes, knock at my chamber window...
> (IV, ii, 39–54)

He's caught by his lust and her skill; and she is immediately brisk with practical details. It is not wholly surprising that he takes her for a common gamester.

That is followed by the most extended of the trap scenes, the exposure of Parolles, in which Bertram plays his part on the other side. Parolles, made a fool of, becomes a self-acknowledged fool – which is wiser than Bertram. It thus gives him the position to make some apt comments:

> Who cannot be crush'd with a plot?
> (IV, iii, 314)

and so to the passage I quoted before, concluding

> Simply the thing I am
> Shall make me live.

and

> Rust, sword; cool, blushes; and Parolles live
> Safest in shame; being fool'd, by fool'ry thrive.
> There's place and means for every man alive.
> I'll after them. (ll. 319–29)

The control of tone is perfect: out of context 'There's place and means for every man alive' could be a rich affirmation; in its place in this play it is an affirmation still, but deprived of its richness – defined in the sense of delimited.

It shadows perfectly the final exposure – of Bertram and Diana – the brilliant last scene. At the start, Bertram's disclaimer that his ring was ever Helena's is – so far as it goes – honest enough. But, confronted with Diana's claims, his tone changes disastrously:

> My Lord, this is a fond and desp'rate creature
> Whom sometime I have laugh'd with. Let your highness
> Lay a more noble thought upon mine honour
> Than for to think that I would sink it here.
> (V, iii, 177–80)

The lie is cheap, and the echo of his reaction to Helena in act II is a sharp irony. Further pressed, he becomes nastier and even more transparent:

Diana. Good my lord,
Ask him upon his oath if he does think
He had not my virginity.
King.
What say'st thou to her?
Bertram. She's impudent, my lord,
And was a common gamester to the camp.
Diana.
He does me wrong, my lord; if I were so
He might have bought me at a common price.
(ll. 183–9)

She is cool enough to catch him logically, and so – like Helena with the Countess, but far more discreditably – he is gradually forced to yield bit by bit of the truth:

King. She hath that ring of yours.
Bertram.
I think she has. Certain it is I lik'd her
And boarded her i'th'wanton way of youth.
She knew her distance and did angle for me,
Madding my eagerness with her restraint,
As all impediments in fancy's course
Are motives of more fancy; and in fine
Her inf'nite cunning with her modern grace
Subdu'd me to her rate; she got the ring,
And I had that which any inferior might
At market-price have bought. (ll. 208–18)

That is still unpleasant and it is still untrue; but it is now what he may plausibly think (given the blind arrogance of the young male). It does have an effective reflex on the cunning with which Diana is now behaving. Under still further pressure he comes a shade, but only a shade, cleaner:

My lord, I do confess the ring was hers.

on which the King comments aptly:

You boggle shrewdly; every feather starts you.
(ll. 230–1)

Bertram is exposed, sharply and precisely, but he does not reach the acceptance of folly which gave Parolles a kind of inverted dignity, partly because he is not a fool in that sense, and chiefly because the final trap is not yet sprung. That is achieved via the less expected tenting of Diana. She, like Bertram, is caught with a ring she should not have (it is notable that we may probably get confused about which ring is which, but never about the degree of truth in anyone's words). Where he blustered, she takes to riddling:

King.
This ring you say was yours?
Diana. Ay, my good lord.
King.
Where did you buy it? Or who gave it you?
Diana.
It was not given me, nor I did not buy it.
King.
Who lent it you?
Diana. It was not lent me neither.
King.
Where did you find it then?
Diana. I found it not.
King.
If it were yours by none of all these ways
How could you give it him?
Diana. I never gave it him.
Lafew.
This woman's an easy glove, my lord; she goes off and on at pleasure. (ll. 264–72)

and after further exchanges, the King comments:

I think thee now some common customer.
(l. 280)

Diana is partly protected by our knowledge that she is not a prostitute (as Bertram was condemned by our knowledge that he was a liar), but the mistake does recall the equivocal tone of her first appearance with her mother and friends to watch the soldiers go by and gaze on the handsome French count who is soliciting her:

Widow. Nay, come; for if they do approach the city, we shall lose all the sight.

Diana. They say the French count has done most honourable service.
Widow. It is reported that he has taken their great'st commander, and that with his own hand he slew the duke's brother. [*Tucket*] We have lost our labour; they are gone a contrary way. Hark! You may know by their trumpets.
Mariana. Come, let's return again and suffice ourselves with the report of it. Well, Diana, take heed of this French earl; the honour of a maid is her name, and no legacy is so rich as honesty.
Widow. I have told my neighbour how you have been solicited by a gentleman his companion.
(III, v, 1–15)

This has more to do with the name of honesty than the fact, as Diana remains a virgin more in fact than spirit. The conventional wisdom leaves the chattering ladies more than half inclined to accept the suit. Diana's name alludes to the goddess, but it is not she; just as Helena's name (altered from the source) has ironic reference to the mythical heroine, stressed in Lavatch's bawdy song about Helen of Troy:

Among nine bad if one be good,
There's yet one good in ten.
(I, iii, 75–6)

Diana's false position at last precipitates the dénouement, Helena's re-appearance:

King. Is there no exorcist
Beguiles the truer office of mine eyes?
Is't real that I see?
Helena. No, my good lord;
'Tis but the shadow of a wife you see;
The name and not the thing.
Bertram. Both, both. O pardon!
(V, iii, 298–302)

Bertram is finally crush'd with a plot, forced to a plain concession. But he recovers enough for a notorious last couplet:

If she, my liege, can make me know this clearly
I'll love her dearly, ever, ever dearly.
(ll. 309–10)

I said 'recovers' advisedly: the flattened affirmation restores something of the false confidence with which Bertram began this scene, assuring the King of his love for Lafew's daughter; still more, its double (feminine?) rhymes recall the equally awful couplet in which Bertram declared his faith to Diana:

Say thou art mine, and ever
My love as it begins shall so persever.
(IV, ii, 36–7)

That flat last couplet (so obviously not an accident) focuses the double nature of the scene. Helena's re-appearance is in one dimension the fairy tale miracle which it appears to the King; but it does not at all so appear to us who know precisely the trick by which it has been devised; hence in its other dimension it is severely naturalistic, the springing of the final trap. The end of *The Winter's Tale* has similar dimensions – a magical resurrection for which a naturalistic explanation can be perceived – but there the proportions are completely reversed: the miraculous is celebrated, and the naturalistic possibility hardly articulated.

The ending here is therefore right for the dominant tone of the play, the limiting and very precise application of a naturalistic vision to a magical motif. My account so far has concentrated almost exclusively on the linguistic and dramatic means for presenting that, and I need now to look at how the romance is established, and how the two are related; for they used to be regarded as merely incongruous and evidence of different dates of composition, which is surely a mistake.

In a sense, of course, the romance structure does not need so much establishing. Folk-tale motifs were doubtless familiar in ballads and oral tradition, and they had been material for the stage at least since Peele's *Old Wives' Tale* and Greene's plays, to say nothing of Shakespeare's earlier comedies. What *All's Well* does, is to take that familiar material and look at it in a very unfamiliar way. The effect seems to me closely analogous to that of the early religious paintings of Caravaggio; indeed, to one in particular, a fairly small picture of Mary Magdalene in the Doria Gallery in Rome (Plate 1). It shows a young servant girl in a nice dress sitting on a kitchen chair in a room that is otherwise totally bare. Her hands are loosely in her lap, her head drooping, perhaps sleepy, pensive, or sad – or all three. There are a few sharply observed objects scattered casually on the floor: a jar of wine, not quite full, two broken gold neck-chains, a torn pearl necklace. At first sight it seems to be a purely naturalistic study of a genre-type more Dutch than Roman. You might even suspect that the title had been added in pious error to a purely secular painting. I did consider that when I first saw it, and found it rather dull. But I was quite wrong. In fact, the nice dress is far too nice; the servant girl appears to be Cinderella after the ball, before her clothes turn back to tatters. And in fact her dress, like her hair, is reddish gold, iconographically traditional for the Magdalene (as are at least some of the objects on the floor).

What Caravaggio has done is to take the familiar iconography and view it with a wholly unfamiliar naturalism, which projects an entirely new image. His Mary is neither crude whore nor glorious saint, but a quiet and plausible girl, very much alone. Once that is seen the painting becomes extraordinarily interesting; and its interest is generated, not by the naturalism alone, but by the juxtaposition of that with the traditional mythology. That is almost exactly the achievement I am attributing to Shakespeare in *All's Well*: not a simple naturalism, but a consistently naturalistic presentation of traditional romance magic. Caravaggio's paintings were frequently rejected by ecclesiastical patrons; they shocked then and, interestingly, they are still startling now. So is *All's Well*.

The equivalent, I suppose, of Caravaggio's iconographic detail, is the romance plot of *All's Well*; it is that which is treated naturalistically. The 'story' is both anticipated and expounded with exceptional clarity and skill, and some of the ways in which that is done have been well analysed by Joseph Price in *The Unfortunate Comedy*;[1] they have been implicit in most of what I have said. But the problem is not what story, but what kind of story, is to be anticipated. Naturalistic language proposes a naturalistic story, and since it is not that at all, it needs another form to mark the difference and to sustain the possibility of non-naturalistic developments. This is done by the couplets into which Helena moves at the end of I, i, and which she uses generally (not exclusively) through her progress to Paris, Florence, and back to Rosillion. They used to be the chief evidence of early composition though it has been recognized that they are not 'early' in form or language. That is certainly true. The language is necessarily slightly less close to speech, but only slightly: it remains generally plain, and the sentence structure most often cuts across the verse structure, resisting its rhythm as much as it does that of the blank verse.

> Our remedies oft in ourselves do lie,
> Which we ascribe to heaven; the fated sky
> Gives us free scope; only doth backward pull
> Our slow designs when we ourselves are dull.
> (I, i, 212–15)

It does incline more towards balanced antithesis,

> What power is it which mounts my love so high,
> That makes me see, and cannot feed mine eye?
> The mightiest space in fortune nature brings
> To join like likes, and kiss like native things.
> (ll. 216–19)

but in that it only intensifies one characteristic of the prose I discussed in the opening dialogue between Lafew and the Countess.

That prose should be seen, therefore, as

[1] Toronto and Liverpool, 1968.

setting a common ground from which the languages of the play can develop: extend it in one direction and you arrive at 'What was he like? I have forgot him', and beyond that Lavatch's cynical bluntness; in another direction you reach riddles, Helena's couplets, or Parolles's affected prose. Either way the development is not very far: the sense of tight control, of modified contrast, of language always related to a common ground, is singularly strong in this play. The restraint is felt in any of the forms of development. Parolles, as people often remark, is not Falstaff; nor is Lavatch quite Touchstone – nor Thersites neither. Though like Thersites, his cynicism expresses a view we might adopt if it were not that it is *he* who expresses it: from that we rebound to a more exact appreciation. Both fools, Lavatch and Parolles, are held within the play's governing tone, just as the blank verse does not soar nor the couplets resonate. In each case the possibilities are glimpsed but restricted. The naturalism imposes a calculated frustration on responses we would like to indulge.

Nonetheless the opposed developments make a sufficiently marked contrast, most conspicuously between Helena's two soliloquies in I, i. The first, in blank verse, I have already discussed: it seems, briefly, to take us inside her, to reveal what makes her tick. The revelation is shown to be incomplete, but it is still revelation, and almost unique in the play; only Parolles's few lines after his exposure come near it; Bertram never reveals himself directly at all – he gives himself away, which is another thing; what he is, or could learn to be, is necessarily enigmatic. Helena's second soliloquy is the couplet speech I have quoted, and it is quite different in effect from her first. It shuts us out, and firmly resists another indulgence we are given to expecting, of sharing the secrets of a character's soul. Helena gives away much (not all) to the Countess; a little to the King, and after that virtually nothing at all. The play depends on exposure, and therefore not on self-revelation. The reticence has another aspect here, insisting on impenetrable surfaces, and the couplets function primarily as barrier. They make the plot develop almost independently of the personalities enacting it.

They are therefore supremely important in what I take to be the play's most difficult achievement, relating naturalism to 'romance'. The form that should take is already recognizable in blank verse in the star image, offering an expansion immediately restricted by its social reference. The fullest development comes with the court scenes of the sickness and cure of the King.

He is said to have a fistula,[1] but of what kind, where, and what its effects are is left vague. When Bertram first arrives at court he is welcomed with reminiscences of his father:

> Would I were with him! He would always say –
> Methinks I hear him now; his plausive words
> He scatter'd not in ears, but grafted them
> To grow there and to bear – 'Let me not live',
> (This his good melancholy oft began
> On the catastrophe and heel of pastime,
> When it was out) 'Let me not live', quoth he,
> 'After my flame lacks oil, to be the snuff
> Of younger spirits...' (I, ii, 52–60)

in other words, with a hangover he was afraid of old age and impotence. That seems to be Lafew's diagnosis of the King in II, i:

> But, my good lord, 'tis thus: will you be cur'd
> Of your infirmity?
> *King.* No.
> *Lafew.* O, will you eat
> No grapes, my royal fox? Yes, but you will
> My noble grapes, and if my royal fox
> Could reach them. I have seen a medicine
> That's able to breathe life into a stone,

[1] Hunter quotes Bucknill to the effect that the word was not so specific then as now, though a rectal abscess would fit well enough.

Quicken a rock, and make you dance canary
With sprightly fire and motion; whose simple touch
Is powerful to araise King Pippen, nay,
To give great Charlemain a pen in's hand
And write to her a love-line.

(II, i, 67–77)

Exactly what the point of King Pippen is the notes don't tell us, but a bawdy sense is fairly obvious. So is Lafew's excited hope that Helena's sexual attractions – 'Doctor she' – will revive the King's spirits.

When he does consent to see her, she offers first her father's medical knowledge; then, as couplets take over from blank verse, she can hint at other powers. The first is divine:

He that of greatest works is finisher
Oft does them by the weakest minister.

(ll. 135–6)

She expands on that and then proceeds to another kind of power:

The greatest Grace lending grace,
Ere twice the horses of the sun shall bring
Their fiery coacher his diurnal ring,
Ere twice in murk and occidental damp
Moist Hesperus hath quench'd her sleepy lamp,
Or four and twenty times the pilot's glass
Hath told the thievish minutes how they pass,
What is infirm from your sound parts shall fly,
Health shall live free and sickness freely die.

(ll. 159–67)

The invocation is now a pagan incantation, and suggests the form of a magic spell, which the couplets can readily do.

The King is persuaded to try, what by he does not say – and what she actually does we do not know, since it is offstage. Total ambiguity is thus set up and maintained. In scene iii Lafew opens (in prose) with the obvious comment:

They say miracles are past.

(II, iii, 1)

In this play they probably are; yet the King is cured; and his entry is greeted by Lafew's excited cry:

Lustique, as the Dutchman says. I'll like a maid the better whilst I have a tooth in my head. Why, he's able to lead her a coranto.

(ll. 41–3)

The last, as the first, suggestion is of sexual arousal, and the scene moves coherently into Helena's choosing of a mate, at once suggestive of Cressida kissing the Greek generals, and yet characteristically less explicit. Whatever cured the King, Bertram's resistance to the enforced marriage and the King's anger at him make no reference to Divine intervention.

So we are left with hints at four different explanations; hints rather than affirmations precisely as the couplets are couplets but not fully resonant. It may be drugs, or miracle, or magic – or it may simply be sexual response (miracle or magic in nature). And in that ambiguity, and in the use of verse, the necessary relationship between naturalism and romance potential is very subtly established. It could not be done without couplets; yet they are not allowed to over-ride the dominance of naturalism.

That may seem to be baffling: I think it does depend on familiarity with the forms of romance thus insinuated but not developed. It would be easy to claim the Elizabethans had such a familiarity and that we have not. But in truth we still have. Fairy stories of various kinds are still common to the vast majority of children; and if the quantity has been reduced as well as the quality become less grim, the appetite emerges in adult cults for the dubiously adult fantasies of Tolkien or C. S. Lewis. No doubt we have not such an exact equivalent for the experience Shakespeare invokes as his own audience would have understood; but a similar point can be made about all his plays. It is, I think, entirely sufficient for this play, as it is for others. Agnostic viewers bred in a Christian tradition, however ignorant of the

Bible, can still be startled by Caravaggio's paintings. So can we be startled by *All's Well*. Conventional contemporaries mistook Caravaggio for an atheist; more perceptive minds (cardinals, as well as painters like Rubens) understood otherwise. It is a narrow criticism which understands *All's Well* as a mere negation of romance. Caravaggio only indicates the religious values he assumes behind his naturalistic treatment; Shakespeare only indicates the values of fiction, which are also those of imagination, which he assumes behind *his* naturalistic treatment. In fact, he indicates rather more fully than Caravaggio, but only as a play has more need to than a painting. In the cure of the King he does it explicitly, however guardedly; there are hints too of another mythology in the names of Helena and Diana; later in the play, it is always implicit in the use of couplets (especially between Helena and the Florentine ladies). It is implicit too in the bed-trick which is teasingly pitched between a folk-tale game and a naturalistic joke. And it is implicit still for nearly the whole of the final scene, which is in motif the testing of the hero, the virtue of the maiden, and the restoration to life of the heroine; but is seen as the exposure of Bertram, the equivocation of Diana, and the stage-management of Helena. The final lines enunciate the romance potential directly, but necessarily minimally, and the apt comment is left to Lafew:

> Mine eyes smell onions; I shall weep anon.
> Good Tom Drum, lend me a handkercher.
>
> (v, iii, 314–15)

I have already claimed for this play a distinctive and very distinguished language. I also think that, so far from being a play that falls apart, it has a controlled unity of a kind rare even in Shakespeare. Its unity is conditioned by its tone; by the refusal ever to let it move beyond the limits which that defines. In that too it resembles Caravaggio: after nearly a century of mannerist variety, his paintings were a shock not only in their naturalism but also in their insistent singularity of vision. Shakespeare started as a mannerist writer: *The Two Gentlemen of Verona* is a gallimaufry with an altogether surprising last act; *Love's Labour's Lost* is explicit about its disrupted dénouement; even *As You Like It*, though it has its own unity, contrives it out of a series of 'turns', like a controlled variety show. *All's Well*, by contrast with these, has on its surface (and it is very much concerned with surfaces) an insistent singularity of vision that is unique.

I can only guess how it might work on the stage. I believe it could, but I have only seen it once,[1] and then it was tricked out in late seventeenth-century style like an odd version of *The Three Musketeers*. Tyrone Guthrie's productions sound as though he deployed all his skills to turn it into the play Shaw wished he'd written. It needs, no doubt, more trust than treatment; its language would surely guide sensitive actresses and actors into a satisfactory number of interesting roles, though they are as severely disciplined as the play itself. But although I believe it could work and be very sharply interesting as well as uncomfortably amusing, I do not suppose it would be exactly 'popular'. Its vision resists too consistently our will to indulgence, whether in sentiment, magic, or psychological identification. Caravaggio, I think, faced the problem that he could not expand on the religious themes to which his paintings allude, and in his last works be explored some curious ways of overcoming that. So did Shakespeare. *All's Well* I take to be a superb achievement in its own terms; but also to be limited by them. It is often said to be a twin play with *Measure for Measure*, but they are certainly not identical

[1] At Stratford, England, in 1955.

twins. The later play is more articulate about its themes because it is not committed to the linguistic unity of *All's Well*: it employs varied and strongly contrasted forms of language. So it does not depend on traps for exposure so much as confrontations, both of people and their several languages. Thus it arrives at Isabella's 'Man proud man, dressed in a little brief authority', or the Duke's 'Be absolute for death,' or Claudio's 'Ay, but to die and go we know not where,/To lie in cold obstruction and to rot' – all of them forms of eloquence impossible in *All's Well*. Technically, they are very different plays. The last plays are more remote still, for they invert the relations of naturalism and romance, obtruding extreme improbability, and giving it surprising local possibility. So, for instance, the motif of the bed-trick reaches its final variation in *Cymbeline*: not with Jachimo's visit where (almost as an in-joke?) it does not take place, but with Cloten's decapitated body dressed in Posthumus's clothes and (as Cloten had claimed) so resembling Posthumus that Imogen feels it and faints upon it. That is marvellously grotesque and therefore the opposite of *All's Well* whose naturalism precludes anything of the kind.

I make these comparisons primarily to identify the uniqueness of *All's Well*, secondarily to place its peculiar achievement and the limitation inherent in that. I do not expect to convince anyone of all my claims, and that is why I made my title out of the scepticism of the play's: for better and for worse, all's well that ends well.

'HAMLET' AND THE POWER OF WORDS

INGA-STINA EWBANK

If the first law of literary and dramatic criticism is that the approach to a work should be determined by the nature of that work, then I take courage from the fact that *Hamlet* is a play in which, in scene after scene, fools tend to rush in where angels fear to tread. That such fools also tend to come to a bad end – to be stabbed behind the arras or summarily executed in England, 'not shriving-time allowed' – I prefer at this point not to consider.

The area into which I propose to rush is the language of *Hamlet*. The method of entry is eclectic. If there is any timeliness about the rush it is that – just as ten years or so ago King Lear was Our Contemporary – Hamlet is now coming to the fore as one of the inhabitants of No Man's Land. A recent book on Shakespeare's *Tragic Alphabet* speaks of the play being about 'a world where words and gestures have become largely meaningless', and even as long as twenty-five years ago an article on 'The Word in *Hamlet*' began by drawing attention to 'the intensely critical, almost disillusionist, attitude of the play towards language itself'.[1] Against these, I must confess a firm (and perhaps old-fashioned) belief that *Hamlet*, the play, belongs not so much in No Man's as in Everyman's Land: that it is a vision of the human condition realized in the whole visual and verbal language of the theatre with such intensity and gusto that from any point of view it becomes meaningless to call that language meaningless; and that in the play as a whole speech is something far more complex, with powers for good and ill, than the 'words, words, words' of Hamlet's disillusionment. My aim is to explore the part which speech plays in the life of this play *and* the function of speech as part of Shakespeare's vision in the play. I must start with an example.

At the opening of act IV – or, as some would prefer to describe it, at the close of the closet scene – Claudius pleads with Gertrude, whom he has found in considerable distress:

> There's matter in these sighs, these profound heaves,
> You must translate; 'tis fit we understand them.

Of course he thinks he knows what the 'matter' is, for he also immediately adds 'Where is your son?'. Gertrude has just been through the most harrowing[2] experience: Hamlet's words to her have 'like daggers' entered into her 'ears' and turned her 'eyes into [her] very soul' where she has gained such unspeakable knowledge of her 'black and grained spots' as might well have made her feel unable to comply with Claudius's request for a 'translation'. Indeed, in a modern play, where husbands and wives tend to find that on the whole they don't speak the same language, the shock of insight might well have led her to make some statement of non-communication – some version of the reply by Ibsen's Nora (that early non-communicat-

[1] Lawrence Danson, *Tragic Alphabet: Shakespeare's Drama of Language* (New Haven and London, 1974), p. 48; John Paterson, 'The Word in *Hamlet*', *Shakespeare Quarterly*, II (1951), 47.

[2] Though Gertrude herself does not use the verb 'harrow', I use it advisedly, as it seems to be a *Hamlet* word. It occurs once in *Coriolanus*, in its literal sense, but Shakespeare's only two metaphorical uses of it are in *Hamlet:* by the Ghost (I, v, 16) and by Horatio describing the impact of the Ghost (I, i, 44).

ing wife) to her husband's wish to 'understand' her reactions:

You don't understand me. Nor have I ever understood you.[1]

In fact, of course, Gertrude does the opposite. She provides a translation of the preceding scene which manages to avoid saying anything about herself but to describe Hamlet's madness, his killing of Polonius, and his treatment of the body. As so often in this play,[2] we have a retelling of an episode which we have already witnessed. And so we can see at once that Gertrude's translation is a mixture of three kinds of components: first, of what really happened and was said (including a direct quotation of Hamlet's cry 'a rat', though she doubles it and changes it from a question to an exclamation);[3] secondly, of what she thinks, or would like to think, happened and was said. She is prepared to read into Hamlet's behaviour such motivations, and to add such details, as she would have liked to find – as Polonius suspected when he appointed himself 'some more audience than a mother, / Since nature makes them partial' (III, iii, 31–2), though even he could not have foreseen that her partiality would come to extend to a fictitious description of Hamlet mourning over his corpse.[4] Thirdly, but most importantly, as it most controls both what she says and how she says it, her translation consists of what she wants the king to think did happen: that the scene demonstrated what Hamlet in a doubly ironic figure of speech had told her not to say, i.e. that he is 'essentially' mad and not 'mad in craft'. Her emotion is released, and her verbal energy spends itself, not on the part of the recent experience which concerns herself most radically, but on convincing her husband that her son is

Mad as the sea and wind, when both contend
Which is the mightier.

Claudius may end the scene 'full of discord and dismay', but – and this seems usually to be the most Gertrude can hope for – things are not as bad as they might have been. She has in a manner protected her son by sticking to her assurance to him that

if words be made of breath
And breath of life, I have no life to breathe
What thou hast said to me;

she has at least not added to Claudius's suspicions of Hamlet's 'antic disposition'; and she has paid some tribute to the victim of the game between the two, the murderer and the revenger: 'the unseen good old man'. I do not think that Gertrude's design is as conscious as this analysis may have suggested, but her translation has worked.

In so far as anything in this play, so full of surprises at every corner, is typical of the whole, the scene seems to me a model for how language functions within much of the play: communicating by adapting words to thought and feeling, in a process which involves strong awareness in the speaker of who is being spoken to. Of course there has not been much truth spoken and on that score, no doubt, the

[1] *A Doll's House*, act III (*Et dukkehjem*, in *Henrik Ibsens Samlede Verker*, Oslo, 1960, II, 474).

[2] Some other examples of 'translated' versions of an episode we have already seen are: Rosencrantz and Guildenstern's slanted report, in III, i, 4 ff., of their meeting with Hamlet in II, ii; Polonius's to Claudius and Gertrude, in II, ii, 130 ff., of how he admonished Ophelia in I, iii; and Polonius's attempt to bolster up Claudius, in III, iii, 30 ff., by attributing to him his own plan hatched at III, i, 184–5. Significantly, at the end of the nunnery scene Polonius and Claudius specifically do not want a report from Ophelia: 'We heard it all' (III, i, 180).

[3] That is, in the punctuation of modern editors (e.g. Alexander and Dover Wilson). In Q 2 Hamlet says 'a Rat,' and Gertrude 'a Rat, a Rat,'; in F 1 the readings are, respectively, 'a Rat?' and 'a Rat, a Rat,'.

[4] As Dover Wilson points out in his note on 'a weeps for what is done', 'the falsehood testifies to her fidelity' (New Cambridge Shakespeare, *Hamlet*, 1934, p. 218).

scene is a thematic illustration of that dreaded pair of abstracts, Appearance and Reality; and the author's attitude is 'disillusionist' enough. And of course the scene in one sense speaks of non-communication between husband and wife. Gertrude has drawn apart, with her unspeakable knowledge and suspicion, much as Macbeth has when he bids his wife 'Be innocent of the knowledge, dearest chuck' (*Macbeth*, III, ii, 45). But, in its dramatic context, the language does a great deal more than that. There is, as Polonius has said, 'some more audience' in the theatre, and to them – to us – the language speaks eloquently of the strange complexities of human life, of motives and responses and the re-alignment of relationships under stress. It speaks of Gertrude's desperate attempt to remain loyal to her son but also (however misguidedly) to her husband and to his chief councillor. Ultimately the power of the words is Shakespeare's, not Gertrude's, and it operates even through the total muteness of Rosencrantz and Guildenstern who, like parcels, are, most Stoppard-like, sent out and in and out again in the course of the scene.

Claudius's verb for what he asks Gertrude to do is apter than he knew himself: 'You must translate'. Presumably (and editors do not seem to feel that annotation is needed) he simply wants her to interpret her signs of emotion in words, to change a visual language into a verbal. But, as anyone knows who has attempted translation in its now most commonly accepted sense, the processes involved in finding equivalents in one language for the signs of another are far from simple. There is a troublesome tension – indeed often an insoluble contradiction – between the demands of 'interpretation' and those of 'change', between original meaning and meaningfulness in another language. That Shakespeare was aware of this – although, unlike many of his fellow poets and dramatists, he was apparently not an inter-lingual translator – is suggested, in the first place, by the various ways in which he uses the word 'translate' in his plays. Alexander Schmidt's *Shakespeare-Lexicon* separates three clearly defined meanings: 1. to transform or to change, as Bottom is 'translated', or as beauty is *not* translated into honesty in the nunnery scene; 2. 'to render into another language (or rather to change by rendering into another language)', as Falstaff translates Mistress Ford's inclinations 'out of honesty into English', or as the Archbishop of York translates his whole being 'Out of the speech of peace . . . Into the harsh and boist'rous tongue of war' (both these examples being rather demanding in the way of dictionaries); and 3. to interpret or explain, as in the Claudius line I have been discussing, or as Aeneas has translated Troilus to Ulysses.[1] Not only do Schmidt and the *OED* disagree over these definitions,[2] but, as the examples I have given indicate, meanings seem to overlap within Shakespeare's uses of the word – so that all three hover around the following lines from Sonnet 96:

> So are those errors that in thee are seen
> To truths translated and for true things deem'd.

That sonnet is in a sense about the problem of finding a language for the 'grace and faults' of the beloved – a problem which haunts many of the Sonnets and can be solved, the poems show, only by fusing change and interpretation into a single poetic act. In much the same way, *Hamlet* is dominated by the hero's search for a way to translate (though Shakespeare does not use the word here) the contra-

[1] See *A Midsummer Night's Dream*, III, i, 109; *Hamlet*, III, i, 113; *The Merry Wives*, I, iii, 47; *2 Henry IV*, IV, i, 46–8; *Troilus and Cressida*, IV, v, 112.

[2] The *OED*, for example, uses both Claudius's line and the one from *The Merry Wives* to illustrate the meaning 'to interpret, explain' ('Translate' II.3. *fig.*)

dictory demands of the Ghost:

> If thou hast nature in thee, bear it not;
> ....
> But, howsomever thou pursuest this act,
> Taint not thy mind...
>
> (I, v, 81, 84–5)

Claudius, we are going to see, finds that his position translates best into oxymorons; and Troilus feels the need to be bilingual – 'this is, and is not, Cressid' – or simply silent: 'Hector is dead; there is no more to say'.

If, then, to translate means both to interpret and to change, it also usually means being particularly conscious of the words used in the process. All of us, surely, are prepared to claim with Coleridge that we have 'a smack of Hamlet' in us; but those of us who have approached the English language from the outside may perhaps claim a special kind of smack. For lack of sophistication we may share that alertness to a rich, hybrid language, to latent metaphors and multiple meanings waiting to be activated, which Hamlet has by an excess of sophistication. With still fresh memories of looking up a word in the English dictionary and finding a bewildering row of possible meanings, or an equally bewildering row of words for a supposedly given meaning, we are also peculiarly prepared to give more than local significance to Claudius's line: 'You must translate; 'tis fit we understand'.

I would not indulge in these speculations if I did not believe that they applied directly to *Hamlet*. George Steiner, in *After Babel*, maintains that '*inside or between languages, human communication equals translation*'.[1] *Hamlet*, I think, bears out the truth of this. Hamlet himself is throughout the play trying to find a language to express himself through, as well as languages to speak to others in; and round him – against him and for him – the members of the court of Elsinore are engaging in acts of translation. The first meeting with Rosencrantz and Guildenstern, in II, ii, would be a specific example of this general statement. Hamlet's speech on how he has of late lost all his mirth – mounting to the much-quoted 'What a piece of work is man!... / And yet, to me, what is this quintessence of dust?' – is only partly, if at all, a spontaneous overflow of his mythical sorrows (let alone of Shakespeare's). Partly, even mainly, it is his translation, in such terms of *fin-de-siècle* disillusionment as clever young men will appreciate, of just as much of his frame of mind as he wants Rosencrantz and Guildenstern to understand. And the verbal hide-and-seek of the whole episode turns what might have been a simple spy / counterspy scene into a complex study of people trying to control each other by words. Here, and elsewhere in the play, the mystery of human intercourse is enacted and the power of words demonstrated: what we say, and by saying do, to each other, creating and destroying as we go along.

No one in the play seems to regret that it is words they 'gotta use' when they speak to each other. Hamlet, unlike Coriolanus, never holds his mother 'by the hand, silent'; and his only major speechless moment is that which Ophelia describes to Polonius, when

> with a look so piteous in purport
> As if he had been loosed out of hell
> To speak of horrors – he comes before me.
>
> (II, i, 81–4)

The Ghost does indeed hint at unspeakable horrors – 'I could a tale unfold' – but he is very explicit about the effects its 'lightest word' would have, and the only reason he does not speak those words is a purgatorial prohibition on telling 'the secrets of my prison-house' to 'ears of flesh and blood' (I, v, 13 ff.). Words govern the action of the play, from the ironical watchword – 'Long live the King!' – which allays Fransisco's fears

[1] *After Babel: Aspects of Language and Translation* (1975), p. 47 (Dr Steiner's italics).

I Michelangelo Caravaggio: *Mary Magdalene* (Doria Gallery, Rome)

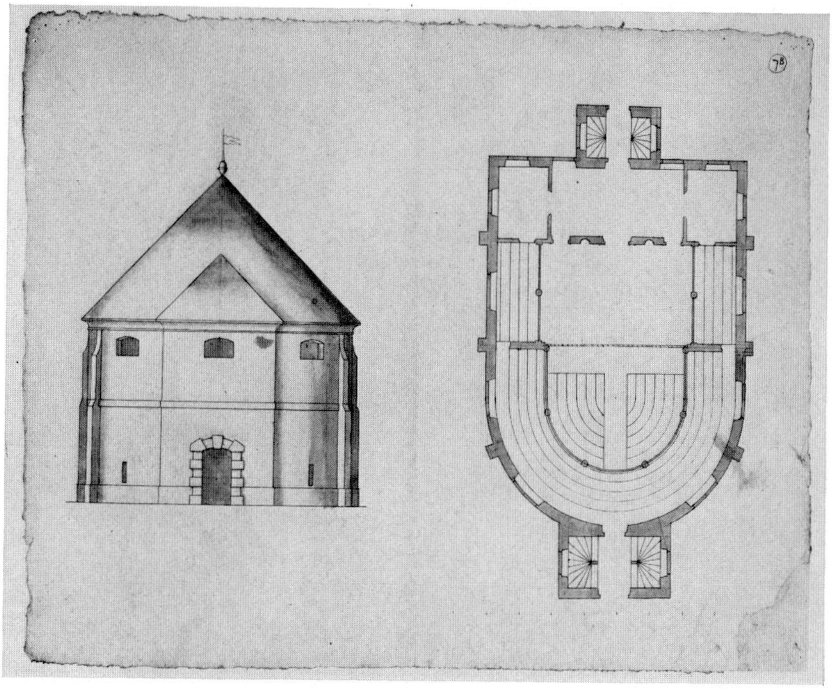

II A and B Theatre designs by Inigo Jones (sheets I/7B and 7C)

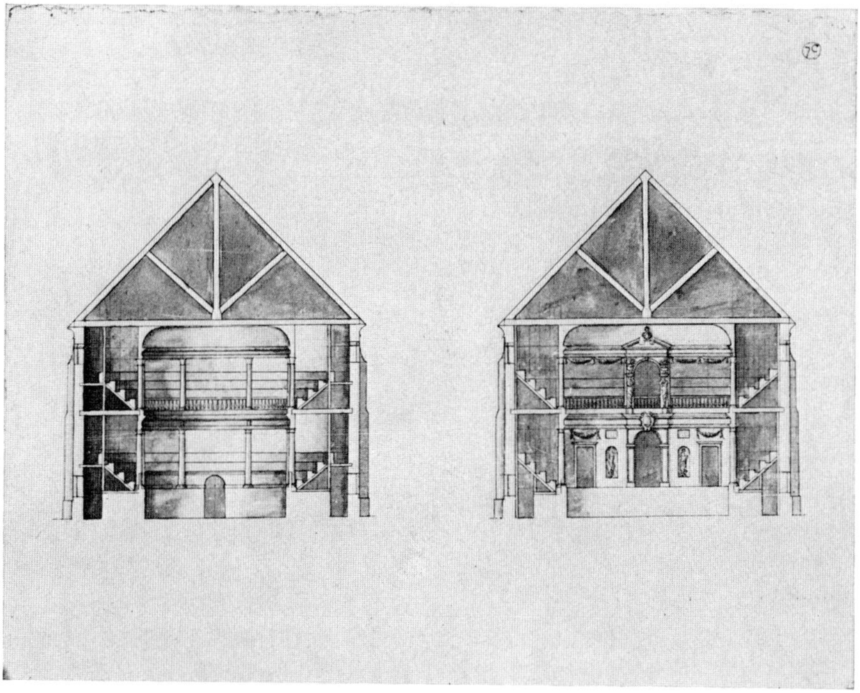

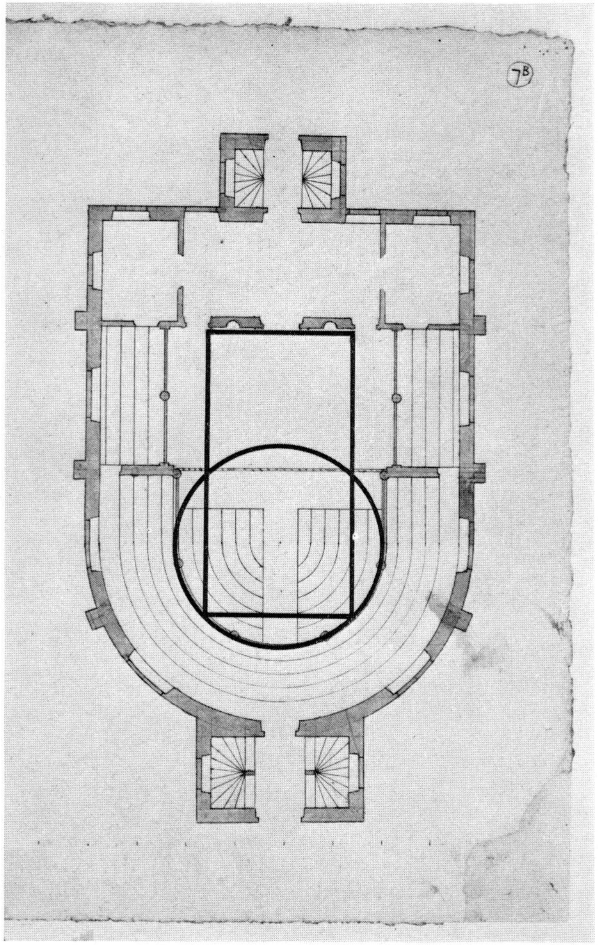

IIIA Two 10-metre squares define the relationship of the pit to the stage

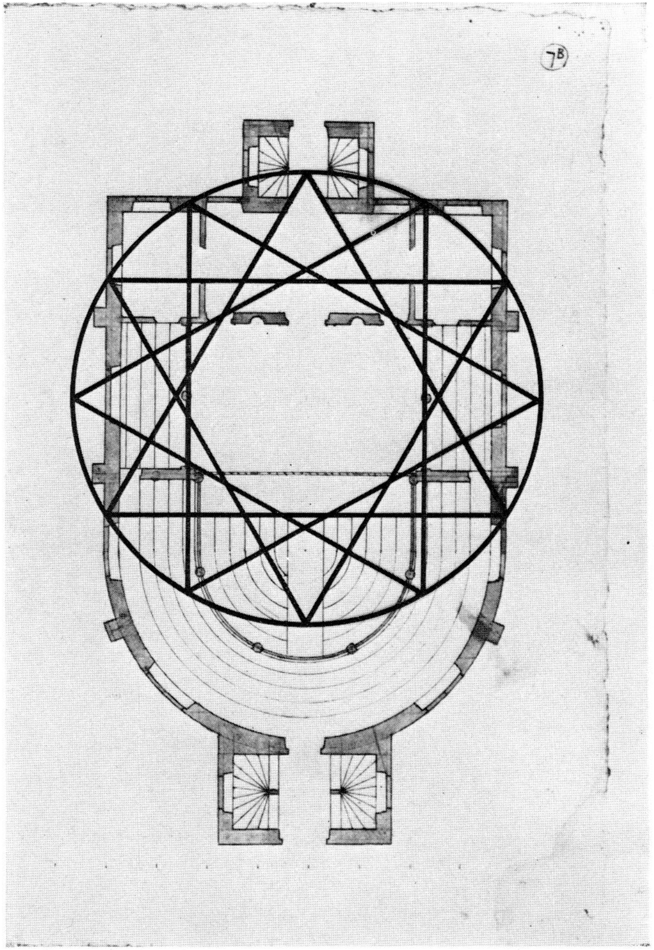

IIIB The Vitruvian pattern of the stage end of the theatre

IV A The Derby pit, from John Speed's *Theatre of the Empire of Great Britaine* (1611)

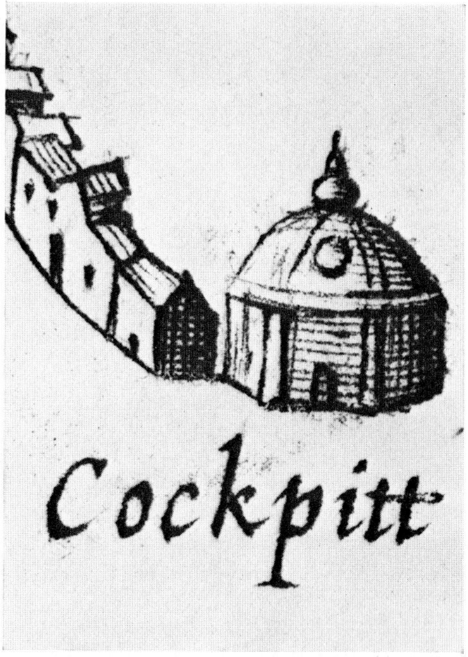

IV B The Leicester pit, from D. Loggan, *Oxonia Illustrata* (Oxford, 1675)

IV C The Oxford Pit, from the same

IV D The Gray's Inn Gardens pit, Holborn, from John Stow, *Survey of the Cities of London and Westminster*, edited by John Strype (1720)

V The Royal Cockpit, Dartmouth Street, from Kip, 'View of Westminster' (1710)

VIA Permanent staging for the Royal Shakespeare Theatre season, 1976, designed by John Napier and Chris Dyer

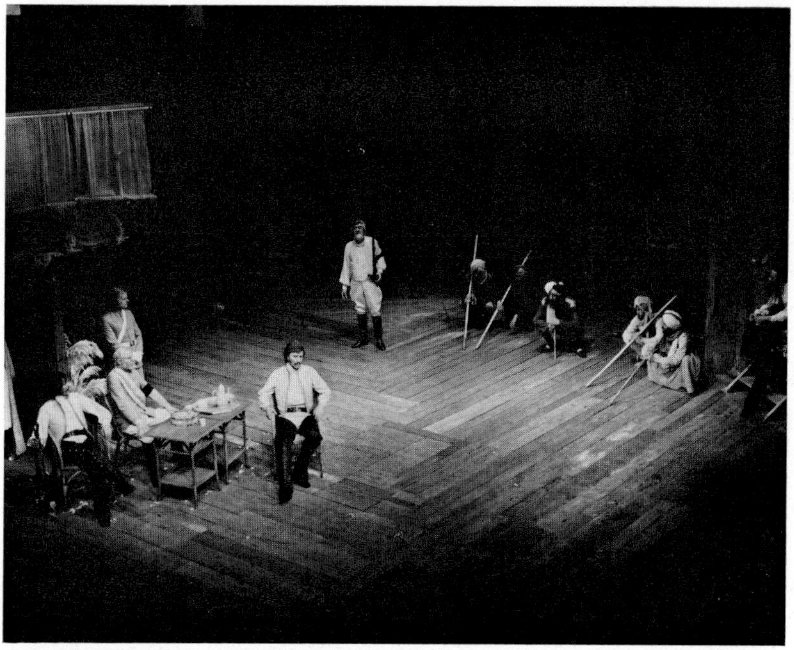

VIB *Much Ado About Nothing*, Royal Shakespeare Theatre, 1976. Directed by John Barton, designed by John Napier. V, i: at table, Claudio (Richard Durden), Don Pedro (Robin Ellis); crouching, Dogberry (John Woodvine) and the watch

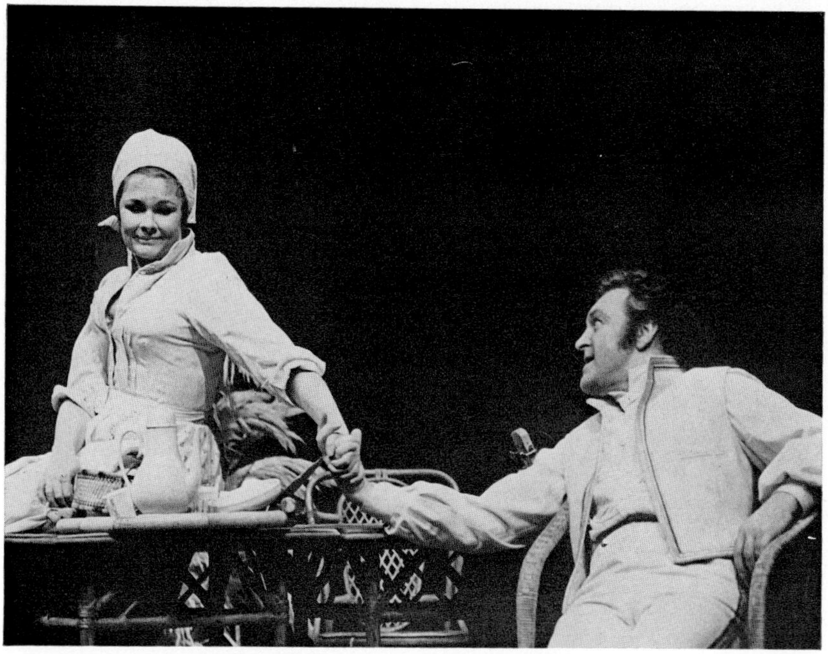

VII A *Much Ado About Nothing*, Royal Shakespeare Theatre, 1976. Judi Dench and Donald Sinden as Beatrice and Benedick

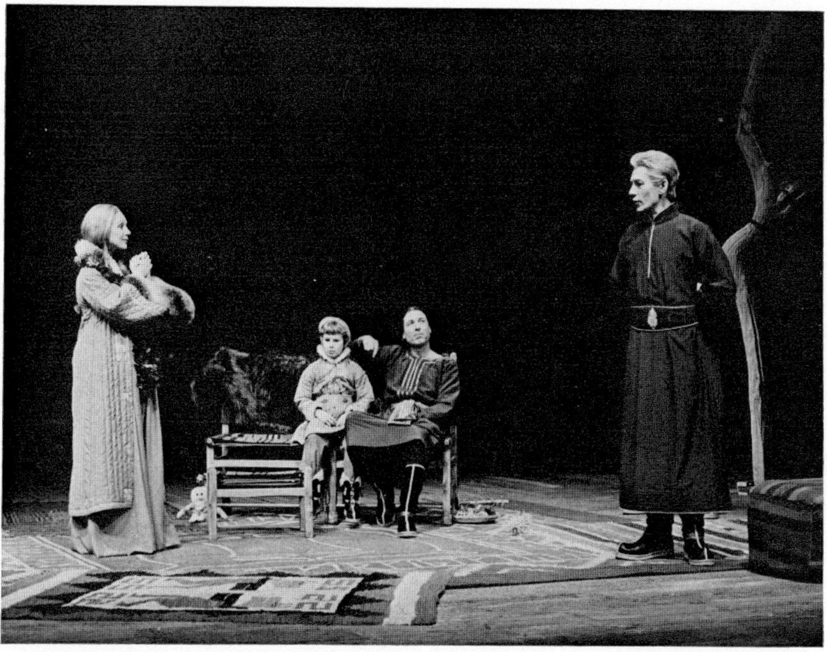

VII B *The Winter's Tale*, Royal Shakespeare Theatre, 1976. Directed by John Barton and Trevor Nunn, designed by Di Seymour. Hermione (Marilyn Taylerson), Polixenes (John Woodvine), Leontes (Ian McKellen)

VIII A *Troilus and Cressida*, Royal Shakespeare Theatre, 1976. Directed by John Barton and Barry Kyle, designed by Chris Dyer. Mike Gwilym and Francesca Annis as Troilus and Cressida

VIII B *Macbeth*. The Other Place, Stratford, 1976. Ian McKellen and Judi Dench as Macbeth and Lady Macbeth

at the opening, to Hamlet's 'dying voice' which gives the throne of Denmark to Fortinbras at the end; and, beyond, to the speech which will be given by Horatio when it is all over, explaining 'to th'yet unknowing world / How these things came about'. Words control the fates and the development of the characters, and not only when they are spoken by the Ghost to Hamlet and turned by him into a principle of action ('Now to my word': I, v, 110). Words can open Gertrude's eyes, help to drive Ophelia mad, unpack Hamlet's heart (however much he regrets it); and if Claudius finds that 'words without thoughts never to heaven go' (III, iii, 98), this merely validates those words which have thoughts. Sometimes the words deceive, sometimes they say what is felt and meant, sometimes they are inadequate – but the inadequacy reflects on the speaker rather than the language. In the study, where the play so readily presents itself spatially and thematically, it may be easy to speak of it as demonstrating the inadequacy of words. In the theatre, the words have to get us through the four-and-a-half hours traffic of the stage, and (when they have not been cut or played about with) they give us a play of relationships, of 'comutual' (as the Player King would call them) interactions and dialogues – a world where it is natural to ask not only 'What's Hecuba to him?' but also 'or he to Hecuba?'. *Hamlet*, for all its soliloquies, may well be the Shakespeare play which most confirms Ben Jonson's statement, in *Discoveries*, that language 'is the instrument of society'; and in exploring the function of speech in the play we may do well to listen to Henry James's words to the graduating class at Bryn Mawr College in June 1905:

> All life therefore comes back to the question of our speech, the medium through which we communicate with each other; for all life comes back to the question of our relations with each other . . .
> . . . the way we say a thing, or fail to say it, fail to learn to say it, has an importance in life that is impossible to overstate – a far-reaching importance, as the very hinge of the relation of man to man.[1]

Looking at the world of 'relations' in *Hamlet* from the outside, we can have no doubt that its hinges are well oiled, by the sheer size of its vocabulary. Long ago now, the patient industry of Alfred Hart demonstrated that *Hamlet* has 'the largest and most expressive vocabulary' of all Shakespeare's plays, and that it abounds in new words – new to Shakespeare and also, in many cases, apparently new to English literature – a considerable number of which do not recur in any later Shakespeare plays.[2] And a new language for new and unique experiences is suggested not only by the single words but by the new structures, images and figures into which they are combined – as indeed by the new uses of old syntactical patterns and rhetorical figures. (It is worth remembering that, seen through the eyes of T. W. Baldwin and Sister Miriam Joseph, Hamlet's forerunners are Holofernes and Sir Nathaniel.)[3] Language is being stretched and re-shaped to show the form and pressure of the *Hamlet* world. The extraordinary variety of language modes is important, too: we move, between scenes or within a scene or even within a speech, from moments

[1] See *Discoveries* CXXVIII, and Henry James, *The Question of Our Speech* (Boston and New York, 1905), p. 10 and p. 21.

[2] Alfred Hart, 'Vocabularies of Shakespeare's Plays', *Review of English Studies* XIX (1943), 128–40, and 'The Growth of Shakespeare's Vocabulary', *ibid.*, 242–3. The subject was freshly illuminated in the paper on 'New Words between *Henry IV* and *Hamlet*' given by Professor Marvin Spevack at the Seventeenth International Shakespeare Conference in Stratford-upon-Avon, August 1976, and by the booklet of word lists which he distributed in connection with his paper.

[3] T. W. Baldwin, *William Shakspere's Small Latine and Lesse Greeke*, 2 vols. (Urbana, Ill., 1944), *passim*; and Sister Miriam Joseph, *Shakespeare's Use of the Arts of Language* (New York, 1947), esp. p. 12.

of high elaboration and formality to moments of what Yeats would have called 'walking naked',[1] where speech is what the Sonnets call 'true and plain' and we call 'naturalistic'.

If we view the world of *Hamlet* from the inside, we find that what the still small voices in the play have in common with the loud and eloquent ones is a general belief in the importance of speaking. The play begins with three men repeatedly imploring a ghost to speak and ends with Hamlet's concern for what Horatio is going to 'speak to th'yet unknowing world', and in between characters are always urging each other to speak. It is as natural for Laertes to part from Ophelia with a 'let me hear from you' (I, iii, 4) as it is for Polonius to react to Ophelia's 'affrighted' description of Hamlet's appearance with 'What said he?' (II, i, 86). In this particular instance there is no speech to report, but the key-note of most of the character confrontations in the play could, again, have been taken from the *Discoveries*: 'Language most shews a man: Speak, that I may see thee.'[2] In *Hamlet*, unlike *King Lear*, seeing is rarely enough. Ophelia's lament at the end of the nunnery scene –

> O, woe is me
> T' have seen what I have seen, see what I see! –

follows upon an unusually (for her) eloquent analysis of both what she has seen and what she is seeing ('O, what a noble mind is here o'er-thrown!'); and Gertrude, we know, soon finds words to translate into words her exclamation, 'Ah, mine own lord, what have I seen tonight!' Often seeing has to be achieved through hearing. 'You go not till I set you up a glass', Hamlet tells his mother, but that 'glass' is not so much 'the counterfeit presentment of two brothers' as Hamlet's speech on Gertrude's lack of 'eyes'. Unlike Edgar, Horatio is left with the exact and exacting task of speaking not what he feels, but what he ought to say. One begins to feel that the ear is the main sense organ in *Hamlet*, and concordances confirm that the word 'ear' occurs in this play more times than in any other of Shakespeare's.[3] Through the ear – 'attent', or 'knowing' – comes the understanding which Claudius asks Gertrude for in IV, i; but through the 'too credent' or 'foolish' ear come deception and corruption. Claudius seems obsessed with a sense of Laertes's ear being infected 'with pestilent speeches' while he himself is being arraigned 'in ear and ear' (IV, v, 87–91). Well he might be, for in the Ghost's speech all of Denmark had, as in a Bosch vision, been contracted into a single ear:

> so the whole ear of Denmark
> Is by a forged process of my death
> Rankly abus'd; (I, v, 36–8)

and the ironic source and sounding-board of all these images is of course the literal poisoning by ear on which the plot of the play rests.

So the characters not only speak, they listen. Not only do we, the audience, marvel at the variety of idioms heard, from Gravedigger to Player King, from Osric, who has 'only got the tune of the time and the outward habit of encounter' (V, ii, 185), to Ophelia whose real fluency comes only in madness. But the characters themselves take a conscious and delighted interest in the idiosyncracies of individual and national idioms, in how people speak, as Polonius says, 'according to the

[1] W. B. Yeats, 'A Coat'. (*Collected Poems*, 1933, p. 142).

[2] *Discoveries* CXXXII (*Oratio imago animi*).

[3] 'Ear' and 'ears' occur, together, 24 (16 + 8) times. The second largest figure is for *Coriolanus*: 17 (3 + 14) times. The different lengths, in lines, make comparisons somewhat unreliable; though *Coriolanus* is less than 500 lines shorter than *Hamlet*, and *King Lear*, with 3,205 lines as against *Hamlet's* 3,762, has only 5 (4 + 1) occurrences of 'ear' and 'ears'. (I take my figures for lengths in lines from Hart, 'Vocabularies of Shakespeare's Plays', and for word frequencies from Marvin Spevack's *Harvard Concordance to Shakespeare*, Cambridge, Mass., 1973).

phrase and the addition / Of man and country' (II, i, 47–8). Hamlet's parodies of spoken and written styles are outstanding, but Polonius – in instructing Reynaldo – is just as good at imitating potential conversations. Seen from our point of view or the characters', the play is alive with interest in how people react to each other and to each other's language.

Like Claudius, in the scene from which I began, the characters, when they urge each other to speak, expect to understand the 'matter', or meaning, of what is said. Hence they are particularly disturbed by the apparent meaninglessness of 'antic' speech – 'I have nothing with this answer, Hamlet; these words are not mine', is Claudius's sharpest and most direct rebuke to his nephew / son (III, ii, 93–4) – and by the dim apprehension, again expressed by Claudius, after overhearing the nunnery scene, that the lack of 'form' in such speech may conceal 'something' (III, i, 162 ff.) Laertes does recognize that mad speech may reach beyond rational discourse – 'This nothing's more than matter' – and be more effectively moving (IV, v, 171 and 165–6). But the first we hear of Ophelia's madness is Gertrude's abrupt opening line in IV, v: 'I will not speak with her', followed by the Gentleman's long account of her language:

> Her speech is nothing,
> Yet the unshaped use of it doth move
> The hearers to collection; they yawn at it,
> And botch the words up fit to their own thoughts.
> (ll. 7–10)

Yielding to Horatio's cautiously applied pressure – ''Twere good she were spoken with' – Gertrude can attempt a dialogue only through the usual request for *meaning*: 'Alas, sweet lady, what imports this song?'; and even Ophelia knows through her madness the kind of question that will be asked about her: 'when they ask you what it means, say you this: ...'

We have returned to the idea of translation, for in their intercourse the characters seem unusually aware of their interlocutors' tendency to 'botch the words up fit to their own thoughts'. One main aspect of this is the belief, demonstrated throughout the play, in the importance of finding the right language for the right person. The opening scene is a model of this. Horatio had been brought in as a translator ('Thou art a scholar; speak to it, Horatio')[1] but, though the Ghost's first appearance turns him from scepticism to 'fear and wonder', he is unsure of his language. His vocabulary is wrong: 'What art thou that usurp'st [a particularly unfortunate verb in the circumstances] this time of night ...?' and so is his tone: 'By heaven I charge thee, speak!'. On the Ghost's second appearance, Horatio's litany of appeals – 'If ... Speak to me' – more nearly approaches the ceremony which befits a king. The second 'If', with its sense of 'comutual' purpose, gets very warm –

> If there be any good thing to be done,
> That may to thee do ease and grace to me –

but Horatio then loses himself in the motivations of generalized ghost lore; and, in any case, Time in the form of a cock's crow interrupts any possible interchange. A 'show of violence' signals the hopeless defeat of verbal communication. Horatio now knows that none but Hamlet can find the language needed, and so the scene ends with the decision to 'impart what we have seen tonight / Unto young Hamlet', for:

> This spirit, dumb to us, will speak to him.

But the gap between speakers which – they are aware – must be bridged by translation is

[1] As Professor A. C. Sprague has pointed out to me, G. L. Kittredge exploded the idea (still adhered to by Dover Wilson; see his note on I, i, 42) that this line refers to the fact that exorcisms of spirits were usually performed in Latin. 'Horatio, as a scholar, knows how to address the apparition in the right way, so as neither to offend it nor to subject himself to any evil influence.' (G. L. Kittredge, ed., *Sixteen Plays of Shakespeare* (Boston, 1939), p. 1021).

not always as wide as the grave. The king appeals to Rosencrantz and Guildenstern as being on the same side of the generation gap as Hamlet –

> being of so young days brought up with him,
> And sith so neighboured to his youth and haviour –
> (II, ii, 11–12)

which should give them a language 'to gather,/So much as from occasion you may glean'; and Hamlet conjures them to tell the truth 'by the consonancy of our youth' (II, ii, 283). When the opening of the closet scene has demonstrated that Gertrude's language and her son's are in diametrical opposition –

> Hamlet, thou hast thy father much offended.
> Mother, you have my father much offended. –

and that he will not adopt the language of a son to a mother ('Have you forgot me?') but insists on a vocabulary and syntax which ram home the confusion in the state of Denmark –

> No, by the rood, not so:
> You are the Queen, your husband's brother's wife.
> And – would it were not so! – you are my mother –

then Gertrude can see no other way out of the deadlock but to call for translators:

> Nay then, I'll set those to you that can speak.

Hamlet's refusal to be thus translated is what leads to Polonius's death. Polonius spends much energy, in his last few days of life, on finding a language for a madman, trying – as in II, ii – at the same time to humour and to analyse Hamlet. But Rosencrantz and Guildenstern are perhaps even more supremely aware of the necessity of different languages for different persons. They take their colour, their style, tone and imagery, from their interlocutors, whether it is a question of speaking the snappy, quibbling dialogue of clever young students with Hamlet on first meeting him, or enlarging before Claudius on the idea of 'the cease of majesty' so that it becomes an extended image of 'a massy wheel,/Fixed on the summit of the highest mount' (III, iii, 10 ff.). They are in the end chameleons rather than caterpillars, and it is naturally to them that Hamlet speaks the words in which the play's interest in suiting language to persons is taken to the extreme of parody:

> Besides, to be demanded of a sponge – what replication should be made by the son of a king?
> (IV, ii, 12)

It is natural, too, that when the programming has gone wrong in their language laboratory they are helpless and can say nothing but

> What should we say, my lord?
> (II, ii, 275)

The characters of the play, then, are on the whole very self-conscious speakers, in a way which involves consciousness of others: they believe in the word and its powers, but they are also aware of the necessity so to translate intentions and experiences into words as to make them meaningful to the interlocutor. And not only vaguely meaningful: they know the effect they want to produce and take careful steps to achieve it. Perhaps the Reynaldo scene is the best model of this. Polonius, in a dialogue of superb naturalism, with its stops and starts, doublings back and forgettings what he was about to say, gives Reynaldo a lesson in translation which is much closer to the heart of the play than any mere plot function might suggest. Anyone who thinks Polonius just a fool ought to look again at the almost Jamesian subtlety with which Reynaldo is instructed to control the *tone* of his indirect enquiries into Laertes's Parisian life, to

> breathe his faults so quaintly
> That they may seem the taints of liberty,
> (II, i, 31–2)

and, in case he has not got the point, to lay

'these slight sullies on my son,/As 'twere a thing a little soil'd wi' th' working' (ll. 39–40). This is a situation less Machiavellian than the Revenge *genre* might seem to demand, and more like the instruction of Strether where, as here, facts tend to refract into opaque impressions rather than moral certainties.

Perhaps I am now being seduced by the power of words – and Polonius's of all people. Not that Shakespeare allows this to happen for very long: the moment that Reynaldo exits, Ophelia bursts in, and the contrast is blatant between the urbanity of the preceding scene and the raw experience of her account – acted out as much as spoken – of Hamlet's speechless visit to her. Clearly, when the characters in *Hamlet* use their language, or languages, for purposes of persuasion and diplomacy, they are generally engaging in duplicity and deception. In the end, the evil underneath is (as James also knew) made more, not less, pernicious by the bland surface of the dialogue. An outstanding example of this is the 'witchcraft of his wits' (as the Ghost is to describe the usurper's 'power/So to seduce') practised by Claudius in the second scene of the play. His opening speech establishes him as a very clever chairman of the board. First he gets the minutes of past proceedings accepted without query, by a carefully arranged structure of oxymorons:[1]

> Therefore our sometime sister, now our queen,
> Th'imperial jointress to this warlike state,
> Have we, as 'twere with a defeated joy,
> With an auspicious and a dropping eye,
> With mirth in funeral, and with dirge in marriage,
> In equal scale weighing delight and dole,
> Taken to wife. (I, ii, 8–14)

The oxymorons, in a relentless series of pairings, operate to cancel each other out, smoothing over the embarrassment (or worse) involved in 'our sometime sister, now our queen', stilling criticism and enforcing acceptance of the apparent logic of the argument, so that by the time we finally get to the verb ('Taken to wife') the 'Therefore' seems legitimate. Then he justifies chairman's action by suggesting that there have been consultations all along, spiking the guns of any potential rebel by thanking him in advance for his agreement:

> nor have we herein barr'd
> Your better wisdoms, which have freely gone
> With this affair along. For all, our thanks.
> (ll. 14–16)

Having dealt with the minutes, he then proceeds to the agenda and polishes off, in turn, the foreign policy problems with Norway, the home and domestic issue of Laertes, and finally the awkward business with Hamlet which – who knows – might be both personal and national, psychological and political. He intends to deal with Hamlet, too, through the technique of dissolving contradictions –

> But now, my cousin Hamlet, and my son –
> (l. 64)

but his briskness here comes to grief, as Hamlet becomes the first to raise a voice, albeit in an aside, which punctures such use of language:

> A little more than kin, and less than kind.
> (l. 65)

Intrepidly, Claudius continues in an image suggesting the tone of decorous grief which ought to be adopted – 'How is it that the clouds still hang on you?' – but this again founders on Hamlet's pun on sun/son. The pun, according to Sigurd Burckhardt in *Shakespearean Meanings*, 'gives the lie direct to the social convention which is language.... It denies the meaningfulness of words.'[2] But in their dramatic context here, Hamlet's puns do no

[1] Danson, *Tragic Alphabet*, p. 26, has some excellent comments on Claudius's use of the oxymoron.

[2] Sigurd Burckhardt, *Shakespearean Meanings* (Princeton, N.J., 1968), pp. 24–5, quoted also by Danson, p. 27, n. 2.

such thing: they deny the logic and sincerity and meaningfulness of Claudius's words but suggest that there is a language elsewhere.

The rest of the scene, until it closes on Hamlet's decision to 'hold my tongue', is a series of contrasts and clashes between different languages. Hamlet's 'common' is not the queen's and implies a far-reaching criticism of hers. Gertrude's reply suggests that she is not aware of the difference, Claudius's that he is trying to pretend that he is not, as he follows Hamlet's terrible outburst against seeming with an, in its way, equally terrible refusal to acknowledge any jar:

> 'Tis sweet and commendable in your nature, Hamlet,
> To give these mourning duties to your father.
> (ll. 87–8)

Hamlet has no reply to Claudius's appeal to the 'common theme' of death of fathers, nor to the request that he give up Wittenberg for 'the cheer and comfort of our eye'; his reply, promising to 'obey', is made to his mother. But it is Claudius who comments on it as 'loving' and 'fair', and it is he who sums up the conversation, translating the tense scene just past into an image of domestic and national harmony –

> This gentle and unforc'd account of Hamlet
> Sits smiling to my heart – (ll. 123–4)

and an excuse for a 'wassail'. The incongruity is as if a satire and a masque by Jonson were being simultaneously performed on the same stage. The ultimate clash comes as, immediately upon Claudius's summing-up, Hamlet breaks into his first soliloquy, giving *his* version of himself and of 'all the uses of this world', particularly those involving his mother and uncle.

The different languages spoken in a scene like this clearly add up to a kind of moral map. That is, the adding up is clear, the map itself not necessarily so. It is not just a matter of Hamlet's words being sincere and Claudius's not. In the dialogue Hamlet is striving for effect in his way just as much as Claudius in his. And Claudius is soon going to be sincere enough, when we learn from his own mouth, in an image that could well have been used by Hamlet, that he is aware of the ugliness of his deed as against his 'most painted word' (III, i, 50–4) and that his words are unable to rise in prayer (III, iii, 36 ff.). Morality and sensitivity to language are peculiarly tied up with each other in this play; and in trying to think how they are related I, at least, am driven back to James and 'The Question of Our Speech': to the importance of 'the way we say a thing, or fail to say it, fail to learn to say it'.[1] In a play peopled by translators, it is in the end the range of languages available to each character – those they 'fail to learn' as well as those they speak – which measures their moral stature. Both Claudius and Gertrude at various times have their consciences stung, but neither seems able to find a language for his or her own inner self. Even Polonius is able to learn and, up to a point, articulate what he has learnt. 'I am sorry', he says about having misunderstood the nature of Hamlet's love for Ophelia, 'that with better heed and judgment/I had not quoted him' (II, i, 111–12). Hamlet himself never has such a moment of recognition in regard to Ophelia. But typically Polonious at once takes the edge off any personal pain of remorse by translating it into a sententious generalization:

> It is as proper to our age
> To cast beyond ourselves in our opinions
> As it is common for the younger sort
> To lack discretion. (II, i, 114–17)

Claudius similarly lacks a really private language. Even when he is alone and trying to pray, his speech retains the basic characteristics of his public 'translations'. Images which in content might seem to anticipate

[1] See note 1, p. 89, above.

Macbeth's,[1] are turned out in carefully balanced phrases – 'heart, with strings of steel' against 'sinews of the new-born babe'; his similes have the considered effect of earlier tragic verse:

> And, like a man to double business bound,
> I stand in pause where I shall first begin,
> And both neglect; (III, iii, 41–3)

and the most trenchant self-analysis is as cleverly antithetical as anything he has to say before the assembled court in I, ii: 'My stronger guilt defends my strong intent'. Unlike Macbeth, Claudius seems to be talking *about* himself, not from inside himself, and his own evil seems to contain no mystery to him, nothing unspeakable. Gertrude has known less evil, and her moral imagination has an even narrower range. Even after the closet scene, her appearances suggest that, like Claudius and unlike Lady Macbeth, she is able to cancel and pass on. The woman who describes Ophelia's death, and strews flowers on her grave, is harrowed within her limits but not marked and changed by her experience, in language and being. The fact that Hamlet and Ophelia are thus changed (however variously) sets them apart. Each of them receives shocks and undergoes sufferings which are taken into their language; and at the extremest point each speaks – whether in madness or not – a language foreign to the other characters.[2]

And yet Hamlet's own language is in many ways that of Elsinore. As others, notably R. A. Foakes, have pointed out, his speech modes and habits are largely those of the court: wordiness, formality, sententiousness, fondness of puns and other forms of word-play, etc.[3] He too uses language in all the ways practised by Claudius and his entourage: for persuasion, diplomacy, deception, and so on. His sheer range, which is as large almost as that of the play itself, has made it difficult for critics to define his own linguistic and stylistic attributes. As Professor Foakes succinctly puts it, 'Hamlet seems master of all styles, but has no distinctive utterance of his own.' Up to a point we can explain this, as Professor Foakes does, by seeing Hamlet as 'the supreme actor who never reveals himself'.[4] But beyond that point we still need a way of talking about Hamlet's language which includes his uncontrolled and (surely) revealing moments, such as the nunnery scene or the leaping into Ophelia's grave, as well as his moments of deliberately antic disposition; and the simple statements in the dialogues with Horatio as well as the tortuous questioning in the monologues. It might be helpful, then, to think of Hamlet as the most sensitive translator in the play: as the one who has the keenest sense both of the expressive and the persuasive powers of words, and also and more radically the keenest sense both of the limitations and the possibilities of words. No one could be more disillusioned with 'words, words, words'. Even before he appears on stage, his mother's rush 'to incestuous sheets' has had an impact which he later describes as having (in contemporary parlance) deprived language of its very credibility:

> O, such a deed
> As . . . sweet religion makes
> A rhapsody of words;
> (III, iv, 45–8)

and, though a Wittenberg scholar could hardly

[1] Claudius wonders whether there is not 'rain enough in the sweet heavens' to wash his 'cursed hand . . . white as snow', and he associates innocence with a 'new-born babe'.

[2] Marvin Spevack has a very interesting discussion of how Hamlet's imagery shows him transforming all he sees, and how he is thus isolated by speaking, as it were, a foreign language; see 'Hamlet and Imagery: The Mind's Eye', *Die Neueren Sprachen*, n.s. v (1966), 203–12.

[3] R. A. Foakes, '*Hamlet* and the Court of Elsinore', *Shakespeare Survey 9* (Cambridge, 1956), pp. 35–43.

[4] R. A. Foakes, 'Character and Speech in *Hamlet*', in *Hamlet*: *Stratford-upon-Avon Studies 5* (1963), p. 161.

have lived unaware of the general maxim that 'one may smile, and smile, and be a villain', the encounter with the Ghost proves it on his own pulses and leaves him permanently aware that language may be a cloak or masque. Yet no one could use his disillusionment more subtly or positively to fit his words to the action, the interlocutor and his own mood – so far indeed that the disillusionment is swallowed up in excitement at the power of words.

No other Shakespearian hero, tragic or comic, has to face so many situations in which different speakers have different palpable designs on him, and where he so has to get hold of the verbal initiative. No other hero, not even Falstaff or Benedick, is so good at grasping the initiative, leading his interlocutor by the nose while – as with Polonius and Osric – playing with the very shape and temperature of reality. Many of the play's comic effects stem from this activity, and the strange tonal mixture of the graveyard scene has much to do with Hamlet, for once, almost playing the stooge to the indomitable wit of the First Gravedigger. No other Shakespearian hero is so good at running his antagonists right down to their basic premisses and striking them dumb, as with Rosencrantz and Guildenstern in the recorder scene. He won't be played upon, and so he listens in order, with lightning speed, to pick up a key-word and turn it into a pun or some other device for playing upon others.

But, unlike many other Shakespearian tragic heroes, Hamlet also listens in a more reflective way – listens and evaluates, as Othello does not (but Hamlet surely would have done) with Iago. In some situations we begin to feel that his linguistic flexibility is founded on a sympathetic imagination. In him, alone in the play, the ability to speak different languages to different people seems to stem from an awareness that, in George Eliot's words, another being may have 'an equivalent centre of self, whence the lights and shadows must always fall with a certain difference'.[1] Other characters meet to plot or to remonstrate, or they step aside for an odd twitch of conscience. To Hamlet, conversations may become extensions of moral sympathy. Even under the immediate impact of encountering the Ghost he can stop to realize and regret that he has offended Horatio with the 'wild and whirling words' which came out of a hysterical absorption in his own experience (I, v, 133 ff.). In retrospect the scene at Ophelia's grave is illuminated by the same sympathy:

> I am very sorry, good Horatio,
> That to Laertes I forgot myself;
> For by the image of my cause I see
> The portraiture of his; (v, ii, 75–8)

and the courtly apology to Laertes (v, ii, 218 ff.), which some critics have taken to be mere falsehood,[2] is surely a genuine attempt at translating his own 'cause' into the language of Laertes. In a case like this, his verbal virtuosity seems to aim at an interchange, a two-way traffic of language between selves. It is worth noting that Hamlet's most explicit tribute to Horatio is to call him 'e'en as just a man / As e'er my conversation cop'd withal' (III, ii, 52–3). Two senses of 'conversation' merge in that phrase – 'the action of consorting or having dealings with others; . . . society; intimacy' (*OED* 2) and 'interchange of thoughts and words' (*OED* 7) – and, one feels, in Hamlet's consciousness.

There is a kinship here between Hamlet and Cleopatra, another character who in her

[1] *Middlemarch*, end of chap. 21 (Penguin ed., p. 243).

[2] For a conspectus of these, see Dover Wilson's note on v, ii, 230, and the Furness *Variorum* edition of *Hamlet*, I, 440. Dr Johnson wished that Hamlet 'had made some other defence; it is unsuitable to the character of a brave or good man to shelter himself in falsehood'; and Seymour believed that the passage was an interpolation: 'The falsehood contained in it is too ignoble.'

language combines intense self-preoccupation with strong awareness of others. In North's Plutarch Shakespeare would have found an emphasis on her verbal powers, even at the expense of her physical beauty which,

> as it is reported, was not so passing as unmatchable of other women, nor yet such as upon present view did enamour men with her; but so sweet was her company and conversation that a man could not possibly but be taken.

Not the least part of the power of Cleopatra's 'conversation' was her ability to speak different languages:

> her tongue was an instrument of music to divers sports and pastimes, the which she easily turned to any language that pleased her. She spake unto few barbarous people by interpreter, but made them answer herself.[1]

It may not be wholly fanciful to imagine that North's comments on Cleopatra's inter-lingual dexterity have in Shakespeare been translated into an intralingual flexibility. Cleopatra is able to speak different languages to Emperor and to Clown as well as to forge her own variety of idioms according to situation and mood – and finally to create, through language, her own reality and Antony's ('Methinks I hear/Antony call. . . . Husband I come'). In her case, as in Hamlet's, the vitality which comes from superb handling of language affects us both aesthetically and morally. To measure it we need only turn to Octavia who is 'of a holy, cold and still conversation'.

Yet by the same measurement there is only a hair's breadth between moral sympathy and callousness, and *Hamlet* shows this too. Hamlet's awareness of others as autonomous beings with 'causes', and accordingly with languages, of their own also helps to explain why he despises Rosencrantz and Guildenstern so, and can so unflinchingly let them 'go to't', recounting his dealings with them as 'not near my conscience' only a few lines before he speaks to Horatio of his regret for what he did and said to Laertes. To him they lack any 'centre of self'; they are instruments used to turn others into 'unworthy' things (III, iii, 353); they are sponges whose only function is to be 'at each ear a hearer' (II, ii, 377). Hamlet's sympathetic imagination falls far short of Stoppard's, and of Christian charity. The killing of Polonius, whom he sees only as an over-hearer and a mouthpiece, affects him no more than a putting-down in verbal repartee:

> Take thy fortune;
> Thou find'st that to be busy is some danger.
> (III, iv, 32–3)

At this point, his whole sense of 'conversation' – of dealings with others – is narrowed onto speaking 'daggers' to Gertrude:

> Leave wringing of your hands. Peace; sit you down,
> And let me wring your heart. (III, iv, 34–5)

Everyone knows that Hamlet speaks rather than acts, and therefore delays; but it is worth pointing out that his peculiar involvement with words can be at the expense of humanity as well as of deeds. It is worth remembering, when we speak of Hamlet as an actor (who can 'act' but not act), that what he remembers from plays are great speeches; and that his own acting – as against his advice to the actors and his full admiration of their art – is almost entirely a matter of handling language: of the ability to control other people's reaction to his words. His self-reproach after the Hecuba speech is not that he can do nothing but that

> I . . . unpregnant of my cause
> . . . can say nothing. (II, ii, 562–3)

[1] *Shakespeare's Plutarch*, ed. T. J. B. Spencer in the Penguin Shakespeare Library (Harmondsworth, 1964), p. 203. Cleopatra, it is pointed out, differs from 'divers of her progenitors, the Kings of Egypt', who 'could scarce learn the Egyptian tongue only'.

Yet, less than twenty lines later he is reproaching himself for saying too much,

> That I, the son of a dear father murder'd,
> Prompted to my revenge by heaven and hell,
> Must, like a whore, unpack my heart with words.
> (II, ii, 579–81)

There is no contradiction here for, while the words with which he unpacks his heart are merely therapeutic, even an anodyne, directed at no object and no audience, the 'saying' which he admires in the First Player is the absorption of the self in a purposeful act of communication, 'his whole function suiting / With forms to his conceit'. The language needed for his own 'conceit' is non-verbal, the act of revenge to which he is 'prompted'. Yet in the logic of this soliloquy, transferring his own 'motive' and 'cue for passion' to the Player and imagining the result, the act is translated into a theatrical declamation:

> He would drown the stage with tears,
> And cleave the general ear with horrid speech;
> Make mad the guilty, and appal the free,
> Confound the ignorant, and amaze indeed
> The very faculties of eyes and ears.
> (II, ii, 555–9.)

It is natural for him to translate intention into language – into verbal rather than physical violence – hence the apparent relief as he finds gruesome reasons not to murder the praying Claudius, or as the 'bitter business' of the 'witching time' can, for the moment, be allowed to be resolved into a matter of words:

> I will speak daggers to her, but use none.

Hence, too, the play to be put on excites him beyond its detective purpose. It is going to speak for him, or he through it – and at least at the outset of II, ii his hopes of the effect of the play seem to hinge on the speech 'of some dozen or sixteen lines' which he has composed himself – to Claudius, to form a translation fully and terribly meaningful only to Claudius. If, besides, it means different things to the rest of the court,[1] all the better a translation. Murder speaks metaphorically in much Elizabethan-Jacobean tragedy, but rarely is the speaking so completely *heard* by the imagination as in Hamlet's plan for the effect of 'The Murder of Gonzago':

> For murder, though it have no tongue, will speak
> With most miraculous organ. (II, ii, 589–90)

Hamlet's excitement with speech as translation of deeds would help to explain, too, why in the graveyard scene it is Laertes's rhetoric which becomes the centre of Hamlet's grievance and object of his aggression. The leaping into the grave is a kind of act fitted to the word, a rhetorical flourish:

> Dost come here to whine?
> To outface me with leaping in her grave?
> . . . Nay, an thou'lt mouth,
> I'll rant as well as thou.
> (V, i, 271–2, 277–8)

We return here to the notion of human sympathy, as well as positive action, being absorbed and lost in speech. For it is in his dealings with Ophelia – which is as much as to say his language to Ophelia – that Hamlet most shows the destructive powers of speech. His vision of the world as 'an unweeded garden' ultimately drives Ophelia to her death, wearing the 'coronet weeds' of her madness. I do not wish to turn the play into a *Hamlet and Ophelia:* the love story is played down in the structure as a whole, its pre-play course known only by the odd flashback and infer-

[1] A. C. Bradley, *Shakespearean Tragedy* (paperback ed., 1955, p. 109, note), finds it strange that while everyone at court 'sees in the play-scene a gross and menacing insult to the King', no one 'shows any sign in perceiving in it also an accusation of murder'. Dover Wilson, in his note on III, ii, 243, points out that 'Hamlet arranges *two* meanings to the Play, one for the King (and Horatio), the other for the rest of the spectators, who see a king being murdered by his nephew'.

ence, and it disappears altogether after the graveyard scene. All the responsibility that Laertes can remember to remove from Hamlet with his dying breath is 'mine and my father's death'. But I still believe that the Hamlet–Ophelia relationship reveals something essential to Hamlet's and his creator's vision of the power of words; and also that it illuminates the way in which Hamlet contracts what Kenneth Muir has called 'the occupational disease of avengers'[1] – how he is tainted by the world in which he is trying to take revenge.

The poisoning of that relationship within the play is full of searing ironies. Hamlet never says 'I love you' except in the past tense and to unsay it at once. By the time he tells the world 'I loved Ophelia', she is dead. The first time he refers to her it is antically, as the daughter of Polonius, the fishmonger. From Hamlet's love-letter – which we are surely meant to take more seriously than Polonius does – we learn that in his wooing he was both as exalted and as tongue-tied as any lover who hesitates to sully the uniqueness of his love by common speech. When he tries to write a love sonnet, the attempt to look in his heart and write turns into a touching version of the conventional idea that the beloved is inexpressible:

> O dear Ophelia, I am ill at these numbers. I have not art to reckon my groans; but that I love thee best, O most best, believe it. (II, ii, 119–21)

When, his world shattered, he came to her in the scene she recounts to Polonius, he was speechless and, though he frightened her, he also, as her mode of telling shows, drew out all her sympathy. But when he actually confronts her on stage, he has translated her into a whore, like Gertrude, and he is only too articulate, in a language which is meaningless and yet desperately hurtful to her – one to which she might well have responded in Desdemona's words:

> I understand a fury in your words,
> But not the words.[2] (*Othello*, IV, ii, 32–3)

Hamlet's vision of Ophelia has changed with his vision of the world. The language to be spoken to her is that current in a world where frailty is the name of woman, love equals appetite, vows are 'as false as dicers' oaths' (III, iv, 45), and nothing is constant. It is a terrible coincidence, and a masterly dramatic stroke, that before Hamlet and Ophelia meet within this vision, Laertes and Polonius have been speaking the same language to her, articulating out of their worldly wisdom much the same view of their love as the one Hamlet has arrived at through his shock of revulsion from the world. In I, iii, while Hamlet offstage goes to meet the Ghost, Ophelia meets with equally shattering (to her world) commands from her father, attacking her past, present and future relations with Hamlet.

Laertes is made to open the attack, all the more insidiously since it is by way of well-meaning brotherly advice, and since it is phrased in the idiom of the courtly 'songs' to which he is reducing Hamlet's love:

> For Hamlet, and the trifling of his favour,
> Hold it a fashion and a toy in the blood,
> A violet in the youth of primy nature,
> Forward not permanent, sweet not lasting,
> The perfume and suppliance of a minute.
> (I, iii, 5–9)

On highly reasonable social grounds he argues that Hamlet's language must be translated:

> Then if he says he loves you,
> It fits your wisdom so far to believe it
> As he in his particular act and place
> May give his saying deed. (ll. 24–7)

[1] Kenneth Muir, *Shakespeare's Tragic Sequence* (1972), p. 57.

[2] I have discussed some aspects of Ophelia's and Desdemona's language, especially the way in which the hero and the heroine in these tragedies become unable to speak the same language, in a short paper to the Second International Shakespeare Congress, held in Washington, D.C., in April 1976.

I need not point out how deeply rooted this is in the language assumptions of the play as a whole. Laertes's tone is not unkind in its knowingness; his final thrust has some of the ineluctable sadness of the Sonnets when contemplating examples of the precariousness of youth and beauty –

> Virtue itself scapes not calumnious strokes;
> The canker galls the infants of the spring
> Too oft before their buttons be disclos'd;
> And in the morn and liquid dew of youth
> Contagious blastments are most imminent –
> (ll. 38–42)

and Ophelia, as her spirited reply suggests, is on the whole able to cope with both the matter and the manner of his preaching. But when Polonius picks up the attack, it is different. His technique is far more devastating: an interrogation where each answer is rapidly demolished. Ophelia does not have the speech-habits of most of the other characters; she is brief, simple and direct – and therefore particularly vulnerable. In a play where rhetorical units of measurement may be 'forty thousand brothers', there is a moving literalness about her statement that Hamlet has 'given countenance to his speech.../With *almost* all the holy vows of heaven'. She does not have the worldly wisdom to produce translations which protect her feelings and hide her thoughts. So to Polonius's opening question – 'What is't, Ophelia, he hath said to you?' – she simply, and vainly, tries to be non-specific:

> So please you, something touching the Lord Hamlet.
> (l. 89)

Some fifteen lines later her confidence is already undermined:

> I do not know, my lord, what I should think.

Polonius's method is particularly undermining in that he lets Ophelia provide the key-words which he then picks up and translates by devaluing them – painfully literally so when Ophelia's 'many tenders/Of his affection' provokes:

> ... think yourself a baby
> That you have ta'en these tenders for true pay
> Which are not sterling. (ll. 105–7)

His translation is partly a matter of devaluation by direct sneer ('think' and 'fashion' are thus dealt with), partly a matter of using the ambiguities of the English language to shift the meanings of words (thus 'tender' is translated into the language of finance and 'entreatment' into that of diplomacy); and partly a dizzifying matter of making one meaning slide into another by a pun. In this last way Hamlet's vows are translated, first into finance, then into religion –

> Do not believe his vows; for they are brokers,
> Not of that dye which their investments show,
> But mere implorators of unholy suits,
> Breathing like sanctified and pious bonds –
> (ll. 127–30)

but always in proof of their falsehood: 'The better to beguile'. What supplies the power of Polonius's words is also a logic which, like Iago's, strikes at the root of the victim's hold on reality:

> You do not understand yourself so clearly
> As it behoves my daughter and your honour;
> (ll. 96–7)

and which has a kind of general empirical truth – such as in the comedies might have been spoken by a sensible and normative heroine:

> I do know,
> When the blood burns, how prodigal the soul
> Lends the tongue vows. (ll. 115–17)

By the end of the scene, Polonius's words have left Ophelia with no hold on her love and with nothing to say but 'I shall obey, my lord'.[1] When there is no one left even to obey,

[1] To 'obey' (which is of course also what Hamlet promises his mother in I, ii, 120) is a troublesome matter in Shakespearean tragedy. Cf. *Othello*, I, iii, 180 and *King Lear*, I, i, 97.

she will go to pieces. But before then she has to be pushed to the limit by Hamlet's verbal brutality which doubly frightens and hurts her because it seems to prove both that Hamlet is mad and that Polonius was right. A first and last intimation of the intimacy and tenderness which might once have prevailed in their dialogues rings out of her greeting to Hamlet in the nunnery scene –

Good my lord,
How does your honour for this many a day? –

but by the end of that scene there is not even a dialogue. The two of them are speaking *about* each other, Hamlet's stream-of-consciousness circling around nuns and painted harlots and Ophelia appealing, twice, to an invisible and silent audience: 'O, help him, you sweet heavens!' and 'O heavenly powers, restore him!' She is left to speak her only soliloquy over the ruins of what used to be her reality, and to lament the most terrible translation of all: 'the honey of his music vows' is now 'like sweet bells jangled, out of time and harsh'.

Hamlet and Ophelia no longer speak the same language. I dwelt at some length on the Polonius–Ophelia scene because it brings out, ironically and indirectly, an important aspect of the 'tainting' of Hamlet. Though he does not know it, and would hate to be told so, his language has moved away from Ophelia's and towards Polonius's. It is a language based on the general idea of 'woman' rather than a specific awareness of Ophelia (to whom he now listens only to score verbal points off her, usually bawdy ones, too). Even his technique is like Polonius's as he picks up words only to demolish them, and her. Thus, in perhaps the cruellest stretch of dialogue in the whole play, Ophelia is allowed, briefly, to think that she knows what Hamlet means, only to have this understanding taken from her:

Hamlet. . . . I did love you once.
Ophelia. Indeed, my lord, you made me believe so.
Hamlet. You should not have believ'd me; for virtue cannot so inoculate our old stock but we shall relish of it. I loved you not.
Ophelia. I was the more deceived. (III, i, 115–20)

Polonius turned her into an object, an instrument, by 'loosing' her to Hamlet in the nunnery scene; Hamlet turns her into a thing – as 'unworthy a thing' as he ever may accuse Rosencrantz and Guildenstern of attempting to make out of him – in the play scene where, in public and listening to a play which from her point of view must seem to be mainly about women's inconstancy and sexual promiscuity, she is all but sexually assaulted by Hamlet's language.[1] We have no evidence that Hamlet ever thinks of her again before he discovers that the grave he has watched being dug is that of 'the fair Ophelia', and no redeeming recognition that the power of his own words has helped to drive her into that grave. In their story speech functions, in the end, as part of a vision of man's proneness to kill the thing he loves.

So we seem in the end to be left with a long row of contradictions: Hamlet's use of language is sensitive and brutal; he listens and he does not listen; his speech is built on sympathy and on total disregard of other selves; his relationship with words is his greatest strength and his greatest weakness. Only a Claudius could pretend that these are not contradictions and only he could translate them into a simple unity. Hamlet's soliloquies are not much help to this end. Even they speak different languages and add up, if anything, to a representation of a man searching for a language for the experiences which are forcing themselves upon him, finding it now in the free flow of I-centered exclamations of 'O, that this too too solid flesh would melt', now in the

[1] I have found Nigel Alexander's study of Hamlet, *Poison, Play and Duel* (1971), esp. chap. 5, 'The Power of Beauty', the most illuminating analysis of Hamlet's relationship with Ophelia.

formally structured and altogether generalized questions and statements of 'To be, or not to be'. It is tempting to hear in Hamlet's self-analytical speeches a progression towards clarity, reaching its goal in the fusion of the individual and the general, of simple form and complex thought, in the speech about defying augury –

> If it be now, 'tis not to come; if it be not to come, it will be now; if it be not now, yet it will come – the readiness is all –

and coming to rest on 'Let be'. It is tempting because many Jacobean tragic heroes and heroines were to go through such a progression, through tortured and verbally elaborate attempts at definition of their vision of life to simple statements of – as in Herbert's poem 'Prayer' – 'something understood'. But to me this seems too smooth a curve, too cathartic a movement, more indicative of critics' need to experience the peace which Hamlet himself happily appears to gain at the end than of the true impact of the language of the play as a whole. That impact is surely much closer to the sense that for a complex personality in an impossible situation – and in 'situation' I include a number of difficult human relationships – there is no single language. This does not mean that the play ultimately sees speech as meaningless, or that Shakespeare (or even Hamlet) is finally trapped in a disillusionist attitude to language. It means that we are given a very wide demonstration of the power of words to express and communicate – it is, after all, words which tell Horatio and us even that 'the rest is silence' – but also, and at the same time, an intimation that there is something inexpressible and incommunicable at the heart of the play.

Shakespeare – whatever the true facts of the *Ur-Hamlet* – must have seen himself as producing a new 'translation' of what the title page of the second Quarto describes as 'The Tragicall History of Hamlet, Prince of Denmark'. Like Gertrude's translation, in IV, i, it meant both changing and interpreting his raw material. Like Gertrude, he concentrated on the speech and deeds of the prince, and their ramifications, merging any personal pressure of experience in a concern for communicating with an audience. The analogy ends here, for Gertrude was, even like Hamlet himself, only part of his translation – a translation which T. S. Eliot criticized for trying to 'express the inexpressibly horrible'.[1] To me the final greatness of the play lies just there: in its power to express so much and yet also to call a halt on the edge of the inexpressible where, to misquote Claudius, we must learn to say ''Tis fit we do not understand'. This, I think, is the hallmark of Shakespeare as a translator, into tragedy, of the human condition.

1 'Hamlet and His Problems', in *Selected Essays* (New York, 1932), p. 126.

HAMLET THE BONESETTER

J. PHILIP BROCKBANK

'The time is out of joint. O cursed spite/That ever I was born to set it right!' It is Hamlet's *moira*, his pitiless lot, that he is cast as bonesetter to the time, and he does not look upon it as a privileged role. The play *Hamlet* is, in one dimension of Aristotle's thought, a goat-song, and in what follows I shall be importunately concerned with the lines of continuity between the tragic play and its primordial spectre, the sacrificial ritual.[1] An interest in Shakespeare cannot in itself be expected to shed light on perplexities that have for so long engaged and divided classical scholars and anthropologists, but when some of Shakespeare's plays are viewed with such perplexities in mind, certain features of their structure and process become, I believe, distinctly visible. In attempting such a perspective there is no necessity to begin with *Hamlet. Titus Andronicus*, for example, in its anthropological as distinct from its historical setting, looks back to rituals of human sacrifice and exemplifies a primitive logic and elemental feeling carried unexpectedly in the vehicle of a decorated and sophisticated art. But the continuities that persist in Shakespeare's maturity are both more obscure and more profound, and to trace them I take my point of departure from a celebrated passage in Gilbert Murray's *Five Stages of Greek Religion*:[2]

> At the great spring Drômenon the tribe and the growing earth were renovated together: the earth arises afresh from her dead seeds, the tribe from its dead ancestors; and the whole process, charged as it is with the emotion of pressing human desire, projects its anthropomorphic god or daemon. A vegetation spirit we call him, very inadequately; he is a divine Kouros, a Year-Daemon, a spirit that in the first stage is living, then dies with each year, then thirdly rises again from the dead, raising the whole dead world with him – the Greeks call him in this phase 'the Third One', or the 'Saviour'. The renovation ceremonies were accompanied by a casting off of the old year, the old garments, and everything that is polluted by the infection of death. And not only of death; but clearly I think, in spite of the protests of some Hellenists, of guilt or sin also. For the life of the Year-Daemon, as it seems to be reflected in Tragedy, is generally a story of Pride and Punishment. Each Year arrives, waxes great, commits the sin of Hubris, and then is slain. The death is deserved; but the slaying is a sin: hence comes the next Year as Avenger, or as the Wronged One re-risen. 'All things pay retribution for their injustice one to another according to the ordinance of time.' It is this range of ideas, half suppressed during the classical period, but evidently still current among the ruder and less Hellenized peoples, which supplied St Paul with some of his most famous and deep-reaching metaphors. 'Thou fool, that which thou sowest is not quickened except it die.' 'As he was raised from the dead we may walk with Him in newness of life.' And this renovation must be preceded by a casting out and killing of the old polluted life – 'the old man in us must first be crucified.'

There may be much here that pedantry, or indeed scholarship, would seek to set aside as speculative, but a little reflection upon the

[1] I am indebted to the indirect encouragement offered to pursue this theme by Walter Burkert, 'Greek Tragedy and Sacrificial Ritual', *Greek, Roman and Byzantine Studies*, (1966), 83–121.

[2] I quote from the 1935 version of the second edition.

literary evidence will convince us that the modes of thought that Murray attributes to ancient ritual are still at work in the tragic, religious and political experience of much later phases in the history of civilization, including our own. The closing sentences of the passage, for example, could remind us that the two parts of *Henry IV* teach us what it means to whip the offending Adam both out of the realm and out of our frail natures. *Henry IV* confesses its debt to the morality play, *Titus Andronicus* betrays one to Ovid and to Seneca, and we may recognize in Shakespeare a convergence of traditions analogous to that which Gilbert Murray observes in St Paul. Because St Paul had assimilated the insights of Greek tragedy into an experience of the significance of Christ (the point could be put the other way round), it becomes possible for us to claim that *Hamlet* is not only a Renaissance tragedy but also a sacrificial tragedy in a tradition older than Christendom, reaching back to Aeschylus and even, perhaps, to the Drômenon. It is, as others have observed, in certain crucial respects like the *Oedipus Rex* of Sophocles,[1] either because Shakespeare knew a version or because he took from Seneca and his English imitators certain imaginative understandings that had also reached him by another route – through the metaphors, teachings and theatre of Christianity.

In both Sophocles's play and Shakespeare's, the survival of the state is threatened by a specific disaster – plague or invasion – which has its source in some more obscure evil which has to be brought to light and eradicated. In the opening lines of *Hamlet* men on guard are a very precise expression of an urgent threat to the state, and offer just the right opportunity for the voicing of misgivings both vague and specific about the nature and direction of a threat which is in the largest sense political – touching the very survival of the *polis*. Coleridge has gone before to admire the detail: the self-control of the guardsmen imposed by a routine ceremony; the disquieting attentiveness to the exact time; the mouse; the impress of shipwrights; the irony of 'long live the king'; the ominous resonance of 'sick at heart'. Horatio's vision dominates – Renaissance sceptic but skilled in medieval ways of thought, comparing Claudius's Denmark with Caesar's Rome, alive to the supernatural signs that prefigure political disaster, knowledgeable about ghosts. A blight is already upon the state of Denmark whose court we meet in the second scene. Turning an ingenuous eye for resemblances upon the *Oedipus Rex*, we may recognize a comparable prelude. This is the priest speaking, in Yeats's translation: 'We all stand here because the city stumbles towards death, hardly able to raise up its head. A blight has fallen upon the fruitful blossoms of the land, a blight upon flock and field and upon the bed of marriage – plague ravages the city.' 'Flock and field' have little place in *Hamlet* (although we may remember the 'mildew'd ear/Blasting his wholesome brother'), but the analogue is clear, and it happens in both plays that the roots of infection are revealed by a sudden dramatic discovery or *anagnorisis*. The messenger in the *Oedipus* and the ghost in *Hamlet*, reveal murder and incest at the head of state.

In the elemental logic of the *Oedipus* it follows that if the state is to survive and renew its failing life, the king must be deposed. We may find the argument metaphoric rather than literal, for it would be surprising (I imagine, even to enlightened ancients) if plague virus responded so directly to a change in government. But the metaphor is powerful (particularly in the theatre) and it seems to express a valid claim about the ultimate connection between public and private events. In *Hamlet*,

[1] See, e.g., Francis Fergusson, *The Idea of a Theater* (New York, 1949).

'The cease of majesty/Dies not alone, but like a gulf doth draw/What's near it with it.' The invasion threat from Fortinbras's 'lawless resolutes' is not directly a consequence of the new king's guilt, but since the death of the elder Hamlet the state has appropriately been supposed 'disjoint and out of frame'. A resemblance to the *Oedipus*, however, must not be allowed to mask conspicuous differences. Oedipus is his own scourge and minister; he bears the guilt and undertakes to purge it, but where the sacrificial role in Sophocles's play is single, in Shakespeare's it is double. From one point of view it is indeed the death of Claudius that restores the equilibrium of the Danish state and (we might add) of the English audience; from another, it is the death of Hamlet, for at his fall a role appears to have been perfected, an end to have been fully shaped. The killing of Claudius is not merely, however, a personal judgement upon the murderer and hypocrite, it is the destruction of the whole moral and political world which he represents and over which he presides – the Denmark of Gertrude, Polonius, Laertes, Rosencrantz and Guildstern, and even Ophelia – and of all the things their words, and our response to them, endorse. Hamlet takes into his consciousness the sins of the realm for which Claudius is responsible. We are made intimately aware of the processes of Hamlet's consciousness, or 'conscience', to use the play's word at a moment in its history when it was particularly ambiguous. It is this intimate transmission of inner consciousness and awareness that calls for the full exercise of Shakespeare's mastery of the conventions of soliloquy, through which so much of Hamlet's presence in the play is expressed. The second scene, which opens with the assured public voice of Claudius, ends with the private, seemingly obsessed, inward-looking utterances of Hamlet. Thus the two great figures of the play are not only made the 'mighty opposites' of the tragic narrative, they reach us through contrasting theatre-conventions, made to engage the attention of the audience in radically different ways. From this point of view the play turns itself about. The first court scene shows us Claudius as a great image of authority, enthroned against the façade, and finishes with Hamlet front-stage, speaking words we are allowed less to hear than to overhear, filling the theatre with the chaos of his mind, already the 'distracted globe'. At the start, to make the same point more archaically, there is apparent order in the macrocosm and disorder in the microcosm. But at the play's end, the most memorable passages suggest quiescence and calm within the mind of Hamlet while the spectacle presents total confusion in the court of Claudius. In the meantime we watch Claudius grow active in self-inquisition; his masks slip and his language, as he begins to soliloquize, grows more like Hamlet's:

> My stronger guilt defeats my sharp intent,
> And, like a man to double business bound,
> I stand in pause where I shall first begin,
> And both neglect.
>
> (III, iii, 40–3)

Under pressure from Hamlet the contrast steepens between what the king seems to be in public and what he reveals himself to be in private, and he becomes, however inadequately, a scourge and minister to his own condition. But for most of the play Claudius is a representative figure, not only because he is the head of state, a crucial fact in an apparently vigorous monarchy, but also because he exemplifies the characteristic moral affliction of Denmark, the hypocrisy which makes moral realities inaccessible.

Hamlet is representative in quite another way, one which invites another comparison with the *Oedipus Rex*. When Sophocles's Oedipus approaches the tragic discovery of his own guilt he has a choice between stopping short, and letting the matter drop without further questioning, or persisting until he masters the full horror of the moral catastrophe. Jocasta, the Shepherd and even Tiresias advise him to take the tactful, politic course and to drop the whole inquiry; but Oedipus owes his tragic stature precisely to his decision to tear off all the veils, to expose the total, desolating predicament, and to take on himself the full consequences both in action and suffering. Jocasta's suicide denies her a tragic death, but Oedipus tears out his eyes and lives on until he is morally fit to die. In *Hamlet* it is the king who tries to cover and the prince to discover the full measure of the realm's distress. Claudius is most guilty, we may say naively, but Hamlet has the keenest sense of guilt. Hamlet exposes his sensibilities to the moral afflictions of the realm, through the mediation of the ghost (unseen by the guilty), through his experience of the events of the play, and through his exercises in introspection. He takes in, not his mother's guilt and his uncle's only, but the pervasive evils of the community:

> The pangs of despis'd love, the law's delay,
> The insolence of office, and the spurns
> That patient merit of th'unworthy takes.
>
> (III, i, 72–4)

'But to the quick of th'ulcer', says Claudius to Laertes, 'Hamlet comes back'. He intends only to 'get to the point', but the play's language works upon our consciousness to remind us that Hamlet returns to probe the inward corruption of the outward condition that Claudius struggles to sustain. For Hamlet, surgeon and bone-setter, not king and queen alone but Polonius and Laertes, Ophelia and himself too, are awry: 'What should such fellows as I do crawling between earth and heaven? We are arrant knaves all; believe none of us. Go thy ways to a nunnery.' If Hamlet's wit here as elsewhere seems malicious, it is because it inflicts pain; but that pain is of the moral kind – consciousness of guilt – and that consciousness, by any religious account in the western tradition and by many ethical wisdoms, has both a destructive and a redemptive energy. In the *Pilgrim's Progress* it is Christian's prerogative to carry his great burden, for many less morally aware figures (including Worldly Wiseman) are without it; but it is also his privilege to shed the burden, since no felicity can be won with it.

In calling the word 'moral' so often into service I do not wish to overlook certain elementary complexities. 'The death is deserved', says Gilbert Murray of the Year-Daemon, 'but the slaying is a sin', and we know the paradox to be fundamental in many plays from the *Agamemnon* to the *Revenger's Tragedy*. In *Hamlet* its application to Claudius and the prince is clear enough, but Shakespeare adroitly allows it also a kind of retrospective force. It is only in Hamlet's vision that his father is unequivocally 'so excellent a king'; by the Ghost's account he is 'confin'd to fast in fires,/Till the foul crimes done in my days of nature/Are burnt and purg'd away'. He recedes into the dawn sky as the glow-worm pales his rival 'uneffectual fires', to submit to a process of spiritual purification which transcends and encompasses the infected bed, body and 'ear' of Denmark. In this perspective Claudius looks like the agent as well as the victim of a continuing and universal sacrificial process. In the *Oedipus Rex* the king is guilty but (I would try to insist) blameless; in *Hamlet* the king is culpable but so, in the operation of the play's language, are we all. With this qualification we may observe of *Hamlet* that the moral imperatives of the plot do not push it towards an act of murderous revenge in obedience to the Ghost and all he stands for, but towards the discovery and assimilation of a communal guilt, in obedience to that higher tragic law which Shakespeare has mastered in the course of shaping the play. Incitement to guilt – that is the motive of the nunnery scene, the play scene and the bedroom scene; and when guilt is everywhere manifest, dis-covered, Hamlet quietens and sheds his more febrile resolution, 'the readiness is all'. He goes into the last scene prepared to die; not prepared to murder; the Ghost, who voices the old revenge law, even while undergoing his purification by fire, fades from the play after failing to 'whet' Hamlet's 'almost blunted purpose', and when the killing of Claudius and the death of Hamlet come at last, they come by accident.

But is it accident? In ancient tragedy, and possibly too in more ancient ritual, there is some recognition or claim that the ultimate moral laws are transcendent and cannot be subdued by the human will. Gilbert Murray locates the mystery in those metaphors of dying-into-life which can be related to the diurnal and seasonal rhythms, and to human mortality. Horatio at the end of the play speaks of 'accidental' events, but his words will bear more than one construction:

> So shall you hear
> Of carnal, bloody and unnatural acts;
> Of accidental judgements, casual slaughters;
> Of deaths put on by cunning and forc'd cause;
> And, in this upshot, purposes mistook
> Fall'n on th'inventors' heads.
>
> (v, ii, 372–7)

'Accidental judgements' may mean 'fortuitous miscalculations' – a lot of things going wrong by chance; or it can mean 'contingent punishments', as if some ineluctable process worked through accidental circumstance towards a fuller realization of justice in the human world. In some moods we might call such a process 'history'; the play speaks of 'a divinity that shapes our ends'. Much happens in the play by significant accident. When Hamlet tries to kill the king, for instance, his sword finds Polonius. Behind the accident and the arras it is possible to glimpse a moral order and even to claim moral cause and effect: Polonius the eavesdropper has been betrayed into hysteria as he witnesses Hamlet's inquisition of his mother. But if Polonius deserves to die, his deserts are not to be found in the Ghost's ethic and command, but only in the larger perspectives in which the Ghost himself is tormented; we *all* deserve to die, as we all deserve whipping.

The tragic effects of both *Hamlet* and the *Oedipus Rex* may be set down, therefore, to a sacrificial law, working through 'accidents' as well as through human choice and disposition, towards the discovery and purgation of guilt. It may be that it needs no ghost come from the grave to tell us that. Gilbert Murray himself, indeed, has been this way before, and among his many heirs and critics I am particularly indebted to Francis Fergusson.[1] But it remains true, I believe, that many of the alleged problems of the play, which persist at least in academic and pedagogic discourse, are much diminished when we attend to them with this tragic structural principle in mind.

Among the first mechanical or technical questions that arise about *Hamlet* is, why is it so long? And the first answer would seem to have little to do with the claims pursued so far, 'Because it is built on a structure of analogues; not on a narrative'. Of these, the most important is that between the world and the stage. If we ask why Shakespeare takes up so much time with the players and their play, we have immediately to acknowledge that their narrative purpose could have been served in, say, a quarter of the lines allowed. The narrative requires that Hamlet should use the mousetrap to catch the conscience of the king, but the structure requires that Shakespeare should use it to explore Hamlet's situation and make the audience more alive to its moral

[1] *Idea of a Theater*, pp. 124–5.

and histrionic complexity. Such is the motive for the scene attending to Hamlet's advice to the players, to their rehearsal, and to the attendant soliloquy. All make us more alert for reflections cast in that mirror held up to nature, the 'abstract and brief chronicle', the Gonzago play. It is often overlooked and underrated, taken to be Shakespeare's sport at the expense of its predecessors. In fact, its bleak, keen, arid rhymes bear the burden of the whole. Whatever defects are attributed to the art of the players' (and Hamlet's) play, Shakespeare's own art, as Fergusson has shown us, is in command. Thus when the Player King speaks of the dislocation between human purpose and accomplishment:

> Our wills and fates do so contrary run
> That our devices still are overthrown,
> Our thoughts are ours, their ends none of our own
> (III, ii, 206–8)

we can find analogues through the play. Thus Laertes to Ophelia:

> but you must fear
> His greatness weighed, his will is not his own.
> (I, iii, 16–17)

And Hamlet's words to Laertes:

> Was't Hamlet wronged Laertes? Never Hamlet.
> ... Hamlet denies it.
> Who does it then? His madness.
> (V, ii, 225, 228–9)

Or again, Claudius's:

> My stronger guilt defeats my sharp intent.
> (III, iii, 40)

But most important, the Player King's conclusion is re-echoed by Horatio at the close of the play, from the 'overthrown devices' to 'purposes mistook'.

Similarly, the Player King is nervous about the transience of human purpose:

> What to ourselves in passion we propose,
> The passion ending, doth the purpose lose.
> (III, ii, 189–90)

It is a spent version of Claudius's still live admonition to Laertes:

> That we would do,
> We should do when we would; for this 'would' changes
> And hath abatements and delays as many
> As there are tongues, are hands, are accidents.
> (IV, vii, 118–21)

Again, the Player King speaks in Hamlet's voice when he finds that:

> Purpose is but the slave to memory
> Of violent birth but poor validity.
> (III, ii, 183–4)

And from the same speech:

> The violence of either grief or joy
> Their own enactures with themselves destroy,
> (III, ii, 191–2)

is an oblique comment on Hamlet, Laertes, Claudius and Ophelia. The Player King, then, reminds us that *Hamlet* is a play about failing human wills and passions, about the need to sustain purpose in face of fading memory and frail resolution; but also, and ironically, about the futility of purposeful action in a society insufficiently aware of the nature and extent of its plight. There are no short cuts. 'Readiness', to use Hamlet's word, comes only when, to linger on the common phrase, 'the time is ripe'; thus, once again, the Player King:

> Which now, the fruit unripe, sticks on the tree
> But fall unshaken when they mellow be.
> (III, ii, 185–6)

Nothing in the play goes according to plan, but everything happens by significant accident and when the time is ripe, when the society and the individual, the *polis* and the *ideotes* (to put it more obscurely), are aware and 'ready'.

The play, in ways that I do not pretend to have exhausted, imitates the situation in the Danish court; but then the situation is reversed, and the prince begins to mimic the play. The

Player King speaks, as Ferguson aptly says, with the clarity and helplessness of the dead; but Lucianus, the king-slayer, momentarily animates, and his reflections upon a deed of darkness, 'Thoughts black, hands apt, drugs fit, and time agreeing;/Confederate season, else no creature seeing', are transposed into Hamlet's soliloquy a few minutes later, ''Tis now the very witching time of night' and 'Now could I drink hot blood'. Shakespeare contrives that the Ghost, the Gonzago play and the traditions of English-Seneca should chime together, all converging on the same idea of moral justice, of dramatic decorum and of behavioural imperative. Thus Hamlet assumes the role of Senecal avenger (English style) and in it he encounters Claudius at prayer and in the same role he spares him. There is no occasion to question Hamlet's sincerity. To obey the Ghost's command Hamlet must by an immense histrionic effort transform himself into a Lucianus, and thus transformed he cannot bring himself to kill his victim at his prayers. The episode becomes yet another in the pattern of self-frustrated purposes, overthrown devices.

It is a necessary critical commonplace about the play that from the moment Hamlet cries, 'These are actions that a man might play', to his, 'Ere I could make a prologue to my brains they had begun the play', we are kept sharply aware of the equivocal compulsion to 'act', meaning both to do something, somehow, to some effect, and to act a part, fulfill a role. Shakespeare's amplitude has this occasion, therefore, that within the larger dramatic rite he mounts a smaller, to an analogous end. But it has other occasions too, some of which can be subsumed by asking again the question that academic courtesy should perhaps never again allow – why does Hamlet delay? Alfred Harbage once reduced two hundred and fifty years of answers to a basic twelve,[1] but I must offer a stingier abstract. Some have argued a psychological defect in Hamlet's character; he is squeamish, or sick with melancholy, or immature, or cowardly, or stricken by an Oedipus complex; all assuming that neither Shakespeare nor the spectator need to challenge the moral authority of the Ghost whom Hamlet would have obeyed if only he had had it in him. A second group find not a psychological but a moral flaw in Hamlet; he resents the call of duty, or is too philosophical to act. A third kind of answer blames the Ghost, finding Hamlet nauseated by the primitive compulsions of a brutal injunction, too sensitive to do as he is told. A fourth set finds neither Hamlet nor the Ghost culpable but points to the obstructions that need to be objectively negotiated before Hamlet can get on with his job – he must test the Ghost's truth, sort out the succession problem or win the populace to his side. The solutions thus curtly surveyed (leaving much patient and sensitive work unacknowledged) appeal to the character and speeches of Hamlet himself. Of solutions appealing to the design of the play the most celebrated is the briskest – 'No delay; no play'. But a meaningless delay, we may reflect in the Philistine temper that Stoll's aphorism induces, is not only bad art but also bad box-office. We must persist with the question in another form, recognizing that Hamlet is not a man but an artefact. Why does Shakespeare make Hamlet delay and, to begin with, what explanations for delay does he make explicit in the speeches he gives to Hamlet himself? These come readily to mind – the Ghost must be tested through the mousetrap and Claudius must not be killed while he is praying, while in soliloquy Hamlet muses on 'Bestial oblivion or some craven scruple/Of thinking too precisely on th'event'. From this excursion it would appear that Shakespeare designed the delay to appear as a problem to

[1] *As They Liked It* (New York, 1947), I, 6.

Hamlet's own bewildered consciousness, and also that the time taken up with this problem is quite short.

'Time taken up' – it is Shakespeare who delays in this sense, not Hamlet. It is he who gives sustained attention to those episodes and speeches not directly connected with the Ghost's command. For Shakespeare takes only a limited interest in Hamlet as an avenger. His deeper interest is in Hamlet the tragic-hero, required to take upon himself the moral distress of the whole community. The delay in *Hamlet* is not of the stock kind associated with the revenge tradition in which Kyd and Marston were active. Shakespeare makes Hamlet delay to say, 'O what a rogue and peasant slave am I', or 'Or my imaginations are as foul as vulcan's smithy', or 'What is this quintessence of dust?', or 'As if increase of appetite had grown by what it fed on', or 'I am very proud, revengeful, ambitious'. He delays to voice his sense of guilt and to make personal the evils and vulnerabilities of the society about him. The process is at work both in the detail of the play's language and in the disposition of its episodes. Thus Hamlet addressing Horatio glances at the sycophancy of the court:

> Why should the poor be flatter'd?
> No, let the candied tongue lick absurd pomp,
> And crook the pregnant hinges of the knee
> Where thrift may follow fawning.
>
> (III, ii, 57–60)

It is an almost subliminal dialect, and to be effective it must find us very quick to perceive the connection between the proclivities of courtiers and the proclivities of dogs – for the dogs breathe in the lines, unnamed. The play's many digressive episodes owe their unity to a related principle, for all mediate between the audience's sense of the human condition and the stage Denmark's accommodation of it.

If, for example, we ask why Shakespeare gives us a scene between Reynaldo and Polonius about Laertes, we find it among the play's many instances of espionage. Spy-traps are set by Polonius and Claudius upon Hamlet, Rosencrantz and Guildenstern upon him, and Polonius again; Hamlet and Horatio upon the king; the Ghost, if we will, upon Hamlet and the queen; and Hamlet upon Rosencrantz and Guildenstern, opening the packet and devising a new commission. But all these are examples of court intrigue, while the Reynaldo scene is outside the narrative intrigues and shows us the routine of Danish manners. While it is not relevant to the story it is relevant to the action. We find the dramatic Denmark a spacious and various society; we know the quality of its guards, gravediggers, courtiers, students, young women and old men, of its leisure, its social habits, its entertainments, literary criticism and proverbial wisdom. The Polonius family scenes yield many graceful, mannered, worldly felicities that are still admired by a wide public and must from the beginning have been capable of winning to a high degree the audience's assent in a norm of privileged domestic behaviour. This is not to deny his public significance; for there is a sense in which he may be constrained in one scholar's stereotype of 'the tyrant's ears',[1] and it is entertaining to see that parallels can be alleged between Polonius's speeches and Burleigh's letter to Oxford of 23 April 1576.[2] But the elegance and worldliness of the wisdom so admired by Dr Johnson gives place in the scene with Reynaldo to an exposition of the significant difference between whoring and drabbing, and of the art of taking truth with a bait of falsehood. Like the scene in which Hamlet meets the Norwegian captain, it contributes to Shakespeare's anatomy of 'the 'imposthume of much wealth and peace,/

[1] L. B. Campbell, in *J. Q. Adams Memorial Studies*, ed. J. B. McManaway and others (1948).

[2] By Percy Allen, *De Vere as Shakespeare* (1930.)

That inward breaks, and shows no cause without/Why the man dies'. In the reflecting but unrepeating mirrors of the play's structure the Reynaldo scene is also one of many to reveal facets of the father–son relationship in Claudius's Denmark. By the image of the causes of both Laertes and Fortinbras Hamlet on different occasions sees the portraiture of his; Hamlet delays a little time to reflect on them, but Shakespeare delays much to present them.

The talk with Reynaldo relates, in another range of the play's analogues, to the process by which Hamlet's sense of his mother's sexual guilt is extended to Ophelia, setting a blister on the fair forehead of an innocent love. Polonius expects Laertes to behave in France much as that young man behaved on St Valentine's eve in the ballad-snatches of the mad Ophelia:

> Then up he rose, and donn'd his clothes,
> And dupp'd the chamber door;
> Let in the maid that out a maid
> Never departed more.
>
> (IV, V, 50–3)

Once again, the relevance is to the action but not to the story. The ballad fragments can tell us nothing about what has happened, only about what is always happening. In the poignancy of her distraction she allows the dead old man ('His beard was as white as snow') the Christian valediction that she herself will be denied in the 'maimed rites' accorded her by the church of the stage Denmark. The bits of popular song and flower lore are the only resources she has to mediate between her catastrophic experience of the general guilt (Hamlet has done to her what Claudius did to Hamlet) and her naive incomprehension of it.

Many complex analogues, some meeting in Ophelia's madness, connect the episodes, speeches and characters expressing human approaches to the experience of death. Between them they display what we may feel as the play enlarges to be an almost exhaustive range of attitudes and apprehensions, from the high social decorum of Gertrude's and Claudius's consolatory speeches of the second scene to the habituated professional jocularity of the grave-diggers, with many modes of fear, pain, nostalgia, exhaustion, protest and acceptance in the moods of Hamlet's soliloquies, and almost as many theological and moral speculations attending the shifts of their thought. Once we content ourselves with this aspect of the play's amplitude, many problems about relevance disappear. We can see, for example, why Hamlet lugs the guts of Polonius into a neighbouring room and leaves him to be nosed out by the stairs into the lobby, and why Gertrude is so long a spectator to Ophelia's muddy death. Questioning the logic of the narrative we get comical answers: Hamlet was hoping to conceal from Claudius a murder his wife had witnessed, and the queen was too preoccupied with composing the felicitous verses she hoped to speak in court to spare time to take a grip on Ophelia's weedy trophies and haul her out. But analogical imperatives, reaching into comprehensive areas of the society and of consciousness, require that death receives alike a brutal presentation and a lyrical. It means, among many other things, a body to be disposed of before it offends the senses, and it can occasion a 'melodious lay' upon the dissolution of a creature native and indued to the element that consumes her. And the same range of analogues takes in Imperious Caesar, the jester and his painted mistress, and those twenty thousand who 'Go to their graves like beds, fight for a plot / Whereon the numbers cannot try the cause'. The techniques of the tragic play, worked out in a Renaissance theatre capable of touching both public and intimate responses, has found new ways of expressing the communities of both human society and human mortality; the

Drômenon is left a long way behind, but its functions are not abdicated.

That Shakespeare was more than usually conscious of the functions of the tragic play within the larger society, and specifically within a monarchy, is clear from the extended attention he gives to the production of the Gonzago play whose thematic content we have already discussed, and I come to the worrying, if slightly gratuitous problem, did Claudius see the dumb show, and if not why not? According to Dover Wilson, Shakespeare needed the dumb-show to signal Hamlet's intention to the audience, but as Hamlet did not need it, he treats it as a meddling intervention on the part of the players.[1] According to S. L. Bethell, Wilson's account is too subtle and makes too severe a demand on the actors' powers of communication.[2] The Elizabethan audience, he thinks, enjoyed a double consciousness of the functions of art: they would know the dumb-show was one thing to the spectators in the Globe (alerting them to a close watch on Claudius), and another for the stage audience of Danes, who would see an 'inexplicable dumb-show', an obscure ritual disclosing little about the Gonzago plot. And certainly Ophelia's question, 'What means this, my lord?', and her observation, 'Belike this show imports the argument of the play', do seem ingenuous and banal when we assume she sees exactly what we see. Nevertheless I find it hard to believe that she sees anything else, and Shakespeare's purpose in measuring more than one distance between art and life seems to have a transparent effect if not a disarming purpose. Hamlet's 'miching mallecho' comment and his, 'the players cannot keep counsel; they'll tell all' are spoken, not with alarmed resentment, as Dover Wilson supposes, but with mounting eagerness. Claudius endures the silent, puppet-like enactment of his crime, but his nerve breaks as the analogues are pressed home in speech. By a process of intensifying articulation the art of the players serves its discovering purpose. Shakespeare is deftly allegorizing the function of his own craft, for this 'abstract and brief chronicle' is meant, in the tirelessly interrelating language of the play, to 'Make mad the guilty, and appal the free'.

The ambition to 'Make mad the guilty' proves an equivocal and reflexive one, connecting Hamlet's first determination to assume 'an antic disposition' and his confession that he was 'punish'd with a sore distraction' when he 'wrong'd Laertes'. In the flux of the play the movements between the antic wit and the madness which is 'poor Hamlet's enemy' leave complicated tracks through territories of moral ambiguity where, for example, 'Our indiscretion sometimes serves us well, / When our deep plots do pall.' And Shakespeare, very aware of the malignant potential of consciousness-of-guilt (not quite co-extensive with 'guilty conscience') attributes to Hamlet many of the characteristics of the Jacobean malcontent or melancholiac, fated to live in a world that is 'weary, stale, flat and unprofitable' even before the Ghost gives specific shape to the general malaise. The personal malaise has been generally described as an incapacity for adult living[3] and more specifically diagnosed as an 'Oedipus-complex'. Ernest Jones's study[4] remains interesting, perhaps, as an event in the history of psycho-analytical criticism, but it is worth re-visiting in the present context because it pursues a connection with the Oedipus story quite different from that which might relate *Hamlet* to the plays of Seneca and Sophocles. For Jones it is Hamlet's 'moral duty to which his father exhorts him,

1 *What Happens in 'Hamlet'* (1935).

2 *Shakespeare and the Popular Dramatic Tradition* (1944).

3 See e.g. G. Wilson Knight, *The Imperial Theme* (1931), and L. C. Knights, *An Approach to 'Hamlet'* (1960).

4 *Hamlet and Oedipus* (1949).

to put an end to the incestuous activities of his mother (by killing Claudius), but his unconscious does not want to put an end to them (he being identified with Claudius in the situation), and so he cannot. His lashings of self-reproach and remorse are ultimately because of this very failure, i.e. the refusal of his guilty wishes to undo the sin. By refusing to abandon his own incestuous wishes he perpetuates the sin and so must endure the stings of torturing conscience.' The postulated nature of the 'unconscious' being what it is, and the word 'ultimately' putting the point at such a distance, there can be no accessible evidence to demonstrate Shakespeare's complicity, as it were, in Ernest Jones's understanding. We are left to assume some obscure collaboration between the unconscious responses of playwright, of character and of audience. Without wishing to rule out this possibility (evidence for its truth might be argued, for example, from Hamlet's double playing of King-slayer and nephew when he identifies with Lucianus), I would suppose this too intimate and too non-political an interpretation of the play, and the point may be pursued through a further comparison with the *Oedipus Rex*. From a reading of Sophocles we may distinguish between the impact of the play and the impact of the myth, and if we ask if the play manifests an understanding of the obscurer sources of the myth in human consciousness, the answer would seem to be emphatically reassuring. Jocasta warns Oedipus not to trouble about the rumours he hears:

> Nor need this mother-marrying frighten you;
> Many a man has dreamed as much.[1]

and Oedipus experiences the revulsions that are attributed uniquely to the double crime of patricide and incest, compounding 'All horrors that are wrought beneath the sun'.[2] Sophocles's treatment does nothing to diminish the force of the myth (for example, by convicting the king of carelessness) and everything to clarify it. The therapy for which the story is made ready, however, is not the private, clinical kind of Dr Jones's day, but the public, tragic kind we may attribute to the Athenian theatre with the aid of Aristotle's term *catharsis*. The tragedy works upon the communities of both human society and human mortality. In Theban society the trap is sprung by the irony which makes Oedipus the state's judge of his own case. In the mortal community, the trap catches every man, inescapably born, as he is, into the basic triangular family situation, inclining him toward excessive love of the mother and an answering jealousy of the father. None can be held responsible for such biologically induced desires, but society holds culpable any who manifest them beyond a certain point. Hence, to ensure social survival, the desires must be repressed, and in the story of the play, the king must abdicate or be deposed, undertaking an ordeal of physical blindness appropriate to the moral blindness with which human circumstance has afflicted him. Freudian treatment of the Oedipus myth therefore cannot yield a complete account of the play; the *Oedipus Rex* is about king and city as well as about mother and son. Similarly, Jones's interpretation of *Hamlet* attends too exclusively to the personal relationship between Hamlet and Claudius. He has it that Hamlet's own evil prevents him from completely denouncing his uncle's, 'his moral fate is bound up with his uncle's for good or ill. In reality his uncle incorporates the deepest and most buried parts of his own personality, so that he cannot kill him without also killing himself.' The play, it is true, seems often to reach towards deep and buried parts of personality, but Shakespeare so constructs it that the relationship between the personal state, the human state and (if the pun can be allowed its relevance) the Danish state,

[1] *Oedipus Tyrannus*, 981–4 (E. F. Watling's translation).

[2] O.T., 1409 (F. Storr's translation).

is frequently acknowledged and regulated in language and episode. He does not let the intrigues of king and prince shape the play and determine its sequence of scenes. Through the personal ordeal of Ophelia, for example, we glimpse the folk-lore and folk-experience of the larger society, and make a discovery about the nature of mortality. Ophelia's destruction in the play-world of *Hamlet* entails her idiocy, her isolation from the community, family and lover whose discords have fractured the complex and delicate relationship between what we conveniently call the individual and the society, or between the personal and social self, the *polites* and the *ideotes*. In Shakespeare's presentation of Ophelia's madness there is much to remind us that as spectators to a play, like the stage audience before whom the alienated girl 'performs', our attention is engaged in changing emotional perspectives. We may be a community watching a community, a family watching a family, or individuals caught up with individuals in the artist's modulation of our personal sympathies. Shakespeare's control of the relationship between the several modes of audience response is what makes the acting of the play a kind of ritual; and it is this control and this range of response that makes it difficult either to acquiesce in Ernest Jones's indifference to the issue of state or to share Arnold Kettle's readiness to set aside the experience of Hamlet the son, as distinct from Hamlet the prince of Denmark ('This sort of thing', he says, referring to the murder, usurpation and marriage, 'was not, after all, so very unusual').[1] For Kettle, Hamlet's protest against the 'feudal world' is manifesting the kind of humanist feeling which was to erupt some thirty years later in the egalitarian aspirations of Cromwell's army. It may well be so, but the play insists that Claudius has usurped the roles of both king and father, figures having related but not identical claims upon respect, allegiance and love. It is not therefore true that the tragedy is valid only for an archaic monarchy, for any 'father-figure' that a society projects as its authority – whether a king or a prime-minister – could call into operation a similar range of experiences and ironies. The play offers no reassurance that men in power may not smile and smile and be villains in other dispensations and other regimes, and the problems of deposing kings may differ only technically from those of deposing, say, presidents and party chairmen. For the son of a king, however, the experience is sharply focused, and in *Hamlet* Shakespeare's control of it is the more certain because the play comes both at a critical moment in the history of the English monarchy and at a moment of maximum expressiveness in the history of a theatre both large enough and small enough for Shakespeare's purpose, capable of providing public spectacle and of being filled with private thought.

Jones treats 'Revenge this foul and most unnatural murder' as if it were the obviously dutiful thing to do. What decent chap wouldn't? And what neurotic outsider wouldn't, after a spell upon the surgery couch? Jones has the powerful ethical tradition of the nordic sources behind him, but it is a tradition that Shakespeare resists. He has no need of that little maxim in the *Atheist's Tragedy*, 'Attend with patience the success of things/ And leave revenge unto the King of Kings', for an equivalent principle has forged his design. The Ghost's awareness of the choices before Hamlet expresses Shakespeare's. The Ghost makes his last appearance precisely when it appears that Hamlet has made the wrong choice; assuming the Lucianus-like posture of killer, he has spared Claudius at his prayers, and committed himself to the rival activity that the Ghost had proscribed, 'Taint not thy mind, nor let thy soul contrive/Against thy

[1] *Hamlet and History* (1971).

mother aught; leave her to heaven,/And to those thorns that in her bosom lodge/To prick and sting her.' In the event, it is the revenge that is left to the 'divinity that shapes our ends', and the mind-tainting contrivances of the soul that are acted out. When the thorns are lodged, there is a sense in which the work is done. Hamlet and the audience submit to a providential movement of events towards what, in a qualified sense of the word, is a sacrificial outcome. The play's shaping providence does not answer to naive expectations – there is nothing miraculous about it. While little happens in the last act in obedience to human design, nothing happens either of which no human account can be given; events take form from propensities, not from purposes. Hamlet's searching inquisition of himself and others has compelled the community to undergo a process of moral *catharsis*.

The word 'sacrificial' is treacherous and complex and must not be barbarously used to impose upon civilized accomplishment an archaic and irrelevant paradigm,[1] yet to call *Hamlet* a 'revenge play' is more culpably to do just that. The point is not that the play is imitating the old rituals but that, with immeasurably greater spiritual and political subtlety, tragic art in the time of both Sophocles and Shakespeare continued in one of its aspects (not all) to acknowledge the persistence of the old mysteries of sin and death. I do not know if anything is gained from calling Hamlet a *pharmakos* or scapegoat, for if we do that we must recognize that he wears his rue with a difference. Like other tragic heroes, he is a victim to the comedy of innocence, whereby we find it necessary to impute guilt to those we kill.[2] The play's leading victim becomes one of its killers, and the cruel discourtesies of his wit do damage to his own humanity. Shakespeare contributes another episode to the history of goat-song, bringing it a long way from its beginnings. For it is finally, not in Denmark's stage court but on the stage of Shakespeare's theatre that the 'sacrifice' of Hamlet and Claudius takes place. Through the attraction and alienation of our sympathies, it is the audience's capacity for life that from generation to generation has been renewed, not that of Fortinbras's fictional state. Hamlet is sacrificed, not because Claudius disposes of him in the interests of Denmark, but because Shakespeare kills him to allow us the satisfaction and exaltation of tragic *catharsis*.

[1] I have examined some aspects of the word in, 'Upon Such Sacrifices', *British Academy Annual Shakespeare Lecture*, 1976.

[2] Burkert, 'Greek Tragedy and Sacrificial Ritual', pp. 106–9.

'HAMLET': A TIME TO DIE

BARBARA EVERETT

'Why does Hamlet delay?' The question has been asked for over two hundred years now. And whether or not it is the best way to interrogate the play, it seems now a natural one. For after every new reading or performance, it's difficult to avoid that prickling, sympathetic and exasperated sensation which formulates itself as: '*Why* does Hamlet delay?' Whatever more correct form the enquiry takes, something to do with time does seem to be at the centre of *Hamlet*: which – to the extent that the play tells this kind of truth at all – makes the whole of life a great waiting game. The prince himself, who doesn't know everything, and whose knowledge is above all that he doesn't know everything, chooses to call what is happening to him, delay; and chooses to find himself guilty of it; or finds himself guilty, whether or not he chooses; and in all these ways, may be right. The qualifications are made necessary by everything in Hamlet that makes the simple and direct 'Why does Hamlet delay?' not the best of questions, though a natural one. All questions are leading, and condition the object of enquiry in the direction of what we want to know about it. To ask this particular one is to push *Hamlet* towards presuppositions about life and literature which are in themselves doubtful, and which almost certainly didn't come into being until the period at which the question about Hamlet began to be asked about: the middle of the eighteenth century. Asking it, we suppose that men are essentially rational and motivated creatures; that in the most important issues of their lives they are free to choose; that choice is an act of will; that will and strength and success are the same thing; and that we know what we mean by *in time*. To pose and answer the question is to make of Shakespeare's play a post-Enlightenment object, whose hero will tend to be neurotic if he isn't rational, and who must be said to fail if he doesn't succeed.

We can only ask the questions we have. But sometimes defining where the questions don't fit is a way of seeing objects more clearly. And Shakespeare's play asks for, and yet sidesteps this one to a degree that is in itself informative. If the enquiry about delay breaks down, then *Hamlet* nonetheless answers another kind of time-question, or manifests another kind of truth about time. An analogy may help to make this point clearer. No work of art is positively like *Hamlet*; but the one most like, I think, with all its enormous differences, is Molière's *Le Misanthrope*, sub-sub-titled 'L'Atrabiliare amoureux' – 'the melancholiac in love'. Half a century nearer to us than *Hamlet*, its very rationality makes its enigmas more lucid. Sad Alceste hates the world but loves its finest flower, Célimène. The question *Why?* may spring to the mind the instant the play finishes, a deference to all its direct power; but it is an evasion of that power, as well as a deference to it. The reasons either don't exist or don't matter: as for instance psychological motivation (Alceste's unhappy childhood) or biographical explanation (Molière's wife) or sociological context (the position of the playwright). Alceste hates the world and loves Célimène. *Love* and *world* are words that have very different meanings for human beings, who may find such meanings irreconcilable, without ceasing however to hunger for their reconciliation. This can be called folly or divine discontent, and may be found either tragic or comic. Alceste is in himself hardly more than a great embodiment of a linguistic difficulty, a man caught forever on one of the more usual human cruces. *Hamlet* can't be summed up like that – and perhaps *Le Misanthrope* shouldn't be either – because Shakespeare's gifts, infinitely more generous and fantastic than Molière's, were so to a degree that forfeited the later writer's economy. All the same, Shakespeare's first quite classic hero, Hamlet, is held in a crux like Alceste's, whose depth consists in its inexpressibility in terms other than its own. Explanations like, for instance, that of the Oedipus complex tend to flow off the play for this reason. Hamlet clearly does have bad nerves. But they exacerbate, not constitute, his situation: in comparison with which a mere Oedipus complex would be child's play. A complex can, after all, be cured; that is the theory of it. What Hamlet has is both incurable and true enough to last some centuries. His situation, which is a situation in time, thus arouses that itch of assent and resentment which both recognizes the incurable and seeks to resolve it with an undermining *Why?*

Why does Hamlet delay in revenging his father? Beyond a certain point, Hamlet didn't delay in revenging his father; because he didn't revenge his father. In the end he revenged only himself. The ghost is a presence that fades. And this fading of the Ghost is a part of the narrative of *Hamlet*, a play which offers such temporal changes and transformations as simply an aspect of the real that we know. The Ghost is first a royal presence coming to the waiting sentries; and then he is the great shadow of a loved father burdening the son with dread; and then a devil in the cellarage, friendly and bad; and finally a man in a dressing-gown whose wife cannot even see him. In the closet scene the Ghost stays just long enough to make us realise that we had almost forgotten him. After it, Hamlet Senior is neither present nor missed, and there is no word of him at the end of the play. The Ghost fades; and Hamlet comes into being, already a dead man. In the graveyard he says suddenly

> This is I,
> Hamlet the Dane (v, ii, 251–2)

taking on, *faute de mieux*, the royal title. Those who survive loss become the dead person; Hamlet ages onstage before us, slowing down into the tiredness of 'Let be'. The prince never does revenge his father; he does something more natural and perhaps more terrible, he becomes his father. He kills Claudius when he recognizes the similarity: 'I am dead, Horatio'.

These events may be given, at will, a psychological explanation: as when one says that a survivor will come to embody the person loved and lost. No doubt a reader so minded could re-tell the Ghost's story in terms of the culpability of memory: 'Why did Hamlet forget?'. But there are other and similar narratives within the play which don't so immediately resolve into psychological process. *Hamlet* contains also the history of Fortinbras, whose travels to and fro through the play delineate a net that tightens around the prince: 'How all occasions do inform against me'. The value of the golden young soldier, all-absorbed in his hunt for honour, lies perhaps mainly in the aching envy he arouses in Hamlet, along with an ironic scepticism. In comparison with that definable military glory, Hamlet's intellectual power dwindles to a single point of acknowledgement: a point that measures how much space Fortinbras has crossed since the play began, and how much time Hamlet has merely lived out. But if Hamlet can understand Fortinbras, he can't stop him – indeed the unstoppability is what he understands: Fortinbras will be there at the end, to inherit the kingdom. The fading of the Ghost, the slow and yet sudden approach of Fortinbras–diminishing Hamlet, overtaking him – are equally the play's rendering of certain great natural and impersonal laws which the individual apprehends but hardly governs. They constitute the real form of the tragedy, that quality of elastic and problematic life which makes the work seem to shift in our hands, but to shift around a centre: the curve of its own plot. The process can be given many true names, but the play leads us unusually often to think of it in terms of the laws of time, and to call *Hamlet*, if we wish, a Time Play. A human experience of living impossibility, Hamlet's crux, can be paraphrased into a very old and frequently recurring philosophical conundrum. This probably came to Shakespeare, though it hardly needed to come from anywhere, from Montaigne's fluid and incessant awareness of a fluid and incessant temporal medium. Its earliest spokesman seems to have been the Heracleitus who said

> You cannot step twice into the same river; for other waters are ever flowing on to you.

The same Heracleitus also said that

> Time is a child playing draughts . . .

and that

> In thirty years a man may become a grandfather.

The amount of time that actually passes in *Hamlet* is debatable. It is short enough for a child's game of draughts, the courtly tit-for-tat that is revenge; it is long enough for a man to become, if not a grandfather, at least much like his father, the King of Denmark, and dead. To neither stretch of time – the game or the growing – does the notion of *delay* seem appropriate.

It is the first of these three sayings of Heracleitus that is the best-known of his utterances: and what has made it, I think, so permanently available is the absoluteness of that 'You cannot' with which the phrase begins in English. The sentence makes a natural epigram for an experience of negation radical to human life, and does so the more believably for the lack of any doctrine. An outdated physics may do very well for wisdom. Shakespeare's tragedies are founded on this acquaintance with impossibilities, and *Hamlet* more than any. At every turning in it, in phrase and image and situation, we meet an inbuilt 'You cannot', a kind of wholly intrinsic 'No Road' sign. And these negations can't in the end be resolved into inhibition, some private trouble of Hamlet's: they are, like the sayings of Heracleitus, laws of nature, statements of human physics. This is why they tend toward, and may be treated as, principles of time; and why a play which is about so many things may nonetheless be thought of as a Time Tragedy.

Time is a concept that we can often only hold by exercising a kind of extreme reach of intellect: and yet it is also true that the sense of time is something that immediately disappears under the impress of consciousness. When we say *Time*, time stops. Dürer's remarkable engraving of that beautiful, wild-eyed Melancholia who is Hamlet's patron saint – a melancholia that is almost the Renaissance word for consciousness – has, up in the right-hand corner, an hour-glass, and the sand is running, and yet also (because we look at it) is completely still. Shakespeare made of his revenge-plot something like the pictured hour-glass. He changed his resources to give father and son the same name, Hamlet old and young: or perhaps he took this brilliant device from the imputed early *Hamlet* of Kyd, whose static rhetoric, violent action and obsession with memory may have become debts that Shakespeare owed gratefully. In Shakespeare's *Hamlet*, whether or not elsewhere, the revenge-plot becomes a mirror-image reversal from generation to generation: Hamlet is killed, Hamlet kills; the king is dead, long live the king. Behind *Hamlet* lie the two interlocking cycles of the Histories, from weak Harry to strong Harry, from the son to the father, from the loser to the winner and so *da capo*. The plot of *Hamlet* is a résumé of the Histories, or of history, just as the play-within-the-play is a résumé of *Hamlet*: an inset which, by the mirror-image logic that governs the entire play, opens out at the heart of its curious individual fable into a grey vista of commonplace history:

> The great man down, you mark his favourite flies;
> The poor advanced makes friends of enemies.

The plot of *Hamlet* maintains this strange static fixity, as of an object balancing its mirrored image. From the opening to the play-scene Hamlet is Revenger, a mere function or shadow of that ghost-father whose appearances frame this half of the play. The dynamic centre of the tragedy lies at that point where Hamlet, with a gesture like that Milton was to give to the tempted Eve in *Paradise Lost* ('she plucked, she ate') waves his arm and impales on his sword – as a pig on a spit – the hapless Polonius. From that vital and ludicrous moment to the end of the play Hamlet is Revengee, an introverted virtual image, a shadow of a shadow. And by this passive and humiliating function he achieves his end, or what seemed the end when he began. Living forwards in time, making history, here becomes what Eliot was to call in 'Gerontion', 'variety in a wilderness of mirrors'. For to any steady consciousness of the situation, the play stands still. 'Denmark is a prison'; the hour-glass does not move. Everything in the court is a frozen shifting, an endless descent of sand: like the movement of that wonderfully distinguished speech in which Claudius sees the laws of his own and his kingdom's dissolution. In the kingdom of power and will,

> That we would do
> We should do when we would; for this *would* changes
> And hath abatements and delays as many
> As there are tongues, are hands, are accidents;
> And then this *should* is like a spendthrift's sigh
> That hurts by easing. But to the quick of the ulcer:
> Hamlet comes back; what would you undertake
> To show yourself indeed your father's son
> More than in words? (IV, viii, 118–26)

In Claudius's dreamy transition, the only paternal bequest is the will to kill. 'Hamlet comes back' in time to this.

Hamlet comes back *in time*. Similarly, Claudius lives 'when we would'. He inhabits a moment of existence conceived by Shakespeare as the time of the politicians. For, ten years after *Hamlet* was written, Claudius's peculiar melancholy, which gives this speech its heavy truth, recurs in the long silences of Alonso. Alonso is a more potent figure than Claudius: there is time and space for him, in the island after the tempest, to define absolutely the futility and the frustrations of the power-hungry will, as he sits withdrawn among the twittering time-passing courtiers. Claudius's more active capacities are embedded in Antonio. And it's an oddity of the temptation scene in *The Tempest* that Antonio seems to have his own time and space; he measures the journey to Tunis, which he left only days earlier, as light-years in length. The fact is that neither past nor future exist for him, though they have for Prospero an intensity of truth to which the play's second scene gives witness. Antonio lives only 'when we would', in the dream-like or posited moment of pure will. He is a man whom the great sea has vomited up

> to perform an act
> Whereof what's past is prologue, what's to come
> In yours and my discharge. (II, i, 243–5)

This abstract state juggles images of time,

but the metaphysic is commonplace. It can be met in the weird mind-changes of any genuinely political personality, unconvinceable that the loyalties or opinions of yesterday have any meaning: too weak, that is, to maintain a truth undermined by the shifts of existence:

It is not very strange, for my uncle is King of Denmark, and those that would make mouths at him while my father lived give twenty, forty, fifty, a hundred ducats apiece for his picture in little. 'Sblood, there is something in this more than natural, if philosophy could find it out. (II, ii, 358–64)

Hamlet's last remark here hesitates between naiveté and a sophisticated irony, as so many of his sayings do. It is both strange, and not strange at all, that courtiers condition their minds to their profit: the matter is both 'more than natural' and very natural indeed. Beyond a certain point, philosophy won't help Hamlet. Similarly, the time-worlds of *The Tempest* don't need metaphysics to explain them. In substance they reflect simple morality; in method they operate merely by Prospero's magic; and both moral and magical systems demand no more than a generous attentiveness from an audience. Dr Johnson once disposed of the unities by saying that we always know in any case that we're in the theatre: a right instinct though a wrong argument. Anyone who understands any work of art knows as much as he needs about the strangenesses of time and space. The symbolisms of art demand a natural acquaintance with conventions, an easiness in taking up and laying down relationship with the actual, that makes of any audience a Prospero in itself. Thus the Chorus of *Henry V*:

'Tis your thoughts that now must deck our kings,
Carry them here and there, jumping o'er times,
Turning th'accomplishment of many years
Into an hour-glass. (Prologue, 28–31)

It's easier than it once was – perhaps almost too easy – to turn that hour-glass, sixty years after the advent of Modernism, which showed that the convention of space in a painting comes to little more than the relation of one brush-stroke to another, and that time is after all only a dimension. The novel started as the story of a lifetime, and George Eliot said that *Romola* took her from youth into age; but a novel doesn't take much longer to read than a twenty-line poem, also perhaps the transcript of a lifetime. Drama, particularly when staged, has a peculiar *vraisemblance* that can make it seem sensible to talk, as several generations once did, of time-schemes, of calendars of days and weeks and months: so that one ought for instance to be able to prove that Hamlet's time is or is not 'enough', that he does or does not *delay*. But even drama, insofar as it is art, is a mental act, and therefore almost timeless, its running-time a metaphor for as long as we like. In Peele's *Old Wives' Tale* an old woman tells a story and its characters walk onstage and are the play. To ask 'When?' would be as misplaced as Laertes's characteristic 'Oh, where?' when he hears his sister's drowned. Peele's people could only say, like Shakespeare's Sir Toby, 'We did keep time, sir, in our snatches'. More formally, one could say that Peele's work balances on a point somewhere between the aesthetic sophistication rediscovered in Modernism, and the simple crude fact that in England in 1590 no clock told the right time. For, if it is Time that is in question, we can't estimate, I think, the subtle but radical changes that four hundred years have brought to the human mind. Queen Elizabeth had a wrist-watch: it was a suitable present for millionaires and monarchs. Clocks became familiar in England only after about 1650; not until the eighteenth century did they become accurate; and absolute accuracy was the product of Greenwich Mean Time. Elizabethan villages lived by the church-bell at their centre. When we think about *delay*, we do so from a standpoint divided from the

Tudor by the age of the satanic mills and factories, when clocks became what human beings clocked in by; and the word *delay* carries locked within it the implicit noise of the machine.

Shakespeare's plays time themselves, as country people did for many centuries, by the sun, and he starts up indoor clocks only as and when he pleases. *Henry IV* Part I opens with Hal rebuking Falstaff for defining time in a way that unmakes clocks; and the play is Falstaff's in this sense, revolving around its great clock-stopping comic occasions, East-cheap nights before the morning after. Part II by contrast belongs to the king and the old Lord Chief Justice, the action dragging itself out in the long dreary shadow of *too late*. Another example: in the middle of *Twelfth Night* Olivia is with finality turned down by Viola. There is – one presumes – a sudden offstage bell-note and Olivia says 'The clock upbraids me with the waste of time'. The death of a fantasy, the pang of a real despised love, are a simple and hard slap in the face strong enough to start up a clock in Olivia's mind. The ghost of Hamlet's father enters at just such another stroke, 'The bell then beating *One!*'. And Hamlet himself says '*One!*' like an echo of the clock, as he gives his first blow to Laertes, to whom he has said 'I loved you ever' and who in response kills him.

The word *One*, used in this way, in fact occurs with weight a third time in *Hamlet*. At the beginning of the last scene, whose packed action so crystallizes into the ritual of the duel as to seem to stand still, to be timeless one might say, Hamlet absently reassures the anxious Horatio:

> It will be short: the interim is mine,
> And a man's life's no more than to say *One*.
> (V, ii, 73–4)

The phrase is definitive though enigmatic. Its resonance has something to do with those two other bell-notes to which it looks forward and back, the clock that strikes at the Ghost's entry and the call of the first blow struck in the duel. The three *One*'s hold together like a linked irregular chain, or like the echoes of a stone going down a deep place. The *One*'s can seem echoic in this way because the first of the sequence, the bell-note that brings in the Ghost, encourages the image, and is, moreover, itself an echo. The entry of the Ghost is an extraordinary dramatic event that helps to define something of what one might mean by calling *Hamlet* a Time Tragedy. And it begins with a man remembering:

> Last night of all,
> When yond same star that's westward from the pole
> Had made his course t'illume that part of heaven
> Where now it burns, Marcellus and myself
> The bell then beating *One* –
> *Enter Ghost.* (I, i, 35–9)

This first appearance of the Ghost is perhaps the most quietly startling moment in all Elizabethan drama. The Ghost brings to their feet the intent seated group of listening soldiers, shattering their circle as it interposes itself within Barnardo's very sentences. It brings its own ending to his unfinished story, a subject relegating his own unspoken object to nothingness: it leaves 'Marcellus and myself' suspended forever in the air, just as it will the next night dislocate Hamlet's life, leaving thirty years unfinished for always. The Ghost's effect is even more radical than this, more transforming and more philosophical: it alters the temporal dimension of the moment. The story that was begun has created on stage that rapt enclosure of the historic where all narratives take place, a security reflected in the lamp-lit circle of listeners. When the Ghost comes on, when the Ghost – unnoticed through the familiar conjurors' distraction of spell-binding anecdote – suddenly *is* on, that security is broken; narrative is drama and the past is present. Theatre and metaphysics come together: the *shadow* behind the soldiers is a true *ghost* because a real *actor*, just as later in the play the Players crowd onstage as 'the brief chronicles of the time', to deny that the past was ever anything but living. In this first scene of the play, time is a great continuum like an open stage. As Barnardo remembers, and the bell beats, and the Ghost comes and stands in the darkness, the present moment dissolves into a receding sequence of shadows, of haunted imagined nights all reaching back for their meaning to a time when 'the king that's dead' really lived. What is here and now grows, like Plato's shadow of a shadow, dependent for its reality on something else, something always behind it to which it traces back in a long tangle of source-relationships. The Player King will say:

> Purpose is but the slave to memory.
>
> (III, ii, 183)

But the Ghost says it first, in silence. For the whole of the rest of the play it will be foolish to think that the past is past, and dishonest to withhold sympathy from a man who finds it impossible to live wholly in the present.

The first appearance of the Ghost is a brilliant stage moment, like a flash of lightning. It is, that is to say, only a moment, but it extends in the mind into concepts and reactions much wider-reaching, their outer limits being the boundaries of the play, which are perhaps the boundaries of human society itself. The moment is a definition, as of law. Barnardo has 'called back yesterday'; from now on, every hour struck in *Hamlet* is a passing-bell. History begins when the bell strikes *One*, and the prince's vocation is to give meaning to the clock, saying *One* until the Ghost is laid at last. For the play's hero is introduced to us as *Young Hamlet*, the child of the Ghost, and the first important thing that we learn about him is that he is, in his black garments, true to the darkness, and incapable of forgetting:

> Heaven and earth,
> Must I remember?
>
> (I, ii, 142–3)

The court of Denmark lives by daylight and survives by forgetting, its time-servers drifting on the present moment as Ophelia will on the brook that finally drags her down. In such a world, Hamlet's only freedom is to follow the Ghost; to be caught into that huge individual act of confronting Time which the play summarizes as memory, or delay: a death in life, but the life, also, of all human civility, and the source from which the prince derives his royalty. While he thus follows the Ghost, life becomes for him 'a time to die'. This is the impasse or crux on which Hamlet rests, and it makes of him a figure not unlike that image of Melancholy which I mentioned earlier, one created at a time when the mechanical clock and the sense of History were together beginning to master Europe. Benighted and moonlit, Dürer's powerful, winged but seated Melancholy lifts a heavy frowning head: and behind her head, next to the hour-glass, there hangs a bell, its rope drawn sideways and out of the picture, about to ring and never ringing. In just such a condition of pause, Hamlet is held: always potential and always too late.[1]

[1] This talk, read at the Shakespeare Conference at Stratford-upon-Avon in 1976, is part of a larger study of *Hamlet* in preparation.

SHAKESPEARE, LYLY AND OVID: THE INFLUENCE OF 'GALLATHEA' ON 'A MIDSUMMER NIGHT'S DREAM'

LEAH SCRAGG

In the words of Anne Barton 'although there is no identifiable narrative or dramatic source for the plot, a good deal of general reading seems to underlie'[1] *A Midsummer Night's Dream*. The nature and extent of that reading has been amply illustrated by previous commentators[2] whose conclusions have almost invariably contained some reference to the influence exerted by Lyly on Shakespeare at this stage of the dramatist's career. Marco Mincoff, for example, maintains that 'with *A Midsummer Night's Dream* comes a new advance'[3] towards the work of a largely uncongenial predecessor, while Anne Barton suggests that Shakespeare's young lovers 'would probably have reminded many members of Shakespeare's audience of equivalent characters'[4] in Lyly's plays. Conversely, writers on Lyly have sought to show the relationship between the first major exponent of the comic form in England and his more illustrious successor, and it is in this area that the most detailed and persuasive analyses may be found. As early as 1902 R. Warwick Bond cited some interesting parallels between Shakespeare's play and Lyly's *Midas*, *Endimion* and *The Woman in the Moon*[5] while, more recently, G. K. Hunter has argued that both *Love's Labour's Lost* and *A Midsummer Night's Dream* are 'completely Lylian in their construction',[6] pointing, in the case of the latter play, to the 'balancing [of] a number of self-contained groups, one against the other', to the introduction of successive groups of characters, each entry expounding 'what is to be its intention and outlook for the rest of the play' and to the 'clearly exposed debate subject of ... imagination versus reason'.[7] Hunter, like Warwick Bond, cites a number of plays in support of his position but neither he, nor any other of the many commentators upon Lyly's influence on Shakespeare, has sought to establish a single play, as opposed to a generalized form of dramatic writing, as a source for *A Midsummer Night's Dream*. It is the purpose of this paper to advance such a claim for *Gallathea*.

The location of the two plays is similarly complex. Lyly's drama is set on the banks of the Humber some time after the Viking invasions, yet its characters, with the exception of the young adventurers Robin, Rafe and Dick, have classical names, largely drawn from Virgil, while their universe is ruled by Neptune

[1] *The Riverside Shakespeare*, textual editor G. Blakemore Evans (Boston, 1974), p. 217. All quotations from *A Midsummer Night's Dream* are from this edition.

[2] See in particular Geoffrey Bullough, *Narrative and Dramatic Sources of Shakespeare*, vol. I (1957), pp. 367–422.

[3] 'Shakespeare and Lyly', *Shakespeare Survey 14* (Cambridge, 1961), p. 20.

[4] *Riverside Shakespeare*, p. 218.

[5] *The Complete Works of John Lyly*, vol. II (Oxford, 1902), pp. 297–8.

[6] *John Lyly: The Humanist as Courtier* (1962), p. 318.

[7] *Ibid.*, pp. 318–19.

as are their hearts by Venus and their forests by Diana. Similarities with the 'Athens' of Shakespeare's play with its very English mechanicals, legendary Duke and folk-lore deities are obvious. The structure of *Gallathea*, like that of *A Midsummer Night's Dream*, involves an alternation between a daylight world and a forest location suggestive of confusion and disorder. The action opens in warm sunshine on the banks of the Humber where a harsh choice between virgin death and instant flight precipitates an exodus to a forest frequented by factious deities and by a group of apprentice artisans, forests in which the emotional confusions of vulnerable youth are compounded by the intervention of a mischief-loving spirit, triangular relationships are established, and resolution, with its accompanying return to the external world, can be accomplished only by the metamorphosis of one of the lovers by the newly reconciled gods who marshal the characters towards a wedding feast in which all social levels are to participate.

The four groups of characters (gods, fathers, lovers, artisans) Lyly involves in this sequence of actions have striking similarities with corresponding groupings in *A Midsummer Night's Dream*. The worlds of both plays are ruled by decidedly emotional deities whose passions bring disorder in the human frame but whose purposes to man are ultimately benign. Thus, though Neptune's anger with humanity once resulted in a state of climatic disorder very like that brought about by the quarrel between Titania and Oberon,[1] he is instrumental in instigating the movement towards resolution with which the play closes, while Venus, like Oberon, manipulates the mis-alliances of the young lovers towards a harmonious outcome. Moreover, the deities of both plays display a disputatiousness that has repercussions in the human sphere. The quarrel between Oberon and Titania involves Bottom, who becomes the instrument of Oberon's revenge as the unsuitable object of Titania's metamorphosed affections. Similarly the strife between Venus and Diana, and hence between Cupid and the nymphs, results in the love-transformed virgin-foresters fixing their affections upon the already bewildered human maidens in their translated shapes. The principal deities – Neptune, Venus, Diana/Oberon, Titania – are attended by a subordinate supernatural being – Cupid/Puck – who delights in promoting the confusion that lies at the heart of the play's action and manipulates affections in the forest world, while the groves of both plays are inhabited by fairies whose appearance is at odds with popular tradition.[2] Those in authority in the mortal sphere, the second separable group of characters within the worlds of the plays, also display a degree of likeness. Fathers and father-figures in both *Gallathea* and *A Midsummer Night's Dream* exhibit a wilful irrationality towards their daughters that is responsible for the movement from an environment conducive to the orderly enactment of ordained rites (the sacrifice to Neptune/marriage between lovers) to the confusion of the wood. Tityrus and Melebeus, blinded by their affections, seek to deceive the all-seeing gods by sleight of hand while Egeus, supported by Theseus, insists upon his preference for the inconstant Demetrius as his daughter's suitor regardless of the obvious merits of Lysander. The young lovers themselves – Gallathea, Phyllida, Diana's nymphs/Helena, Hermia, Demetrius, Lysander – have even more obvious similarities. All are the idealistic victims of a mating game that is complicated by cross-affections, by the doubts and hesitancies of youth and by

[1] Compare *Gallathea*, I, i, 12–34 with *A Midsummer Night's Dream*, II, i, 88–117. Some verbal correspondences between these passages are discussed below.

[2] That Lyly's fairies are as attractive as Shakespeare's is borne out by Rafe's remark that 'so fair faces never can have . . . hard fortunes' (II, iii, 6–7).

uncertainty as to the nature and feelings of the desired object. Diana's nymphs, like Lysander in acts II and III and Demetrius up to III, ii, love beings whose affections are committed elsewhere, while Gallathea and Phyllida, like Hermia in act III and Helena up to III, ii, love those who require some kind of metamorphosis before love can be fulfilled. But it is the fourth group of characters, the apprentices/artisans, who display many of the most interesting correspondences with one another, some of which will be discussed below in relation to theme. Lyly's apprentices, like Shakespeare's mechanicals, display their inadequacies in the face of uncongenial occupations, exhibit the least grasp of the nature of their world and manifest the most assurance in confronting it. Like Bottom, Rafe (the central figure) is involved in a process of 'translation' and contemplates with equanimity the possibility of being 'hail-fellows with the gods'. It is this group of characters in both plays which is to provide entertainment for the rest at the marriage feast.

It is, however, on thematic grounds that a case for relationship may be most forcibly argued and here misconceptions about the principal concerns of *Gallathea* may well have been responsible for blurring its affinities with Shakespeare's play just as they have obscured the relationship between the levels of its dramatic action. Anne Begor Lancashire, for example, in the most recent edition of the play, declares that '*Gallathea* is a play about the nature of love, and how it physically and mentally affects man', contending that it is 'centered on a debate theme familiar to the court of Elizabeth: which is better, love or chastity?'[1] G. K. Hunter exhibits a similar confidence that 'the play is, of course, basically ... about love'[2] though he notes that 'almost all the plot material is made out of one motif – the attempt to defeat destiny by disguise'[3] and elsewhere declares, somewhat confusingly, that 'what the play is about [is] the interrelation of gods and men, obedience and deceit'.[4] Such commentators have inevitably found difficulty in accommodating the area of action devoted to the apprentices (who are not involved in the activities of the lovers) to this kind of framework. Anne Lancashire, lacking Warwick Bond's temerity (the 'comic matter [is] entirely unconnected with the plot'[5]) resorts to the specious ('the subplot scenes partly serve, through their many sexual jokes, to emphasize the physical inevitability of love for humans [while making] the love debate of the main plot a part of the larger perception of reality'[6]) while G. K. Hunter simply omits the boys from his account of the structure of the play even while maintaining that *Gallathea* is 'one of the most beautifully articulated plays in the period'.[7] That *Gallathea* is, in part, 'about' love, in the same way that *A Midsummer Night's Dream* might be said to be about the same subject, can hardly be doubted. It is the super-fondness of the shepherds for their daughters that initiates the action, the love between Gallathea and Phyllida, Diana's nymphs and the disguised maidens, which forms a large part of the central interest, and it is in the framework of a love versus chastity debate that the complexities of the action are resolved (compare the love between Hermia

1 *Gallathea and Midas*, Regents Renaissance Drama Series, General editor Cyrus Hoy (1970), p. xxiv. All quotations from *Gallathea* are from this edition.

2 *John Lyly*, p. 201.

3 *Ibid.*, p. 198.

4 *Ibid.*, p. 195.

5 Warwick Bond, *Complete Works of John Lyly*, p. 419.

6 *Gallathea and Midas*, pp. xxv–xxvi.

7 *John Lyly*, p. 198. Hunter does, however, discuss the role of the boys in his analysis of Lyly's use of the sub-plot, relating them to the 'estates-satire' tradition and suggesting, not very convincingly, that their masters are ridiculed because they lack 'the all-round gracious dilletantism of the gentleman' (p. 234).

and Lysander that sets *A Midsummer Night's Dream* in motion, the central interest in the exchanging of partners in the wood and the framing quarrel between Oberon and Titania over the Indian boy[1]). Similarly the irrationality of love looms large in both plays with Cupid playing havoc with the affections of the nymphs much as Puck exposes what fools these mortals be through his confusion over the 'Athenian garments'. But in both plays a larger vision of a universe characterized by flux 'places' the experience of the lovers as an instance of a pervasive process of metamorphosis that extends far beyond the sphere of human affections. Though the attitudes of Shakespeare and Lyly differ, and Lyly is characteristically ambivalent as to the sources of change in his world, it is this vision of 'translation' that forms the primary link between the two plays.

The importance of the transformation theme in *A Midsummer Night's Dream* has been analysed at greater length and much more persuasively than could be attempted here in David P. Young's *Something of Great Constancy*[2] and it would be pointless to urge the matter further, but the pervasive 'change' motif in *Gallathea* remains unexplored, commentators having failed to note the connection between the characters' persistent assumption of disguise and the sex change in the final act. In fact, as in *A Midsummer Night's Dream*, the concept of mutation informs both the dramatic action and the language of the play, linking groups of characters whose activities are barely connected in formal terms.

The play opens with Gallathea, already metamorphosed (in terms of outward appearance) in her disguise as a boy, listening to her father's account of the origin of the virgin sacrifice, the custom which threatens her life. The flux of time has, we learn, bred an act of impiety that has stirred Neptune to transform the natural world.

> In times past, where thou seest a heap of small pebble, stood a stately temple of white marble, which was dedicated to the god of the sea... Hither came all such as either ventured by long travel to see countries or by great traffic to use merchandise... but Fortune, constant in nothing but inconstancy, did change her copy as the people their custom, for the land being oppressed by Danes, who instead of sacrifice committed sacrilege, instead of religion, rebellion, and made a prey of that in which they should have made their prayers, tearing down the temple even with the earth, being almost equal with the skies, enraged so the god who binds the winds in the hollows of the earth that he caused the seas to break their bounds, sith men had broke their vows, and to swell as far above their reach as men had swerved beyond their reason. Then might you see ships sail where sheep fed, anchors cast where ploughs go, fishermen throw their nets where husbandmen sow their corn, and fishes cast their scales where fowls do breed their quills. Then might you gather froth where now is dew, rotten weeds for sweet roses, and take view of monstrous mermaids instead of passing fair maids.
>
> (I, i, 12–34)

It is to escape a world in which the wrath of the gods enforces the sacrifice of the fairest and the most chaste, where it is thought 'as dishonourable to be honest as fortunate to be deformed' (V, iii, 19–20), that Gallathea changes her outward form and seeks the shelter of the woods and her action initiates a sequence of like situations. To quote G. K. Hunter, 'From this starting-point one can see the play being built up by methods almost exactly analogous to those of fugue in music'.[3] Gallathea's transformation to a boy is echoed in I, iii by Phyllida's assumption of a masculine shape at her father's bidding and mirrored in Cupid's device, conceived in I, ii and executed in II, ii, of assuming the form of a virgin in order to betray Diana's nymphs. Finally, Neptune himself joins the minuet of

[1] This account does not, of course, exhaust the richer canvas of Shakespeare's panorama of love.

[2] New Haven and London, 1966, pp. 155–66.

[3] *John Lyly*, p. 198.

maskers, commenting upon their performance as he does so:

Do silly shepherds go about to deceive great Neptune, in putting on man's attire upon women, and Cupid, to make sport, deceive them all by using a woman's apparel upon a god? Then, Neptune, that has taken sundry shapes to obtain love, stick not to practice some deceit to show thy deity, and having often thrust thyself into the shape of beasts to deceive men, be not coy to use the shape of a shepherd to show thyself a god. (II, ii, 17–24)

From this point, 'changes' proliferate. Gallathea's disguise involves her in the activities of a boy ('I will now use for the distaff the bow, and play at quoits abroad that was wont to sew in my sampler at home'), Phyllida finds herself forced to 'transgress in love a little of [her] modesty', the nymphs are transformed from cold condemners of love to ardent suitors to the 'boys' (Gallathea and Phyllida), Cupid, once captured, declines from 'Venus' son' to 'Diana's slave' (III, iv, 99) and is forced to unpick love knots rather than tie them, while at the close of the play, resolution is achieved by the permanent and total metamorphosis of either Phyllida or Gallathea, one of whom becomes a youth.

This sequence of transformations, the majority of which bring misfortune,[1] is punctuated by the activities of three boys who also seek to triumph over destiny (in the shape of poverty) by a series of ill-conceived attempts at 'translation'. They first appear, shipwrecked, in I, iv, in company with a mariner who claims, ambiguously, to be able to 'shift the moon and sun' (ll. 30–1) but who has failed to avert the disaster at sea and who accepts without question the fact that to take to the oceans is to assume the habits of a fish without its capacity for survival in a liquid element. The boys, more perturbed by the incongruous fact that 'a little cold water should kill a man of reason, when you shall see a poor minnow lie in it that hath no understanding' (ll. 26–8) decide to forsake the waves for the woods and to separate, Rafe appearing alone in II, iii to confront Peter, the Alchemist's boy and to meet his master whose 'powers' are set forth in lyrical terms which have obvious reference to the main plot:

I durst undertake to make the fire as it flames, gold, the wind as it blows, silver, the water as it runs, lead, the earth as it stands, iron, the sky, brass, and men's thoughts, firm metals. (ll. 122–5)

Rafe embraces his service in the hope of obtaining 'a golden body' (compare the physical transformations of the main plot) only to quarrel with him in III, iii and devote himself to an Astronomer whose promises are yet more alluring than those of his previous master:

Astronomer. I will make the heavens as plain to thee as the highway. Thy cunning shall sit cheek by jowl with the sun's chariot. Then shalt thou see what a base thing it is to have others' thoughts creep on the ground, whenas thine shall be stitched to the stars.
Rafe. Then I shall be translated from this mortality.
Astronomer. Thy thoughts shall be metamorphosed, and made hail-fellows with the gods. (ll. 74–80)

Rafe, though initially impressed,

O fortune! I feel my very brains moralized, and, as it were, a certain contempt of earthly actions is crept into my mind, (ll. 81–2)

soon discovers that the Astronomer's assumption of godhead is as hollow as the Alchemist's claim to mutate the physical properties of matter and by V, i he has abandoned his service to be re-united with Robin, only to hear from Peter that his other brother, Dick, has learned a means by which to transform himself from

[1] Only the transformations wrought by the more powerful deities have beneficial effects. Those designed to cheat the gods are potentially disastrous. The disguises of Phyllida and Gallathea threaten the girls with emotional attrition and the country with destruction. Cupid's disguise as a nymph places him in Diana's power and brings misery to the virgin huntress's train.

the youngest member of the family into the eldest. Rafe at first is incredulous but for once Peter is speaking the truth:

Rafe. That's as true as thy master could make silver pots of tags of points.
Peter. Nay, he will teach him to cozen you both and so get the mill to himself. (ll. 67–70)

The three boys are brought into relationship with the main plot characters in formal terms only in the last act (compare the mechanicals in *A Midsummer Night's Dream*) but Rafe's pursuit of change clearly relates to the transformations of the main plot while his successive masters highlight the folly of those who seek to usurp the role and function of the gods. The actualities of the world of Gallathea and Phyllida remain hypotheses in the world of Rafe and Peter (cf. Rafe's *desire* for a golden body and the ragged Alchemist's *claim* to be disguised) but a concern with metamorphosis is clearly common to both.

All three areas of action – the virgin sacrifice, the love tangle and the adventures of the boys – are permeated by references to the protean nature of the universe. The transformations wrought by Neptune in his rage at man's impiety have been noted already but the pervasive references to mutability in the actions framed by the virgin sacrifice deserve notice. Telusa, for example, one of Diana's nymphs, laments the effects of love upon her in the following terms:

Is thy Diana become a Venus, thy chaste thoughts turn'd to wanton looks, thy conquering modesty to a captive imagination? Beginnest thou with pyralis to die in the air and live in the fire? (III, i, 2–5)

and she concludes that love can make

the bashful impudent, the wise fond, the chaste wanton, and [work] contraries to our reach. (ll. 110–11)

Gallathea concludes the play in similar terms:

Venus can make constancy fickleness, courage cowardice, modesty lightness, working things impossible . . . and tempering hardest hearts to softest wool. (*Epilogue*, 2–4)

Similarly the conversations among the boys and between Rafe and his masters are fraught with such phrases as:

for often times of smoke he has made silver drops (II, iii, 87–8)

he is able to make nothing infinite (II, iii, 95)

you may then make a dram of wind a wedge of gold (III, iii, 20–1)

He would of a little fasting-spittle make a hose and doublet of cloth of silver. (V, i, 28–9)

The action of *Gallathea*, therefore, like that of *A Midsummer Night's Dream*, is concerned with metamorphosis on every level and, as in the later comedy, this dominating interest radiates into the language of the play. Like *A Midsummer Night's Dream*, *Gallathea* presents us with an image of a world in which fortune is inconstant, affections unstable and gods and men alike find themselves assuming roles seemingly at odds with their basic natures. And in both plays the transfigurations experienced by human and superhuman personages alike are internal as well as external. Just as Bottom is physically changed into an ass (compare Puck's ability to transform himself into a joint stool) either Gallathea or Phyllida is to undergo a corporeal change after the end of the play and Rafe yearns to have his body turned to gold. Similarly, just as Lysander changes his affections twice during his sojourn in the wood, the nymphs swing from chastity to amorousness under the influence of Cupid, and Rafe's thoughts are 'translated' by the 'power' of the Astronomer. Even the stable framework of the universe is subject to the mutability inherent in the processes of time. The onset of Neptune's wrath turns dry land to ocean and natural fertility to fruitless decay, a state of chaos which in turn is reversed as his anger is appeased, just as the natural disorder bred by the quarrel between Oberon and Titania is assumed to be brought to an end by their reconciliation. In Lyly's play the cause of the transformations that take place is primarily assigned to the misuse of man's intelligence. The wrath of Neptune, for example, and the consequent turmoil in the elements are seen as direct consequences of the overthrow of reason in the conduct of human affairs: the god 'caused the seas to break their bounds, sith men had broke their vows, and to swell as far above their reach as men had swerved beyond their reason' (I, i, 26–8). Similarly, the disguises of Gallathea and Phyllida spring from the fact that their fathers 'fearing to become unnatural [have] become unreasonable' (IV, iii, 5), while the loves that are engendered in the woods are irrational in every instance (all the parties being girls) and the conduct of the boys and their masters displays a lamentable absence of true 'cunning' throughout. Thus far similarities with *A Midsummer Night's Dream* might still be cited. Shakespeare's mechanicals display much the same reasonable unreasonableness as Lyly's boys while his lovers are equally ready to deny the relevance of the head to the affairs of the heart. But whereas the climax of Lyly's play brings a return to stability that extends into the future, with the virgin sacrifice remitted, Cupid restored to Venus, and either Gallathea or Phyllida permanently transformed to allow their union – a movement pointedly initiated by a return to rationality (*Neptune.* 'It were unfit that goddesses should strive, and it were unreasonable that I should not yield' (V, iii, 67–8)) – *A Midsummer Night's Dream* ends far otherwise. Though Demetrius's transformation, like Gallathea/Phyllida's, will be permanent and Shakespeare's deities, like Lyly's, bring the action to a close, the play ends in the moonlight world that has alternated with the daylight world throughout, and the fairies' benediction, performed without the knowledge of the lovers, does not reflect the conscious acquiescence of humanity in divine processes. Puck's first speech in V, i, with its emphasis on death, places the present happiness of the lovers in the context of mortality and locates the 'swing toward constancy'[1] with which the play closes within a larger concept of mutability. Above all, the very appearance of the fairies to bless both their former favourites and the lovers they have manipulated reminds us that the statuesque positions assumed in the final act are no more than momentary points of stasis in a world of flux. Titania, we remember, has once led the 'rational' Theseus through the 'glimmering night' as she has led Bottom (and Puck has led the lovers) in the course of the play. Oberon has once loved Hippolyta as Demetrius once loved Hermia and now loves Helena. The newly-reconciled fairies were at enmity in the forest as were the newly-reconciled maidens. Thus the exchanging of roles, the shifting of personalities and merging of individuals are recalled rather than forgotten at the close of the play – suggesting that inconstancy and change are not merely the products of irrationality in the human and divine frames, they are the basic characteristics of a world instinct with the revolution of the seasons, the changing of the moon, the alternation between day and night. Yet, even here, the hint may have been supplied by Lyly. Though a great deal of emphasis is placed upon irrationality as the motivating force behind the action of *Gallathea*, Lyly is characteristically ambivalent as to whether inconstancy and change are to be regarded as the products of a moral aberration or as the symptoms of a universal condition. At the start of the play we are informed that fortune is 'constant in nothing but inconstancy' (I, i, 19) and at the close, though the goddesses are ostensibly reconciled, the positions they

[1] Young, *Something of Great Constancy*, p. 158.

assume are mutually exclusive and pregnant with future strife:

Venus. I will be wary how my son wander again. But Diana cannot forbid him to wound.
Diana. Yes, chastity is not within the level of his bow.
Venus. But beauty is a fair mark to hit.
(v, iii, 81–4)

Above all, the supreme deity, Neptune, who is most committed to reason, has assumed the shape of beasts in the past to prosecute his lusts, and admits, at the close of the play, the sovereignty of love over his heart. Thus the 'swing toward constancy' (in the widest sense) at the close of *Gallathea* is more pronounced than in *A Midsummer Night's Dream* but it certainly does not preclude a return to the opposite state.

The affinities between Shakespeare's play and Lyly's in terms of location, plot, character and theme are thus remarkable enough to suggest a conscious use of the earlier play by the later dramatist and such a supposition may be supported by a number of minor, but significant, liguistic echoes. Names from the earlier play are heard in the later. Oberon is very conscious of Cupid, Venus and Neptune: Titania, angry with Oberon, accuses him of 'versing love/To amorous Phillida' (II, i, 67–8). Roles are seen in similar terms. Oberon calls Helena a 'nymph' and thinks of the forest through which she is wandering as a 'grove' (II, i, 245), while Venus's reference to Cupid as an 'elf' (*Gallathea*, v, iii, 89) finds an echo both in the role Puck plays and in the 'small elves' (II, ii, 5) attendant on the fairy queen. There are similarities between the creatures who inhabit the woods of Lincolnshire and Athens. Rafe is conscious of 'screaking... owls, croaking... frogs, hissing... adders' (II, iii, 3–4) while the 'clamorous owl', 'newts and blind-worms' and 'spotted snakes with double tongue' are banished from Titania's resting place (II, ii, 6–11). The wood itself furnishes a pun in both plays: Rafe, disgusted with his fruitless fortune-hunting through the forest, exclaims 'Would I were out of these woods' (II, iii, 2) while Demetrius, frustrated by his failure to find Hermia, declares himself 'wode within this wood' (II, i, 192). The griffin is used as an object of comparison by both dramatists: the Alchemist compares his beggarly appearance and concealed wealth to the feathery exterior of the griffin whose nest is constructed from gold (II, iii, 111–13) while Helena sees her flight after Demetrius in terms of a dove's pursuit of the same mythical beast (II, i, 232). Terms of abuse are echoed: Rafe runs from the Alchemist with 'concur, condog, I will away' (III, iii, 25) while Hermia berates Demetrius with 'Out, dog, out, cur' (III, ii, 65). More tentatively, Oberon's account of the origin of the power of 'love-in-idleness' may owe something to the Cupid scenes of Lyly's play. Oberon describes how he saw:

Cupid all arm'd. A certain aim he took
At a fair vestal throned by [the] west,
And loos'd his love-shaft smartly from his bow,
As it should pierce a hundred thousand hearts;
But I might see young Cupid's fiery shaft
Quench'd in the chaste beams of the wat'ry moon,
And the imperial vot'ress passed on,
In maiden meditation, fancy-free.
(II, i, 157–64)

The passage has been taken as complimentary to Elizabeth and is in part conventional but its occurrence in this context may well derive from Shakespeare's recollections of the relationship between Cupid and Diana at the heart of Lyly's play and the earlier dramatist's presentation of the imperious virgin huntress.

The most important echoes, however, are undoubtedly heard in passages concerned with the disorder consequent upon the passions of the gods and in episodes relating to the 'translation' of irrational mortals. General resemblances between Tityrus's speech in I, i, and Titania's in II, i, have been noted already but the analogous symptoms of disorder cited by the two speakers are worthy of further comment. In both plays, wind and water work together to produce like dire effects. In *Gallathea* Neptune, 'who binds the winds in the hollows of the earth', caused 'the seas to break their bounds' (I, i, 25–6) while in *A Midsummer Night's Dream* 'the winds.../...have suck'd up from the sea/Contageous fogs; which falling in the land,/Hath every pelting river made so proud/That they have overborne their continents' (II, i, 89–92). The result, in both cases, is detrimental to the ploughman ('Then might you see...anchors cast where ploughs go' (ll. 28–9)/'The ploughman lost his sweat' (l. 94)) and productive of a state of decay rather than growth ('Then might you gather froth where now is dew, rotten weeds for sweet roses' (ll. 32–3)/ 'the green corn Hath rotted ere his youth attain'd a beard' (ll. 94–5)). And both dramatists associate this disorder with impiety (the Danes 'instead of sacrifice committed sacrilege' (l. 21)/'No night is now with hymn or carol blest' (l. 102)).[1] But by far the most convincing link between the two plays is forged by the use of the term 'translated' in related contexts. Lyly employs the word once in III, iii when Rafe, on hearing the promises of the Astronomer, declares 'I shall be translated from this mortality' and is assured that he will soon be 'hail-fellows with the gods' (ll. 78–80). The word occurs twice in *A Midsummer Night's Dream* and in both cases the linguistic and thematic contexts are similar. In III. i Bottom, ingloriously crowned with an ass's head (one might compare Rafe's stupidity), terrifies Quince into exclaiming 'Bless thee!/Thou art translated' (ll. 18–19) at the very moment Titania is about to wake, salute him as an equal, offer to 'purge his *mortal* [my italics] grossness' (l. 160) and encourage her elves to 'hail' him. The word recurs again in the following scene where the association between 'translation' and intimacy with the gods is maintained. Puck tells Oberon

> [I] left sweet Pyramus translated there;
> When in that moment (so it came to pass)
> Titania wak'd, and straightway lov'd an ass.
> (ll. 32–4)

In the face of so many correspondences (and this list is by no means exhaustive) it might not be too hazardous to suggest that Rafe's haunting remark that to be a mariner is to be 'within an inch of a thing bottomless' (I, iv, 21) may have set up reverberations in the mind of the later dramatist of which the phrase 'because it hath no bottom' (IV, i, 216) may be merely symptomatic.

That Shakespeare was both familiar with and conscious of *Gallathea* at the time when *A Midsummer Night's Dream* was composed is attested by other evidence beyond doubt. It has long been accepted that act IV, scene iii of *Love's Labour's Lost* is modelled on act III, scene i of Lyly's play[2] and critics concur in linking *Love's Labour's Lost* with *A Midsummer Night's Dream* as the last of the early comedies and the two plays written most directly under Lyly's influence. No doubt other plays by the older dramatist formed a part of that 'general reading' upon which *A Midsummer Night's Dream* was based. The epilogue seems to have been furnished by *Saphao and Phao* and the ass's head may owe something to *Midas*. But the primary influence on *A Midsummer Night's Dream* appears to be the play which, as the most brilliantly structured comedy of its period, would have

[1] It is notable that Titania refers to Neptune in her next speech where she also uses the word 'merchandise' and a trading image – both to be found in the first half of Tityrus's speech in *Gallathea*.

[2] See Hunter, *John Lyly*, pp. 340 ff. Shakespeare's familiarity with the play is also borne out by his later use of it in the mature comedies.

been most likely to appeal to a dramatist deeply concerned at this time with the projection of theme through the relationship between levels of action.

It remains to relate this paper to Ovid. Stanley Wells has recently remarked that 'There is no comprehensive study of the important influence of Ovid' on Shakespeare[1] and this lack is nowhere to be more deeply regretted than in relation to *A Midsummer Night's Dream*. The pervasive concern with 'translation' and the direct borrowing of the Pyramus and Thisby story from the *Metamorphoses* invite comparison with Ovid's work, but the nature and extent of the Roman poet's influence has remained elusive. If in fact *A Midsummer Night's Dream* is as heavily indebted to *Gallathea* as this paper has suggested much of that elusiveness may well be accounted for by the intervention of Lyly between Shakespeare and Ovid since elements of *Gallathea* themselves look back to the *Metamorphoses*.[2] Ovid's influence on Shakespeare in this play may therefore be both direct and indirect, and his concept of 'translation' filtered through more than one sensibility.

That Shakespeare's play is both different from and superior to Lyly's comedy is beyond dispute. It is a poetic drama at once richer and more profound than anything of which the earlier dramatist was capable. Like Bottom's dream it defies final critical analysis, plunging the audience into an anatomy of love and an exploration of the nature of art and reality through the most brilliantly articulated plot that Shakespeare was ever to produce. But *Gallathea* is no mean achievement. It too may claim a place among the best constructed plays of the period, it too handles love with grace and mutability with perception. It would not be surprising if Shakespeare turned to the greatest work of his most polished predecessor when constructing the finest comedy he ever wrote.

[1] *Shakespeare*, Select Bibliographical Guides (Oxford, 1973), p. 5.

[2] See Lancashire, *Gallathea and Midas*, pp. xvi–xvii.

MAKING A SCENE: LANGUAGE AND GESTURE IN 'CORIOLANUS'

JOYCE VAN DYKE

It has often been noticed that North's Plutarch describes Coriolanus as 'eloquent'[1] whereas Shakespeare has often represented him as inarticulate or at a loss for words, and has Menenius remark several times that Coriolanus is not a good speaker. Coriolanus's critics tend to agree with Menenius's judgement: 'Lacking the verbal resources and the confidence in language required for effective argument, he remains taciturn whenever possible . . . [He is] insensitive to the tone or connotative qualities of words . . . there is very little of the lyric in his speech . . . Nor does he engage in word-play'.[2] All of these statements are partially true, or true in certain circumstances, but taken together they are an inadequate description of Coriolanus as a speaker. His peculiarity is not an insensitivity to words; rather, he is uncommonly sensitive to them. For Coriolanus, words have virtually a material existence:

> As for my country I have shed my blood,
> Not fearing outward force, so shall my lungs
> Coin words till their decay . . . (III, i, 76–8)[3]

and they can register with physical impact upon him:

> I have some wounds upon me, and they smart
> To hear themselves rememb'red. (I, ix, 28–9)

To say that words are virtual things for Coriolanus perhaps does not differ much from saying he is unresponsive to 'tone or connotative qualities', to the variable nature of language, but hypersensitivity explains more about the ways he responds in linguistic situations than insensitivity does. If Aristotle's dictum that 'He that is incapable of living in a society is a god or a beast' is applicable to Coriolanus, as G. K. Hunter suggests,[4] then the linguistic implications of this statement may be applied as well. God is the figure of ultimate articulateness, whose word is (for the Christian God) materially realized, whose desires and commands are immediately enacted. (Coriolanus sometimes has this power: 'What he bids be done is finish'd with his bidding' (V, iv, 23). The beast is, at the other extreme, ultimately inarticulate, a creature whose expressive capacities are not verbal but physical, instinctual, gestural. Coriolanus, it seems to me, unites both tendencies.

The scenes which Coriolanus makes reveal his fundamentally gestural habits of response; for whether speech is god-like in its articulateness, or inarticulate, it tends to the condition of gesture, it becomes an act of pure self-expression. Coriolanus first appears in the play just after Menenius's narration of the Belly fable, and particularly after such a jocular and pacific speech our first impression of Coriolanus is

[1] *Coriolanus*, ed. Reuben Brower (New York, 1966), p. 247.

[2] James L. Calderwood, '*Coriolanus:* Wordless Meanings and Meaningless Words', *Studies in English Literature* VI (1966), 214–15.

[3] Quotations from Shakespeare are made from *The Complete Works*, ed. Peter Alexander (1951).

[4] G. K. Hunter, 'The Last Tragic Heroes', *Later Shakespeare*, *Stratford-Upon-Avon Studies 8*, (New York, 1967), p. 20.

shocking. Hereafter we are prepared for the temperament revealed in his rejection of Cominius's praises, in the corn speech, and in his response to banishment.

For the moment, it may be noted that all of these explosions occur in a context of civil, legally or ceremoniously controlled discourse, not in military action. This is not to say that Coriolanus does not express rage and impatience on the battlefield; he does, but there it is functional, not a wasted discharge. On the battlefield, Coriolanus is immensely efficient, even mechanically so. Whether or not we regard this as more horrific than ordinary human violence, Coriolanus has no bloodlust, at least, none of the sort which motivates the warriors in *Troilus and Cressida* to perform their deeds of extraordinary violence in battle. Coriolanus has no lines like Aufidius's graphic threat to

> Wash my fierce hand in's heart.
>
> (I, x, 27)

When Coriolanus extols to his troops

> this painting
> Wherein you see me smear'd
>
> (I, vi, 68–9)

the blood is appreciated for its symbolic value.

In keeping with his lack of bloodlust, he is a remarkably chaste warrior, and values the idea of chastity highly, as his apostrophe to Valeria in act V suggests. In fact he demonstrates no physical appetites, unlike Timon with his material luxuries and feasts, unlike Antony, unlike Menenius in this play, with his gustatory preoccupations. It is notable that, except for his weary call for wine after battle, in a play which concerns the problem of hunger, we never see or even hear of Coriolanus eating. All this is meant simply to suggest that if we talk of Coriolanus's violence, bestiality, passion, it ought to be recognized as a peculiarly rarefied, intellectually or idealistically determined passionateness. Or, to put it another way, he is animalistic to the degree that he is physically and instinctually responsive, but not to the point of being controlled by bestial appetites.

His first outburst reveals him as an angry man, but one whose violence of feelings finds its outlet in abstract, tightly controlled speech. His very first words perhaps tell us more about him than we consciously assimilate in the shock of their occurrence. As he enters, Menenius greets him:

> *Menenius.* Hail, noble Marcius!
> *Marcius.*
> Thanks. What's the matter, you dissentious rogues
> That, rubbing the poor itch of your opinion,
> Make yourself scabs? (I, i, 161–4)

In retrospect, it is the disjunction between the courtesy to Menenius and the insult to the people which is more shocking than the insult itself. The man who could without apparent strain accommodate those opposed feelings simultaneously, making a clean about face, yet expressing himself succinctly, is not a man who lacks verbal resources. In grammatical terms, he is a man who omits conjunctions, but this syntactical characteristic penetrates his habits of feeling and perception as well. It is not merely a soldier's taciturnity which prevents Coriolanus from introducing transitions into his speech; his habits of perception seem inherently disjunctive, and he makes this sort of abrupt reversal repeatedly.

> then we shall ha' means to vent
> Our musty superfluity. See, our best elders.
>
> (I, i, 223–4)

> these base slaves
> Ere yet the fight be done, pack up. Down with them!
> And hark, what noise the general makes! To him!
>
> (I, v, 7–9)

Such speeches suggest Coriolanus's 'pseudo-precise, black or white view of things';[1] they

[1] Calderwood, '*Coriolanus*: Wordless Meanings and Meaningless Words', p. 216.

also suggest, in the violence of their shifts from one mood to an antithetical one, a mind which will be capable of Coriolanus's apostacy.

But his language, however pseudo-precise or reductive or disjunctive it may be, is not illogical in the way that Leontes's passionate rants are. It is in fact strongly marked by parallel constructions and antitheses:

What would you have, you curs,
That like nor peace nor war? The one affrights you,
The other makes you proud. He that trusts to you,
Where he should find you lions, finds you hares;
Where foxes, geese; you are no surer, no,
Than is the coal of fire upon the ice
Or hailstone in the sun. (I, i, 166–72)

Even in the fury of his final speech to the Romans, parallelisms abound. In contrast to Menenius's narrative powers, it is clear that Coriolanus's language depends for its force on a principle of elemental repetition and accretion. R. P. Blackmur has suggested that 'any word or congeries of words can be pushed to the condition of gesture . . . by simple repetition.'[1] In such a case language loses its normal meaning and social function and tends to become more simply self-expression.

It is true that although Coriolanus seems able to articulate his thoughts in general, the logic, the communicative capacity of what he is saying, is often dissipated. For all his passionately reasonable speech about why corn should not be given gratis, the general significance of what he is saying is wasted.

Tell me of corn!
This was my speech, and I will speak't again –
(III, i, 61–2)

The entire repeated speech functions as an extravagant gesture, a repeated assertion of himself and the truth that he stands for.

It is when Coriolanus is compelled to use language as a purely symbolic form rather than a literal or gestural one that we see him inarticulate or at a loss for words:

Volumnia. I have heard you say
Honour and policy, like unsever'd friends,
I' th' war do grow together; grant that, and tell me
In peace what each of them by th' other lose
That they combine not there.
Coriolanus. Tush, tush!
Menenius. A good demand.
(III, ii, 41–5)

But if in this instance his inadequacy is glaring, why should he have admirable verbal resources and confidence in language in other situations? (i.e., insofar as he is able to express himself well: *he* may be frustrated when cursing the people, but his language is not.) How could such a man deliver the stunning speech banishing the Romans, or the biting rejoinder to the citizen who accuses him of not loving the common people? The problem is not that he lacks verbal resources, but that for him language, as a symbolic medium, seems useless for purposes of argument, which after all is intended to issue in action. Coriolanus's tendency is always to convert verbal altercations into physical ones; if words seem impotent to effect change, gestures or acts have an immediate and significant effect.

One of the reasons then that Volumnia is always victorious is that Coriolanus is literally not able to argue with her. At the start of their final interview, he begs of her (and it seems an admission of just this vulnerability):

Do not bid me
Dismiss my soldiers, or capitulate
Again with Rome's mechanics. Tell me not
Wherein I seem unnatural; desire not
T'allay my rages and revenges with
Your colder reasons. (V, iii, 81–6)

Do not argue with me for I will not be able to refute you.

Coriolanus's answer in the first scene to the

[1] R. P. Blackmur, *Language as Gesture* (New York, 1935), p. 13.

people's charge finally proves to be inexpressible in language.

> They say there's grain enough!
> Would the nobility lay aside their ruth
> And let me use my sword. (I, i, 194–6)

Action is eloquence, Coriolanus could say, appropriating his mother's phrase. Gesture is the only truly satisfactory mode of expression because it is both literal and symbolic; bodily movements are actual in themselves and they have significance, for they express the inner man. And gesture is a sufficient mode of communication if, as Coriolanus believes, that which it is important to express consists of a number of simple, stable truths. If gesture is the essential mode of expression, if physical posture and movement are the outward signs of an inward state, as is the case for the soldier whose swordblows are the expression of his patriotism, then it is no surprise that the corruption of gesture, the 'body's action', involves corruption of the mind and can teach it a 'most inherent baseness' (III, ii, 122–3).

There are two more features of Coriolanus's language which recur when he makes scenes and these are cursing and trigger response. Cursing and its analogue, praying (which Coriolanus also does frequently[1]), are the verbal expressions of a desired action which it is beyond the power of the speaker to accomplish. Both thus can be seen as a use of language as a substitute for action or gesture. It is only the gods who have the superhuman power to fulfil curses and prayers. Coriolanus curses the Romans when he is banished, but he could only realize the verbal gesture of his curse, as he nearly does, by denying his own humanity.

When talking to Menenius about the people in the first scene, his repetitive curses punctuate his speech like a tic, expressing a consistent emotion which is an undercurrent to the momentary discourse riding above it. There is a difference between this frustrated, abbreviated, apparently inadvertent cursing and the full-blown imaginative cursing he does when directly addressing the object of his anger. This difference in fluency can perhaps be explained by the fact that in the first case, discursive language keeps collapsing into the more natural mode of gesture, whereas in the second case, language *is* gesture, the two are fused as completely as is possible.

When he is not exploding into periodic curses under the constraints of ordinary discourse, Coriolanus often treats language as gesture in another way. Certain words seem to have such an impact on him that he cannot assimilate them, and he throws them back at the speaker as if he were returning a hurled weapon. Such an instance occurs in the first scene when Menenius voices the people's desire:

> *Menenius.*
> For corn at their own rates, whereof they say
> The city is well stor'd.
> *Marcius.* Hang 'em! They say!
> They'll sit by th' fire and presume to know
> What's done i' th' Capitol,
> ... They say there's grain enough!
> (I, i, 187–90, 194)

This sort of harping upon a word or phrase seems to have, or attempt, a curative, purgative function, especially if we recollect Coriolanus's own equation of words and wounds. For all the words which thus provoke him are words that threaten to wound either him or the state. The whole of his final speech to the Romans is simply an elaboration of this sort of habitual response. To their 'banished' he retorts in kind, and then rephrases it in terms of a symbolic gesture:

> Despising
> For you the city, thus I turn my back;
> (III, iii, 135–6).

Such responses are utterly predictable, and

[1] e.g., I, iv, 10–12; III, ii, 33–7; V, iii, 70–4.

indeed it has often been noticed that there is a virtual automatism in the way he responds. Michael Goldman, for example, says that 'As Antony is the most unpredictable, Coriolanus is the most predictable of men' like a 'mechanical toy'.[1] There seems to us something petty and childlike in such automatism, but I think it is a distortion of Coriolanus to see him strictly in these terms. He is a man of deeply ingrained habits of thinking and feeling, and his automatism is not a senseless mechanical response. It is closer to the automatic (in other words, the instinctual) response which an animal makes to a provocation which touches it at the profoundest levels of life.

I have been trying to suggest some of the ways in which Coriolanus typically expresses himself; part of the way we perceive him is also via the responses from his immediate audiences. We receive a number of reports which suggest that the effect of his looks, tone of voice, and posture is potent: there is language in his very gesture. Brutus and Sicinius remember 'his lip and eyes' (I, i, 253) when they were chosen tribunes; Lartius commends the fear created in his enemies by 'thy grim looks' and the 'thunder-like percussion of thy sounds' (I, iv, 59–60); Brutus says of the triumphant Coriolanus that it is

> As if that whatsoever god who leads him
> Were slily crept into his human powers,
> And gave him graceful posture.
>
> (II, i, 209–11)

After Coriolanus receives the vote of the people, Sicinius says,

> He has it now; and by his looks methinks
> 'Tis warm at's heart. (II, iii, 148–9)

Menenius later says of Coriolanus:

> Yet to bite his lip
> And hum at good Cominius much unhearts me.
>
> (V, i, 48–9)

And Cominius tells how he was dismissed 'Thus with his speechless hand.' (V, i, 67). The climax of these descriptions of Coriolanus (and this list is by no means exhaustive) comes in Menenius's grotesque catalogue in act V, scene iv. It seems clear that if, as Menenius says, 'What his breast forges, that his tongue must vent' (III, i, 258), his facial and body movements must vent his feelings as well.

In the scenes Coriolanus makes, we see an interaction between himself and the crowd which involves the wavelike systolic-diastolic rhythm Goldman describes.[2] The action of wave and repulse does not concern bodies only though: it is also created by verbal assaults and repudiations. People are always impinging upon Coriolanus, literally and figuratively, and he is always pushing them away. In act I, scene ix, Cominius begins by conjuring up the Roman audience which will hear him report Coriolanus's deeds. Then Lartius enters with a real audience, and begins to swell the praise. Coriolanus repeatedly tries to silence all of them, but by accident he himself enlarges the encomiastic audience. He protests,

> [I] stand upon my common part with those
> That have beheld the doing.
>
> (I, ix, 39–40)

The commons, responding to this as an appeal to themselves, create a commotion, throwing up their caps. This is the limit of pressure; Coriolanus explodes, and he does so into the oaths, curses, the gestural language which we have seen as typical.

Coriolanus has just made his appearance as consul in act III, scene i when the tribunes block his path, and their opposition sets him off again. This time the brakes are applied by his auditors: Menenius, Cominius, the Senators, even the tribunes once they think Coriolanus has said enough to damn himself, try repeat-

[1] Michael Goldman, *Shakespeare and the Energies of Drama* (Princeton, 1972), p. 118.

[2] *Ibid.*, pp. 112–16.

edly to silence him. But his vehemence is aroused by verbal pinpricks as we have seen earlier, and from each attempted interruption he gains new impetus. Shakespeare found most of his text for the corn speech in Plutarch, where it occurs as a single, apparently uninterrupted speech. But his rendering of it in this scene makes it much more than a position statement by Coriolanus. What Coriolanus is speaking *about* is what he considers to be the abrogation of order within the state, fomented by the people and the tribunes, condoned by the patricians – caused in fact by everyone. But to his audience, it is Coriolanus who is disrupting order, making a scene when the appropriate thing to do would be to go on to the marketplace and 'answer by a lawful form', (III, i, 325) as Menenius says. Ironically, when for once he wants his words and his logic to register, the gestural aspect of his speech predominates; what he is doing is so much more significant to his audience than what he is saying, that his most eloquent, emotionally charged statements fall on deaf ears:

Coriolanus. . . . and my soul aches
To know, when two authorities are up,
Neither supreme, how soon confusion
May enter 'twixt the gap of both and take
The one by th' other.
Cominius. Well, on to th' market-place.
(III, i, 108–12)

We can say that Coriolanus has no sense of timing, that it would be impolitic for Cominius to encourage him in the presence of the tribunes. But the problem is that Coriolanus takes the threat of disorder and ruin of the state personally. Menenius may tell the fable of the Belly, illustrating that the life of the body politic must imitate the life of the human body, but it is Coriolanus who says 'my soul aches' when he perceives a threat to the life of the state. There is a peculiarly vulnerable tone to these lines, almost a revelation of nakedness, and A. P. Rossiter picks them out as 'heart-felt' but somehow felt by Shakespeare, who puts them 'in Marcius' mouth'.[1] I see no reason not to credit Coriolanus with all the feeling that lies behind them. If we see him as a man for whom the sense of ordered and stable relationships, in the state and in the family, is supremely important, then it is perfectly in character for him to make such a statement and such a scene. I don't think it is an exaggeration to say that while the verbal substance of this speech defends the life of the state, the gesture that it makes in the act of delivery defends the identity of the man. For Coriolanus defines his identity by Rome and Rome's ideals, as he conceives them. Antony's character may be called unpredictable or large or magnanimous – the words suggest that he carries resources within himself, and for Antony, to be Antony is primarily a personal matter involving his own will and his relationship with Cleopatra. But for Coriolanus, to be Coriolanus requires the existence and co-operation of a viable Roman state; it is only bravado which declares that there is a world elsewhere.

Coriolanus is not the only person who makes scenes in the play. Virgilia too makes a scene, without any show of temper, yet one which shows how closely attuned her nature is to her husband's. Act I, scene iii begins with Volumnia's energetic speeches about Coriolanus in battle, rising to a rather grotesque pitch in this quiet domestic context. But then Valeria enters and the conversation descends to small talk, marked only by Virgilia's strange obstinacy in refusing to go out with the other women. Strange, because the request seems normal, and because Virgilia gives no reasons:

Valeria. Fie, you confine yourself most unreasonably; come, you must go visit the good lady that lies in.
Virgilia. I will wish her speedy strength, and visit her with my prayers; but I cannot go thither.

[1] A. P. Rossiter, *Angel With Horns*, (New York, 1961), p. 243.

Volumnia. Why, I pray you?
Virgilia. 'Tis not to save labour, nor that I want love.
(I, iii, 76–81)

When Virgilia says I *cannot* go (and she refuses six times), it sounds to the other women like an absurd exaggeration. What she really means, it seems to them, is that she doesn't want to go, and Valeria even accuses her of being a duplicitous Penelope. But Virgilia means it literally. Valeria has commanded,

Come, lay aside your stitchery; I must have you play the idle huswife with me this afternoon.
(I, iii, 69–70)

But Virgilia is solemn, as both the others complain; she is concerned about her husband, a concern which must have been recently aggravated by Volumnia's bloody imaginings, and she cannot 'play the idle huswife' at anyone's request. Valeria tries to bribe her with the promise of news, but Virgilia has made a vow and will not budge. In her own fashion, she proves herself as stubborn as her husband, but the significance of her refusal of the ladies is that she will sacrifice their opinion to her own integrity. She will not 'play' the woman she is not, even though to refuse is a disagreeably disobedient act for her. Coriolanus, of course, exhibits the same character to an even more marked extent.

II

Coriolanus does not have much of a sense of play. We have very few glimpses of him when he is not in the thick of very serious matters, but we do get one early in the play which warns us of his habitual earnestness. Coriolanus and Lartius are with the troops before Corioli, watching a messenger arrive. They wager their horses on what the news will be, and Coriolanus loses.

Lartius. So, the good horse is mine.
Marcius. I'll buy him of you.
Lartius.
No, I'll nor sell nor give him; lend you him I will
For half a hundred years. (I, iv, 5–7)

Even a wager made to pass time before battle Coriolanus takes completely seriously; for him, the wager is literal, a bond with material consequences, whereas Lartius's banter emphasizes its insubstantial nature. Coriolanus only engages in wordplay when he is in disguise, wearing the gown of humility or the 'mean apparel' he appears in at Aufidius's house. In both cases he begins to speak ironically, mocking himself and his audience, making plays on words, all in all behaving most uncharacteristically. This wittiness is an indication of his own discomfort; and its apparently compulsory nature suggests, to adapt Coriolanus's phrase, that the body's action is teaching the mind a most inherent ironic attitude. Under the constraint of unnatural appearance and action, his language assumes strange disguises and facetious appearances as well.

Coriolanus, under ordinary circumstances, is playing the man he is (III, ii, 15–6), by which I think he means that he is behaving naturally, being true to himself, but also that he is quite conscious that this is what he is doing. We have noted how responsive the public is to Coriolanus's appearance. He too seems frequently aware of the impression he is making, especially when he thinks that that impression might be misleading. He draws attention to any divergence between his being and seeming, and attempts to reconcile them: though I seem to be thus, I am really thus and so. There are numerous examples of this situation. When Coriolanus meets Aufidius at Corioli, battle-weary and covered with blood, he hastens to represent himself as a threatening opponent:

Within these three hours, Tullus,
Alone I fought in your Corioli walls,
And made what work I pleas'd. 'Tis not my blood
Wherein thou seest me mask'd. (I, viii, 7–10)

He tells the citizens, when they ask why he is standing for their voices, that his 'desert' not, as they may suppose, his 'desire' has brought him there (II, iii, 64–6). In his farewell to his mother, he assures her that he is still her son: she will hear nothing 'But what is like me formerly' (IV, i, 53),

> – though I go alone,
> Like to a lonely dragon, that his fen
> Makes fear'd and talk'd of more than seen –
> (IV, i, 29–31).

Conscious of the mean disguise in which he seeks Aufidius's hospitality, he says,

> A goodly house, The feast smells well, but I
> Appear not like a guest. (IV, v, 5–6)

And as he is about to name himself, to assume his true form, he prompts Aufidius to make a consistent response: 'Prepare thy brow to frown' (IV, v, 63). Coriolanus reports to the Volscians that for Menenius's

> old love I have –
> Though I show'd sourly to him – once more offer'd
> The first conditions. (V, iii, 12–14)

The same discomfiture which provokes such remarks is in little that which provokes his violent outbursts at being called traitor or boy. He is enraged at the possibility that he could seem to be a boy when in fact (even in the annals) he is a hero; he insists upon seeming what he is.

It is not surprising then that some of the most notable scenes Coriolanus makes concern just this situation. Menenius asks him, just as Valeria requested Virgilia, to perform a normal, customary act, and Coriolanus responds just as his wife had responded:

> I do beseech you
> Let me o'erleap that custom; for I cannot
> Put on the gown. (II, ii, 133–5).

To Menenius, the protest is nonsense or petulance, but to Coriolanus it is an occasion on which he fully expects that to the people he will seem what he is not; he will show them his scars which they will perceive

> As if I had received them for the hire
> Of their breath only! (II, ii, 147–8).

He not only anticipates the event as playing a part, he anticipates gesture, words, and audience response, all the trappings of a role. When the approach of the citizens is imminent, he stands in the gown of humility 'rehearsing' what he must perform:

> What must I say?
> 'I pray, sir' – Plague upon't! I cannot bring
> My tongue to such a pace. 'Look, sir, my wounds!
> I got them in my country's service, when
> Some certain of your brethren roar'd, and ran
> From the noise of our own drums.'
> (II, iii, 48–53)

The rehearsal quickly modulates from prescription to an ironic undercutting of his 'lines', and the tone he achieves here is sustained during his encounter with the people.

Throughout, Coriolanus attempts to withdraw as far as possible from the part he is constrained to play. His language sophistically suggests to the people that he is playing up to them when he is clearly demonstrating his disdain, 'I have here the customary gown' (II, iii, 84), he says, as though he were holding it at arm's length. He holds the people at arm's length too; instead of performing his ritual obligations and instead of ingratiating himself, he says he *will* do so, conjuring up a degraded future image of himself: 'since the wisdom of their choice is rather to have my hat than my heart, I will practise the insinuating nod and be off to them most counterfeitly' (II, iii, 95–6). As one of the citizens says, 'But this is something odd' (II, iii, 80). Quite probably, as Coriolanus is promising to take his hat off to them in this ingratiating fashion, the citizens are perceiving that what he is actually doing is waving it in scorn, as one complains later on.

The ritual act of wearing the gown of humility dictates what Coriolanus must do here, and he is not inherently opposed to custom and ceremony; he is proud to wear the oaken garland, and to receive the name Coriolanus. But his next role is harder to accept, and it is dictated only by policy. The mutiny in the marketplace which he aroused in part by playing the man he is, is now to be appeased by his assumption of an artificial role. Everyone recognizes the 'lawful form' Menenius has requested as an occasion for acting. Volumnia, backed up by Menenius and Cominius, becomes a prompter and director.

Volumnia's argument is essentially that performing a part is not difficult or perverted but easy and quite natural. We have just heard Menenius say 'His heart's his mouth' (III, i, 257) but Volumnia strives to separate the two. His heart is what 'prompts' his tongue; Coriolanus normally speaks 'by [his] own instruction' (III, ii, 54–4). Even natural speech thus is described as a response to prompting, to rehearsal, as opposed to Coriolanus's automatic responses. It is not much different in operation then from false-speaking, in which the tongue is also instructed, but by another agent.

Volumnia's rhetoric dismembers heart and mouth, but when Coriolanus decides to take the part, he views it as a total fracturing of identity, the destruction of 'This mould of Marcius' (III, ii, 103). Just as before, he anticipates himself in the role, and responding to his mother's gestural directions, anticipates or rehearses what he must do. (Volumnia's directions call for a gesticulating, flattering, puppet-like Coriolanus perilously like the one he conjured up to mock the citizens.)

Well, I must do't.
Away, my disposition, and possess me
Some harlot's spirit! My throat of war be turn'd,
Which quier'd with my drum, into a pipe
Small as an eunuch or the virgin voice
That babies lulls asleep! The smiles of knaves
Tent in my cheeks, and schoolboys' tears take up
The glasses of my sight! A beggar's tongue
Make motion through my lips, and my arm'd knees,
Who bow'd but in my stirrup, bend like his
That hath receiv'd an alms! (III, ii, 110–20)

This catalogue of disjunct entities – harlot, eunuch, virgin, knaves, schoolboys, beggar – demonstrates the complete confusion of identity which acting entails for him. (The confusion of identity is no longer even human when Coriolanus next assumes disguise: like an asocial animal, he dwells under the canopy in the country of kites and crows.) It is a grotesque vision, and so eloquently grotesque that in speaking it, Coriolanus persuades himself that he cannot go through with the part. The speech is virtually a string of curses, and by the end of it he indeed realizes that to accept such a role would be to accomplish his own damnation.

If we have seen in these scenes that Coriolanus considers acting and disguise to be fearful and self-destructive, what then must be the effect of his entry in act IV, scene iv '*in mean apparel, disguis'd and muffled*' (IV, iv)? (The disguise is in Plutarch, but the prior emphasis on Coriolanus's attitude to disguise is not.) Surely this voluntary assumption of a beggar-like disguise is a potent visual suggestion that something in the man himself, not just in his circumstances, has changed. His own explanation that the disguise is expedient is rather remarkable in light of the fact that we have just watched him allow himself to be banished, rather than speak one expedient fair word. And the irony is that here there is no need to be expedient. There is a comic pathos in the very idea of the hero making allowance for the 'wives with spits and boys with stones' (IV, iv, 5) who would try to slay him, and in his certainty that disguise is necessary to avoid recognition, since it becomes absurdly clear from his treatment by the servants and Aufidius that no one has the faintest idea who he is. If hitherto Coriolanus insisted he could not perform a part without destroying or degrading himself, are we to understand that now he can assume a disguise because he has been destroyed?

Part of the difficulty in assessing Coriolanus's response to banishment is that he offers such scant assessment of the situation himself. When Antony flees at Actium, he recognizes that his dishonourable act has in some sense destroyed him, and although he rallies, as he does from the actual suicide blow, he repeatedly returns to the realization of the present difficulty or impossibility of being Antony. Now the great hero must

> To the young man send humble treaties, dodge
> And palter in the shifts of lowness,
> (*Ant. & Cleo.*, III, xi, 62–3).

This is exactly what we see Coriolanus doing and yet his own verbal responses seem grossly inadequate to his circumstances. Look at his analysis of what has happened. In soliloquy he discusses the revolutions of fortune: inseparable friends 'On a dissension of a doit' become enemies, while enemies 'by some chance,/Some trick not worth an egg' (IV, iv, 17–21) become allied. The generalization clearly refers to his own situation, yet there is a curious depreciation or suppression of the cause of change, as if there were no real connection between one state and another. Here we see again Coriolanus's disjunctive habit of perception, but in this case the transition he deprecates happens to be the most violent and earth-shaking experience of his life. His lack of response seems to reveal a deadness of feeling which is not mitigated by the violence of his statement to Aufidius when he has unmuffled, for he offers to fight against Rome or to present his throat to Aufidius's knife as equal alternatives (and it is one of the ironies fulfilled by the play that in fact they are identical choices). His banishment from Rome, his loss of the political and familial orders which defined him, have mortally stricken Coriolanus, and though he may not speak of his wounds, his altered behaviour reveals them.

This incident is not his only voluntary assumption of a disguise or role subsequent to banishment. He also deliberately 'shows sourly' to Menenius: he pretends to be divorced from his family, though he fails 'Like a dull actor' (V, iii, 40); he enters Corioli greeting the lords of the city as a triumphant hero even though he has confessed to Aufidius that he has been forced to compromise. Laurence Kitchin's very interesting review of a Memorial Theatre production with Laurence Olivier suggests that Coriolanus can very plausibly be played along the lines that his beggarly disguise initially suggests, and that this scene shows us the beginning of his disintegration.[1]

The behaviour of Aufidius's servants to him recapitulates Coriolanus's banishment from Rome; as he notices,

> I have deserv'd no better entertainment
> In being Coriolanus.
> (IV, v, 9–10)

The servants keep trying to rid the house of a nuisance, while he echoes their words and gestures of banishment, once pushing and once beating them away. Subsequent to his banishment from Rome, we can see Coriolanus's behaviour as one long reactive series, pushing

[1] Laurence Kitchin, *Mid-Century Drama* (1960), p. 144: 'There was no doubt at all where the play's climax comes. It is on the sealing of their pact, or so I shall always believe after Olivier's extraordinary handshake. He had been very quiet during the scene. There was a deathly, premonitory misgiving in the way he eventually shook hands; and his eyes were glazed. Whatever integration the character of Marcius had possessed fell apart at that moment. The rest was crumble, detonation and collapse, with part of him fatalistically detached.'

away the servants, dismissing Cominius, saying 'Away!' (v, ii, 76) to Menenius as well, physically turning away from his family, and again turning away from Rome even as he had first turned his back.

In their last confrontation, Coriolanus attempts to face Volumnia

> As if a man were author of himself
> And knew no other kin. (v, iii, 36–7)

He is performing a part, in other words, and this time it is Volumnia's task to persuade him to be a natural man again, to be Coriolanus, her son, a Roman. He is also, however, in performing this part, being true to himself, to the vow he has made and his sworn loyalty to the Volscians. He is hopelessly divided against himself: witness the fact that now it is not play-acting which he thinks would make him effeminate and childlike, but natural behaviour, obedience to instinct, which would make him a 'gosling' (v, iii, 35) or 'of a woman's tenderness' (v, iii, 129).

Previously, Coriolanus has proved himself a most unable actor, particularly in the matter of gesticulation, since gesture is for him the mode of expression least susceptible to corruption by the will or intellect. Volumnia (and her party), arguing for the natural man, has all the influence of this potent form of expression on her side, while Coriolanus has only his verbal and intellectual resolve to counter it with. It is their physical presence and gestures which move him; Coriolanus melts, in fact, before a word has been exchanged, at the sight of Virgilia, his mother's bow, his son's 'aspect of intercession' (v, iii, 32). The instinct he swears he will not obey has been throughout the overriding motive for all his conduct, including his turn against Rome, and it cannot now be wilfully ignored.

The scene begins with a series of ceremonially heightened gestures: Coriolanus's embrace of Virgilia; his salute to his mother by kneeling; Volumnia's reciprocation of that gesture; Coriolanus's lyric apostrophe to Valeria; his benediction of his son; and the boy's genuflection in response. Once Coriolanus has turned to her, it is Volumnia who orchestrates these exchanges, confirming relationships. Her first long plea is full of bodily and gestural images of the sort which must impress themselves on Coriolanus's imagination: she offers him the alternative images of himself led manacled through Rome or treading triumphantly on his mother's womb. Then, when she finds she must yet intensify her plea, she does so by emphasizing the immediate, their physical presence, their actions as pleaders, and finally by acting, directing and interpreting dramatic gesture for Coriolanus who is the unwilling audience:

> He turns away.
> Down, ladies; let us shame him with our knees.
> To his surname Coriolanus' longs more pride
> Than pity to our prayers. Down. An end;
> This is the last. So we will home to Rome,
> And die among our neighbours. Nay, behold's!
> This boy, that cannot tell what he would have
> But kneels and holds up hands for fellowship,
> Does reason our petition with more strength
> Than thou hast to deny't. Come, let us go.
> (v, iii, 168–77)

The impact of such a reversal must be breathtaking to Coriolanus. After insisting by word and gesture during the entire course of the scene on the physical and emotional bonds between him and themselves, and at this climactic moment of unified gestural appeal, Volumnia rises, snaps the bond, and denies the existence of any relationship whatsoever:

> This fellow had a Volscian to his mother;
> His wife is in Corioli, and his child
> Like him by chance.
> (v, iii, 178–80)

It is that denial and withdrawal which finally provokes Coriolanus's instinctive response; his hand binds her to him.

Though we see Coriolanus fail 'like a dull actor' in the face of his family's appeal, his inability to act is no longer the converse, as it once was, of the absolute integrity of his character. If there is no longer such a strain between playing a role and playing the man he is, it is because the man he is is no longer a clearly definable entity. Certainly he is no longer the singular incomparable hero, for after he has conceded to Volumnia, he asks,

> Were you in my stead, would you have heard
> A mother less, or granted less, Aufidius?
>
> (v, iii, 192–3)

With its appeal for emotional support, and its implication that he is behaving as any other man would have behaved, such a question is startlingly new for Coriolanus.

His failure to act the solitary hero has led to an admission of his common humanity. As an ordinary man, no longer exalted by a proud idealistic integrity, he is groping towards the ordinary man's refuge: the capacity to pose, to act, to be politic. After his banishment Coriolanus can no longer play the man he is, but because of this very loss of integrity he can play a role; and the role he plays upon re-entering Corioli is that of the man he once was.

He enters Corioli with fanfare and the public adulation which previously had been repugnant to him. Here, he offers no such response; the stage direction reads that 'the Commoners [are] with him'. Coriolanus's speech to the lords of the city rings unbearably hollow: it poses as a tale of the triumphs Coriolanus used to tell, or rather which he heard told of him. But there is no triumph involved; there is instead political rhetoric:

> You are to know
> That prosperously I have attempted, and
> With bloody passage led your wars even to
> The gates of Rome. Our spoils we have brought home
> Doth more than counterpoise a full third part
> The charges of the action. We have made peace
> With no less honour to the Antiates
> Than shame to th' Romans;
>
> (v, vi, 74–81)

His real glory and real triumph lie in the past, when he *was* Coriolanus, and it is to this he reverts when he is insulted. The oaths, exclamations, acts, all of the last scene which Coriolanus makes, must be seen as the shadow of his earlier scenes, for his furious indignation is no longer pure self-defense or pure self-expression. At the last, crying out to use his sword, it is what is written in the annals, the historically recorded Coriolanus, which his gesture would defend.

FREEDOM AND LOSS IN 'THE TEMPEST'

CLIFFORD SISKIN

When Leontes gazes upon the statue of his wife in the last scene of *The Winter's Tale*, his initial reaction is not one of unrestrained wonder:

> But yet, Paulina,
> Hermione was not so much wrinkled, nothing
> So agèd as this seems. (v, iii, 27–9)

This unblinking perception of old age inextricably blends the miraculous with a sense of loss. Despite the brilliant spectacle of a younger generation coming to maturity, Shakespeare continues to focus on the problematic situation of their parents. As in *Pericles*, he moves beyond the recovery of the lost child to stress the renewal of the older generation; the reunion of husband and wife culminates both plays. Not until Thaisa is recovered does Pericles proclaim: 'You gods, your present kindness/Makes my past miseries sports' (v, iii, 39–40). Similarly, Leontes's redemption requires Hermione's resurrection; Shakespeare concentrates his, and our, energies on that act by placing the father–daughter recognition scene off-stage.

Northrop Frye classifies this tendency to contain the action of the play within 'the shadow of an older generation' as a structural technique common to all Shakespearian romances. He claims that 'everything' in *The Tempest* 'is subordinated to the return of Prospero'.[1] Thus the recovery of Prospero's dukedom parallels Pericles's reunion with Thaisa and Leontes's reconciliation with Hermione.

If Prospero's reward is to be as revivifying, then a great deal of stress must be placed on the political significance of the plot. The Caliban–Stephano–Trinculo and Antonio–Sebastian conspiracies undoubtedly reenact the events in Milan twelve years earlier, providing Prospero with the opportunity to demonstrate convincingly his new political acumen. An undercurrent throughout the play, however, suggests that his most profound concerns lie elsewhere. For example, as Michael Goldman has observed, there is a curious twist to the argument of the 'revels' speech. If Prospero was truly immersed in the real-life problems of politics he might have been expected to offer a slice of conventional wisdom:

> Don't worry, this is an illusion, and now I have to turn to something real; life is serious, though under control, and we must put aside vanities. But this is not what he says, and in fact there is little reason to be disturbed by the threat Caliban poses, as the audience knows.[2]

Instead, stressing his age and 'infirmity', he articulates a haunting vision of life as dream and illusion; he appears strangely disturbed, as if forced to confront a formidable dilemma. Prospero manifests this unsettled feeling in his somewhat severe behavior towards Miranda and Ariel in the opening scenes, his treatment of Ferdinand, the strange manner in which he interrupts the wedding masque, and, most explicitly, in the statement: 'Every third

[1] Northrop Frye, *A Natural Perspective: The Development of Shakespearean Comedy and Romance* (New York, 1965), pp. 87–8.

[2] Michael Goldman, *Shakespeare and the Energies of Drama* (Princeton, 1972), p. 144.

thought shall be my grave' (v, i, 312). Critical explanations for his morbid demeanor have ranged from an uncontrollable desire for revenge to the 'poverty of the plot'.[1]

Almost universally ignored has been *The Tempest*'s unique handling of the two fundamental relationships to which Shakespeare clearly attached special significance: husband–wife and father–daughter. Prospero's wife is only mentioned once (in a humorous context: I, ii, 56–7) during the entire play, and we assume that she is dead;[2] in fact, Miranda is the only human female who appears on stage. Thus Prospero is deprived of the possibility of a renewing reunion with his wife. His dukedom may provide some satisfaction, but it certainly fails to carry the emotional and redemptive impact of a Hermione. Like Leontes, Prospero cannot dismiss sorrow and age, but he wants the consolation miraculously provided for his counterpart: 'the sweet'st companion that e'er man / Bred his hopes out of' (*The Winter's Tale* v, i, 11–12).

Because there has been no previous separation between father and daughter, *The Tempest* also lacks a Periclean recognition scene. In a profound turn-about from his earlier romances, Shakespeare uses Prospero and Miranda to explore the dynamics not of recovery, but of loss: a father yielding up his daughter to her husband. Although a less dramatic separation than those described in *Pericles* or *The Winter's Tale*, it is an equally agonizing one, and a problem of apparently absorbing interest to Shakespeare. Lear's estrangement from reality, for instance, originates in a tragic inability to cope with Cordelia's avowal that the 'lord whose hand must take my plight shall carry/ Half my love with me, half my care and duty' (I, i, 103–4). This universal human dilemma informs *King Lear* and *The Tempest*; both plays anchor their myriad concerns in the bedrock of familial passion.

Although Shakespeare plants Prospero's rocky isle with the greenery of romance, it is misleading to see *The Tempest* as basically a repetition, within a new form, of its immediate predecessors.[3] The burden of Prospero's past is not the loss of a wife and daughter, but the unnatural betrayal that forced him out of his dukedom; reunion and reconciliation do not occur within the familiar romance patterns. But political victory and renewed friendships cannot remedy the fundamental isolation of a widower, who, even as he prepares to reveal the culminating miracle of young love, exclaims: 'I/Have lost my daughter.' By examining *The Tempest* in terms of that loss, its profound nature can be comprehended without resorting to the extravagant allegorical speculations marring much of the previous criticism.

The 'accident most strange' (I, ii, 178) which brings Alonso and his party into Prospero's power was the marriage of Claribel to the King of Tunis. According to Sebastian, she did so against her will, and the king himself seems to regret his action:

> Would I had never
> Married my daughter there! For, coming thence,
> My son is lost; and, in my rate, she too,

[1] John P. Cutts, *Rich and Strange: A Study of Shakespeare's Last Plays* (Pullman, Washington, 1968), pp. 86–105. E. E. Stoll, '*The Tempest*', in *Twentieth Century Interpretations of 'The Tempest'*, ed. Hallett Smith (Englewood Cliffs, 1969), p. 33.

[2] The seemingly irrelevant references to 'widow Dido' and 'widower Aeneas' (II, i, 79–106) might be related to the crucial fact that Prospero is a widower and therefore deprived of the possibility of a renewing reunion with his wife.

[3] Stanley Wells, for instance, recognizes structural differences between *The Tempest* and the earlier romances, but his observation that 'the story works toward reunion, reconciliation, and the happy conclusion of the love affair' distracts him from the major thematic reorientation implied by that change (Stanley Wells, 'Shakespeare and Romance', in *Later Shakespeare*, Stratford-upon-Avon Studies 8, ed. John Russell Brown and Bernard Harris [New York, 1967], p. 70).

Who is so far from Italy removed
I ne'er again shall see her. (II, i, 112–16)

His feelings for his son, however, render him generally apathetic to her fate. Prospero, on the other hand, who has no son and whose relationship with his daughter has been intensified by their isolation, is passionately heedful of Miranda and her marital possibilities. He affirms his preoccupation early in the play: 'I have done nothing but in care of thee,/Of thee my dear one, thee my daughter' (I, ii, 16–17). To Ferdinand he reveals: 'I/Have given you here a third of mine own life,/Or that for which I live' (IV, i, 2–4).

This arithmetic is echoed in the final scene. After seeing their 'nuptial' in Naples he will return 'to my Milan, where/Every third thought shall be my grave'; the idea of separation from Miranda, who is a third of his life, turns his every third thought towards death. The remaining two thirds of Prospero's life have engendered much speculation. Frank Kermode's list of possibilities in the Arden Shakespeare omits the most obvious answer;[1] Prospero is most likely referring to the three beings with whom he dwells: Miranda (the daughter), Ariel (the 'chick,' meaning 'child') and Caliban (the 'bastard'). Even if inapplicable to this specific arithmetical context, however, this familial pattern does place Prospero's actions within a structure sustained throughout the play. The Duke of Milan's dealings with his two 'adopted' charges, in fact, are the means by which his internal tensions concerning the loss of his real daughter can best be understood.

Shakespeare initially links Ariel and Miranda[2] by introducing them in the same scene with remarkably similar techniques. An overwrought Prospero demands Miranda's absolute attention as he recounts her past. Ignoring her protestations of interest, continually chiding her for a lack of concern which we have little reason to believe is present, he seems at certain points to disregard her responses altogether:

Prospero.
Mark his condition, and th' event; then tell me
If this might be a brother.
Miranda. I should sin
To think but nobly of my grandmother.
Good wombs have borne bad sons.
Prospero. Now the condition. (I, ii, 117–20)

Treating Ariel in much the same manner, Prospero berates his child, rejecting any response in order to make his point:

Dost thou forget
From what a torment I did free thee?
Ariel. No.
Prospero. Thou dost. (I, ii, 250–2)

By freeing Ariel from the 'knotty entrails' of a pine, Prospero has given him a second life; in return, Ariel must serve out a term of service. The mechanics of the relationship echo *King Lear*: Cordelia serves her father according to her 'bond, no more nor less' (I, i, 95). Once she reaches a certain age she must be freed from total servitude to take a husband.

Ariel also desires to be free. But what does freedom mean to a spirit? Ariel is not exhausted by his tasks, and he certainly does not harbor the physical desires of a Caliban; in fact, he seems to enjoy his work and love his master. Yet he remains deeply committed to eventual liberation, his very insistence demanding a precise appreciation of Shakespeare's use of the word 'free'. Two meanings are especially relevant: 'emancipation from some type of bondage' and 'innocence'. The distinction turns on the possibility of an innocence produced by emancipation from the corrupting influence of the past.

Such an ambiguity informs the famous

[1] William Shakespeare, *The Tempest*, ed. Frank Kermode (1954), p. 93.

[2] In Frye's structural analysis of the romances, Ariel, as an 'Eros' figure, is linked to Miranda, as an 'Andromeda' figure (Frye, *A Natural Perspective*, pp. 90–1).

Dover Cliffs scene of *King Lear*. Having just been convinced that the gods have saved him from a terrible fall, Gloucester exclaims:

I do remember now: henceforth I'll bear
Affliction till it do cry out itself
'Enough, enough,' and die. That thing you speak of,
I took it for a man; often 'twould say
'The fiend, the fiend' – he led me to that place.
(IV, vi, 75–9)

Edgar replies: 'Bear free and patient thoughts.' Russell Fraser, in his Signet edition, apparently believes that 'free' refers to the first part of Gloucester's statement, and so glosses the word as 'emancipated from grief and despair, which fetter the soul'.[1] G. B. Harrison and Robert F. McDonnell, however, in their Harcourt sourcebook, suggest that Edgar is referring to the second part of his father's statement, in that he will not yet reveal to Gloucester that he was the 'fiend' who led him to the cliff; they define 'free' as 'innocent'.[2]

A similarly ambiguous use of the word carries crucial implications for *The Winter's Tale*. Hermione has just given birth to Perdita, and Paulina decides to take the babe to Leontes in the hope that it will end his jealous rage. As she tries to leave the jail, the following exchange occurs:

Jailer.
Madam, if't please the Queen to send the babe,
I know not what I shall incur to pass it,
Having no warrant.
Paulina. You need not fear it, sir.
This child was prisoner to the womb, and is
By law and process of great Nature thence
Freed and enfranchised – not a party to
The anger of the King, nor guilty of,
If any be, the trespass of the Queen.
(II, ii, 55–62)

'Freed' refers both to emancipation from the womb and that innocence which is the birthright of all children. The 'law and process of great Nature' not only causes children to be born, but frees them from the guilt and despair of the older generation.

Ariel's desire to protect his own birthright led to enclosure in the pine; he refused to obey the 'earthy and abhorred commands' of Sycorax (I, ii, 273). Although Prospero is a 'white' witch, his commands also taint Ariel's natural purity. The spirit's desire for freedom, therefore, signifies a longing to regain his indigenous innocence. Significantly, at the end of the play, as he helps Prospero don the trappings of an Italian duke, he sings:

Where the bee sucks, there suck I;
In a cowslip's bell I lie;
There I couch when owls do cry.
On the bat's back I do fly
After summer merrily.
Merrily, merrily shall I live now
Under the blossom that hangs on the bough.
(V, i, 88–94)

Clearly, Ariel is anticipating his future freedom in terms of harmony with nature: a vision of innocence.

Since a human child like Miranda possesses a similar birthright, then within the familial structure of *The Tempest*, Ariel's quest for freedom comments in a profound manner on Miranda's relationship with Prospero. When her childhood expires, she must also be emancipated from her father, but rather than returning to nature she must seek a husband. Together, they can preserve that native-born innocence essential to the perception of a 'brave new world'. Despite his benevolent intentions, the world is not 'new' to Prospero (V, i, 184), and so he must be excluded from their unsullied vision.

Neither Miranda nor her spirit brother, however, engages in actual combat with their

1 William Shakespeare, *King Lear*, ed. Russell Fraser (New York, 1963), p. 149.

2 William Shakespeare, *King Lear*, ed. G. B. Harrison and Robert F. McDonnell (New York, 1962), p. 36.

father. Both Ariel's freedom ('Before the time be out? No more!' I, ii, 246) and the match with Ferdinand ('It goes on, I see,/As my soul prompts it' I, ii, 420–1) have been preordained. With Prospero in total command of the action, the only real struggle must be internal; he must confront the emotional ramifications of his plan. He *knows* that Ariel must be free and that Miranda must marry, but as these events begin to unfold he becomes increasingly aware that they mean the loss both of the powers he has enjoyed for so long and the total affection and physical presence of the daughter for whom he lives.

His behavior mirrors this vacillation between conviction and emotional backlash. Early in the play, Prospero reacts violently to being reminded of his promise to free the spirit, but after a lengthy outburst he immediately reaffirms that pledge: 'after two days/I will discharge thee' (I, ii, 298–9). The lovers shall also be 'free,' but until then they too must 'exactly do/All points of my command' (I, ii, 499–501). The commands themselves reflect Prospero's wisdom, but his matchmaking demeanor demonstrates his growing irritability. Admittedly, the log-piling episode does not violate the lovers' innocence, and it may well add greater clarity to their vision of a brave new world in which love transforms even the most menial tasks into 'pleasures' (III, i, 7). But surely these lessons do not necessitate Prospero calling his daughter his 'foot' and telling her he will 'hate' her if she speaks another word. The severity of his language echoes his unsettled condition in the opening dialogues and anticipates his unarguably disturbed behavior during the wedding masque.

As Prospero prepares to give away that for which he lives, his intensified asperity contrasts sharply with the light-hearted behavior of Ariel and the lovers. Northrop Frye may be correct in attributing the demand for chastity to a 'magical rather than a moral anxiety',[1] but it is an anxiety nonetheless. The warning is couched in unduly harsh terms which betray a certain tension on Prospero's part:

> barren hate,
> Sour-eyed disdain, and discord shall bestrew
> The union of your bed with weeds so loathly
> That you shall hate it both. (IV, i, 19–22)

Shakespeare highlights Prospero's growing instability by providing Ariel with his most playful speech of the play:

> Before you can say 'Come' and 'Go,'
> And breathe twice and cry, 'So, so,'
> Each one, tripping on his toe,
> Will be here with mop and mow.
> Do you love me, master? No?
> (IV, i, 44–8)

By playfully teasing Prospero, Ariel attempts to allay his tension; he gently mocks his master's tendency to use the word 'so',[2] and, in the last line, he apparently looks over Prospero's shoulder and, noticing the lovers' embrace, precociously asks his father if he loves him. Similarly, Ariel explains his hesitation to warn Prospero of the conspiracy ('When I presented Ceres,/I thought to have told thee of it, but I feared/Lest I might anger thee' IV, i, 167–9) not from any mysterious impulse – Kermode asks, 'Why does Ariel mention this?'[3] – but because throughout the entire scene he has recognized Prospero's disturbed state and has endeavored not to aggravate it.

Despite the spirit's efforts, however, Prospero does interrupt the masque, emphatically excluding himself from a vision accessible only to the younger generation. The end of this 'vanity' of his art marks the end of Prospero's control over that generation: Miranda has been

[1] Frye, *A Natural Perspective*, p. 153.

[2] Prospero constantly uses the word 'so': 'so dear the love my people bore me', 'tutors not so careful', etc. When excited, he uses the word to patch together his hurried thoughts: see I, ii, 165.

[3] Shakespeare, *The Tempest*, p. 105.

lost to Ferdinand. Prospero is 'distempered' not merely because he has again displayed the irresponsibility that cost him his dukedom, but because he is emotionally overwhelmed by his sense of loss. Quite naturally, therefore, his speech to the lovers dwells on a feeling of emptiness emphasizing the dream-like nature of all of life:

> the great globe itself,
> Yea, all which it inherit, shall dissolve,
> And, like this insubstantial pageant faded,
> Leave not a rack behind. We are such stuff
> As dreams are made on; and our little life
> Is rounded with a sleep. (IV, i, 153–8)

Prospero concludes the speech by telling the lovers that 'A turn or two I'll walk/To still my beating mind' (IV, i, 162–3). On two other occasions in the play there are references to *beating* minds:

> I pray you, sir –
> For still 'tis beating in my mind – your reason
> For raising this sea storm? (I, ii, 175–7)

> Do not infest your mind with beating on
> The strangeness of this business. (V, i, 246–7)

In each instance the individual's mind is beating because he is asking the question 'Why?'. That is precisely Prospero's condition; he wants to know why he must experience this agonizing loss. Of his island family, only Caliban will remain, and it is within that character's relationship to Prospero that the answer lies.

In the second scene of the play, Shakespeare places Caliban in the familial structure by revealing Prospero's initial step-father attitude towards the monster:

> When thou cam'st first,
> Thou strok'st me and made much of me; wouldst give me
> Water with berries in't; and teach me how
> To name the bigger light, and how the less,
> That burn by day and night. And then I loved thee
> And showed thee all the qualities o' th' isle.
> (I, ii, 332–7)

As the two corporeal (in contrast to the spirit Ariel) children under Prospero's care, Miranda and Caliban can easily be compared. Kermode lists the most obvious parallels:

> The Miranda–Caliban comparison persists; it began with the accounts of their education, was continued in the linked accounts of their reactions to the first encounter with men; and ends here with the parallelism of these lines [O Setebos, these be brave spirits indeed!' V, i, 261] and ll. 181–4 ['O brave new world'].[1]

For Kermode, the essence of these parallels is the nature–nurture controversy explicitly invoked by Prospero after the interruption of the masque:

> A devil, a born devil, on whose nature
> Nurture can never stick; on whom my pains,
> Humanely taken, all, all lost, quite lost!
> And as with age his body uglier grows,
> So his mind cankers. (IV, i, 188–92)

Undoubtedly, the nature–nurture problem is central to the passage, but the emotional picture it conveys is that of a father despairing over his delinquent son.

Shakespeare's most infamous 'born devil' or 'bastard' is Edmund in *King Lear*. Just as Lear's troubles stem from his inability to accept the loss of his daughter, so Gloucester's difficulties erupt from careless handling of his bastard son. Edmund symbolizes the darkness of Gloucester's past from which he cannot escape and for which he must accept responsibility; Edgar explicitly connects Edmund's begetting with Gloucester's blindness: 'The dark and vicious place where thee he got/Cost him his eyes' (V, iii, 174–5). The legitimate son recognizes that the 'thing of darkness' must be acknowledged:

> Let's exchange charity.
> I am no less in blood than thou art, Edmund;
> If more, the more th' hast wronged me.
> My name is Edgar, and thy father's son.
> (V, iii, 168–71)

[1] *Ibid.*, p. 129.

Another Shakespearian 'demi-devil', Parolles in *All's Well That Ends Well*, also demands acknowledgement.[1] When he 'seeks for grace' at the play's conclusion, the following conversation ensues:

Parolles. O my good lord, you were the first that found me.
Lafew. Was I, in sooth? And I was the first that lost thee.
Parolles. It lies in you, my lord, to bring me in some grace, for you did bring me out.
Lafew. Out upon thee, knave! Dost thou put upon me at once both the office of God and the devil? One brings thee in grace and the other brings thee out. [*Trumpets sound*.] The King's coming; I know by his trumpets. Sirrah, inquire further after me. I had talk of you last night; though you are a fool and a knave you shall eat. Go to, follow.
Parolles. I praise God for you. (v, ii, 45–58)

This exchange places the idea of grace, of acts of kindness between individuals, in the context of a special kind of responsibility. Lafew is in no way to blame for Parolles's acts, but he realizes that as a person in need, and as a part of his own past, Parolles is, in a very profound way, his responsibility; if we do not have it within us to perform 'God's office' and pardon 'fools', how can we expect God to pardon us?

Similarly, Prospero is not directly to blame for Caliban's actions, yet he too realizes that just as Alonso must 'know and own' Stephano and Trinculo, so he must acknowledge 'this thing of darkness... mine' (v, i, 274–6). The character of Caliban is central to the question that disturbs Prospero during the wedding masque because he symbolizes the past, the responsibilities that bind a man to the world and prevent him from escaping from it; it is the memory of Caliban's conspiracy that forces Prospero to leave the brave *new* world of the masque. He must suffer the agonizing loss of his daughter because her world is no longer his. She must be free of him if she is to grow and forge a new life by pursuing a vision of innocence.

Prospero is left to seek consolation in reunion and reconciliation not with a wife or daughter, but with Alonso and his party.[2] After being pardoned, the king suddenly remembers Ferdinand and complains about his loss. Prospero replies by claiming that he has had a 'like loss' which is

As great to me, as late, and supportable
To make the dear loss, have I means much weaker
That you may call to comfort you; for I
Have lost my daughter. (v, i, 145–8)

There is no reason to accept Frye's contention that Prospero only 'pretends' to lose Miranda.[3] The Duke of Milan *has* lost a daughter 'in this last tempest', for she has met Ferdinand and she is now his; Prospero's grief is less 'supportable' than Alonso's because he has suffered a real, and irreversible loss. His only consolations are 'patience' (v, i, 143) and the recovery of his dukedom.

Just before he discovers Ferdinand and Miranda playing at chess, Prospero tries to equate his political gain with the vision he is

[1] Like Caliban, Parolles is a threat to virginity (I, i, 116–71), and just as the monster's nature is reflected by his outward appearance, so Parolles's true self is revealed by his outrageous clothes. Lafew, an old nobleman like Prospero, is the first to find him out, and tells him: 'The devil it is that's my master' (II, iii, 251). Both Parolles and Caliban are eventually undone by a 'trick' and gain a measure of self-knowledge: cf. *The Tempest*, v, i, 295–8 and *All's Well That Ends Well*, IV, iii, 348–51.

[2] Prospero's famous renunciation of magic is ironically modeled after a speech by Medea in Golding's translation of *The Metamorphoses*. Medea conjures the spirits in order to perform her most ambitious act of magic: the rejuvenation of Jason's aged father. Prospero, on the other hand, struggling to reconcile himself to the onset of old age symbolized by the loss of Miranda, invokes the spirits in order to 'abjure' such 'rough magic'. For Golding's text see W. H. D. Rouse, ed., *Shakespeare's Ovid* (Carbondale, 1961).

[3] Frye, *A Natural Perspective*, p. 151.

about to present:

> Pray you look in.
> My dukedom since you have given me again,
> I will requite you with as good a thing.
> (v, i, 167–9)

He finds, however, that he has to qualify his statement: 'At least bring forth a wonder to content ye/As much as me my dukedom' (v, i, 170–1). Prospero's remarkable comparison demands that he be as satisfied with his dukedom as Alonso is contented and filled with wonder by the sight of his son, alive, and in the company of a 'goddess'.[1] Shakespeare emphasizes the obvious discrepancy by engaging the two lovers in a dialogue mocking the value of kingdoms:

> *Miranda.*
> Sweet lord, you play me false.
> *Ferdinand.* No, my dearest love,
> I would not for the world.
> *Miranda.*
> Yes, for a score of kingdoms you should wrangle,
> And I would call it fair play. (v, i, 172–5)

Except for his recovered 'kingdom', Prospero's condition parallels Paulina's in the concluding act of *The Winter's Tale*. Her final words are tinged with bitterness:

> Go together,
> You precious winners all; your exultation
> Partake to every one. I an old turtle,
> Will wing me to some withered bough, and there
> My mate, that's never to be found again,
> Lament till I am lost. (v, iii, 130–5)

Like Prospero, she has not been reunited with a daughter or a 'mate' and the future appears dismal. Leontes provides her, however, with a substitute husband, Camillo, with whom she will apparently be happy for the rest of her life. For Prospero, there is only retirement to Milan where 'Every third thought shall be my grave'.

Viewing *The Tempest* in terms of its familial relationships clarifies the unique ways in which it differs from the other romances; it centers not upon a husband–wife or father–daughter reunion and reconciliation, but upon the loss of a daughter through marriage. Prospero's relationship with Miranda is informed both by his treatment of Ariel, who exemplifies the need for innocence, and by his reaction to Caliban, who symbolizes the past, the responsibilities that bind a man to the world. The intermittent harshness characterizing Prospero's behavior, therefore, issues not from external causes, but from an internal struggle with the emotional ramifications of his loss.

Prospero's providential status spares him Lear's madness but not his pain. The agony erupts most conspicuously when the wedding masque is brought to its abrupt end and Miranda joins Ferdinand in a new world from which Prospero is excluded. In the previous romances a link exists between the generations in the form of the recovered wife. Hermione's return not only provides Leontes with consolation for his losses, but the physical likeness of his wife and daughter fills the king with a sense of continuity between the old world and the new.

The special quality, the tremendous profundity, which readers sense in *The Tempest* arises from the lack of an obvious consolation. We are confronted with the bare facts of loss. The new world of the young lovers is as bright as it is in the other plays, but there is a gap between it and the old world. It is that gap which has caused almost every critic to note that the ending of *The Tempest* seems to be touched by despair – what D. C. R. Marsh calls 'a certain world-weariness'.[2] It is also

[1] Francis Neilson's analysis of the final scene supports my contention that Prospero is not really 'contented' by his dukedom (Francis Neilson, *Shakespeare and 'The Tempest'* [Rindge, N. H., 1956], pp. 180–1).

[2] D. C. R. Marsh, *The Recurring Miracle: A Study of 'Cymbeline' and the Last Plays* (Lincoln, Nebraska, 1962), p. 191.

that gap which Prospero asks us to help him cross in the epilogue.

A speech by Gower in *Pericles* evidently served as a prototype for Prospero's plea:

> Now our sands are almost run;
> More a little, and then dumb.
> This, my last boon, give me –
> For such kindness must relieve me.
> (v, ii, 1–4)
>
> Now my charms are all o'erthrown,
> And what strength I have's mine own,
> Which is most faint. Now 'tis true
> I must be here confined by you,
> Or sent to Naples. (Epilogue, 1–5)

In the earlier play, this appeal bridges the gap between Pericles's reunion with Marina and the resurrection of Thaisa. *The Tempest*, however, *ends* with Prospero's request. He must die in 'despair' on the island, which is now 'bare' after the departure of Ariel and Miranda, unless we help send him to Naples, the kingdom over which the young couple rules. Prospero reveals that in the end it is not his power, but our own, which constructs the bridge between the old world and the new, providing continuity when it is not given to us. We must break the 'spell' cast by our own indifference and so freely enter into the 'innocent' vision of a brave new world without abdicating our responsibilities in the old.

INIGO JONES AT THE COCKPIT

JOHN ORRELL

Historians of the English stage have always had to do without that most desirable of source documents, a set of detailed drawings of a known and significant theatre of the early seventeenth century. The best picture of a pre-Caroline theatre we have is a rough copy of a traveller's thumb-nail sketch of the interior of the Swan. It is useful but ambiguous, and even when supported by the building contracts for the Fortune and the Hope it cannot give historians the kind of information they want: an exact rendering of the plan, elevation and section of a major theatre of Shakespeare's age.

In the collection of architectural drawings at Worcester College, Oxford, there are two sheets of designs by Inigo Jones for a U-shaped theatre which has so far remained unidentified.[1] D. F. Rowan has performed a valuable service by publishing them in *Shakespeare Survey* and elsewhere,[2] but with two exceptions to be discussed below no-one has found evidence directly to connect them with a known building. So imprecise is the theatre history of the seventeenth century that Mr Rowan finds that he can place the designs no more accurately than as a 'missing link' between the Swan (*c.* 1596) and the Cockpit-in-Court (1629).[3] Professor Glynne Wickham speculates that they belong at the very latest point in this time scale, with the Salisbury Court theatre built in 1629.[4] I cannot produce the single piece of 'hard' evidence that would settle the matter once and for all, but I believe there are good circumstantial reasons for setting the theatre about midway in Mr Rowan's range. For the evidence shows that the designs are probably for the Cockpit in Drury Lane, which was built in 1616.

This identification is not altogether new. Iain Mackintosh reviewed some of the evidence for it in a little-known article published in 1973,[5] and I know of two scholars who have suggested it in private, but so far no whole-hearted attempt has been made to confirm what promises to be so interesting a piece of information about the seventeenth-century stage. The matter seems worth investigating in some detail.

We must begin this necessarily rather roundabout search with a study of Jones's drawings. Mr John Harris, Keeper of Drawings at the Royal Institute of British Architects, has already assigned them to the period 'between *c.* 1616 and *c.* 1618.'[6] In matters of this sort the

1 Worcester College Library, Jones/Webb drawings I/7B and 7C. See plates IIA and B.

2 'A Neglected Jones/Webb Theatre Project: "Barber-Surgeons' Hall Writ Large,"' *Shakespeare Survey 23* (1970), pp. 125–9, abstracted from an article of the same title in *New Theatre Magazine* 9 no. 3, (1969), 6–15; and 'The English Playhouse: 1595–1630', *Renaissance Drama*. n.s. 4 (1971), 37–51.

3 'A Neglected Jones/Webb Theatre Project, Part II: a Theatrical Missing Link', in David Galloway (ed.), *The Elizabethan Theatre II* (Toronto, 1970), pp. 60–73.

4 *Early English Stages 1300–1660* (1972), II, part 2, pp. 144–7.

5 'Inigo Jones – Theatre Architect', *TABS* 31, no. 3 (1973), 99–105.

6 John Harris, Stephen Orgel and Roy Strong, *The King's Arcadia: Inigo Jones and the Stuart Court* (1973), p. 109, article initialled by John Harris. Mr Harris is sure enough of his dates to discount any association of the designs with the reconstruction of the Fortune in 1621–2, because 'the style of the drawing is too early'.

layman must accept the findings of the expert, for much depends on an intimate knowledge of the whole Jones canon, but it is not difficult to see the similarity between the theatre drawings and others made between 1616 and 1618, such as the design for Fulke Greville's house (>1619) or that for an entrance bay dated 1616 by Jones himself.[1] Nor is it difficult to see how far they differ from the freer style of the drawings for the Whitehall Banqueting House (< 1619).

If we accept Mr Harris's dates, as we must do unless we find hard facts which override the stylistic evidence, then we cannot agree with Professor Wickham that the designs show the Salisbury Court theatre, which was not undertaken until 1629.

The drawings are certainly in Jones's early hand, yet the building shown in the elevation is hardly typical Jones, even early Jones. There are no orders, no pediments, no evident classicism at all on the outside. The segmental-headed windows do recall some the architect used at the rear of the Prince's Lodging in Newmarket,[2] but otherwise the shell of the building might have come from almost any mason's hand. The outer wall seems to be of brick, and for some reason it is buttressed; the roof is of tile with a steep pitch, and the whole is topped by an egg-shaped finial and a breezy little pennant. This last touch is also characteristic of Jones's early designs.

The plan has a lot more to tell us than the elevation, but before I try to coax its secrets from it I must give a word of caution. Measured analysis of architectural drawings cannot be done from ordinary photographs, which distort the periphery of the area they show. The reproductions in *Shakespeare Survey 23* are unfortunately less accurate than most, since they stretch the plan longitudinally to the point where geometrical analysis becomes impossible.[3] To prevent such errors I have measured the drawings at Oxford with some care, and in what follows I give the readings in millimetres, to the nearest 0.5mm. The scales on seventeenth-century designs tend to be unreliable, and although there seems to be little wrong with the ones we are dealing with here, I have thought it best to use the direct measurements wherever possible. The analysis begins, however, with Jones's modular system, which must be expressed in feet and inches, so I shall compromise by giving the direct measurements in brackets.

It was Jones's usual practice to assemble his designs using a simple module from which the proportions of the whole derived. Where orders were employed the module was normally the diameter of a column, though the plan might be laid out using a larger unit. The Whitehall Banqueting House interior, for example, is 110′ long and 55′ wide, and its plan is developed from a five-foot unit, which represents the width of the windows between their reveals.[4] A similar unit is used for the outer wall of the theatre in the Worcester College designs, but it applies to the exterior dimensions, which are all multiples of five feet. The radius of the 'round' is 20′ (69·5 mm on the drawing), the rectangle forming the rest of the U is 40′ by 35′ (139 mm by 122 mm) and the overall length excluding the attached stair turrets is 55′ (191·5 mm). The details of the elevation do not fit the five-foot unit. True, the

[1] The design for Fulke Greville's house is at Chatsworth and is reproduced in *The King's Arcadia*, p. 105 (no. 189); the entrance bay drawing is at the R.I.B.A. (Jones/Webb no. 73) and is reproduced in *The King's Arcadia*, p. 107 (no. 192).

[2] Worcester College Library, Jones/Webb drawing I/73 verso. See John Harris, 'Inigo Jones and the Prince's Lodging at Newmarket', *Architectural History* 3 (1959), 26–40.

[3] *Shakespeare Survey 23* (1970), plates I and II.

[4] John Summerson, *Inigo Jones* (Harmondsworth, 1966), p. 50, fig. 13. For the relation of the module to the orders see R. Wittkower, 'Inigo Jones, Architect and Man of Letters', *R.I.B.A. Journal* 60 (1953) 83–8.

string-course is 15′ (52 mm) above the grade, but the main door and upper windows are 4′ 6″ wide (15·5 mm) and the narrow lower windows are 3′ tall (10·5 mm). Evidently these parts of the design derive from a 1′ 6″ module, which is incompatible with that of the U-plan.

These inconsistencies are not at all surprising. It is only when we turn to look at the internal layout that they assume any significance. Much of the interior is assembled from the smaller module, which I shall call M. The pit door is 2M wide (10·5 mm), the centrepiece of the *frons scenae* is 4M across (21 mm), the benches are 1M apart (5 mm).

One measure, however, fits both modules because it is a multiple of both. This is 10M (i.e. 15′, or 52 mm on the drawing), and it is precisely the depth of the stage. Moreover, the outer stage doors are separated by 10M, so that a square 10M across based centrally at the front of the stage defines both the depth of the stage and the placing of its entrance doors. The stage front bisects the overall length of the theatre (again, excluding the stairs), so that it is just 5M (i.e. 7′ 6″, or 26 mm) distant from the centre of the 'round'. The gallery rail above the pit has a diameter of some 21′ 2″ (73·5 mm), a dimension which at first sight appears to have nothing to do with either module. It is, however, 15′ × $\sqrt{2}$, or the diameter of a circle described around a square 15′ across. A 10M square, constructed on the auditorium side of the stage front, thus defines both the width of the pit (as indicated by the inner face of the gallery rail) and the relation of the pit to the stage (plate IIIA).

The plan of the outer wall, then, is designed in multiples of five feet, but details of the elevation and of the interior use a 1′ 6″ module. The modular armature of the interior, a pair of 15′ or 10M squares either side of the centre line, fits both systems. But why did Jones not use the 1′ 6″ module for the exterior, and so achieve a fully consistent plan? The difference would have been very small, and it is hard to see why he should have fixed on a width of 40′ instead of say 42′ unless he was constrained in some way. Certainly the inconsistency looks looks like a practical concession, and not at all like a theoretical demonstration.

The modular systems account for all the major features of the plan, with two exceptions. The width of the stage, at a fraction over 23′ (80·5 mm) remains unaccounted for, as does the depth of the 'post scene'[1] between the front pit benches and the stage rail, about 3′ 10″ (13·5 mm). Although these figures look arbitrary, they are not, and the solving of the riddle of their relation to the rest of the design leads to a new conclusion: that this drawing of Jones's, made before 1618, incorporates in somewhat unconventional fashion the layout of the ancient theatre as reported by Vitruvius and publicized by his Renaissance commentators.

Vitruvius began his description of the plan of a theatre thus:

> Having fixed upon the principal centre, draw a line of circumference equivalent to what is to be the perimeter at the bottom, and in it inscribe four equilateral triangles, at equal distances apart and touching the boundary line of the circle, as the astrologers do in a figure of the twelve signs of the zodiac, when they are making computations from the musical harmony of the stars.[2]

From the positions of the triangles within the circle the relative positions of the stage, the *frons scenae*, the five stage entrances and the seven auditorium gangways could all be calculated. We know that Jones absorbed this diagram thoroughly, for in 1620 he made a

[1] I adopt the term 'post scene' from the English translation of Serlio made in 1611, which uses it for the Italian's 'proscenio', changed in the editions of 1566 and later to read 'piazza della scena.' All these terms refer to the space between the front of the stage and the seats closest to it.

[2] Vitruvius, *The Ten Books of Architecture*, translated by Morris Hicky Morgan (Cambridge, Mass., 1914), p. 146.

survey of Stonehenge and came to the strange conclusion that it was Roman work, chiefly because he saw the Vitruvian pattern somehow living within its stones.[1] If he could so forcefully impose the pattern on those mute ruins, it is no wonder that he should have used it in a real theatre design a few years earlier.

The clue lies in the width of the stage, which at just over 23′ (80·5 mm) is precisely equal to the width of the theatre divided by $\sqrt{3}$ (139 mm ÷ 1·732 = 80·5 mm, to the nearest 0.5 mm). $\sqrt{3}$ is the height of an equilateral triangle whose sides are 2, so if we are to account for this peculiar measure's presence we must look for a geometric construction involving equilateral triangles. The Vitruvian diagram is just such a construction, and if we build it from the stage centre within a circle whose radius equals the width of the stage we find that the width of the theatre, the location of its back wall, the width of the stage and the depth of the 'post scene' are all brought into relation with one another. No simpler diagram will do this, and of course it is beyond belief that the measurements are arbitrary and their conformation a matter of coincidence. Nevertheless the thickness of the lines in my diagram (plate IIIB) might well hide a multitude of approximations; indeed it does, for the lines cover the distortions of the photograph on which they are superimposed. The accuracy of the diagram must be checked arithmetically against the measurements taken directly from the Worcester College drawing.

We have seen already that the actual widths of the stage and the theatre bear a $\sqrt{3}$ relation to each other. The centre of the diagram falls on a line which connects the centres of the posts in front of the boxes flanking the stage. This line is just 20′ (69·5 mm) from the back wall of the theatre. The distance from the front pit bench ends to the back wall is 109.5 mm, measured on the plan. In the diagram this distance is equal to that between the base of a triangle and the centre, plus half the side of a triangle. If the side of a triangle is 40′ (or 139 mm), the former value is 40′ ÷ $2\sqrt{3}$ = 11′ 6½″ (or 139 mm ÷ $2\sqrt{3}$ = 40 mm), and the latter is 20′ (or 69·5 mm). Added together they come to 31′ 6½″ (or 109·5 mm): the diagram agrees precisely with the readings taken from the drawing itself.

This is not, however, a 'Vitruvian' theatre. Although Jones had visited the Teatro Olimpico, had marvelled at its almost archaeological response to ancient ideas and brought home drawings of it,[2] he was hardly aiming to repeat Palladio's achievement here. The present designs show a theatre whose layout chiefly represents a modular ordering of conventional Jacobean parts, in which the Vitruvianism is almost an afterthought. It is worth noting that the diagram gives the correct five points to the stage and seven to the auditorium, but also that the centre of the circle would naturally form the centre of a 'heavens' painted over the stage, with clouds in the midst and the twelve signs of the zodiac all around, echoing the Vitruvian theme in very Jacobean style. Its location means that the pattern of triangles is relevant to the stage end of the theatre and not to the round of the auditorium at all, an emphasis that looks strange on paper and suggests that Jones thought of the two parts as essentially disjunct, for all their linking in the modular systems.

Taken all together, the evidence from this analysis suggests that the width of the theatre was a datum from which Jones began, and not something he arrived at by his usual methods. The stage end, with its nod to Vitruvius, consorts a little awkwardly with the round of the auditorium, as if it were an addition rather

[1] Inigo Jones [and John Webb], *The Most Notable Antiquity of Great Britain, Called Stone-Heng, on Salisbury Plain, Restored* (1655), p. 70.

[2] For Jones's collection of Palladio drawings see W. G. Keith, 'Inigo Jones as a Collector,' *R.I.B.A. Journal* 33 (1925–6), 101.

than a fully integrated part of the whole. Above all, the curious assortment of methods suggests that the design was a practical one and not a theoretical exercise.

The practical theatre projects undertaken in London between Harris's authoritative dates '*c.* 1616 and *c.* 1618' were two. One was the abortive project at Puddle Wharf, begun in 1613 and persisted with until finally suppressed in January 1616/17. Since Jones was out of the country in 1613–1614, he is unlikely to have been concerned with this theatre. The other was the Cockpit in Drury Lane. If Jones's designs were ever realized, the circumstantial evidence of date points unambiguously to the Cockpit as their object.

The Cockpit was not built *ab ovo* in 1616. In that year Christopher Beeston leased the site from John Best, who had built a regular cockpit there in or shortly after 1609.[1] Some accounts of Beeston's theatre say that it was newly erected in 1616, while others speak of his converting the original cockpit building to dramatic uses. Thus Camden said it was 'nuper erectum' and Edward Sherburne called it 'a newe playhouse',[2] while to John Chamberlain it was 'a new play house (somtime a cockpit)'.[3] The Benchers of Lincoln's Inn complained of 'the convertinge of the Cocke Pytte in the Feildes into a playe house'.[4] Taken together these allusions indicate a conversion so far-reaching as to provide a substantially new building. We know that the resulting theatre was made of brick with a tile roof,[5] in conformity with the Proclamations on building.

It is among the Proclamations and the measures taken to enforce them that we find the next clue to the identity of the Jones drawings. James I issued a series of Proclamations beginning in 1603 aimed at controlling, indeed almost at preventing, further development in and around London. The policy and its effects are handsomely described in Norman Brett-James's *Growth of Stuart London:* the main object seems to have been to prevent overcrowding, while a good deal of attention was also given to the prevention of fire. The chief means to the latter end was to insist on building in brick or stone, and the former was to be achieved by limiting all new buildings to old foundations, so that little expansion was legally possible. Of course the Proclamations were especially aimed against residential development, but in practice they were held to cover buildings of all sorts, including theatres.[6]

Not infrequently offending houses were pulled down. One such belonged to Christopher Beeston, the principal in our story about the Cockpit. On 18 September 1616 the Privy Council sent the High Sheriff of Middlesex a list of houses it wanted demolished, including a tenement in Clerkenwell which Beeston had erected separate from his house there, in spite of an undertaking not to.[7] The Sheriff started his work, but his term of office soon expired. When his successor made his report he found that some of the buildings complained of did not exist, others had been pulled down, and 'For Christopher Bastones house, it is for the most parte puld downe, not to be inhabited.'[8] In the following year, however, the Council complained that the house

1 The lease is quoted in G. E. Bentley, *The Jacobean and Caroline Stage* (Oxford, 1942–68), VI, 48.

2 William Camden, *A Complete History of England* (1706), II, 647; for Sherburne's letter see Bentley, *Jacobean and Caroline Stage*, VI, 54.

3 Chamberlain's letter is printed in Bentley, *Jacobean and Caroline Stage*, VI, 55.

4 *Ibid.*, p. 50.

5 For the bricks see Thomas Middleton, *Inner-Temple Masque, or Masque of Heroes* (1619), sig. $B3^v$; for the tiles see Sherburne's letter.

6 The building proclamations are printed in James F. Larkin and Paul L. Hughes (eds), *Stuart Royal Proclamations* (Oxford, 1973–), I, nos 25, 51, 78, 87, 120, 121 and 152. For their implementation see Norman Brett-James, *The Growth of Stuart London* (1935), pp. 80–100.

7 *Acts of the Privy Council, 1616–17*, p. 15.

8 *Ibid.*, p. 36, dated 7 October 1616.

was 'buylt up agayne, and his Majesty of late passing that way hath taken speciall notice thereof, being highly offended with the presumption.'[1] Beeston's tenement was evidently too 'neere unto his Majesties passage' to escape scrutiny, and the Sheriff was ordered to pull the house down to the ground and utterly demolish it.

This little tale of Beeston's Clerkenwell tenement has two points of relevance to our inquiry. It shows that the king took a personal interest in the execution of his Proclamations on building; and it proves that Christopher Beeston had no special influence over the Privy Council, at least at the time when he was building the Cockpit.

Among the developments particularly at risk from the Proclamations were those that the king actually saw on his journeys in and about London. It happened that close to the Cockpit site in Drury Lane there was a private royal road leading out of Westminster towards the hunting country of Theobalds, Royston and Newmarket. East of Drury Lane it became known as Queen Street, after Anne of Denmark, and ran where Great Queen Street runs now.[2] It is not entirely clear whether this section of the route was still private in 1616, but the part north of Holborn certainly was, and James was travelling the whole road frequently during the construction of the Cockpit. From it he could see the new buildings springing up around Drury Lane, and he took exception to them.[3] Doubtless he could see the Cockpit too, and while there is nothing to suggest that he was the source of complaint against it, the Middlesex Justices could hardly ignore so flagrant a violation of the Proclamations when it was so obviously visible little more than a hundred yards from the king's 'ordinary way'.

That the Justices did move against Beeston in the matter of the Cockpit is plain from the entries in their registers. At the Middlesex Sessions of 5 and 6 September 1616 the following order was made:

> Whereas this Courte is informed that there is a new buildinge in hand to be sett up and erected in Drury Lane nere Lincolnes Inne Feildes att and adjoyninge to the Cocke-pitt, contrary to the Lawe and His Majesties Proclamacione; It is therefore ordered that the said new building shall presently be staid and the workemen committed to prison, that shall hereafter presume to goe forward in the said New Buildinge and also such as shall sett them on worke, havinge had warninge alreadye to forebeare, And further it is ordered that all other new buildinges whatsoeuer be likewise stayed.[4]

In the language of the Proclamations a new building is one that is set on new foundations. Evidently the Justices believed that the development 'att and adjoyninge to' the Cockpit involved the use of new foundations, and indeed an earlier record from the same Sessions appears to confirm the matter (I quote from the calendared version):

> John Shepperd of 'Lillypott Lane', London, bricklayer, committed for working upon a new foundation in Drury Lane, and handed in bail to Richard Smith of Holborn upon condition that he shall appear before the Lords of the Council at their first sitting at Whitehall, and in the meantime not to go on in the building and withall to do his best endeavour to bring forth Mr. Beeston to-morrow in court, then his appearance to be spared and Beeston to be bound. On 10 September, A.D. 1616, discharged by order of the Justices.[5]

Since there is no record of any building in Drury Lane by Beeston other than his work at the Cockpit, it is certain that the theatre is referred to here, and that Shepperd was the builder at least of its foundations.

Despite the actions of the Justices the building went ahead, for all we know undisturbed.

[1] *Ibid.*, p. 334, dated 29 September 1617.

[2] *L.C.C. Survey of London*, v, 36.

[3] Many of the buildings listed for demolition by the Privy Council were situated close to the king's road to Royston. See *Acts of the Privy Council 1616–17*, p. 15 and *1617–19*, p. 175.

[4] *Middlesex County Records*, II, 125–6.

[5] *Ibid.*, n. s. III, 310.

It duly opened before Shrove Tuesday 1616/17 by which time it had already worried the Benchers of Lincoln's Inn. Yet the court's determination to stop the building cannot be doubted. What prevented it from succeeding? Five days after making its staying order it discharged Shepperd and, we must conclude, closed the case, yet there is no record that the crafty Beeston ever appeared before it to state his position.

Who called off the Middlesex dogs? Beeston had no personal pull with the Council, as the affair of his Clerkenwell tenement proves. But had he the wit to involve the King's Surveyor in his theatre project he might confidently have expected some special favour, even during this singularly inauspicious time when the Puddle Wharf proposal was being so energetically scotched.

There remains the more interesting probability that the new building was set largely on old foundations, the foundations, that is, of the cockpit which had stood on the site since about 1609. One of the provisions of the Proclamation of 12 October 1607 allowed for the extension of buildings set on old foundations up to a third larger than their original size.[1] If the cockpit were to be adapted to theatrical use under the regulations of the time, good sense required the incorporation of its original plan, together with an extension built outwards on new foundations continuous with the old, and so limited that the new part could plausibly be represented as no more than a third of the size of the old. The magistrates stayed the work 'att and adjoyninge to' the cockpit, using a phrase which precisely indicates that just such a scheme was afoot. Any excuse that it did in fact meet the requirements of the Proclamations (and the original cock-houses and sheds on the property would have entered into the calculations of area) would have been lent colour had it been made by Jones, who as Surveyor was among those charged with seeing that the building policy was carried out.

Plainly we need to know more about John Best's cockpit of 1609. Unhappily the design of cockpits in the seventeenth century has gone virtually unrecorded. Much information about cockfighting in general lies scattered in documents and pamphlets, but all too little of it relates to the size and structure of the buildings in which the matches were held. We know most about the elaborate pit put up by Henry VIII in Whitehall, but that was an unrepresentative building, quite unlike the more modest ones established elsewhere.[2] A great many are recorded in England before 1700, but apart from Whitehall only five are illustrated in engravings (see plates IV and V). These are at Derby and Leicester (illustrated in Speed maps of 1610), Oxford (built by 1672), Dartmouth Street, Westminster (the 'Cockpit Royal,' built *c.* 1671) and Gray's Inn Gardens, Holborn (built by 1700).[3] The engravings show that

[1] Larkin and Hughes, *Stuart Royal Proclamations*, 13, no. 78: '... if any person shall erect ... for the inlargement of his dwelling house, any building joyning to the same, hee shall not be taken or held to be an offendor against this Proclamation, so as the precinct of ground within the said addition or enlargement, amount not to any more then a third part of the precinct of ground within the olde foundation, and that it be used with the former for one onely habitation.'

[2] For Jones's conversion of the Whitehall cockpit into a theatre in 1629–30 see Bentley, *Jacobean and Caroline Stage*, VI, 270–9.

[3] For Derby and Leicester see John Speed, *The Theatre of the Empire of Great Britaine* ... (1611). 'The Cock Pitt' is keyed no. 26 in the 'Darbye' map in error for 27. The Leicester pit, on the outskirts of the town, is drawn very large, but it clearly bears no relation to the scale of the rest of the map. The Oxford pit stood at the corner of Holywell and Church Streets, and appears in D. Loggan, *Oxonia Illustrata* (Oxford, 1675), plate II. On its origins see H. E. Salter (ed.), *Surveys and Tokens* (Oxford, 1923), p. 101. For the Dartmouth Street pit see *L.C.C. Survey of London*, X, part 1, p. 81. It may have been built when Sir Edward de Carteret leased the site from

Footnote 3 *continued page* 164

each of them was an enclosed, centrally-planned building of no great size. Two – those depicted by Speed – were polygonal in plan, while the two close to London were round. To judge from the print, the Oxford pit might have been either. Leicester was domed, and the rest had conical roofs. Both the Holborn and the Westminster pits are marked on various London maps, usually with a circle, but little credence can be given to the scale of what may well be no more than a partly conventional sign.[1]

No seventeenth-century view of the interior of a regular cockpit is extant, though the Dartmouth Street pit – usually known as the Cockpit Royal – appears in an early guise in the frontispiece of R[obert] H[owlett]'s *The Royal Pastime of Cock-fighting* (London, 1709). The round pit is ringed by three tiers of benches, rising to a balustrade behind which runs a level promenade by the perimeter wall. A similar layout appears in Rowlandson's famous print of the same building as it was *c.* 1808.[2] Hogarth's engraving of a cockpit, usually said to represent this Dartmouth Street building, in fact shows something quite different, a straight-walled, apparently windowless room in which the circular pit and concentric degrees have been arranged on the Westminster pattern. The presence of jockeys shows Hogarth's pit to be the one at Newmarket.[3]

Fortunately we have a description of one of the London pits, possibly that at Shoe Lane, made by Thomas Platter in 1599, a mere decade before the Drury Lane pit was built.

> ...I saw the place which is built like a theatre (theatrum). In the centre of the floor stands a circular table covered with straw and with ledges round it, where the cocks are teased and incited to fly at one another, while those with wagers as to which cock will win, sit closest around the circular disk, but the spectators who are merely present on their entrance penny sit around higher up....[4]

The Holborn pit was described in similar

Christ's Hospital in 1671. It is illustrated in Kip's 'View of Westminster' (1710). The Gray's Inn Gardens pit was called 'new' in an advertisement of 1700 cited by J. P. Malcolm, *Anecdotes of the Manners and Customs of London during the Eighteenth Century*, 2nd edn (1810), II, 115. It appears in the background of the 'Prospect of Gray's Inn' engraved by Sutton Nicholls for John Stow, *A Survey of the Cities of London and Westminster*, edited by John Strype (1720), book IV, plate facing p. 69. In 1731 Nicholls engraved another view which shows the cockpit in rather more detail. It is reproduced in Hugh Phillips, *Mid-Georgian London* (1964), pp. 202 and 203. In an article in *Notes and Queries* 7th series 9 (1890), 258, S. A. T. claimed that the Gray's Inn pit was built well before 1660, but gave no source for his information.

[1] The Cockpit Royal, Dartmouth Street, is marked by a circle on Robert Morden and Philip Lea's 'Actuall Survey of London and Westminster...' (*c.* 1690), and on John Rocque's 'Plan of the Cities of London and Westminster...' (1746). It is marked by a symbol on the map of Saint Margaret's, Westminster, included in Strype's edition of Stow. The 'Mapp of St. Andrews Holbourn Parish' in the same work marks the Gray's Inn pit by a circle, apparently to scale, indicating a diameter of about 37'.

[2] Reproduced by Wickham, *Early English Stages*, II, part 2, plate XVII.

[3] See William H. Holden, 'Hogarth's *Cockpit*,' *Notes and Queries* 14th series 161 (1931), 352. With the single exception of Whitehall, no representation of a seventeenth-century cockpit gives any indication that there were interior posts supporting the roof. They would not be required for the domes or conical roofs shown in the exterior views, and they are not present in the interior views. Neither are they mentioned in any verbal description. The Whitehall building was of a type derived from monastic kitchens and employed, for example, in the Livery Kitchen at Richmond. There is no reason to believe that any other cockpit imitated its unusual design. Glynne Wickham's reconstruction (*Early English Stages*, II, part 2, pp. 84–9) of the Drury Lane conversion is based on the assumption that Best's building 'followed the same ground-plan as that of the Royal Cockpit [Whitehall],' and makes much of the posts which are held to be an irremovable part of its structure. Since these posts are unlikely to have existed, Professor Wickham's fascinating account literally lacks support and must now be set aside.

[4] *Thomas Platter's Travels in England*, translated by Clare Williams (1937), pp. 167–8. On the location of the pit see Hans Hecht, *Thomas Platters des Jüngeren Englandfahrt in Jahre 1599* (Halle, 1929), p. 152 n.

terms in the eighteenth century by another European traveller, Zacharias von Uffenbach:

A special building has been made for [cockfighting] near 'Gras Inn'... The building is round like a tower, and inside it resembles a 'theatrum anatomicum,' for all round it there are benches in tiers, on which the spectators sit. In the middle is a round table, which is covered with mats, on which the cocks have to fight.[1]

That these descriptions made more than a century apart agree so well with one another and with Rowlandson's nineteenth-century print suggests that the main features of the cockpit were early standardized in much the same way as those of a tennis court or a cricket pitch. Specific regulations governing the size of the pit come too late to be relevant here, but the need for them must have been recognized from the beginning.

Although no direct description of it survives, it is safe to assume that the Drury Lane pit was a round or polygonal building with a conical roof, and that inside there was a circular pit with degrees ranged about it rising up to an ambulatory by the wall. It was probably not very big. The Royal Cockpit engraving shows four degrees before the ambulatory, while in Rowlandson's version there are only three, with another two beyond the balustrade. Hogarth found three degrees and an ambulatory at Newmarket. Allowing 20′ for the diameter of the pit, the usual sort of cockpit building was probably no more than 40′ across in all, and sometimes it was less. In one case – that of Royston – no guesswork is necessary because a precise survey is extant. The cockpit at Royston formed part of James I's 'court house', and was most likely built as part of the general development there between 1607 and 1611.[2] It was surveyed by the Parliamentary Commissioners in 1649:

All that Round bricke buildinge called the Cockpitt conteyninge 30.ty foote of Assize in widenes, and 17.tn foote of Assize in heighte, with a substantiall Tymber roofe couered with Tyles....[3]

The public pits of London were doubtless somewhat larger than this, for they depended on a paying audience and needed to attract enough of a crowd to cover their costs. Nevertheless the diameter of 30′ was not greatly exceeded by any commercial cockpit of later times whose dimensions are known to me: that built in 1785 at Lowther Street, Carlisle, for example, was an octagon 40′ across.[4] None was large enough to be converted into a regular professional theatre without extensive structural alterations. There is no reason to suppose that the Drury Lane pit differed from the rest in this respect.

The Drury Lane pit was built at much the same time as the one at Royston by John Best, a member of the Grocers' Company whose name often appears in the county records of Middlesex, where he emerges as a small businessman occasionally involved in local government. His interest in cockfighting was not, however, merely speculative. In the Diet Book of Prince Henry's household, 1610, there is a list of miscellaneous tradesmen qualifying for wages. Among them is 'John Beast Cockemaster.'[5] He must have known the Royston pit, and he must have known much else of relevance to this study, for the name at the head of the short list in which his own appears is 'Mr Inico Joanes Suruayer of the Workes'.[6]

It is time to return to Jones and his drawings. In 1616 he had newly succeeded to the king's surveyorship and was engaged on various projects for Anne of Denmark, including the silkworm room at Oatlands and the Queen's House at Greenwich. Any involvement with

1 *London in 1710*, translated by W. H. Quarrell and M. Mare (Oxford, 1928), p. 48.

2 See Joseph Beldam, 'Royston Court House and its Appurtenances,' *Archaeologia* 40 (1866), 119–37.

3 PRO E317/Cambs. 4.

4 *Victoria County History: Cumberland*, II, 479.

5 B. L. Harleian MS 642, fol. 260.v

6 *Ibid.*, fol. 260r.

Beeston would hardly have been part of his official work, but since Beeston represented the interests of the company of actors called the Queen Anne's Men an informal connection would not be unlikely. Between his return from Italy in 1615 and *c.* 1618 Jones designed what appears to be a practical enclosed theatre, and the only new theatre building in the period – besides the ill-fated Puddle Wharf – was the conversion of the cockpit in Drury Lane to house the Queen Anne's Men. But are the drawings consistent with such a conversion?

Beeston had to expand the cockpit because it was too small for a theatre. The Proclamations required that he should retain as much as possible of the foundations of the original building, but even had they not done so he would have been forced to demolish and begin anew or to adopt a U-shaped plan like that in the Jones drawings. There is no other way of expanding a centrally-planned building. Simply to erect a similar but larger building on the same site would require the destruction of the first and the provision of a complete set of new foundations, a possibility excluded as much by common sense as by the Proclamations. If we now turn again to Jones's drawings we can understand their odd use of two modular systems. The round of the auditorium coincides with half the plan of the original cockpit, with its diameter of 40′. The stage end is an addition built on the new foundations 'att and adjoyninge to' the cockpit which worried the Middlesex Justices, and which may have been allowed under colour of the provision for expansions up to one third the size of the previous building. It is laid out on the lines of a Vitruvian diagram, albeit unobtrusively, and it sits a little awkwardly against the semicircle inherited from John Best's fighting birds. How much confidence Jones had in the structural viability of this compromise may perhaps be judged from his provision of extra support, longitudinally in the stair turrets and laterally in buttresses, a most unusual feature in designs from his hand. Possibly part of the original wall was retained. Its height is not absorbed into Jones's modular system, and it may well have been defined by the height of Best's cockpit. Certainly the elevation of the theatre in the Worcester College drawing retains a general resemblance to the seventeenth-century cockpits illustrated in the surviving engravings.

Here, then, is circumstantial evidence of a new identification of some importance to English theatre history. Like most such evidence it lacks certainty but not persuasiveness. If it is accepted the Worcester College drawings will emerge as documents of outstanding interest, more useful than de Witt's sketch of the Swan. They give a precise, detailed reading of a major private theatre of the Jacobean age, one moreover that carried the traditions of its time through the theatrical depression of the Commonwealth well into the Restoration. I have no space to enter into the larger issues of stage history raised by these drawings of the Cockpit, if that is what they are, though their Vitruvian element is of singular interest in the light of Frances Yates's theory, developed in *The Theatre of the World*,[1] that the Elizabethan theatre derived from Vitruvian principles. Neither can I enter here into what would have to be an intricate discussion of John Webb's work for the Cockpit in the 1650s, when he designed scenes for Davenant's *Siege of Rhodes* whose dimensions precisely fit the theatre shown in the Jones drawings.[2]

[1] (1969), *passim.*

[2] Since the publication of W. G. Keith's article, 'The Designs for the First Movable Scenery on the English Public Stage,' *Burlington Magazine* 25 (1914), 29–33 and 85–98, it has been assumed that the six setting designs for *The Siege of Rhodes* now at Chatsworth show the same stage as a plan and section in B. L. Lansdowne MS 1171, fols 11 and 12, and that this stage is the one Davenant set up at Rutland

Footnote continued on page 167

One detail of the Cockpit's subsequent career which tends to confirm the identification can, however, be dealt with quite briefly. Among the drawings from Jones's hand at Chatsworth is a rough sketch[1] showing an arched proscenium with a railed stage set with wings, cloud borders and a 'citti of rileve' before a backcloth. The paper is endorsed, 'for y[e] cokpitt for my lo Chāberalin 1639.' This sketch is hard to identify, chiefly because the shape of the proscenium is quite unlike any that could reasonably be fitted into the Cockpit-in-Court theatre at Whitehall.[2] Part of the difficulty lies in its clear direction to the Lord Chamberlain, within whose care the Whitehall Cockpit certainly lay, while Drury Lane did not. By 1639, however, much had changed at the Cockpit. Christopher Beeston, who in 1616 had so little influence at court that his illegally-built house was pulled down at the instance of the Privy Council, had by now established a unique and very convenient relationship with the Lord Chamberlain himself. In that officer's warrant book there is an entry dated 21 February 1636[/7]: 'A Warrant to sweare M[r] Christopher Bieston his M[tes] servant in y[e] place of Gouuernor of the new Company of the Kinges & Queenes boyes.'[3] This status of Governor was, as G. E. Bentley remarks, 'unprecedented since the time of the Elizabethan and early Jacobean boy companies.'[4] A short time later, moreover, and despite a flagrant violation of the plague prohibition at the Cockpit, Beeston was granted unusual privileges by the Lord Chamberlain in the matter of the possession of disputed playscripts. After Christopher's death in 1639 his son William inherited the special relationship, and by a warrant of 5 April he was sworn 'vnder the Title of Gouuernor & Instructer of the Kings & Queens young Company of Actors'.[5]

In 1639, then, first Christopher and then William Beeston enjoyed a contact with the Lord Chamberlain so direct that it appears for a time to have bypassed the authority of the Master of the Revels.[6] This is the context in which Jones's drawing 'for y[e] cokpitt for my lo Chāberalin' must be placed. The particular

House in 1656. However discrepancies between the two sets of drawings show that if the scene designs were for Rutland House, the stage drawings must have been for somewhere else, presumably the Cockpit, to which Davenant transferred the production in 1658. The Cockpit stage had been dismantled in 1649 and rebuilt in 1651 by William Beeston at a cost of £200. See Leslie Hotson, *The Commonwealth and Restoration Stage* (Cambridge, Mass., 1928), p. 96. The Lansdowne MS section shows a raked stage 2′ 6″ high at the front. If the Rutland House proscenium were mounted on it, the total height would be 13′ 6″, or precisely the distance from the floor to the ground story entablature in the elevation of the *frons scenae* in the Worcester College drawing which I hold to be of the Cockpit. Moreover, while the whole width of the stage in the Jones plan is just over 23′, measured between the rails of the boxes which flank it, the elevation shows an empty space ready to take a stage structure, and this space is exactly 22′ 4″ wide, just the width of the stage shown in Webb's plan. Mackintosh, 'Inigo Jones – Theatre Architect', p. 104, notes the similar widths of the Webb frontispiece and the Jones stage, but does not allow for the inconsistencies between the two sets of Webb drawings. The facts must be presented more fully than is possible in this note, but it would appear that Davenant, who had been connected with the Cockpit since 1640, set up his Rutland House theatre with its stage in mind and was able to transfer Webb's settings to it without alteration.

1 Stephen Orgel and Roy Strong, *Inigo Jones: The Theatre of the Stuart Court*, 2 vols. (1973), II, 786, drawing no. 443.

2 See the discussions in Bentley, *Jacobean and Caroline Stage*, VI, 51–2 and Orgel and Strong, *Inigo Jones*, II, 787–8.

3 Quoted by Bentley, *Jacobean and Caroline Stage*, VI, 68.

4 *Ibid.*

5 *Ibid.*, p. 70.

6 There is no mistaking Herbert's satisfaction when, a year later, he notes in his Office Book that William Beeston has been committed to Marshalsea for putting on an unlicensed play which upset the king. See Joseph Quincy Adams (ed.), *The Dramatic Records of Sir Henry Herbert* (New Haven, 1917), p. 66.

play for which the design was made remains unknown, but the difficulty of trying to fit it into the Cockpit-in-Court now disappears. The proscenium, although only roughly drawn, is accurately contained within a square. As Iain Mackintosh has shown,[1] it would, without adjustment, fit the stage of the cockpit in Drury Lane as we know it from the Worcester College drawings. There the railed front of the stage, which is included only in the plan, measures about 21′ 6″ between the centres of the gallery posts closest to it which define its visible width. The height of the ceiling above the floor of the stage is also 21′ 6″, and an arch made to the pattern of Jones's sketch would neatly fill the opening onto the stage as seen from the auditorium. Now at last the 'lo Chāberalin' sketch makes sense. It is the earliest stage design for the professional theatre in England, dashed off by Inigo Jones to fit a theatre which, there is every reason to believe, he had himself created almost a quarter of a century before.

[1] Mackintosh, 'Inigo Jones – Theatre Architect' p. 103.

THEORY AND PRACTICE: STRATFORD 1976

ROGER WARREN

In an article in *The Sunday Times* a few days before the 1976 Stratford season opened, Trevor Nunn showed a healthy distrust of current cliché:

> 'Free Shakespeare! Banish conceptions. End the tyranny of Directors' Theatre. Let the plays speak for themselves.'
>
> I disagree with these essentially academic slogans.[1]

His distrust of academic cliché had positive results, especially in *Macbeth*. As Robert Cushman put it in his review in *The Observer*, Macbeth

> is the most self-aware of tragic heroes, and the play makes us free of his mind. (Here of course lies its greatness – not ... in the piling up of external symbols of chaos to point a perfectly obvious moral.)

Since Mr Nunn's production brought this out, 'the play gets into your bones'.[2] The implications of the imagery were made clear, but with a lightness of touch, and through character. Again, his imaginative independence enabled him to re-value the second half of *Romeo and Juliet*, or at any rate to turn its weaknesses to positive account.

On the other hand, some of Mr Nunn's own slogans don't always correspond to what we actually see. He made two basic policy statements. He re-iterated that the RSC is 'first and foremost ... a company':

> however well people may be type-cast and however much the public responds to famous names dropping in for their short stints in the theatre, nothing can replace the ability to listen, adapt, reveal, and risk acquired by actors who work and develop together over many years.

Second, the RSC would continue its pursuit of 'simplicity' of staging. Although Mr Nunn denied that his permanent stage for the 1976 season (see plate VIA) was a 'reconstruction' or an 'attempt to be nostalgic about past ages', this basic set was quite obviously based on Elizabethan models:

> there will be places for the public not only at the sides of the stage but also (as in the de Witt drawing of the Swan Theatre, and as in a number of conjectural reconstructions of Elizabethan playhouses) above and behind the playing area.

In fact, very few members of this Stratford company had worked with the RSC 'over many years'. Many of them were newcomers; the company as a whole had the inevitable strengths and weaknesses of any *ad hoc* group. The notable successes of the season came from Ian McKellen as Macbeth and Leontes, certainly a 'famous name dropping in', and from Judi Dench (Beatrice and Lady Macbeth) and Donald Sinden (Benedick), both appearing occasionally rather than regularly with the RSC. The best team-work came in *Much Ado*, from four complete newcomers to the RSC; in general the company no longer appears to command the powerful middle-range talent it once did. Sometimes Mr Nunn appears to neglect such matters in favour of inventing general exercises which give minor actors as much to do as major, most notably in the song-and-dance routines of *The Comedy of Errors*. But when it comes to delivering the

[1] *The Sunday Times*, 28 March 1976.
[2] *The Observer*, 12 September 1976.

text, some of these actors simply let the performances down. In *Macbeth*, for instance, it was the 'famous names' who realized Mr Nunn's ideas superbly, and the non-famous (Duncan, Lennox, the Sergeant, the Doctor, especially the Porter and Ross) whose ineptitude seemed to me to imperil entire scenes.[1]

I don't feel that you establish a 'company' atmosphere merely by having your bit-part actors in *Romeo and Juliet* strenuously practising fencing while the audience assembles; still less by having your Chorus (in trendy denim, as opposed to the aggressive – and scrappily ugly – Renaissance clothes of the others) wandering amongst them, swiping other people's lines, making a terrible mess of them in the interests of irrelevant, ingratiating community contact, and nearly wrecking the (finely achieved) grief of the finale by sidling on to close the play with the prince's last lines. This was a grotesque example of how Mr Nunn can allow theory to get in the way of successful practice.

As for simplicity, it would be a great mistake to confuse *Romeo and Juliet*'s real simplicity with, or attribute its success to, its 'Elizabethanisms'. The lighting was either bright or very bright throughout, and people carried torches which weren't lit, as presumably they did in the Elizabethan daylight. The balcony and tomb scenes would have been just as good if atmospherically lit – and the ball scene might have worked. It is mere pedantry to deny lighting effects in a modern theatre. This affectation was not repeated in the other productions, and I do not raise such issues to attack the company or this production. Quite the reverse: the opening *Romeo* worked, for the simple reason that Mr Nunn had some extremely imaginative ideas about essential passages, had quite obviously rehearsed his company assiduously, and cast good actors in certain crucial roles. Its success derived, that is, from the talents of director and actors, which is precisely whence good productions always derive their strength, not from peripheral decorations.

I

This was the only *Romeo* I have seen to avoid collapse half-way through, actually to gain in power, and to culminate in a superb (and even moving) final scene. For all that strenuous fencing, Mercutio and his friends were tiresome rather than vivid, and the ball was exceptionally pedestrian. But thereafter Mr Nunn began to show his hand. The lovers were human and touching in the balcony scene, which Mr Nunn encouraged them to pace and time with great naturalness, conviction, and even humour. Then Mr Nunn played his first real trump card – David Waller's Friar, not the usual pious contemplative, but a vigorously earthy man, an enthusiastic seeker after the 'virtues excellent' in the world of nature. He communicated his enthusiasm to us in the punch and committed force with which he outlined the dual capacity of that 'weak flower' which

> being smelt, with *that* part cheers each part;
> Being tasted, slays all senses with the heart;

and this seemed also to underline the two-edged quality of the lovers' passion, positive yet destructive. Mr Nunn's achievement was to allow the Friar's viewpoint full conviction without in any way, as some commentators have done, cheapening that of the lovers by contrast; rather, balcony and cell were held in finely-judged balance.

From here the production gained and gained in power; the sympathetic treatment of the lovers, and so our sense of waste at the end, was given an extra twist by Mr Nunn's finest

[1] It is only fair to record that both *The Observer* and *The Sunday Times* of 12 September 1976 singled out the Porter/Ross for commendation, and that *The Observer* found 'the supporting playing . . . the best all round at Stratford for years'.

invention: Romeo died cradling Juliet in his arms; just *before* he took the poison, her arm around his neck began to move; swamped by grief, he didn't notice that she was in fact alive. And so what has usually seemed a blemish, the purely accidental nature of the tragedy, was turned into a positive feature: stressing what a close thing it was intensified the pathos of their deaths. What is more, the reconciliation of the Houses was for once genuinely convincing, because prepared for: John Woodvine's violent Capulet had to be forcibly restrained from assaulting Juliet, and indeed, at the end, the Friar as well; so when this man took his adversary's hand and called him '*brother* Montague' (to the amazement of all present) the perfunctorily written close acquired genuine humanity. This moment, like Juliet's reviving, typify Mr Nunn's real qualities – not following manifestoes, but an ability to bring out the human realities of situations. Often his finest inventions are his simplest; but this *human* simplicity is a very different matter from an affected scenic simplicity derived from the modish trends of academic or theatrical theory.

II

It may seem perverse that, after criticizing superficial Elizabethanisms, I should pine for an Elizabethan *Much Ado*, but it would be a change; of the six productions I've seen, only one was not set in the Nineteenth Century. The case for such a setting has been best put by a perceptive review of Stratford's first Victorian version:

> For all its undertones of seriousness, *Much Ado* is . . . about the behaviour of largely superficial people in a superficial society: what is important is that the society should be real and recognizable.[1]

The argument is that Shakespeare's presentation of a group of people who behave outrageously in pursuit of their shallow ideas of 'honour' can be grasped more clearly in terms of Nineteenth-Century 'officers and gentlemen' than in Renaissance ones.

John Barton, staging the play in Imperial India, sharpened the distinction between the civilian and military worlds; as Anne Barton's programme note put it, 'the offence done not only to his honour but to that of Don Pedro, his superior officer, is all that counts' to Claudio. So when tremendous gaiety gives way to the play's dark centre, Claudio's 'tomorrow in the congregation, where I should wed, there will I shame her' was both chilling and completely comprehensible. The transition from one mood to another was underlined at the end of the scene (and of the first half): Ursula appeared on a balcony, singing peacefully in the warm night air; suddenly Claudio and Don Pedro drew the pistols with which they had been shooting game earlier and shattered the peace by firing them menacingly into the audience as the lights faded for the interval.

Despite this preparation, the church scene, oddly, was the one scene that didn't come off. It was too intimate, too un-elaborate a ceremony. Part of the cruelty of the behaviour of these honourable men is that Hero is shamed *in public*, 'in the congregation'. Here, there was no congregation; it hardly seemed worth all the effort. But by contrast, what Anne Barton's note called the 'imposed ritual of empty atonement' before Hero's tomb was superbly and daringly realized. 'Round about her tomb they go', indeed: Claudio and Don Pedro marched in a formal circle with military precision, half drew and then completely drew their sabres by numbers, then reversed the process to sheathe them again. These mechanical military honours exactly fitted the mechanical formality of the text. But then dawn broke,

[1] *Leamington Spa Courier*, 29 August 1958.

and Don Pedro gave full value to his warmly flexible lines about the gentle day as the play moved up into (literally) the light again. It was the strength of Mr Barton's scheme that it could accommodate all the shifts of that very tricky scene v, i, where Don Pedro and Claudio joke after Hero's supposed death, resuming their camaraderie with Benedick as if nothing had happened; and that it could enable them to move from shock at Borachio's revelation to humorous conversation with Dogberry in a few lines with no sense of strain at all – which is, of course, exactly what Shakespeare's text (but by no means every production) achieves (plate VIB).

Part of this strength derived from finding a real place for Dogberry in the scheme. He and his Watchmen were Indian natives, and the malapropisms were imperfectly assimilated English – imperfections delivered with the absolute confidence of sublime innocence and genial condescension towards those less well endowed than he by John Woodvine's beautifully timed, entirely unforced Dogberry, a blessed change from the routine figure of tedious farce. The structure of the production enabled Robin Ellis and Richard Durden to give first-rate performances of Don Pedro and Claudio, consistent and thoroughly convincing – the best Claudio I recall, indeed, and the best Hero too: an attractively open, honest performance from Cherie Lunghi, informing Claudio in no uncertain terms that 'surely as I live, I *am* a *maid*'.

In a very interesting lecture, which indicated that at any rate *his* theory and practice don't conflict, Mr Barton implied that there was no reason for the others to think Don John a 'villain'; but wasn't the war they've just come back from against *him*? Isn't that why he has just been 'reconciled to the prince', and why he particularly hates Claudio: 'that young start-up hath all the glory of *my overthrow*'? This whimpering Don John, farcically falling over his trailing sabre, couldn't indeed have won anything; but a dubious interpretation became disastrous because of the sheer hopelessness of the execution, even technically, all the more noticeable in the sophisticated company of this prince and Claudio. But this was the only jarring note in a scrupulously consistent show; and the permanent set looked much better with its Elizabethanism totally disguised as an outpost of the Empire; the oatmeal of John Napier's canopies, muslin curtains, giant feathers and cane furniture blended perfectly with the bleached look of the timbers when softly lit, and set off the costumes, mostly in black and white.

So there was much to enjoy before even touching upon the main triumph of the production – Judi Dench and Donald Sinden as Beatrice and Benedick (plate VIIA). Predictable, of course; but that didn't decrease the sheer delight of hearing those brilliant lines delivered with such panache and relish, but more important still with such awareness of the human realities they imply: their wit reveals humanity and strength of feeling, that of the court potentially explosive frivolity. All the great moments went off superbly, and all were related to character and situation: 'Against my will (*pause*) I am sent (*pause; glower; then very emphatically*) to bid you (*then very fast, very loud*) come in to dinner!': Judi Dench underlined this by emphatically beating a small portable dinner gong. After this unappetizing invitation, Mr Sinden's triumphant 'There's a double meaning in that' justly brought the house down. Again, Beatrice obsessively swept up the scattered flowers left over from the calamitous wedding to control her feelings as her dialogue with Benedick began; the business would no doubt work with a lesser actress – but this dry account can't begin to capture the way it was used, nor to communicate the life, command, control, and sheer human feeling of two superb actors at the height of their powers.

III

The Winter's Tale, co-directed by John Barton and Trevor Nunn, underlined both the advantages and drawbacks of a company whose work is based on one dramatist: on the one hand, a new production can develop discoveries made in earlier ones; on the other, there is a constant temptation to avoid last time's solution, however successful. *The Winter's Tale* presented this temptation in an acute form, since Trevor Nunn's 1969 version had been outstandingly successful, one of the half dozen most imaginative productions of Shakespeare I have seen. Mr Nunn carried over into the new production the most crucial feature of the previous one, the switch from normal stage lighting to weird coldness in order to emphasize the sudden way in which fantasies seize upon Leontes's fevered brain.

This basic effect has two important consequences. First, it greatly aids the actor, since it uses an extreme, startling technical effect to parallel Shakespeare's own extreme, daring psychological technique for Leontes – one moment a man engaged in domestic intimacy, the next possessed by violent jealousy. The lighting device has the effect of enabling Leontes to deliver those convoluted speeches with an uncanny clarity; the whole play becomes much easier to follow than usual. Thus set up, Ian McKellen proceeded to deliver the text with an unfussy, direct power which gained immeasurably in emotional impact and conviction from his abandonment of all those fidgety mannerisms, vocal and physical, which he has in the past found necessary to suggest passion.

The other main result of that lighting effect is that, since it by-passes irrelevant conjectures about 'gradual' jealousy by emphasizing the sudden shifts of style, it frees the actors to make the very most of those domestic exchanges that precede Leontes's first outburst. This essential domestic, family atmosphere was conveyed by comfortable chairs, rugs, and clothes in Scandinavian furs and folk-woven materials, hot reds and oranges predominating, bathed in amber light (plate VIIB). This intimacy was reinforced by enclosing the stage with curtains decorated by primitive symbols; a shattered wintry tree intruded incongruously into the middle of the set, much as Leontes's suspicions intrude into that family atmosphere. This tree also provided a stark background for Hermione's defence, a suggestion of 'this place i' th' open air'. This suggestion was badly needed, since the permanent set robbed the trial of a sense of space, of sinister occasion, as it did the church scene in *Much Ado*.

Even so, Marilyn Taylerson's frail, delicate Hermione rose splendidly to a powerful defence, though she pushed the climax into rant; earlier on, her 'I never wished to see you sorry: now/I trust I shall' had been petulant rather than moving; and though she was good at the domestic opening, I prefer something stronger and warmer in this role, that mature glow which made Judi Dench such a remarkable Hermione in the earlier version, 'as rare and precious as the text suggests', as one critic put it, speaking for all.[1] Miss Taylerson lacked the sheer distinction to convey that; and so, not for the first time in a production of this play, it was Paulina rather than Hermione who balanced Leontes: Barbara Leigh-Hunt unerringly achieved every humorous effect which Shakespeare has so carefully placed in the baby scene, both to ease the tension and then to screw it up again; and her 'thousand knees' speech after the trial was, like Mr McKellen's speeches, charged with a powerful clarity totally free from rant: a superb performance to match his.

In Bohemia the designs became schematic

[1] Hilary Spurling, *The Spectator*, 22 May 1969.

and constricting, instead of liberating as in the abandoned *joie-de-vivre* of the earlier version; this was where deliberate avoidance of an earlier solution was most noticeable. The Bear was another primitive folk emblem, an actor in a huge mask *guiding* Antigonus off to slaughter. I thought it worked, because unnatural shock is of the essence in this bizarre scene. But after the interval, the 'folk' element verged on the pedantic: the costumes now seemed Serbo-Croatian, and Perdita was 'pranked up' less like the goddess Flora than like some Byzantine icon; Michael Williams's Autolycus worked so hard that the effort showed, though he had his moments, introducing his wares like glove puppets through a curtain before emerging as a trinket-laden Father Christmas; and though Mr Barton and Cherie Lunghi strove prodigiously to bring out the 'thematic' points behind Perdita's flower speeches, the effort was again evident. I begin to suspect that those speeches, lovely as they are, are insufficiently integrated into the basic dramatic pointing of the scene to be grasped immediately – quite unlike the craggy verse of the court scenes which, however difficult or austere on the page, always works superbly in the theatre.

The re-appearance of the contrite Leontes made the point at once; Mr McKellen's delivery was very moving in its simplicity, and so was Miss Taylerson's return to life, her brief utterance skilfully suggesting how strange it seemed to be among people again after that long seclusion. As in 1969, the moving quality of the scene was intensified by having Leontes and his family touching hands in a silent circle of reunion, filling the stage, as one critic finely put it, 'with a sense of mystery and strangeness that passes rational explanation or the power of language to describe'.[1]

[1] Michael Billington, *The Guardian*, 4 June 1976.

IV

John Barton's close involvement with *Troilus and Cressida* over several productions has its dangers. He knows it *so* well that he sometimes appears to forget that what the audience needs, primarily, is to have the main points of an exceptionally difficult text, and especially the main sense of the *arguments*, made as clear as possible. He achieved this in 1960, but his later versions have tended to lose sight of main issues in the exploration of a particular passage or detail or relationship. The result has sometimes been bewildering rather than, as he obviously intends, enriching: 'Shakespeare invites tragic, comic, satiric, intellectual and compassionate responses almost at the same time.' Quite so, but with a text so complex that it's often hard to grasp the basic sense, there is a limit to what an audience can take in all at once.

Mr Barton carried over several features from his controversial 1968 version: the Trojans were virtually naked when they went into battle, and so were the Myrmidons throughout; Achilles was showily effeminate; Thersites was covered with bleeding sores and wore a grotesque mouth-shaped codpiece with a dangling red tongue/penis; Thersites and Pandarus had a song-and-dance routine for the epilogue. My objection to these things was not that they were offensive, as some found them, but that they distracted one from concentrating on that complicated language, without being closely enough related to the text to act as visual symbols of it. His most successful innovation last time was a Helen who was not a caricatured whore but a 'glimpse of a human woman'; but Helen this time was led on by Paris, who drew her by a golden chain around her neck, and compelled to speak the unexceptional lines about unarming Hector grimly and slowly, as if the Helen/Paris relationship was growing stale – one of the few deteriorations, surely, *not* suggested by the text: 'Sweet, above thought I love thee.'

In underlining the text's deflation of the heroes, Mr Barton has tended in fact to undermine both the possibility of characterisation and often of simple comprehension: Agamemnon carried a frying-pan to the first council, and wore a bucolic straw hat; but 'satire' was carried to the self-defeating point of sheer inaudibility in his case and of having Ulysses rise again and again during Agamemnon's and Nestor's speeches in an attempt to stop the flow of senseless rhetoric and get a hearing; a similar jokiness underlined Aeneas's and Ajax's verbosity with apparently unending trumpet-calls; the balletic posturings of the Hector/Ajax duel were simply ridiculous. Shakespeare certainly satirizes heroes' feet of clay, but if Achilles, for instance, doesn't even *seem* a warrior-hero to start with, what is there to satirize? More seriously still, Mr Barton equipped Cressida with a stock courtesan mask, fitted to the back of her head-dress, which she suddenly revealed as she walked off at the end of the betrayal scene. This gross schematic ostentation flatly contradicted both the ambiguity of Cressida's feeling, and Francesca Annis's subtle presentation of it.

This device emphasized what seems an uncertainty in Mr Barton's approach. He once said in these pages, 'what happens, by the end, to Troilus and Cressida and Hector is not [black comedy]. ... I feel a great compassion for what becomes of Troilus and Cressida'.[1] And certainly Troilus and Cressida for the first time in my experience held the centre of their play. Francesca Annis perfectly caught the 'slippery' changeability of Cressida, sophisticated one moment, the next giving intense value to the haunting solemnity with which Cressida swears truth,

> When time is old and hath forgot itself,
> When waterdrops have worn the stones of Troy.

This scene, with its magnificent juxtaposition of present and future, and of passionate seriousness and bawdy wit, was the high point of the play, superbly realized by Miss Annis, David Waller's expert Pandarus, and Mike Gwilym's coherent and un-mannered Troilus.

All the more surprising, then, that Mr Barton should seem to satirize Troilus's savage outburst of disillusion by making Ulysses ironically applaud it. Perhaps the idea was to satirize Ulysses's lack of understanding, though this is unlikely since Troilus here, and only here, fell into the ranting of the conventional Troiluses; but whatever the motive, the presentation of both Ulysses and Hector reinforced my feeling of uncertainty about Mr Barton's viewpoint. It's true that there is a 'shiftingness of view ... in the play's presentation of character', a contrast between a character's 'beliefs' and his 'actions'. But it's surely enough to make very clear (as this production certainly did) Hector's *volte-face* in the Trojan council; elsewhere the presentation of Hector was 'shifting' to the point of confusion rather than complexity. Michael Pennington achieved another of those haunting, magical moments, juxtaposing past and present, when he saluted Nestor with humanity and gravity, stilling the theatre:

> Let me embrace thee, good old chronicle,
> That hast so long walk'd hand in hand with time.

But the next moment he was ostentatiously flexing his muscles (as again in the farewell to Andromache) and appeared to be tipping the character into overt parody.

Again, it is one thing to stress the contrast between Ulysses's elaborate stratagem to bring Achilles back to the battle line, and the human motive, Patroclus's death, which actually brings him back. But you can't grasp such an irony unless you have followed the

[1] *Shakespeare Survey 25* (Cambridge 1972), pp. 67–8.

detailed arguments of Ulysses in the first place. While Tony Church certainly made all the points very clearly, with full relish for the language, Mr Barton maddeningly distracted from his Time speech by having Achilles constantly play with the book that Ulysses had been reading. I don't understand the motive for this at all. Of course we need to see Achilles's reactions; but first and foremost we need to follow Ulysses's speech, in detail and without distractions. Even if Ulysses's attitudes are subsequently undermined, they need to be established clearly first.

Yet for all these reservations it was a consistently interesting and absorbing occasion; the long evening seemed to pass very quickly. Whatever Mr Barton's over-emphasis or over-ingenuity, he enabled his cast to bring out the 'shifting' ambiguous quality of much, at least, of the play, and certainly much more than in his previous version.

V

For *The Comedy of Errors*, John Napier transformed the permanent set into a contemporary, cluttered Turkish market; Aegeon was clearly in the rag trade, and garments festooned the balconies; the balcony of Adriana's house overlooked this market; the Porpentine and the Tiger were bars in the market, complete with a group to provide a backing for Guy Woolfenden's interpolated musical numbers. Again and again, a scene would stop for a song based on fragments of the text at that point, or simply on doggerel supplied for the occasion. Adriana and Luciana had a duet, 'A man is master of his liberty', Antipholus of Syracuse a solo based on 'Am I in earth'; a large-scale ensemble illustrated his

> There's not a man I meet but doth salute me
> As if I were their well-acquainted friend

which turned into a nightmare of illusions; Pinch's exorcisms were built up into an even longer ensemble; both Dromios had extended numbers, one to illustrate the feeble jokes about Time and baldness, the other to elaborate on the beatings he receives. Although these numbers appeared to derive from the text itself, they in fact had the effect of superimposing one medium on another.

Trevor Nunn rightly says that the play works 'when it genuinely uplifts us, when it makes us feel better'. The RSC's previous celebrated version (1962–72, directed by Clifford Williams) achieved exactly that, but there the 'company' feel derived not from generalized routines but from the characters being sharply detailed individuals, reacting to each other and to their situations, out of which the humour arose. Here, the spoken text was again packed with appropriate invention, often very funny, especially the shutting out of Antipholus of Ephesus and the contradictory evidence of the finale, played as a courtroom drama, complete with 'exhibits'; but the sung ensembles tended to merge everyone into puppets, and to blunt personality. These interpolations may have been good for the general morale of the company but they did not seem to me actually to help the performances of its individual members in any way.

Roger Rees's Antipholus of Syracuse, for instance, was potentially excellent, but the director's routines did not help him develop that potential into a complete characterization. Luciana was a bespectacled bookworm, trotting out Renaissance clichés on order and male mastery from her reading, preserved from caricature by Francesca Annis's natural charm and poise. Both she and Judi Dench (Adriana) had suddenly to switch off their performances of the text itself in mid-scene and concentrate on singing; these moments did nothing to support their interpretations; I thought they strained them unnecessarily. Smaller roles stood even less chance of being sustained: the Duke was a Greek military dictator, switching from declarations of the law over a public address system to private sympathy for Aegeon; but he made absolutely nothing of the moment-to-moment bewilderment of the finale, which a succession of very human Dukes in the Williams version made much more of than was allowed to emerge here. Mr Nunn certainly appeared to 'give the audience a really good time', but I thought he did so by imposed routines rather than, as the Williams production did, by emphasizing Shakespeare's distinctive humanizing of his rather inhuman Plautine models.

VI

Trevor Nunn's *Macbeth* at the Other Place (the RSC's studio theatre) was the best example of the company's developing work on a single play. Mr Nunn's elaborate version at Stratford in 1974 (which opened too late for review in these pages) was drastically simplified for the Aldwych in 1975; it had been further refined for the small confines of the Other Place, where it was played within a black magic circle painted on the floor, outside which the cast sat on boxes until needed; and, as at the Aldwych, there was no interval, which helped prevent the second half from winding down.

Much of the approach and detail was carried over, particularly the clash between religious purity and black magic. Purity was embodied by Duncan, very infirm (in 1974 he was blind), dressed in white and accompanied by church organ music, set against the black magic of the witches, who even chanted 'Double, double' to the *Dies irae*. The 1974 version used black masses, church services, and the coronations of, in turn, Duncan, Macbeth, and Malcolm. Here a gold robe and crown simply passed from one to the other, with the additional point that, by the end, ceremony had become meaningless because Macbeth had so desecrated the office: a stunned weariness overcame Malcolm and the surviving lords, and instead of a coronation, robe and crown were simply carried away after his weary exit, leaving the stage to the weapons and shattered trappings of Macbeth's regime.

Other striking effects reappeared: Lady Macbeth sat on the stool to emphasize that Banquo's ghost was an illusion; the witches were practical and down-to-earth, the first carrying a handbag and mixing her brew in an old kettle, and only the second having any obvious link with the supernatural; Macbeth was compelled to *drink* their brew and was blindfolded to 'see' the inheritance of Banquo and his heirs as an appalling insight of his own. The sharpest development was in the presentation of the besieged Macbeth. When in 1974 he sat on top of a precarious pile of chairs to look for Birnham Wood, it seemed merely a quirky trick. This time, he sat surrounded by the boxes that had served as seats earlier and by the ceremonial robe and crown, completely the focus of attention; the besieging lords played their brief scenes outside the circle while he still sat there; he looked for Birnham Wood by putting just one box on top of another so that he could reach an overhead spotlight which he directed first towards Birnham and then all round the theatre; it then began to sway wildly of its own accord, the estate of the world all undone.

The vital development, though, was that these ideas, interesting in themselves, were forged into a convincing whole because, this time, Mr Nunn had two players able to rise to all the challenges of Macbeth and Lady Macbeth. Ian McKellen, with greased-back hair, black-shirted and coldly efficient, recalled the fascist image of the 1930s. Judi Dench, slight and dressed in sober (drab?) black with a headscarf, was simple and direct, her invoking of the spirits uncluttered by the 1974 trappings of black magic; from this simplicity it was an easy step to the welcome of Duncan, so deceptively open that Duncan dismissed Macduff, who was supporting him ('By your leave') and took *her* arm ('Hostess!') so that she could smilingly lead him to his death. As they left the circle, Macbeth rapidly entered it from the other side and began 'If it were done... then 'twere well it were done *quickly*' very fast, neatly underlining their *combined* handling of the situation.

They certainly seemed husband and wife (plate VIIIB), not merely in passion but in the quiet, natural, almost colloquial handling of their conversations. She brought out Lady Macbeth's essentially practical qualities: 'It *must* seem / their / guilt' was a slow, emphatic explanation; 'there are two lodged together' was an attempt to calm his fears of the supernatural by stressing the ordinary and the reasonable; her 'Come on!' meant 'snap out of it' in response to 'after life's fitful fever he sleeps well'. All this made the cracking of their relationship especially successful: Macbeth ordered her out of the room ('God be with you') before plotting Banquo's murder; 'Come, seeling night' was addressed directly to her, and at 'scarf up the tender eye' he covered her face, thereby adding to her bewilderment in the text. After the banquet, her hysterical 'go at once!' instantly gave way to an attempt at graciousness ('a kind good night'); there they sat, she bleakly smiling and he waving goodbye in the aftermath of a foaming fit, both total wrecks, a marvellous image of the hollow kingship they risked so much to gain. But then she collapsed; he dragged her up at 'young in deed' and pulled her away, firmly replacing her as the more resolute of the two.

Fine as these scenes were, best of all was the scene with the murderers. Macbeth was at his most briskly administrative, busy with papers, as he blackened Banquo; then he suddenly turned a cold, beady eye upon them to make the distinctions about dogs and men; once the business of the meeting was over, a dismissive jerk of the head to Seyton to get rid of them contrasted with the affable 'abide within' to them. At the end, his vision was one of total nihilism, with no touch of conventional sentimentality at 'troops of friends'.

Mr Nunn, for all his emphasis on black magic versus white purity, also avoided sentimental over-emphasis of those images or passages which are said to embody the 'poetry of the commonweal': John Woodvine's 'temple-haunting martlet' was a genially paternal lesson for Fleance, and the 'positive' value of the image lost nothing by being expressed lightly. If Malcolm was dressed in symbolic white sweater and jodphurs, as opposed to everyone else's black, there was no forcing in the English scene: Roger Rees was encouraged to play his deception of Macduff and the description of the King's Evil easily and naturally.

On the other hand, Macduff was variable, dour, devoid of personality (as in the text?) and Duncan was so mannered and so infuriatingly holy that he simply cried out for assassination, at total variance with Mr Nunn's setting-up of the character. It is also hard to see how Mr Nunn can encourage (or permit) the presentation of the Porter as a stand-up comedian, hopelessly wrecking his ironic commentary on the main action ('porter of hell-gate', 'devil-porter it no further'), quite apart from the inadequacy of the performance, to which I referred at the beginning of this article.

This production, in fact, presented the strengths and weaknesses discussed above very clearly, and added another doubt about the theory: I did not feel that this production *needed* to be in a studio. It is I daresay a relief to the company to play in a small theatre (though Mr McKellen spared himself nothing in the projection of sheer intensity); while it is good in theory for the audience to be close to the actors, in practice most scenes were laid out as if *all* the audience was in front, as were all the productions in the main house, so that if you sat at the back of the main stage, or at the sides in the Other Place, you missed much. I should dearly have liked to have seen Judi Dench's face, for instance, as she greeted Duncan. If the general impression of Stratford 1976 is that it was pretentious in theory but impressive in practice, that is surely very much the right way round.[1]

[1] I should put my personal view in perspective by saying that the press was divided over *Romeo*, *Troilus*, and *Winter's Tale*, virtually unanimous in enthusiasm for *Much Ado* and *Macbeth*, and in finding that permanent set crampingly unhelpful.

THE YEAR'S CONTRIBUTIONS TO SHAKESPEARIAN STUDY

1. CRITICAL STUDIES

reviewed by R. F. HILL

Giorgio Melchiori's[1] brilliant book on the Sonnets (a re-working of the original Italian version published in 1973) has as its sub-title *An Experiment in Criticism.* Although relying significantly on structuralist analytical techniques it is, nonetheless, critical of their rigorous and abstract application which runs the risk of 'imprisoning [the poem] in pre-established categories which precede the very act of creation, so as to suppress all truly critical considerations'. Melchiori's own method is therefore a convergence of a variety of critical approaches, taking into account, for example, structural and linguistic features, sociological and political backgrounds, ideological links with Shakespeare's other works and those of his contemporaries. Using computer statistical data he points out in what respects Shakespeare's sonnet sequence is atypical in comparison with those of his contemporaries, notably in its high incidence of the second person and the presence of a dramatic I–thou relationship. However, where such a relationship is not set up and we have 'meditative' sonnets a drama is still acted out within the speaker's mind. Of these, nos. 94, 121, 129, 146 are exceptional in their themes being dramatic meditations on power, social behaviour, sex, and religion, and the book comprises in the main a critique of these four sonnets. Subtle and penetrating throughout the work is especially impressive in its demonstration of the interrelationship of formal and semantic structures and in its tracing of ironies and ambiguities in the minutiae of form. The formal excellence of supposedly unsatisfactory sonnets is convincingly shown, although some of his readings will doubtless be challenged. For example, his rejection on rhythmic and grammatical evidence of modern emendations to Sonnet 129 seems to push structuralism too far. This book makes heavy demands on the reader but rewards one with an enriched sense of the man-centredness of Shakespeare's universe and his ambivalent attitude towards its workings.

Rather less critical rigour is displayed in J. H. Padel's[2] brief speculations about the human drama inspiring and shaping the Sonnets. Although likely to convince few the account is worth recording for the new vistas it opens up on a topic which one supposes will never cease to stimulate the curious. Launching off from Dover Wilson's hypothesis that the first seventeen sonnets were commissioned by the Countess of Pembroke for William Herbert's seventeenth birthday in April 1597 Padel notes that these sonnets, urging marriage and the begetting of an heir, were written by a man who had eight months previously lost his own son and heir. Thence it is a short step to Shakespeare's identification

[1] *Shakespeare's Dramatic Meditations. An Experiment in Criticism* (Oxford University Press, 1976).

[2] '"That the thought of hearts can mend". An Introduction to Shakespeare's Sonnets for psychotherapists and others', *Times Literary Supplement* (19 December 1975), 1519–21.

of his dead son with William Herbert and his passionate preoccupation with giving him eternal life; other and stranger unconscious identifications follow. The trip is an intriguing one however irrelevant it may be for literary criticism of the Sonnets. Placing less strain on one's credulity is Eliot Slater's[1] modest note on Sonnet 62, which is seen not so much as a compliment to the Friend as an intuition of a modern psychological commonplace – that identification with another is the means of escape from the prison of self. In an essay concerned with the thematic rather than the biographical organization of the Sonnets C. F. Williamson[2] analyses the two contrasting experiences involved in the Poet's relationship with Friend and Mistress, concluding, with something less than novelty, that man's love partakes of both Divine and Satanic natures.

Public, not private, backgrounds are the concern of Sidney Shanker[3] who attempts to chart, in selected plays from *Henry VI* to *The Tempest*, a development in response to contemporary 'ideologies', a term which embraces concepts of order and justice, stoicism, ambition, social and political currents. While no-one would deny that the plays reflect such materials, nor that Shakespeare would attune his plays to audience interests, Shanker may be thought to exaggerate the extent to which the plays are governed by a direct response to 'ideologies', and perhaps also their orientation to instruction in such matters. The evidence he adduces from the plays can be forced (Bottom and Sly seen as examples of social climbing, 'the deepest meaning' of *Twelfth Night* seen as 'the symbolic rejection of Malvolio', the puritan); or questionable (the Duke's speech in *Measure for Measure*, 'Be absolute for death' seen as 'An idea of purest Stoic derivation'). Moreover, as in the case of *Twelfth Night*, the complex overall effect of plays is not always sufficiently considered; the Stoic doctrine of acceptance is seen as an important part of the vision of *King Lear*, but have Lear and Kent in the end learned this? Again, in tracing a development in Shakespeare's thought from Christian orthodoxy to Stoicism in the tragedies, Shanker does not discuss the surely orthodox *Macbeth* which is treated separately under ambition. Confidence in the book is undermined by some doubtful interpretations of Shakespeare's sense, and there are errors not all of which can result from faulty proof-reading – emplastic (esemplastic), introduction (induction), dulce et decorum (utile dulce), wilful suspension of disbelief. It is an earnest book and contains some good sections, as, for example, on the 'neutrality' of *Coriolanus* and on the 'vanishing ideology' of *Antony and Cleopatra*. But, having regard to the defects noted and to the dangers of inferring Shakespeare's own beliefs from the plays, it needs to be read with caution.

John Weld[4] studies Elizabethan romantic comedy in relation to the religious dramatic tradition. His investigation of meaning in romantic comedy is confessedly restricted: 'The meaning proposed merely purports to be what a significant number of well-educated Elizabethan spectators might be expected to see in the play.' Actually the study is narrower than that definition suggests, being concerned principally with the comedies as metaphors of religious import and such could not have been their only meaning for an Elizabethan audience. The first half of the book is a critical survey of the largely moral and religious dramatic tradition in which audiences had been trained. Weld stresses the 'frequent radical indepen-

1 'Sinne of self-love', *Notes and Queries*, n.s. XXIII (1976), 155–6.

2 'Themes and Patterns in Shakespeare's Sonnets', *Essays in Criticism*, XXVI (1976), 191–208.

3 *Shakespeare and the Uses of Ideology*, (Mouton, The Hague, 1975).

4 *Meaning in Comedy. Studies in Elizabethan Romantic Comedy* (State University of New York Press, 1975).

dence of dramatic vehicle and tenor' in the morality drama, and the semantic complexity of a wide range of theatrical representation; a drama of layered meanings, employing personified abstractions whose social realism was often oddly suited to the simple tenor of their names, was familiar. Thence follows an allegorical reading of comedies by Lyly, Greene, and Shakespeare. Since Weld is arguing not for *the* meaning but *a* meaning the critic is somewhat disarmed. However, while there may be no objection to seeing *The Comedy of Errors*, *The Taming of the Shrew*, *A Midsummer-Night's Dream*, and *The Merchant of Venice* in a general way as comedies of 'natural man', showing his error and irrationality, his ultimate salvation being mirrored in their happy conclusions, the reductive process can be alarming in its slighting of detail. Antonio's melancholy supposedly arises from his being trapped in the world, a creature of fortune, while Bassanio in the ring episode learns, like Antonio, that he must rely on mercy; Antonio, however, was not saved by mercy but by the strict application of the law. For all that, the book does service in drawing our attention to the worldly/other-worldly aspects of the comedies, and the reading of the conclusion of *A Midsummer-Night's Dream* is especially persuasive.

Ronald F. Miller[1] delicately treads familiar ground in considering the problem of the nature of the fairies and of reality in *A Midsummer-Night's Dream*. The strength of this essay is partly its insistence on the plurality of Shakespeare's vision (to say that the fairies are natural disorder mythologized as well as the projection of some immanence behind events is only to begin to define their multivalency) and partly its refusal to labour an intellectual content so gracefully carried by the play. Vera M. Jiji[2] spells out for us the unconscious aspects of *The Merchant of Venice*; both Shylock and Portia are threatening castration figures, and the play's unity is unconsciously determined by related sexual implications in bond, casket, and ring plots. Psychological interpretations are notoriously resistant to proof or disproof, and the case presented here, even if acceptable, offers but a small part of the play's meaning. For R. F. Hill[3] the role of Shylock determines a portrayal of male friendship and heterosexual love in *The Merchant of Venice* which is unique among the romantic comedies, since the two kinds of love, united in values against the common enemy, must themselves be untroubled by such traditional romantic strains as jealousy, folly, and self-interest. Kent Talbot van den Berg's[4] complex essay on *As You Like It* studies the function of dramatic form as metaphor of meaning. The conspicuous narrative artifice of the opening scenes is displaced by the theatrical artifice of the forest scenes, which reflects the movement from limitation to self-realization. Further, the play's action of withdrawal from, and return to, 'normal' life is said to reflect the audience's experience of withdrawal in the theatre, and to objectify the development of love in Rosalind and Orlando. Also writing on *As You Like It* Harry Morris[5] believes that the 'somber counterpoint' to gaiety is intensified by the presence in the play of the related *memento-mori* and *et in Arcadia ego* motifs. The case

[1] '*A Midsummer-Night's Dream:* The Fairies, Bottom, and the Mystery of Things', *Shakespeare Quarterly*, XXVI (1975), 254–68.

[2] 'Portia Revisited: The Influence of Unconscious Factors upon Theme and Characterization in *The Merchant of Venice*', *Literature and Psychology*, XXVI (1976), 5–15.

[3] '*The Merchant of Venice* and the Pattern of Romantic Comedy', *Shakespeare Survey 28* (Cambridge University Press, 1975), pp. 75–87.

[4] 'Theatrical Fiction and the Reality of Love in *As You Like It*', *Publications of the Modern Language Association of America*, XC (1975), 885–93.

[5] '*As You Like It:* Et in Arcadia Ego', *Shakespeare Quarterly*, XXVI (1975), 269–75.

for the latter is not strong, and were it stronger would not much affect the play's acknowledged tonal ambivalence. Shanti Padhi's[1] 'Production Notes' on *Twelfth Night* assign to Maria a more significant role in the play's marriage patterns than is customary and, specifically, refer the 'him' of 'make him believe thou art Sir Topas the curate' to Sir Toby rather than to Malvolio. Some of her interpretations force the evidence of the text. In a suggestive essay, but one which moves rather too quickly over the difficult ground, Peter Bryant[2] examines in several comedies, especially in *Twelfth Night*, the comic and critical effects achieved by the interplay of characters as theatrical roles and as 'real' persons.

The 'problem' plays have stimulated some good contributions. For A. C. Kirsch[3] formal objections to *Measure for Measure* rest largely upon a misapprehension of the play's ideas, and his fine exegesis of the latter demonstrates a coherence arising from the play's foundation on a close nexus of scriptural texts. Although less convincing in its dealings with modulations of tragic and comic moods, this essay is a distinguished piece of criticism giving the play its due as a masterly whole in its integration of tenor and dramatic vehicle. Instructive as a companion piece is Arthur H. Scouten's[4] essay on *Measure for Measure* which, while directing interpretation by reference to a variety of historical contexts, is also a trenchant attack on the errors of other historical critics of the play. Where Kirsch finds humility in Isabella's plea for Angelo's life, Scouten finds female vanity, although they agree that she achieves an enlarged understanding of the needs of others. A. D Nuttall[5] reasserts the disquiet aroused by *All's Well that Ends Well* and *Measure for Measure* resulting from the tangle of theory and practice in marriage contracts, and the combination of fairy-tale story with psychological complexity. His resolution, that Shakespeare 'brought the two modes together, quite deliberately, in a strange and quickening relationship', that the mystery and joy of marriage both co-exists with, and over-rides, legal vexations, is too briefly sketched. Robert Grudin[6] studies Ulysses in his double role as moralist and deceiver, finding an unsuspected irony in his more famous speeches which implicitly judges the values of his fellows and 'forms the only attitude expressed in *Troilus and Cressida* which comes close to what our own matured understanding of the play should be'. In Ulysses, as in the Duke in *Measure for Measure* and in Helena, we see characters forced to depend on deceit in the pursuit of virtuous ends in a corrupt world.

David Kaula[7] adds an interesting dimension to a very different kind of deceiver, Autolycus, in showing the popish associations of his peddling; the textual evidence is slight but well supported by contemporary references. Less convincing is the detection of religious symbolism in Florizel and Perdita. Starting from the (not inevitable) assumption that the statue scene in *The Winter's Tale* is offering a solution to the problem of death Robert R. Hellenga[8] dismisses moral, psychological, symbolic, and aesthetic interpretations as reductive or inadequate. His own interpreta-

[1] 'Queen of Misrule: Maria in *Twelfth Night*', *The Literary Criterion*, University of Mysore, XII (1975), 46–57.

[2] *Shakespeare's Comic Perspectives* (University of Port Elizabeth Publications, 1975).

[3] 'The Integrity of *Measure for Measure*', *Shakespeare Survey 28* (Cambridge University Press, 1975), pp. 89–105.

[4] 'An Historical Approach to *Measure for Measure*', *Philological Quarterly*, 54 (1975), 68–84.

[5] '*Measure for Measure:* the Bed-trick', *Shakespeare Survey 28* (Cambridge University Press, 1975), pp. 51–6.

[6] 'The Soul of State: Ulyssean Irony in *Troilus and Cressida*', *Anglia*, 93 (1975), 55–69.

[7] 'Autolycus' Trumpery', *Studies in English Literature*, XVI (1976), 287–303.

[8] 'The Scandal of *The Winter's Tale*', *English Studies*, 57 (1976), 11–18.

tion remains unclear, and the case against the others is weakened by his treating them as if they were mutually exclusive. Walter F. Eggers, Jr[1] shows that Gower in *Pericles* belongs to a tradition of 'authorial presenters' of plays, but that he proves exceptional in the final inadequacy of his moral commentary on the tale he has presented.

Irene Naef's[2] book on the songs in the comedies (including the romances) analyses their dramatic and thematic functions. An examination of the individual songs in context is followed by a summarizing section in which the diversity of the songs is ordered into categories, and general critical conclusions advanced – in particular that the development of Shakespeare's use of songs shows their increasing integration into the structure of the plays. The critical value of the study would have been improved by more consideration of the songs in the context of other musical features.

Essays on the English history plays include a defence of the style of the *Henry VI* plays by Ronald Watkins[3] which urges the expressiveness of some verbal and metrical features found therein; one misses reference to other work on Shakespeare's early style. Writing on *Richard II* S. Schoenbaum[4] describes the varying portraiture of Richard in narrative and dramatic accounts and, while dissociating Shakespeare from any direct political concern with the Essex rebellion, sees in Shakespeare's portrait a monarch of considerable political acumen in his handling of the Mowbray–Bolingbroke quarrel. No attempt is made to relate this Richard to the Richard of the subsequent acts but Schoenbaum's purpose is more general, to offer us a Shakespeare who is a political realist. Noting Shakespeare's expansion in *1 Henry IV* of the brief source references to Sir Walter Blunt, Margaret B. Bryan[5] argues persuasively for his importance in Shakespeare's thinking about true honour, while Gillian West[6] is convinced by source comparisons and alleged parallels between King Henry and Falstaff that we are meant to find Henry's conduct at Shrewsbury 'futile and contemptible'. Roy Battenhouse's article, 'Falstaff as Parodist and Perhaps Holy Fool', reviewed in last year's number of *Shakespeare Survey*, has been the subject of attack and amplification by Roger L. Cox and James Hoyle respectively, and of further comment from its author.[7] An article by John Jump[8] conveniently takes us forward to the Roman histories. He argues that while Shakespeare was a sincere supporter of the Tudor myth of history he may have been conscious, especially in the writing of *Henry V*, of its restrictiveness, and so for his next essay in dramatizing history he chose Roman history, the conspiracy against Caesar, a field which gave his political imagination more scope.

Michael Platt's[9] study of the Roman plays considers Shakespeare's moral evaluation of Roman political and social structures as they developed from the foundation of the republic to the emergence of the empire. The study begins with *The Rape of Lucrece* since here is indicated the transition from tyrannical rule to

1 'Shakespeare's Gower and the Role of the Authorial Presenter', *Philological Quarterly*, 54 (1975), 434–43.

2 *Die Lieder in Shakespeares Komödien*, (Francke Verlag, Bern, 1976).

3 'The Only Shake-Scene', *Philological Quarterly*, 54 (1975), 47–67.

4 '*Richard II* and the Realities of Power', *Shakespeare Survey 28* (Cambridge University Press, 1975), pp. 1–13.

5 '"Sir Walter Blunt. There's honor for you!"', *Shakespeare Quarterly*, XXVI (1975), 292–8.

6 'Bolingbroke at Shrewsbury: the Recreant King of *1 Henry IV*', *Neophilologus*, LX (1976), 460–5.

7 'Interpreting Falstaff', *Publications of the Modern Language Association of America*, XC (1975), 919–22.

8 'Shakespeare and History', *Critical Quarterly*, 17 (1975), 233–44.

9 *Rome and the Romans According to Shakespeare* (Universität Salzburg, 1976).

republic, and in the conduct of Lucrece focuses that devotion to honour which is to be the guiding principle of the republic. The limitations of the Roman concepts of honour and nobility are treated in long studies of *Coriolanus* and of *Julius Caesar*. The Roman city is seen as resting upon insecure foundations because owing no allegiance to the transcendent or universal and, because insecure, repeatedly at strife until the thrust of Caesar drove towards Godhead. *Antony and Cleopatra* heralds the decline of Roman honour and the shift from martiality to eros, itself imperfect but to be perfected in a new order of love inaugurated in the birth of Christ which 'lies in pointed obscurity behind the foreground sterility of Rome and Egypt'. This résumé reflects little of the book's complex musings and challenging detail. The author proposes no neat theses to answer all the questions which the plays provoke but prefers to leave his readers with questions. The resulting book is not easy to read and one's passage through it is intermittently subject to such irritants as verbosity, truism, heavy erudition, and faulty proof-reading, lapses which can perhaps be traced to the book's origin in a Ph.D. dissertation. There are some odd eddies of thought – for example, because Shakespeare showed such political awareness in his plays he could, had he chosen, have been a master politician in life. Nonetheless, the book gives the group of Roman plays a coherence and stimulates some re-thinking, notably of the characters of Caesar and Brutus.

Patricia K. Meszaros[1] distinguishes the supposedly immutable laws embodied in the concept of the commonwealth and the reality of power politics connoted by the word 'state', and sees Coriolanus as crushed by political forces which have outrun the absolute values to which he adheres. Ray L. Heffner[2] offers a brief discussion of the way in which messengers, necessary bits of stage machinery, are in *Antony and Cleopatra* made dramatically expressive as extensions of the personalities of the senders. In an impressive essay Morris Weitz[3] argues strongly for the legitimacy of philosophical literary criticism, and proves his point in a survey of a varied crop of imagery of generation and corruption in *Antony and Cleopatra*, which suggests as one philosophical theme in the play a form of generation that destroys itself in its perfection. As a theme unique to the kind of love shared by Antony and Cleopatra it distinguishes the play from *Hamlet* and *King Lear* which, arguably, carry philosophical theses of universal applicability.

The most startling of three books on the tragedies is Michael Long's[4] humanist study. Any interpretation based on a fixed system of ideas, even if flexibly deployed, and with an awareness of the reductive pitfall, is likely to falsify the picture at some points, and the likelihood is greater when such ideas are pursued in a crusading spirit. The 'thought-model' seen as underlying the tragedies derives from the Law/Nature conflict of the festive comedies, and related concepts in the tragic theories of Schopenhauer and Nietzsche. *Measure for Measure*, *Troilus and Cressida*, and the tragedies are interpreted as various manifestations of a single social-psychological vision, the opposition of cultural rigidities and the Dionysiac, releasing energies of the world of kinesis. Evil is located in the flawed cultural systems of Troy, Greece, Rome, Elsinore, Venice, and Vienna, which stunt the rich vitality of man's natural potentialities, with tragic consequences. Analysis in these

1 '"There is a world elsewhere"': Tragedy and History in *Coriolanus*', *Studies in English Literature*, XVI (1976), 273–85.

2 'The Messengers in Shakespeare's *Antony and Cleopatra*', *English Literary History*, 43 (1976), 154–62.

3 'Literature without Philosophy: *Antony and Cleopatra*', *Shakespeare Survey 28* (Cambridge University Press, 1975), pp. 29–36.

4 *The Unnatural Scene* (Methuen, 1976).

terms complements more familiar readings of the plays and, in particular, affords new insights into the complex coherence of *King Lear*. However, going along with such insight – notable again in the detection of transferred eroticism in *Coriolanus* – there is exaggeration, distortion, and slighting of detail, especially in the studies of *Othello* and *Measure for Measure*. The religious dimension in both plays is passed over, or mocked, or implicitly assimilated to the flawed cultures of Venice and Vienna. One wonders how, if Desdemona is 'civilized almost out of existence' she could ever have married a Moor. The reading of *Measure for Measure* is determinedly eccentric, selective, and vulgarizing, the polarities of law and kinetic energy riding rough-shod over the play's intricate patterning of idea and character. In the shrill tirade against law Lucio is a victim of the system while Angelo's marriage is a 'derisory fate'. Original the book certainly is but its moral stance and attendant emotive writing are, to say the least, serious drawbacks to objective assessments.

In a less provocative study of the tragedies Larry S. Champion[1] traces the development of Shakespeare's tragic vision and of the technical means by which he manipulates the spectators' view of it. The role of society as a destructive force in the tragic process is not seen as an important preoccupation until the final group of tragedies, *Timon of Athens*, *Coriolanus*, and *Antony and Cleopatra*, and even in these Shakespeare does not minimize the culpability of the tragic hero. The greater social emphasis of these plays is related to a modulation of that 'double vision', pervasive in the tragedies, in which the spectator is simultaneously drawn to share the protagonist's suffering and pass judgement on his culpability; in these last tragedies the emotional rapprochement is diminished, with a consequent shift of attention from the individual to the societal nature of evil. This 'double vision', together with the nature and effectiveness of the mediating dramatic means – soliloquies, asides, subplots, character parallels and foils, anticipatory devices – are central concerns. The strength of the book lies in the systematic analysis of such means; it does not claim novelty of interpretation but seeks 'to establish the fundamental constraints within which ... interpretation must take shape'.

Writing on a similar subject E. A. J. Honigmann[2] produces a very different kind of book, partly because more pragmatic and diverse in the apprehension of dramatic devices, and partly because he presents some marked readjustments of interpretation. Unlike Long's book this one is fighting no cause but the demonstration of Shakespeare's incomparable skills, and can be as coolly persuasive about the rightness of Hamlet's sensibility as impartial in assessing a bond of 'sympathy' between Iago and the audience. Although Honigmann, like Dr Johnson on another matter, is 'almost frighted at [his] own temerity' he determinedly focuses upon character. The life-likeness and inwardness (the justice of these terms is convincingly argued) of Shakespeare's characters creates a 'sympathetic' bond which the dramatist is forever manipulating this way and that, eliciting complex and even contradictory responses. If there is a cause in this book beyond the demonstration of Shakespeare's dramatic skills it is resistance to reductive interpretation, whether in response to character or tragic meaning. In respect of complex response and the detection of 'secret motives' Honigmann is a subtle guide despite occasional questionable reading of detail. It is an absorbing and important study, analysing manipulatory techniques in such a way as to shed fresh light on some central interpretative questions as, for

[1] *Shakespeare's Tragic Perspective* (University of Georgia Press, 1976).

[2] *Shakespeare: Seven Tragedies. The Dramatist's Manipulation of Response* (Macmillan, 1976).

example, the nobility of Brutus, the motives of Iago, the functioning of Lear's mind, the supposed clarity of *Coriolanus*.

After judicious assessments of various theories that have been proposed to explain difficulties in the *Hamlet* play scene W. W. Robson[1] tentatively advances a theory of multiple viewpoint; the play scene resolves Hamlet's doubts about the Ghost's 'honesty' and the king's guilt but not those of the theatre audience. This multiple view of the play scene is extended to embrace the play as a whole, announcing the tragic period with its contradictions and pressures of feeling. Martin Stevens[2] finds stronger evidence in the text than many would allow that Hamlet's encounter with the pirates was planned, and Alan Warren Friedman[3] believes that Hamlet is the reverse of inactive but that his actions are from the point of view of revenge perverse or gratuitous because as a moral being he is incapable of premeditated murder. For Ralph Berry[4] the 'one' of Hamlet's 'and a man's life's no more/Than to say one' is both the thrust that will kill Claudius and also what that action signifies for Hamlet, an affirmation of self which includes important features of the Hamlet consciousness, self-vindication and self-dramatization. *Hamlet*, taken out of historical and dramatic contexts, serves T. Manocchio and W. Petitt[5] in considering the psychology of the family. Whether or not a serious analysis of the play is intended one does get the impression that some straight talking would have sorted out the problems at Elsinore. Alan Sinfield[6] also uses a psychological approach to analyse the power–love confusions in the relationship of Lear to his daughters; his detection of the 'double-bind' to which Cordelia and then Lear himself fall victim is especially interesting, as also is his tracing of Lear's loss of identity. Neil McEwan[7] contends that the Fool in *King Lear* is indeed a boy as he is called by Lear and shows how this interpretation contributes to the thematic life of the play. However, doubts will persist if only because there is a considerable gap between the repartee of Lylian pages and the bitter insights of the Fool. In a short article on De Quincey and *Macbeth* V. A. De Luca[8] is more concerned with De Quincey's mind than with the play, but interestingly relates the knocking at the gate to the awakening from a dream since in both cases it is the point of total realization of the other mode of being from which we have just emerged. Horst Breuer,[9] approaching the meaning of time in Macbeth's 'To-morrow, and to-morrow, and to-morrow' speech from the perspective of Samuel Beckett's writings and the relationship of time to order, purpose, and sanity, finds that the disintegration of a meaningful sense of time for Macbeth results from his challenge to feudal conceptions of order. Further, and less convincingly, Macbeth is seen as representative of 'an historically progressive individualism'. Inga-Stina Ewbank's[10] inaugural lecture gives deep consideration to the kinds and the conveyance of the unspeakable experience in

1 'Did the King See the Dumb-show?' *Cambridge Quarterly*, VI (1975), 303–26.

2 '*Hamlet* and the Pirates: A Critical Reconsideration', *Shakespeare Quarterly*, XXVI (1975), 276–84.

3 'Hamlet the Unready', *Modern Language Quarterly*, 37 (1976), 15–34.

4 '"to say one": an Essay on *Hamlet*', *Shakespeare Survey 28* (Cambridge University Press, 1975), pp. 107–15.

5 *Families Under Stress: a Psychological Interpretation* (Routledge & Kegan Paul, 1975).

6 'Lear and Laing', *Essays in Criticism*, XXVI (1976), 1–16.

7 'The Lost Childhood of Lear's Fool', *Essays in Criticism*, XXVI (1976), 209–17.

8 'De Quincey's "Knocking at the Gate in *Macbeth*": Dream and Prose Art', *English Language Notes*, XIII (1976), 273–8.

9 'Disintegration of Time in Macbeth's Soliloquy "Tomorrow, and tomorrow, and tomorrow"', *Modern Language Review*, 71 (1976), 256–71.

10 *Shakespeare, Ibsen and the Unspeakable* (Castle Cary Press, 1976).

literature, particularly in the work of Shakespeare and Ibsen. The topic stimulates some fine insights, especially into *Macbeth* and *Othello*, and leaves us to reflect that although the spoken word may be made to bear the weight of the unspeakable, most language delimits, and at the end of the tragedies there is a climbing down to the speakable for 'life goes on' and 'life must be lived within language'.

The fourth of Brian Vickers's[1] volumes on Shakespeare's reception from the seventeenth to the nineteenth centuries makes a welcome appearance. Particular attention has been given to Shakespeare in the theatre during the hey-day of Garrick, with illustration of the striking disparity of opinion concerning both his acting and his Shakespearian adaptations. The passages printed from his and the adaptations of others show the pressure of both neo-classic and less elevated tastes. The range of critical opinion assembled indicates, predictably, the stultifying effects of neo-classic critical canons, yet there are also signs of restiveness, of challenge to the view that Shakespeare wanted art, and the volume affords an excellent context for the assessment of Johnson's Shakespearian criticism. An article by René Wellek[2] demonstrates the roots of A. C. Bradley's thought in German idealistic philosophy and English romantic poetry, and within that perspective offers a reasoned case for the increase of respect which Bradley's Shakespearian criticism seems to have been gaining.

There remains a heterogeneous group of pieces which have refused to fit in tidily elsewhere. References to Plato and Sir Thomas Elyot prop W. R. Streitberger's[3] limited reading of *Venus and Adonis* in which Adonis is seen as an 'ideal Renaissance schoolboy' dedicated to duty, and his riderless lusting stallion as an exemplum of reason abandoned to passion. Ernest Schanzer[4] illustrates from a range of plays Shakespeare's dealings with the neo-classical doctrine of the unity of time. He sees in Prospero's numerous references to the time of day an expression of Shakespeare's sense of the absurdity of the doctrine, Prospero being depicted as 'the harassed designer of the plot, who is obliged by the critics' demand to bring his action to a close by a certain hour of the day'. Heinz Zimmermann[5] studies personification in Shakespeare's plays against the background of contemporary definition and varied usage in morality plays, pageants, masques, emblem books, and the visual arts. Personification is here considered as a stylistic device, for Shakespeare rarely makes use of it as a mode of characterization. A classification of types of the device in Shakespeare's usage is followed by an evaluation of its function, the most interesting part of the book, showing how personification in dialogue helps to define character and theme. Three scholarly, well-documented and perceptive studies by Maria Manuela Delille from Portugal deserve mention. She has written on Shakespeare's imagery[6] and on the influence of his *Julius Caesar* on eighteenth-century Portuguese tragedy,[7] but the most interesting of the three articles examines the Hamlet and Ophelia theme – following the pre-Raphaelite 'decadent' fashion – in the work of the important nineteenth-century Portuguese poet, António Nobre.[8]

[1] *Shakespeare. The Critical Heritage. Volume 4: 1753–1765* (Routledge & Kegan Paul, 1976).

[2] 'A. C. Bradley, Shakespeare, and the Infinite', *Philological Quarterly*, 54 (1975), 85–103.

[3] 'Ideal Conduct in *Venus and Adonis*', *Shakespeare Quarterly*, XXVI (1975), 285–91.

[4] 'Shakespeare and the Doctrine of the Unity of Time', *Shakespeare Survey 28* (Cambridge University Press, 1975), pp. 57–61.

[5] *Die Personifikation im Drama Shakespeares* (Quelle & Meyer, 1975).

[6] *As Imagens nas Tragédias de Shakespeare* (Coimbra University, 1974).

[7] *Una Tragédia Portuguesa do século XVIII: 'Morte de Cezar'* (Coimbra University, 1975).

[8] *'A Sombra': Poema Hamlético e Ofélico de António Nobre* (Coimbra University, 1975).

The central assertion of Michael Goldman's[1] original and absorbing study is of the actor not as a mere imitator but as an experiencing being whose reality in the theatre has important consequences for audience response. In addition it encompasses fundamental questions of dramatic theory, realism, mimesis, dramatic modes, the dramatic hero, and most searchingly, the nature of identification – the actor's relationship to character, and the audience's relationship to actor-as-character. Although the study offers only limited specific discussion of Shakespeare, in particular the roles of Hamlet, Othello, and Cleopatra, it deserves the attention of Shakespearian critics in emphasizing the mediating power of the actor and what that implies for the power of Shakespeare's plays. Ruby Cohn's[2] book on modern transformations and adaptations of Shakespeare provokes astonishment at their variety and number, particularly since the survey confines itself largely, though not exclusively, to dramatic offshoots written in English, French and German, and concentrates on *Macbeth*, *Hamlet*, *King Lear*, and *The Tempest*. Another response might be some coolness towards such creations since, on the evidence here assembled, they have used Shakespeare for their own purposes, whether propagandist for modern theatrical modes – epic, absurdist, concrete, collage – or sociopolitical ends. Some good plays have been produced under direct Shakespearian influence although one gets the impression that on the whole dramatic offshoots are less impressive than those in other fictional genres. The book will be valued most by those interested in modern theatrical developments; for the Shakespearian critic it offers lively and informative guidance into much unfamiliar territory.

This review may fittingly conclude with two moral tributes to Shakespeare. Madeleine Doran[3] considers the idea of excellence in the plays, particularly as manifested in the women characters. She relates Shakespeare's use of hyperbole and comparison to the inexpressibility topos, and the strain of idealism to that of his age, insisting that his unequivocal prizing of excellence in character is something which modern criticism too easily loses sight of. For M. Grivelet,[4] in his British Academy Shakespeare Lecture, the myth of Proteus has lessons for us about both the relationship of Shakespeare to his dramatic creations and our criticism of the plays. Pico della Mirandola saw man in his unlimited and various potential as symbolized by Proteus, while Homer's story of Menelaus and Proteus characterizes the quest for truth as a tireless struggle with illusions. Thus the power of Protean Shakespeare is 'rooted in a fearless humanity', and our quest to know him is a struggle 'with the many changing illusions that conceal and reveal him'. Grivelet has risen to the challenge of his occasion with a ranging scholarship, but the clear plea is for a response to the plays that is not a detached aestheticism but an engaged quest for the mind of a poet who is himself 'an allegory of the dignity of man'.

1 *The Actor's Freedom. Toward a Theory of Drama* (The Viking Press, 1975).

2 *Modern Shakespeare Offshoots* (Princeton University Press, 1976).

3 'The Idea of Excellence in Shakespeare', *Shakespeare Quarterly*, XXVII (1976), 133–49.

4 'A Portrait of the Artist as Proteus', *Proceedings of the British Academy*, LXI (1975).

2. SHAKESPEARE'S LIFE, TIMES, AND STAGE

reviewed by N. W. BAWCUTT

This year there are fewer full-length books to review in this section than is normally the case, though of course articles continue to appear in large numbers. There is little to report on the biographical side. Parvin Kujoory deals with the development of Shakespearian biography from the seventeenth to the late eighteenth centuries, from casual anecdotes to the scholarly approach of Malone.[1] His essay contains no fresh material, however, and adds nothing to Samuel Schoenbaum's magisterial *Shakespeare's Lives* (Oxford, 1970), which Kujoory, rather surprisingly, does not mention.

One way of placing an author in his 'times' is to ask what the relation is between the artistic culture of a given age and the state of its politics. Joel Hurstfield suggests that the greatest period of Elizabethan society was ending as Shakespeare came to maturity, and goes on to debate what is meant when we describe late Elizabethan and early Jacobean political life as corrupt.[2] Administrators of the time expected a fee for their service which must not necessarily be considered a bribe. The deepest corruption came in the later Jacobean period, when the king's favourites failed to consider the national interest as well as their personal interest. Hurstfield's discussion, though not primarily a piece of literary criticism, should be read by all literary students who are interested in Shakespeare's political themes.

Other attempts to relate Shakespeare to his age are more narrowly theatrical. The title of Stephen Orgel's new book, *The Illusion of Power: Political Theater in the English Renaissance*,[3] may perhaps mislead some readers into assuming that it deals with the great Elizabethan and Jacobean tragedies of politics, rather like J. W. Lever's *The Tragedy of State* (1971). In fact the book deals with the court masques of the Stuart period, and Orgel emphasizes that the masques are not mere entertainment but rather overt political statements which glorify the monarchy as a god-like power controlling every aspect of national life. There are several pages on *The Tempest*, since the figure of Prospero illustrates, according to Orgel, Shakespeare's 'profound understanding of court theater and the quintessentially courtly theatrical form of the masque'. It is a stimulating essay, handsomely produced and illustrated, though scholars who have already studied Orgel's earlier writings on Inigo Jones and the Stuart masque will be familiar with many of the ideas contained in it.

The annual volumes of *Renaissance Drama* throw a good deal of light on Shakespeare's background. Volume v of the new series, dated 1972 but published in 1974, is entitled 'Essays Principally on Comedy';[4] it includes a number of articles on English and Italian Renaissance comedy, including essays on Jonson and Marston, but the only item which is unmistakably relevant to this review, by Brownell Salomon, is summarized below in the section dealing with the Elizabethan theatre. Volume vi (1973, published in 1975) contains 'Essays on Dramatic Antecedents', several of which

1 'From Fact to Fiction', *Shakespeare Jahrbuch 1975*, pp. 99–111.

2 'The Politics of Corruption in Shakespeare's England', *Shakespeare Survey 28* (Cambridge University Press, 1975), pp. 15–28.

3 University of California Press, 1975.

4 Northwestern University Press, 1974.

merit detailed attention. Bruce R. Smith opens by showing that productions of Plautus and Terence during the Renaissance were by no means exclusively academic – there were several productions for the court of Henry VIII – but the taste of the time was not severely 'classical', and the plays were accompanied by masque-like mythological and chivalric shows which were sometimes more popular than the plays themselves.[1] Gail Kern Paster argues that the urban setting of Plautus's plays finds its closest parallel in the city comedies of Thomas Middleton, though she does not consider how far Middleton may be thought to have been consciously imitating Plautus.[2]

Robert C. Jones notes that the vice-figures in morality plays are usually livelier and superficially more attractive than the virtues, and tries to explain how the dramatists controlled a tendency which could have ruined their moralizing purpose.[3] Jones answers that the vices play upon the audience just as they do upon the central figure in the play, so that the audience sooner or later realizes that it too is being put to a moral test. (A somewhat different answer to this problem by J. A. B. Somerset is mentioned below.)

Catherine Belsey touches upon the vexed question of Senecan influence in Elizabethan drama.[4] She suggests that Seneca's expression of mental conflict in his heroes and heroines helped to influence the expression of moral conflict by sixteenth-century English dramatists. But she does not see the matter simply as a question of indebtedness; the native traditions and the Senecan blended and mutually interacted. Rosemary Woolf shows how the mystery plays influenced three tragedies from the 1560s, *Apius and Virginia*, *Cambises*, and *Horestes*,[5] while Ervin Beck surveys English plays on the theme of the prodigal son; he defines the genre in such a way that it includes *All's Well That Ends Well* and *Henry IV*, and gives a list of 'prodigal son' plays from 1515 to 1635.[6]

In a closely-packed article, to which a brief summary cannot do justice, G. K. Hunter demonstrates that the only form of Italian drama to be significantly popular in Renaissance England was the pastoral tragicomedy best exemplified by Guarini's *Il Pastor Fido*.[7] He offers an explanation for this, and discusses the influence of Guarini on Marston's *The Malcontent* and the problem plays of Shakespeare. Finally, David Riggs argues that the gap between the popular traditions of Renaissance drama and neoclassical theory derived from Aristotle was not as absolute as some modern scholars assume.[8] Sixteenth-century commentators conflated Aristotle with Horace and Donatus, and their ideas about the construction of plays were closer to contemporary practice than we might realize.

Many scholars have dealt with Shakespeare's sources. The longest single study, David Kaula's *Shakespeare and the Archpriest Controversy*, suggests possible sources for six plays from Shakespeare's middle period – *King Lear*, *Hamlet*, *Troilus and Cressida*, *Measure for Measure*, *Othello*, and *Macbeth*.[9] According to Kaula Shakespeare made extensive borrow-

1 'Sir Amorous Knight and the Indecorous Romans: or, Plautus and Terence Play Court in the Renaissance', *ibid.*, pp. 3–27.

2 'The City in Plautus and Middleton', *ibid.*, pp. 29–44.

3 'Dangerous Sport: The Audience's Engagement with Vice in the Moral Interludes', *ibid.*, pp. 45–64.

4 'Senecan Vacillation and Elizabethan Deliberation: Influence or Confluence?', *ibid.*, pp. 65–88.

5 'The Influence of the Mystery Plays upon the Popular Tragedies of the 1560s', *ibid.*, pp. 89–105.

6 'Terence Improved: The Paradigm of the Prodigal Son in English Renaissance Comedy', *ibid.*, pp. 107–22.

7 'Italian Tragicomedy on the English Stage', *ibid.*, pp. 123–48.

8 '"Plot" and "Episode" in Early Neoclassical Criticism', *ibid.*, pp. 149–75.

9 Mouton, 1975.

ings in these plays of words and phrases taken from pamphlets provoked by an internal controversy among the English Catholics during the early 1600s. At the heart of the matter was a struggle for power and authority between the Jesuits on the one side, and the secular priests, who regarded themselves as the true heirs of pre-reformation Catholicism, on the other. The English government did its best to stimulate the quarrel, and used it to discredit Catholicism as a whole, even conniving at the publication of anti-Jesuit pamphlets by the secular priests, which were printed in London and were freely available in England.

It is clear, then, that Shakespeare could have read the pamphlets without much difficulty; whether he actually did so is another matter. Some of the phrases Kaula derives from the pamphlets (such as 'close prisoner' and 'young fry') were stock phrases of the time, for which no source is needed. Some of the suggested parallels will not stand up to close examination. When Laertes, returned to Denmark, 'keeps himself in clouds' (*Hamlet*, IV, V, 89), the word 'clouds' has nothing to do with building castles in the air, as Kaula suggests; Dover Wilson's edition glosses 'in clouds' as 'in obscurity', and there may be an echo of the clouds that hang on Hamlet at I, ii, 66. In the same play, 'there is nothing either good or bad but thinking makes it so' (II, ii, 246–7) is not the same as 'thoughts of what matter soeuer good or bad', and in any case closer parallels to Shakespeare's idea can be found elsewhere.

Sometimes Kaula stretches the meaning of a Shakespearian term in order to link it with one of the pamphlets. The 'moated grange' in *Measure for Measure*, III, i, 257, may indeed have some religious associations; the Arden editor glosses it after *O.E.D.* as 'an outlying farm-house belonging to a religious establishment'. But does it really have any connexion, as Kaula asserts, with the seminaries in which the English priests were trained? A few of Kaula's suggestions are more plausible, but none, it has to be said, carries immediate conviction in the same way as some of the resemblances between (for example) *King Lear* and Harsnet's *Declaration*. Until material of this kind is forthcoming, Shakespeare's indebtedness to the pamphlets of the Archpriest controversy must remain problematical.

In a distinguished article Robert Ellrodt has taken a fresh look at the relationship between Shakespeare and Montaigne.[1] He considers that there is only one indisputable borrowing (in, of course, *The Tempest*), and that some suggested parallels are fanciful, but feels that a small group of resemblances between *Hamlet* and Montaigne's *Essays* is close enough to be convincing. Montaigne and Shakespeare are then discussed for their part in the remarkable growth of self-consciousness and introspection during the sixteenth century.

We may now turn to individual plays, beginning with the early tragedies. Pierre Legouis discusses the reference to Tarquin and his queen begging at the gates of Rome in *Titus Andronicus*, III, i, 298–9.[2] There is no mention of this incident in Livy, but material exists in Dionysius of Halicarnassus which might have suggested the idea to Shakespeare. Writing on the same play, Jørgen Wildt Hansen argues that Shakespeare's debt to Seneca's plays, especially *Hercules Furens* and *Thyestes*, is fuller and more specific than earlier scholars were prepared to allow.[3] Ann Thompson's perceptive comparison of *Romeo and Juliet* with Chaucer's *Troilus and Criseyde* is perhaps more valuable as a piece of criticism than as a source-

1 'Self-consciousness in Montaigne and Shakespeare', *Shakespeare Survey 28* (Cambridge University Press, 1975), pp. 37–50.

2 '*Titus Andronicus*, III, i, 298–9', *ibid.*, pp. 71–4.

3 'Two Notes on Seneca and *Titus Andronicus*', *Anglia*, XCIII (1975), 161–5.

study in the normal sense.[1] She begins by suggesting that Chaucer's poem was 'very much in Shakespeare's mind if not actually in front of his eyes', but there is not a great deal of evidence to prove indebtedness, and the conclusion is rather tentative. Gary M. McCown throws light on Juliet's soliloquy (*Romeo and Juliet*, III, ii, 1–31) by relating it to the traditions of the epithalamium in classical and English poetry.[2]

The items on *Hamlet* and *Othello* concern themselves with points of detail. Joan Larson Klein suggests that Hamlet's image of the sponge (IV, ii) may be derived from one of Whitney's *Emblems*,[3] and Lawrence Rosinger notes a few rather faint verbal parallels between *Hamlet* and two of the Homilies ('Of the State of Matrimony' and 'Against Adultery').[4] Rodney Poisson accepts the Quarto reading of 'base Indian' in Othello's last speech, and believes it to refer to the indifference shown by the natives of the West Indies to gold and precious stones.[5] He cites a number of printed allusions to their behaviour, some hitherto unnoticed, all of which derive ultimately from the letters of Amerigo Vespucci. This is immediately followed in the same journal by Richard S. Veit's defence of the Folio reading 'Judean'.[6] Veit argues that 'tribe' in Shakespeare is associated with Jews (e.g. in *The Merchant of Venice*) but never with Indians, and that Othello's reference to his earlier execution of a 'turbaned' and 'circumcised' Turk reinforces the Middle Eastern flavour of the whole speech.

O. B. Hardison acknowledges that the source-material for *King Lear* comes basically from history (or pseudo-history), but is convinced that the myth of Ixion is of fundamental importance for the play.[7] The myth does not organize the plot-structure; rather it provides Shakespeare with 'the philosophical issues in terms of which the action of the play is developed'. Harbison's argument is perhaps a little strained at times, but he does succeed in showing that the allegorical interpretations of the myth available to Shakespeare give it a stronger connexion with *King Lear* than would seem probable at first glance. H. F. Lippincott compares the Fool in *Lear* to the Fools in Robert Armin's *Foole upon Foole*, first published in 1600 and revised in 1608.[8] The conclusion seems to be that Shakespeare had little to learn from Armin's book, and the 1608 revisions may even be due to Shakespeare's influence upon Armin.

In a new contribution to the 'Salzburg Studies in English Literature' Dorothy Nameri has made a detailed comparison of the anonymous *King Leir*, published in 1605, Shakespeare's *King Lear*, and Nahum Tate's adapted version of 1681.[9] Unfortunately it is painfully obvious that the book is a thesis which has been put into print without revision; it is clumsily written and does not add a great deal to previous work on the topic. The point that Miss Nameri seems most concerned to argue is that Tate borrowed from *King Leir* as well as from Shakespeare's play, but her case is based on unconvincing verbal parallels, sometimes involving no more than a single key word. If the series of Salzburg Studies wishes to redeem

1 '*Troilus and Criseyde* and *Romeo and Juliet*', *The Yearbook of English Studies*, VI (1976), 26–37.

2 '"Runawayes Eyes" and Juliet's Epithalamium', *Shakespeare Quarterly*, XXVII (1976), 150–70.

3 '*Hamlet*, IV, ii, 12–21, and Whitney's *A Choice of Emblemes*', *Notes and Queries*, n.s. XXIII (1976), 158–61.

4 '*Hamlet* and the Homilies' *Shakespeare Quarterly*, XXVI (1975), 299–301.

5 'Othello's 'Base Indian': A Better Source for the Allusion', *ibid.*, pp. 462–6.

6 '"Like the base Judean": A Defense of an oft-rejected Reading in *Othello*', *ibid.*, pp. 466–9.

7 'Myth and History in *King Lear*', *ibid.*, pp. 227–42.

8 '*King Lear* and the Fools of Robert Armin', *ibid.*, pp. 243–53.

9 *Three Versions of the Story of King Lear* (Universität Salzburg, 1976).

itself from criticisms made by several reviewers it will need to be much more selective in future.

Michael Lloyd published an essay some years ago in *Shakespeare Survey* on Shakespeare's Cleopatra as the goddess Isis;[1] this has been supplemented and to some extent corrected by John Adlard.[2] In a more general article Dimiter Daphinoff examines the sources of *Antony and Cleopatra* to illustrate his point that we must be sure our source-material is authentic before we start drawing conclusions from it.[3]

Little has been published on the histories. Richard Helgerson argues that Shakespeare's indebtedness to *Woodstock* in *Henry IV Part I* is more elaborate than has been so far recognized, and points out various similarities between the two plays.[4] Helgerson's note prompts J. C. Maxwell to express scepticism about the traditional dating of *Woodstock* at *c.* 1592.[5] Parallels between the play and Shakespeare's plays do not prove that Shakespeare was the borrower, and *Woodstock* ends its blank-verse scenes with a rhyming couplet in a way which (according to the investigations of John Weeks) is very rare in Elizabethan drama but fairly common in early Jacobean drama.

Work on the comedies has dealt with the late plays, with the one exception of Alan Taylor Bradford's discussion of Jaques's speech on the seven ages of man in *As You Like It*.[6] He points out that Jaques distorts and departs from the traditional pattern of the seven ages, of which Bradford quotes an unfamiliar example from Henry Cuffe's *The Differences of the Ages of Man's Life* (London, 1607), in order to reinforce his melancholy and pessimism.

Karl Haffenreffer does his best (with some success) to demolish Jan Kott's argument[7] that IV, ii, 251–2 of *Cymbeline* are a direct borrowing from Lucian's *Charon*.[8] It has already been known for some time that several of the character-names in *The Winter's Tale* seem to be derived from names in Plutarch's *Lives*; F. N. Lees notes that some of these names can be found together in the *Life of Dion*, and that the treatment of Dion's widow, who gives birth to a child in prison, and is then treacherously murdered at sea with her child, has distinct resemblances to Shakespeare's play.[9]

Three items have appeared on *The Tempest*, two of them by Jacqueline Latham. She suggests that Shakespeare had read or seen Jonson's *Masque of Queens* before writing his play; there was no direct influence, but Jonson's organization of his materials helped Shakespeare to unify his play.[10] She has also examined Caliban and his parentage in the light of contemporary discussions of witchcraft and demonology.[11] Unfortunately her attempt to assert that King James's *Daemonologie* has a particular relevance to *The Tempest* seems weakly-based and unconvincing. Ann Thompson suggests that 'Our revels now are ended',

1 'Cleopatra as Isis', *Shakespeare Survey 12* (Cambridge University Press, 1959), pp. 88—94.

2 'Cleopatra as Isis', *Archiv*, CCXII (1975), 324–8.

3 'Zur Behandlung der Quellenfrage in der englisch-deutschen Studienausgabe der dramatischen Werke Shakespeares', *Deutsche Shakespeare-Gesellschaft West Jahrbuch 1975*, pp. 179–93.

4 '*I Henry IV* and *Woodstock*', *Notes and Queries*, n.s. XXIII (1976), 153–4.

5 'Doubts on the Date of *Woodstock*', *ibid.*, pp. 154–5.

6 'Jaques' Distortion of the Seven Ages Paradigm', *Shakespeare Quarterly*, XXVII (1976), 171–6.

7 'Lucian in *Cymbeline*', *Modern Language Review*, LXVII (1972), 74–4.

8 'Jan Kott's "Lucian in *Cymbeline*"', *The Yearbook of English Studies*, VI (1976), 38–40.

9 'Plutarch and *The Winter's Tale*', *Notes and Queries*, n.s. XXIII (1976), 161–2.

10 '*The Tempest* and *The Masque of Queens*', *ibid.*, pp. 162–3.

11 '*The Tempest* and King James's *Daemonologie*', *Shakespeare Survey 28* (Cambridge University Press, 1975), pp. 117–23.

IV, i, 148, echoes 'And farewel, our revel all was ago' in Chaucer's *Franklin's Tale*.[1]

A lively interest continues to be shown in theatre-history and the Elizabethan stage, both as a physical object and as an influence on techniques of production. John C. Coldewey examines the final collapse of local drama in Essex in the middle years of Elizabeth's reign, and argues that Puritan hostility to drama, though important, was not the sole cause of the decline.[2] For example, the availability of Catholic religious garments for use as stage costumes provoked a temporary resurgence of drama in the earlier years of Elizabeth's reign, but when the vestiarian controversy became fiercer most of the clothing was sold or destroyed. There were also difficulties in finding suitable play-texts not tainted with Catholicism, and the popularity of 'conferences' (in effect, theological debates in public) provided a kind of counter-attraction to drama.

The evidence of Greene's *Groatsworth of Wit* and Shakespeare's obvious knowledge of several of the plays in the repertory of the Queen's Men is used by G. M. Pinciss to suggest that Shakespeare began his career as an actor with that company.[3] Pinciss also conjectures that the company called Pembroke's Men, which existed for about a year from 1592 to 1593, was formed from a section of the Queen's Men when the company split up because of financial difficulties. In 1974 Mary Edmond published an important new document, the will of an actor called Simon Jewell, and made various deductions from it.[4] Scott McMillin now argues that Jewell probably belonged to the Queen's Men rather than Pembroke's Men (though he agrees with Pinciss that Pembroke's Men may possibly have been an offshoot of the older company) and suggests that the man called Johnson mentioned in the will was William Johnson, not Ben Jonson.[5]

There have been many attempts to reconstruct an Elizabethan playhouse; D. A. Latter bravely tries yet again, using the evidence of the Fortune and Hope contracts, but paying more attention than earlier scholars to the problem of sight-lines (in other words, the extent to which the stage was visible to the audience).[6] Latter believes that the more aristocratic spectators sat above, and sometimes on, the stage, and like many recent scholars he does not believe that Elizabethan theatres were equipped with an 'inner stage'. In 1973 C. Walter Hodges published his reconstruction of the Second Globe;[7] Richard Hosley now questions some of his conclusions.[8] It is not certain that there were no posts on the stage; the large superstructure above the stage, which Hodges sees as an empty shell, may have provided storage space or even accommodation, and Hosley's calculations suggest that Hodges slightly under-estimated the dimensions of the theatre.

We may be tempted to assume that provincial playhouses did not exist in Shakespeare's time. We should be wrong to do so; Kathleen M. D. Barker has published some interesting evidence that a privately-owned indoor theatre existed in Bristol during the

[1] '"Our revels now are ended": an allusion to *The Franklin's Tale*', *Archiv*, CCXII (1975), 317.

[2] 'The Last Rise and Final Demise of Essex Town Drama', *Modern Language Quarterly*, XXXVI (1975), 239–60.

[3] 'Shakespeare, Her Majesty's Players, and Pembroke's Men', *Shakespeare Survey 27* (Cambridge University Press, 1974), pp. 129–36.

[4] 'Pembroke's Men', *Review of English Studies*, n.s. XXV (1974), 129–36.

[5] 'Simon Jewell and the Queen's Men', *ibid.*, n.s. XXVII (1976), 174–7.

[6] 'Sight-lines in a Conjectural Reconstruction of an Elizabethan Playhouse', *Shakespeare Survey 28* (Cambridge University Press, 1975), pp. 125–35.

[7] *Shakespeare's Second Globe: The Missing Monument* (Oxford University Press, 1973).

[8] 'The Second Globe', *Theatre Notebook*, XXIX (1975), 140–5.

first twenty years of the seventeenth century.[1] In a brief appendix to this article Sybil Rosenfeld reminds us of evidence published in 1926 that a playhouse was built in York in 1609, but the owner, Richard Middleton, antagonized the corporation, which put an end to the venture.

Warren D. Smith's *Shakespeare's Playhouse Practice: A Handbook* discusses various features of Shakespeare's dramatic technique and relates them to the physical characteristics of the Elizabethan playhouse.[2] For example, entrance announcements (of the 'Look where he comes' variety) are not there to identify the newcomer – often his name is not mentioned – but to draw attention to his presence, to give him time to cross the deep Elizabethan stage, and to indicate to those already on the stage that they will need to re-group themselves. Exit cues are more frequent than in modern plays because the Elizabethan repertory system did not allow the actor to settle into the comfortable routine which results when a play has a long run.

Several of the points made in Smith's book were published as articles more than twenty years ago, and occasionally Smith fails to answer criticisms of them by other scholars. His theory that a small portable scaffold, with four steps leading to the top level, was used for a hillock or similar minor elevation has been endorsed by Bernard Beckerman (in *Shakespeare at the Globe, 1599–1609*, 1962) but Beckerman's cogent objections to the use of this scaffold as Cleopatra's monument are ignored by Smith (who does not in fact give detailed references to any recent work on the Elizabethan stage).

Brevity is often a grace in scholarship, but sometimes Smith's conclusions are too briefly stated to be fully convincing, and the reader may feel that relevant factors are ignored. It would have been useful, for example, to see whether any distinctions can be made, as far as stage-directions are concerned, between texts based on prompt-copy and those derived from foul papers. It is not always clear whether the practices under discussion are particularly Shakespearian or are stock features of Elizabethan drama. But when all reservations are made the book remains valuable. Smith's theory that stage-directions in Elizabethan plays should be regarded simply as brief notations for the benefit of the prompter is challenging, and it is to be hoped that his book will stimulate fuller discussion of the minutiae of Shakespeare's stagecraft.

Producers frequently remind academic critics that drama does not consist exclusively of a spoken text, and Brownell Salomon, using evidence from a large number of plays by Shakespeare and his contemporaries, shows that some of the most striking effects in Elizabethan drama are created visually or aurally, by such means as gesture, costume, music, and sound-effects.[3] The point is a necessary one, though Salomon's somewhat pretentious introduction on semiology seems to add little to his argument. And it might also be noted that all Salomon's evidence is derived from a reading of the printed texts of the plays, including, of course, their stage-directions; it presumably follows that an academic in his study can bring a play fully to life if only he reads it sensitively enough.

Working on a smaller scale than Salomon, Klaus Büchler points out that in addition to the explicit stage-directions in *The Tempest* there are often detailed indications in the text of how the characters are intended to appear and behave.[4] Neil Carson discusses a specific aspect

[1] 'An Early Seventeenth Century Provincial Playhouse', *ibid.*, pp. 81–4.

[2] University Press of New England, 1975.

[3] 'Visual and Aural Signs in the Performed English Renaissance Play', *Renaissance Drama*, n.s. v (1972), 143–69.

[4] 'Explizite und implizite Bühnen- und Spielanweisungen in Shakespeare's *Tempest*', *Deutsche Shakespeare-Gesellschaft West Jahrbuch 1975*, pp. 174–8.

of stage-behaviour, the way in which the Elizabethan actor delivered his soliloquies.[1] There is much in Heywood's plays to suggest that he went, as Carson puts it, 'to considerable trouble... to disguise or otherwise eliminate direct communication between actor and audience'; in other words, Heywood tried to provide realistic stage-action in order to make asides and monologues seem as plausible as possible. The same may well be true of other dramatists of the period.

The Elizabethan Theatre V, edited by George Hibbard, is a worthy addition to an already distinguished series, and its articles show that an awareness of theatre-history is a valuable asset to the literary critic of drama.[2] David Bevington agrees with those recent scholars who argue that the late medieval vernacular cycles did not develop out of church drama in Latin, and asserts that this discontinuity is shown in the casting of performers: the church drama used chiefly men, most of whom were trained singers, while the cycles used a variety of casts including sometimes professional actors.[3] R. W. Ingram discusses the production of religious drama in Coventry during the sixteenth century, using evidence from the records of the Cappers' Company which shows that this dramatic activity went on until remarkably late in the century.[4] The development of the vice-figure is studied by J. A. B. Somerset, who argues that comedy is an essential part of his role, and has a theatrical function which is deeper than mere 'comic relief'.[5]

In the remaining articles T. W. Craik looks at staging problems in a number of plays by Marlowe and other dramatists,[6] and D. F. Rowan examines various problems connected with the staging of *The Spanish Tragedy*.[7] Peter Saccio considers what qualities make *Endimion* unique among Lyly's plays,[8] and Inga-Stina Ewbank discusses the relation between language and spectacle in the plays of George Peele.[9]

Bernard Grebanier's *Then Came Each Actor* is a history of Shakespearian actors in England and America from Elizabethan times to the present day, with a few brief references to actors like Fechter and Salvini whose native language was not English but who acted before English-speaking audiences.[10] The book moves forward chronologically, while separate chapters are allotted to major figures like Garrick and Kean. Grebanier has an obvious enthusiasm for Shakespeare and the theatre, and his book is written with a gusto and liveliness which make it very easy to read.

It is hard, however, not to have serious reservations about the book. There are, for example, some startling inaccuracies. Grebanier quotes the song 'Black Spirits and White' from D'Avenant's adaptation of *Macbeth* to illustrate D'Avenant's 'tasteless re-writing' of the play and his mediocre abilities as a poet. Grebanier seems unaware of two facts: that the song comes from Middleton's *The Witch* and is not by D'Avenant at all, and that the Folio text of *Macbeth* has a stage-direction in IV, i, '*Musicke and a Song. Blacke Spirits, &c.*', which suggests that the song was inserted into

1 'The Elizabethan Soliloquy – Direct Address or Monologue?', *Theatre Notebook*, XXX (1976), 12–18.

2 Macmillan Company of Canada, 1975.

3 'Discontinuity in Medieval Acting Traditions', *ibid.*, pp. 1–16.

4 '"To find the pleyers and all that longeth therto": Notes on the Production of Medieval Drama in Coventry', *ibid.*, pp. 17–44.

5 '"Fair is foul and foul is fair": Vice-Comedy's Development and Theatrical Effects', *ibid.*, pp. 54–75.

6 'The Reconstruction of Stage Action from Early Dramatic Texts', *ibid.*, pp. 76–91.

7 'The Staging of *The Spanish Tragedy*', *ibid.*, pp. 112–23.

8 'The Oddity of Lyly's *Endimion*', *ibid.*, pp. 92–111.

9 '"What words, what looks, what wonders?": Language and Spectacle in the Theatre of George Peele', *ibid.*, pp. 124–54.

10 David McKay, 1975.

the play decades before D'Avenant had anything to do with it.

Grebanier's second chapter accepts far too uncritically some of the legends about Shakespeare which sprang up during the seventeenth century. The anecdote on the opening page of this chapter, in which a younger brother of Shakespeare vaguely recollects in old age a performance by the dramatist of Adam in *As You Like It*, is sheer rubbish; Shakespeare's younger brothers all predeceased him, and though Edmund Shakespeare became an actor, and might possibly have seen William perform, he died in 1607 at the age of twenty-eight. Shakespeare may have been living in London by 1588, but there is no documentary evidence for this, and it is misleading, to say the least, to say that Shakespeare collaborated with Burbage 'in painting and gilding a shield for the Earl of Rutland'.

These blemishes could be regarded as trivial, but it has to be said that Grebanier's approach to acting is not strikingly thoughtful or perceptive. We should expect a book of this kind to contain plenty of biographical information, but all too often the approach is simply in terms of anecdotes, many of which seem to have been inserted for entertainment only. Grebanier clearly has strong prejudices, but lacks a controlling purpose to shape and direct the book; it is obviously intended to be more than a biographical dictionary, but does not give us a full sense of the different ways in which actors have approached Shakespeare from century to century.

Charles H. Shattuck's *Shakespeare on the American Stage* has a more limited scope than Grebanier's book.[1] It begins in 1752, when Lewis Hallam's company gave in Williamsburg, Virginia, the first significant productions of Shakespeare in America, and ends just over a century later with Edwin Booth, the greatest American actor of Shakespeare in his time. Wisely Shattuck does not overburden himself with too much detail, and restricts himself to a dozen or so of the more significant actors and actresses.

Shattuck's book shows the academic virtues at their best. It is aimed at a popular audience, but attains lucidity and readability without any sacrifice of quality. We are given the main biographical facts about each actor, as well as a discussion of his (or her) sensitivity to Shakespeare and conception of the craft of acting. Shattuck even manages to find space to discuss some of the theatres and the costumes and scenery used in them. Most of the leading Shakespearian actors in America up to the early nineteenth century were imported from England and sometimes tensions arose among both Americans and Englishmen from outraged patriotism. Shattuck deals with this theme judiciously and impartially (he gives, for example, a much more illuminating account than Grebanier of the rivalry between Macready and Edwin Forrest which led to the Astor Place riots of 1849). One other feature of this book must be mentioned: it contains over a hundred illustrations, a few of them in colour, which have been skilfully chosen and well reproduced.

Articles on theatre-history will be placed in chronological order. The earliest is negative but necessary: David M. Bergeron takes a fresh look at a letter from Sir Edward Hoby to Sir Robert Cecil containing an allusion to 'K. Richard' which many scholars have interpreted as referring to a private production of Shakespeare's *Richard II*.[2] But the king could have been Richard II or Richard III; there may not have been any question of a play, and even if there was a play it need not have been by Shakespeare. Bergeron sadly notes that several earlier attempts to destroy

[1] The Folger Shakespeare Library, 1976.

[2] 'The Hoby Letter and *Richard II*: A Parable of Criticism', *Shakespeare Quarterly*, XXVI (1975), 477–80.

the myth have been unsuccessful. Judith Milhous has compiled a useful list of the roles played by Thomas Betterton from 1659 to 1710.[1] Taken as a whole the list suggests that we should not overstress Betterton as a Shakespearian actor, for he repeatedly took on completely new roles. Furthermore, he was extremely energetic and versatile, and it would be wrong to think of him chiefly as an actor of tragedy. J. D. Hainsworth suggests that Garrick's production in February 1756 of John Brown's *Athelstan*, whose ending has some resemblance to the ending of *King Lear*, may have been planned by Garrick in order to test whether eighteenth-century audiences would accept Shakespeare's play in its original version rather than Tate's revision.[2] But the reception of *Athelstan* did not encourage Garrick to abandon Tate's version, and one reviewer of Brown's play made the same objections to it that had earlier been made to the original ending of *Lear*.

Two scholars deal with aspects of the French reaction to Shakespeare during the nineteenth century. In the first part of a substantial article Barry Vincent Daniels considers in detail the reception of Alfred de Vigny's translation of *Othello* at and after its first production in Paris on 24 October 1829; the second part considers its accuracy as a translation and its impact (not, apparently, very profound) on the development of French theatre.[3] Jacques Gury describes the three productions of *Romeo and Juliet* in Paris in 1827 and 1828,[4] The first began on 16 June 1827; it used the Ducis version and aroused very little reaction. The second, beginning on 15 September 1827, was by the visiting English players with Charles Kemble and Harriet Smithson in the leading roles, using Garrick's acting version. The realism of their acting caused a sensation in Paris. In 1828 a new adaptation by Frédéric Soulié was performed, but his version was timid and feeble, and had the unfortunate effect of preventing the appearance of a more authentic translation.

Herbert Beerbohm Tree is usually thought of as an old-fashioned actor–manager who liked to take the central role in spectacular productions. But George Rowell's account of Tree's Shakespeare Festivals, held from 1909 to 1913, shows him in a different light: for example, he encouraged other companies to contribute guest productions, and staged *Hamlet* in a remarkably simple way with the minimum of scenery.[5] We may conclude these notes on theatre-history in a small way by noting the discussion by Fritz Däbritz of some recent productions of Shakespeare's plays in the puppet-theatre of Eastern Europe.[6]

Shakespeare's influence on later writers is illustrated in a note by Robert Folkenflik pointing out several unnoticed allusions to *Othello* in Fielding's *The Author's Farce*.[7] Fielding, he suggests, travestied *Othello* as a means of ridiculing the pretensions of Italian opera. Three scholars contribute footnotes to the history of Shakespeare criticism. Brian Vickers makes a short survey of English critics of Shakespeare in the earlier eighteenth century;[8] F. W. Price discusses Mrs Radcliffe's views of Shakespeare as shown in a conver-

[1] 'An Annotated Census of Thomas Betterton's Roles, 1659–1710', *Theatre Notebook*, XXIX (1975), pp. 33–44 and 85–94.

[2] '*King Lear* and John Brown's *Athelstan*', *Shakespeare Quarterly*, XXVI (1975), 471–7.

[3] 'Shakespeare à la Romantique: *Le More de Venise* d'Alfred de Vigny', *Revue d'Histoire du Théâtre*, XXVII (1975), 125–55.

[4] 'Fortune et infortunes de Roméo et Juliette à l'age romantique', *ibid.*, pp. 156–75.

[5] 'Tree's Shakespeare Festivals (1909–1913)', *Theatre Notebook*, XXIX (1975), 74–81.

[6] 'Shakespeare auf dem Puppentheater', *Shakespeare-Jahrbuch 1975*, pp. 123–33.

[7] '*The Author's Farce* and *Othello*', *Notes and Queries*, n.s. XXIII (1976), 163–4.

[8] 'Die ersten Shakespeare-Kritiker', *Deutsche Shakespeare-Gesellschaft West Jahrbuch 1975*, pp. 10–30.

sation between two characters in her last unfinished novel *Gaston de Blondeville*;[1] and Ursula Klein considers the reaction to *Hamlet* of Goethe and Friedrich Schlegel, and then moves on to modern German criticism of the play from a Marxist viewpoint.[2]

Many notes have been published explaining points of detail in Shakespeare's plays. G. Lambin tries to throw light on the puzzling reference to 'the charge-house on the top of the mountain' in *Love's Labour's Lost*, v, i, 69–70.[3] Lambin believes that Holofernes teaches at the Collège de Montaigu in Paris. 'Charge-house' is explained by the fact that scholars at this institution were forced to carry out various kinds of manual work as part-payment for their education. Lambin also has some suggestions concerning *The Merchant of Venice*.[4] The word 'Rialto', he claims, does not refer specifically to the bridge, but to a district of Venice where a great deal of commerce went on. 'Gobbo' means 'hunchback', and 'Lancelot' makes us think of 'Lancelot of the Lake': the Venetian lagoons and canals were called 'lakes' by contemporaries like Thomas Coryate.

Robert F. Fleissner argues that *Much Ado About Nothing* was originally only a sub-title, and this play is really the mysterious *Love's Labour's Won* mentioned in Meres's *Palladis Tamia*.[5] However, Fleissner's explanation of why the sub-title became the main title seems rather strained and implausible. Hallett Smith quotes evidence from a jest-book of 1637 that an actor once ludicrously reversed the nouns in a line from *Henry VI Part II*, III, i, 71, 'As is the sucking lamb or harmless dove', and suggests that Shakespeare may have had this slip in mind in giving the phrase 'sucking dove' to Bottom in *A Midsummer Night's Dream*.[6] S. Viswanathan conjectures that 'medlar' in *As You Like It*, II, ii, 107, can mean 'nymphomaniac', and wonders whether it was also a cant term in the Elizabethan theatre for the 'boy-actress' whose voice might break and ruin his career (so that he would be rotten before ripe).[7] In similar vein Robert F. Willson discovers a number of implications, sexual and otherwise, in the name 'Falstaff'.[8]

Harold Jenkins puts forward an elegant and convincing explanation of Hamlet's use of the term 'fishmonger' in II, ii, of the play.[9] The primary significance of the phrase is in relation to Ophelia rather than to Polonius; passages in Ben Jonson and Hugh Platt indicate that Elizabethans felt that 'the womenfolk of fishmongers have a special aptitude for procreation', and this clearly links up with Hamlet's later reluctance that Ophelia should be 'a breeder of sinners'. James Gray queries one of Dr Johnson's annotations to *Hamlet*.[10] Johnson glosses *Hamlet*, I, v, 154, 'Swear by my sword' by saying that 'it was common to swear upon the sword, that is, upon the cross which the old swords always had upon the hilt', and justifies his interpretation by reference to a passage in the writings of Brantôme shown him by Garrick. He does not, however, quote the passage;

[1] 'Ann Radcliffe, Mrs Siddons, and the Character of Hamlet', *Notes and Queries*, n.s. XXIII (1976), 164–7.

[2] 'Zur *Hamlet*-Rezeption – ein Vergleich', *Shakespeare-Jahrbuch 1975*, pp. 81–96.

[3] 'The Charge-House at the Top of the Mountain', *Études Anglaises*, XXVIII (1975), 466–9.

[4] 'Lancelot Gobbo', *ibid.*, p. 470.

[5] '"Love's Labour's Won" and the Occasion of *Much Ado*', *Shakespeare Survey 27* (Cambridge University Press, 1974), pp. 105–10.

[6] 'Bottom's Sucking Dove, *Midsummer Night's Dream*, I, ii, 82–3', *Notes and Queries*, n.s. XXIII (1976), 152–3.

[7] 'The Medlar in the Forest of Arden', *Neuphilologische Mitteilungen*, LXXVII (1976), 93–4.

[8] 'Falstaff in *I Henry IV*: What's in a Name?', *Shakespeare Quarterly*, XXVII (1976), 199–200.

[9] 'Hamlet and the Fishmonger', *Deutsche Shakespeare-Gesellschaft West Jahrbuch 1975*, pp. 109–20.

[10] '"Swear by my Sword": A Note in Johnson's *Shakespeare*', *Shakespeare Quarterly*, XXVII (1976), 205–8.

Gray can find nothing in Brantôme with precisely this meaning, and wonders if Johnson made a mistake.

The 'Sagittary' mentioned twice in act I of *Othello* is usually taken to be a house or inn; T. Sipahigil presents evidence to suggest that the word may refer to a kind of ship.[1] According to Adrienne Lockhart 'the cat is grey' at III, vi, 45, of *King Lear* alludes to the proverbial saying that at night all cats are grey, and can be interpreted as a reference to Lear's inability to make sound judgements of character.[2] Some years ago G. T. Buckley asserted that strictly speaking Edmund in *King Lear* was not a traitor;[3] Raymond V. Utterbuck now argues in opposition to Buckley that Edmund was indeed a traitor, especially towards Lear who was still technically the king.[4]

Marie-Madeleine Martinet believes that the 'rare Italian master, Julio Romano' referred to in *The Winter's Tale*, V, ii, 95, was in fact the historical Giulio Romano, who was famous for *trompe-l'oeuil* effects.[5] He is mentioned by several English writers of the time, or in Italian treatises translated into English which Shakespeare could have read. A well-known problem in the same play is the sea-coast of Bohemia. According to Siegfried Koss part of Northern Italy, with its own sea-coast, could be described as 'Bohemia', though Koss does not produce any sixteenth-century evidence for this, and does not explain why Ben Jonson failed to understand the point.[6] Raymond A. Urban explains why Caliban in *The Tempest* worships the man in the moon; Caliban is being inducted into the religion of drunkards, a comic Bacchanalian sect that took the man in the moon as its god and the liquor bottle as its bible.[7]

A sidelight is thrown on the history of Shakespearian scholarship by the publication of *Frank Sidgwick's Diary*, edited and introduced by his daughter Mrs Ann Baer.[8] Sidgwick was assistant to A. H. Bullen, and did a good deal of the hard work necessary to start the Shakespeare Head Press at Stratford-upon-Avon in 1904. The book also contains an obituary of Bullen by H. F. B. Brett-Smith, first published in 1921, and a recent lecture on Bullen by Paul Morgan, which makes it sadly clear that Bullen lacked the business sense and organizing ability to turn his grandiose publishing projects into reality. It might be suggested that the fragmentary letter reproduced on page 56 was addressed to Sir Walter Greg; the top lines seem to refer to publications of the Malone Society.

A few miscellaneous articles remain which do not obviously seem to fit in anywhere else. Karl Adalbert Preuschen traces the origins of the myth of Phaeton and its development during the sixteenth century, and then surveys Shakespeare's use of the myth.[9] We are told in *Hamlet*, V, i, that a tanner's body will last for nine years in the earth; Cay Dollerup believes that this, taken in association with the various Danish allusions in the play, may allude to a lost play, *The Tanner of Denmark*, recorded in Henslowe's *Diary* as having been performed by Strange's Men on 23 May 1592.[10]

1 '"Sagitary / Sagittar" in *Othello*', *ibid.*, pp. 200–1.

2 'The Cat is Grey: *King Lear*'s Mad Trial Scene', *ibid.*, XXVI (1975), 469–71.

3 'Was Edmund Guilty of Capital Treason?', *ibid.*, XXIII (1972), 87–94.

4 'Edmund: A Most Vile Traitor', *ibid.*, XXVII (1976), 201–3.

5 '*The Winter's Tale* et "Julio Romano"', *Études Anglaises*, XXVIII (1975), 257–68.

6 'Gab es ein Küstenland Böhmen?', *Deutsche Shakespeare-Gesellschaft West Jahrbuch 1975*, pp. 209–11.

7 'Why Caliban Worships the Man in the Moon', *Shakespeare Quarterly*, XXVII (1976), 203–5.

8 Shakespeare Head Press, 1975.

9 'Zur Verwendung der Mythologie in der englischen Literatur des 16. Jahrhunderts, dargestellt am Beispiel des Phäeton-Mythos', *Deutsche Shakespeare-Gesellschaft West Jahrbuch 1975*, pp. 194–208.

10 'A Shakespeare Allusion to a Lost Play (*Hamlet*, V, i, 162)?', *Notes and Queries*, n.s. XXIII (1976), 156–7.

George Walton Williams suggests that some lines in the anonymous *The Pedlar's Prophecy*, printed in 1595, contain a fragment of the old lost play on Hamlet which was presumably the source of Shakespeare's play.[1] Finally, James C. Bulman argues that the anonymous *Timon* could have been written soon after 1601, thus making it possible to suggest that Shakespeare borrowed from it in *Timon of Athens*.[2]

[1] 'Another Line from the Ur-*Hamlet*?', *ibid.*, pp. 157–8.

[2] 'The Date and Production of *Timon* Reconsidered', *Shakespeare Survey 27* (Cambridge University Press, 1974), pp. 111–27.

3. TEXTUAL STUDIES

reviewed by RICHARD PROUDFOOT

Although this review is not the appropriate place for extended obituary comment, the deaths, within one year, of A. C. Cairncross, J. W. Lever and J. C. Maxwell, must mark 1975–6 as a season of dreadful and irreplaceable loss to Shakespearian editing and textual studies and cannot pass unnoted. All three made important contributions to the revised Arden Shakespeare and Maxwell had the unique distinction of belonging as well to Dover Wilson's team for the new Cambridge Shakespeare.

Coriolanus and *Pericles*, which may have been written in the same year but have little in common either as plays or in the tasks they offer to editors, are the latest volumes to appear, respectively, in the New Arden and New Penguin Shakespeares, the former edited by Philip Brockbank, the latter by Philip Edwards.[1]

Brockbank's long introduction to *Coriolanus*, for all its divisions into sections on 'The Text' and 'The Play', is a seamless garment. His deepest engagement with the play is revealed in his commentary on Shakespeare's handling of his sources and in his pages on 'The Tragedy of Coriolanus', but the same questioning alertness which distinguishes his critical discussion is equally apparent in his treatment of the historical and technical issues of dating, stage history and text. If one aspect of the play is slightly neglected, it is the theatrical: little is said of the scenic structure and overall balance of the action, in spite of its importance in presenting contrasts of character and theme, while the stage history has more to say of adaptors than of actors. In the section on sources, no reference is made to Shakespeare's earliest allusion to the story, in *Titus Andronicus* (IV, iv, 67–8), which isolates the vindictiveness of Coriolanus against Rome as the point of a simile. The verbal parallel between I, i, 187 and the Hand D addition in *The Book of Sir Thomas More*, adduced on p. 37, would be more impressive if *More* really did include the words 'woold feed on one another': its true reading is 'woold feed on on another', which could as well mean 'one on' as 'on one'.

The textual part of Brockbank's introduction is well balanced and properly cautious about the practical value of information about

[1] *Coriolanus*. Methuen, 1975; *Pericles*. Penguin Books, Harmondsworth, 1976.

the printing of F1 for editors of Shakespeare. In arguing for the likelihood of authorial copy for F *Coriolanus*, he makes much of Hand D in *More* as a source of evidence about Shakespeare's spelling habits: he concedes, however, that most features of the text in F could have survived in a scribal transcript and finds 'some evidence for the intervention of the book-keeper at some stage in the transmission'. One question not raised is whether music cues requiring '*Cornets*' (I, x, SD and II, i, 202) may indicate revival at the Blackfriars rather than performance at the Globe. The relining of verse mislined in F, which is among an editor's most extensive jobs in *Coriolanus*, is sensibly handled and soundly defended. Brockbank makes heavier weather of one other topic, the confusion and misspelling of proper names in F (pp. 21–4). For instance, compositor A's 'sustained use of *Latius* [for *Lartius*] in II.i' can only be 'proof that it stood in copy there' if we rule out the possibility that variation in the spelling of this name, both within A's stints and between A and B, could result from inconsistency in interpreting a consistent copy form in which *ar* and *a* were easily confused (as in many secretary hands of the early seventeenth century). Such misreading of the name must account for the error of '*Lucius*' for '*Lartius*' at I, i, 238. The fact that '*Lartius*' is sometimes misprinted as '*Latius*' in the 1595 and 1603 editions of North's Plutarch seems to prove little more than that the error was an easy one for a compositor to make, even when working from printed copy. The two occurrences of '*Marcus Caius Coriolanus*' and one of '*Marcius Caius Coriolanus*' (all in A's pages) may indeed be authorial in origin and may indicate that 'By a kind of tactical mistake, Shakespeare treats *Martius* as a more intimate name than *Caius*' (though a desire to stress the connection of his hero with the god Mars might afford a more conscious motive), but a possible explanation of the readings as compositorial errors which is not considered is that in each instance one of the forenames, *Caius* or *Martius*, was initially omitted by author or scribe and was subsequently interlined above the other without clear indication of whether it should precede or follow it. Here, as elsewhere, Brockbank shows a faith in the survival of copy detail in the printed text which may be a practical editorial necessity but which will hardly serve as the basis for more elaborate conjecture.

The New Arden text of *Coriolanus* is conservative, and could have afforded to be even more so. Thus, in I, i, Capell's reassignment to *1 Citizen* of speeches given in F to *2 Cit.* is accepted in aid of 'apparent consistency of character', without direct comment on the fact that the F error, if indeed it is one, must presumably go back to copy. Again, at line 91 of the same scene, Theobald's easy and logical 'stale't' is preferred to F 'scale't', which a note characterizes as 'almost acceptable' (though without reference to the recent defence of F by W. F. Bolton[1]). Here the principle of *difficilior lectio* might be thought applicable. F readings of comparable difficulty are elsewhere retained, e.g. 'appear'd', IV, iii, 9; 'verified', V, ii, 17. Hilda Hulme's suggestion of 'ovator' for the major crux at I, x, 46 is here first adopted by an editor of *Coriolanus*, though the required sense of 'triumpher' or 'recipient of an ovation' is not attested before 1626, and a fresh adjustment of F is offered at IV, v, 165–6. At II, iii, 1, 'Once, if he do' is a fussy change of F's 'Once if he do' and may mistake the sense, viz., 'if once [= only] he do'. Established emendations which are accepted, but which may be due for reappraisal, are the omission of 'in peace' at III, i, 231 (where the removal of 'go' from F's 'go to' earlier in the line would be an easier solution) and Capell's 'hate' for 'haue' at IV, iv, 23, which gives the

[1] *English Language Notes*, X (1972), 110–11.

strong antithesis of 'hate' and 'love', but cannot wholly still a suspicion that copy 'leaue' is as likely to underlie F 'haue'.

Commentary on the language of *Coriolanus* is notoriously difficult and might become inordinately ponderous if it tried to catch all or even most of the play's pervasive ambiguity and irony. The reader of the New Arden notes will find help with most points of difficulty (though there are gaps, such as 'Spies', I, vi, 18). He will find less in them to alert him to ironic premonition or cross-reference, such as occurs in the earliest speeches in which Martius refers to Aufidius, at I, i, 232–4, where no hint is given of the ambiguity in the words 'to make/Only my wars with him', or at I, vii, 1–2, where the premonition of promise-breaking goes unnoted. If such critical comment be held inappropriate in a commentary which must select, still the apportioning of space may raise doubts. Thus, in I, iii, a seven-line note is given on the common exclamation 'la' (1.67), but none on 'verily' (1.91), which, on the evidence of *The Winter's Tale*, I, ii, 46–7, is equally characteristic of the social affectation of Valeria. Meanwhile, at line 81, 'labour' receives no comment, in spite of a context suggesting ambiguity (both trouble and child-bearing are involved). The note on lines 76–7 is confused by the misprint of 'Volumnia's' for 'Valeria's'. The edition is usefully completed by an Appendix, which reprints Plutarch's *Life of Coriolanus* from the 1579 edition of North's translation, with collation of some variants from the editions of 1595, 1603 and 1612, together with Camden's version of the fable of the belly and the members.

Pericles presents a uniquely difficult task for the editor of Shakespeare, but Philip Edwards approaches it from a position of strength, having previously made a major contribution to the study of the first Quarto of 1609. Accepting that the editor's task is the 'rather gloomy' one of 'trying to make the most of a poor text which he can never hope to bring back to its pristine condition', Edwards has carried to a more consistent and thoroughgoing point than his predecessors two policies which have increasingly recommended themselves. He treats the quarto text conservatively as his view of its memorial origins demands (short of printing nonsense), but he also makes full use of the evidence embedded in George Wilkins's *The Painful Adventures of Pericles, Prince of Tyre* (1608), which has some claim to be regarded as a second report of the play. The use of Wilkins includes both the importation of four short passages into the text, in square brackets, and some reference in the commentary to his version of passages which appear to be corrupt in Q. Nine new emendations are mainly attempts to improve on previous suggestions for the mending of major disruptions of sense or metre, or of less obvious corruption in the form of stilted or unidiomatic language. The most clearly persuasive are the reassignment of two speeches near the end of III, i to the First Sailor and the simplification of the opening stage direction of III, ii to read '*two Servants*' in place of the usual variations on Malone's '*and some Persons who have been shipwrecked*', which leave the single '*seruant*' of the Q direction with no visible function in the scene.

The tactfully edited text is preceded by an introduction which achieves a *tour de force* of critical tact. In it, Edwards conducts a full critical analysis of the play in relation to its medieval antecedents, its Renaissance analogues and its internal structures before even embarking on the vexed and inconclusive issue of its authorship and without such detailed dependence on the verbal texture as would be inconsistent with his view that the surviving text is a report of strikingly variable quality. The edition does much to extricate *Pericles* from its formidable thicket of scholarly dispute and to restore it to the student of Shakespeare in simple and apprehensible form and with many and useful aids to appreciation and understanding. These range from a map of what childhood memories of its Pauline equivalent prompt me to refer to as the missionary voyages of Pericles, to a full but pointed and relevant commentary.

Mention may still be made (though a few years overdue) of *The Macmillan Shakespeare*, a series for which some dozen of the most studied plays have been edited, with readable, informative and critically stimulating introductions and brief annotation (conveniently arranged to face the text page), by a strong team of editors including N. Alexander, E. A. J. Honigmann and P. Edwards. Although designed for school use, these volumes have much to offer to amateur performers, and to that paragon, the common reader – if he still exists – they hold out the fruits of Shakespearian scholarship with less than the usual proportion of rind and pips.[1]

No. 16 of the Clarendon Press *Shakespeare Quarto Facsimiles*, Q1 *Othello* (1622), reproduced from the copy in the Pierpont Morgan Library,[2] fills one of the larger gaps in the series. The editor, Charlton Hinman, has made a long study of the Quarto and his intimate knowledge of it is reflected in an unusually full account of the printing (which draws also on the work of Dr Millard Jones) and of the recorded copies (though this is not detailed enough to record the transposition of two leaves, C2 and C4, in the Garrick copy in the British Library). The demonstration that Q was set by formes and that the casting-off of copy may not have been done with great accuracy is likely to affect future studies of the relation between Quarto and Folio *Othello*. The facsimile itself, though perfectly useable and a great improvement on the Praetorius facsimile of 1885, is less pleasing to the eye than might be expected, given the stated 'excellent condition' of the Morgan copy. Not only has the format necessitated the removal of its large margins, reducing the $7\frac{5}{8} \times 5\frac{3}{4}''$ of the original to about $7 \times 4\frac{9}{16}''$, but variation in colour between pages is such as to suggest variable photographic results rather than discolouration in the original. In most pages the paper of Q comes out as a deeper grey than is usual in other facsimiles in the series and shinethrough is obtrusive in many places. Even in facsimiles of quartos, a case could perhaps be made for reproducing a composite copy, using clean pages representing chosen states of correction from several copies of the original. Hinman's own successful use of this technique for the Norton facsimile of the First Folio further recommends its use in the remaining volumes of *Shakespeare Quarto Facsimiles*. It is to be hoped that we shall not have to wait many more years for *The First Part of the Contention* (1594), Q1 *Romeo and Juliet* (1597), *2 Henry IV* (1600) and Q1 *A Midsummer Night's Dream* (1600).

1976 has been a lean year for printing analyses of Shakespeare, but while we await such promised studies as that of P. W. M. Blayney on the texts of *Lear*, the labours of the investigators of compositors in the First Folio continue to add periodic accretions and qualifications to the already large record. S. W. Reid[3] performs the useful, if retrospective, task of sorting out the spelling preferences of compositor B in the seven plays in which he worked from identified quarto copy. His work will help in the reassessment

[1] Macmillan Education Ltd., London and Basingstoke: *The Tempest*, ed. A. C. & J. E. Spearing; *Macbeth*, ed. D. R. Elloway (1971); *Twelfth Night*, ed. E. A. J. Honigmann (1972); *Hamlet*, ed. Nigel Alexander (1973); *Richard III*, ed. Richard Adams (1974); *King Lear*, ed. Philip Edwards (1975).

[2] Clarendon Press, Oxford, 1975.

[3] 'Some Spellings of Compositor B in the Shakespeare First Folio', *Studies in Bibliography*, 29 (1976), 102–38.

of B's role swingeingly initiated by A. C. Cairncross and progressing more cautiously in the work of T. H. Howard-Hill.[1] Reid's reference to the work of B in the 1619 'Pavier' quartos is more questionable. He shows no detailed awareness of the work of Blayney or of J. F. Andrews,[2] and weakens his general argument for spelling as evidence for B's presence by assuming that B alone set those quartos. The reprinting of two classic essays in Shakespearian bibliography, 'An Examination of the Method of Proof Correction in *King Lear* Q1 (1947)' and 'The Folio *Othello*: Compositor E (1959)' in Fredson Bowers's *Essays in Bibliography, Text, and Editing*[3] may provide the stimulus to further work in this strenuous field.

Middleton and Massinger do not properly belong in a review of Shakespearian textual studies, but David J. Lake's study of *The Canon of Thomas Middleton's Plays*[4] and the edition of Massinger's *Plays and Poems* by P. Edwards and C. Gibson[5] have some claim to passing mention. The edition of Massinger is the first English edition of a major dramatist for some decades to appear in its entirety and in a form which reasserts the needs of the whole reader against the regimen of a textual scholarship which has confined its efforts to the constitution of texts and to recording the history of their transmission. Not only has a relatively inaccessible author been given to us complete (in the works of his sole authorship), but a model of editing has been established which should encourage and inspire editors of Elizabethan plays for many generations to come. That a book on the canon of Middleton's plays should spread into Shakespeare studies is, at first sight, surprising. The disintegration of Shakespeare is a game that has lost much of its once heady attraction under the stern eyes of its critics, from Chambers to Schoenbaum. D. J. Lake starts *his* game in a different court and expresses his own surprise when his ball bounces into Shakespeare's works. If the mechanical and formidably accurate application of a wide range of linguistic tests (quantitatively assessed without reference either to variable literary intentions or to the mediating influence of compositors in a wide range of Elizabethan printing-houses) to a substantial number of English plays of the early seventeenth century can afford an adequate basis for the confident attribution of authorship, then we are to believe that Thomas Middleton's participation in *Timon of Athens* is proved and that he also wrote the pseudo-Shakespearian *A Yorkshire Tragedy*. If we can harbour doubts about a method of attribution which does not start from the indubitable evidence of the extant Middleton autograph manuscripts, which discounts the need to justify lines of type as an influence on printed linguistic forms and which builds up its list of 'Middleton' characteristics by drawing on the resources of each new play alleged to be his as if the attribution could safely be assumed as fact, then we may wish to continue to regard *Timon* as Shakespeare's (and *A Yorkshire Tragedy* as anonymous).

Disquiet about recent or current editorial assumptions and practices provides the linking theme for a number of disparate publications. H. J. Oliver's[6] disquiet is aroused by the new editorial freedom to emend encouraged by 'modern bibliography... for all its protestations about being scientific', and especially by a tendency he discerns among the biblio-

1 See *Compositors B and E in the Shakespeare First Folio*. Columbia, South Carolina, 1976 (privately circulated).

2 See P. W. M. Blayney, 'The Compositors of the Pavier Quartos', *Library*, XXXI (1976), 143–5.

3 ed. I. B. Cauthen. University Press of Virginia, Charlottesville, 1975.

4 Cambridge University Press, 1975.

5 Clarendon Press, Oxford, 1976. 5 vols.

6 *'Cur'd, and Perfect': The Problem of Shakespeare's Text*. Sydney University Press, Sydney, 1971.

graphers to rationalize an editorial preference with an allegedly objective argument from textual theory or printing analysis. From the opposite corner of the ring, and in more general terms, Fredson Bowers[1] expresses *his* disquiet about the steeply rising expense of scholarly editions and tells sad stories of the sins of printers. He also asserts the primacy of author over editor, but deduces the moral (wherein resides his opposition to Oliver) that the editor's responsibility to edit, in Greg's sense of taking 'the risks of backing his own judgement', is increased rather than diminished if his eye is on his author's glory (where it belongs) rather than his own. Disquiet about the state of Shakespeare editing is shared by Ulrich Suerbaum[2] and Jürgen Schäfer.[3] Praising the achievement of John Dover Wilson in the new *Cambridge Shakespeare*, Suerbaum remains uneasy in his realization that all modern editions are in some sense translations of Shakespeare (a notion that might be seen as applying in some degree to *all* modernizing reprints or editions since, and even including, that of 1623). He wishes that the impetus given to textual work by Dover Wilson showed more signs of being sustained today. Schäfer regrets our continued lack of a 'definitive' old-spelling Shakespeare and fears that the bibliographical studies once confidently aimed at the achievement of such an edition have instead led us into a new era of doubt. Concluding that a 'definitive' Shakespeare is an unattainable goal, he finds some comfort in the existence of facsimiles and concordances which have at least increased the availability to students of the materials for an edition.

The respective sources of disquiet which have prompted Sidney Thomas,[4] Eleanor Prosser,[5] and Michael L. Hays[6] to publish their views are specific. Thomas challenges the received opinion that the 'good' quartos were printed with the authorization of Shakespeare and his company. His motive is to impugn the authority of Q2 *Romeo and Juliet*, which he does to some effect by conjuring up the vision of 'a Shakespeare who turns his foul papers over to the printer without checking or correcting them in any way, and who then takes not the slightest interest in the printing of the book or the correction of the proofs – all this in pursuance of his aim to replace a bad text with a good text'. Where he goes too far is in wishing to deny the possibility that *any* of the 'good' quartos was authorized, at which point he merely seeks to replace one assailable general assumption with another. It must remain possible that the appearance of the 'good' quartos of 1600 bears some direct relation to the strain on the finances of the Chamberlain's Men imposed by the building of the Globe in the previous year. Eleanor Prosser challenges the claim of G. B. Evans to have provided, in the textual notes for the *Riverside Shakespeare*, the materials for study of Shakespeare's text 'in depth'. She illustrates the selective, and in some respects inconsistent, nature of the notes, while conceding that Evans made no secret of their selectivity. Hays lays rather heavy hands on the palaeographic evidence in support of the identification of Hand D in *Sir Thomas More* as Shakespeare. Quoting the forensic judgement of E. Huber (of the Royal Canadian Mounted Police) that the evidence wouldn't stick in a court of law,

[1] 'Scholarship and Editing', *Papers of the Bibliographical Society of America*, 70 (1976), 161–88.

[2] 'Der "Neue Shakespeare": John Dover Wilson und die moderne Textkritik', *Shakespeare Jahrbuch West* (1975), 62–92.

[3] *Die Krise der Shakespeare-Edition*. Ernst Vögel, München, 1975.

[4] 'The Myth of the Authorized Shakespeare Quartos', *Shakespeare Quarterly*, XXVII (1975), 186–92.

[5] 'The Riverside Textual Notes: A Word of Caution', *ibid.*, 193–9.

[6] 'Shakespeare's Hand in *Sir Thomas More*: Some Aspects of the Paleographic Argument', *Shakespeare Studies*, VIII (1975), 241–53.

he proceeds to remind us that the six Shakespeare signatures usually accepted as genuine afford an inadequate control and even to raise some question of their authenticity. The weakness of his own palaeographic qualifications is demonstrated by his wish to challenge Greg's discrimination between Hands D and C.

Another dissatisfied student of Shakespearian textual matters is Robert E. Burkhart, who has devoted a short book to the important and interesting subject of *Shakespeare's Bad Quartos*.[1] The first part of his contention is that the whole theory of 'memorial transmission' is a comedy of errors; his true tragedy is that he has distorted a healthy scepticism into a rigid alternative hypothesis which depends on a flat denial that the five quartos he chooses to consider transmit a seriously corrupt text. On his theory, the quartos of *Henry VI*, Parts 2 and 3 (1594–5), *Romeo and Juliet* (1597), *Henry V* (1600), *The Merry Wives of Windsor* (1602) and *Hamlet* (1603) all represent authentic abridgements made by and for Shakespeare's company of the time for use as provincial acting versions of the plays. In favour of this view, he proposes that all reduce the casting demands of the play (though the reduction from twenty-two roles to twenty in *Merry Wives* still requires a minimum cast of twelve, as in the Folio text) and that all omit the kind of elaborate or allusive passages which might prove caviare to the peasantry. Against it may be urged the facts that some of these editions contain matter not paralleled in the 'good' texts and therefore not to be explained in terms of abridgement (e.g. Q1 *Hamlet*, sc. xvi) and that all of them impressed scholars as deeply corrupt long before hypotheses to explain that corruption began to be developed. Burkhart omits to discuss either *Pericles* or *The Taming of A Shrew*, nor does he refer to such studies as D. L. Patrick's on the texts of *Richard III*, which includes a full account of 'memorial' features of Q1 of that play. This expedient allows him to avoid accounting for memorial conflation of passages from different plays, which is frequent in *A Shrew*. It further enables him to give the impression that the detection of memorial stigmata is the merest matter of subjective scholarly whim. He makes no attempt to explain by what process a scribe employed by Shakespeare's company, with a full manuscript of any of the five plays before him, could have produced, not only the few selected types of variation which he considers but the whole transmutation which has led to the categorization of these editions as 'bad'. Furthermore, in what purports to be a theoretical discussion, it is unsatisfactory to find no systematic reference to the twenty-odd non-Shakespearian 'bad quartos' so far identified. To cite Greg, as Burkhart does, in favour of the existence of provincial abridgements, on the strength of his analysis of *The Battle of Alcazar*, without also citing his parallel study of *Orlando Furioso* as evidence for the existence of memorial corruption, is simply disingenuous and merits instant delivery to the mercy of 'Tygers of *Arcadia*'. Was it Q1 *Hamlet*, 'as it hath beene diuerse times acted by his Highnesse seruants . . . in the two Vnuiersities of Cambridge and Oxford', that moved Gabriel Harvey to think the play worthy 'to please the wiser sort'? 'I there's the point'.

The 'bad quartos' are better served in the latest volumes of Marvin Spevack's monumental *Complete and Systematic Concordance to the Works of Shakespeare*.[2] Volume 7 is devoted to stage directions and speech prefixes from the plays already concorded in volumes 1 to 6; volume 8 concords the five hardcore 'bad quartos' and adds *A Shrew* (1594) and *The Troublesome Reign of King John* (1591) for full measure (volume 9, the last projected, is to contain the substantive variants for all the plays). The claims to system

[1] Mouton, The Hague, 1975.

[2] Georg Olms, Hildesheim: New York, 1975.

and completeness which in earlier volumes have been to some extent undermined by the choice of a single edited text as the basis for the concordance are fully justified by the new volumes, and the modern-spelling text is now equipped with exhaustive old-spelling apparatus. The stage directions are collated through the early editions, up to and including F1, and are then twice concorded, first play by play, then all together. Quite why these pieces of dramatic apparatus should be displayed and arranged on a scale so much ampler than that of the substantive readings of the early editions is not explained and the uses of volume 7, except to editors of the plays most often reprinted before 1623, are hard to imagine. Volume 8 is much more obviously useful and should facilitate further close analysis of the 'bad' texts in respect of their language and likely origins, one of the most urgent outstanding textual investigations of Shakespeare. The translation of old-spelling texts into computer-readable form involves the usual awkwardnesses, but one at least, the retention of 'vv' for 'w', could reasonably have been avoided as this spelling is of exclusively printing-house origin and is devoid of linguistic significance.

Jeanne Addison Roberts[1] provides a full and informative history of developing scholarly opinion about the Quarto and Folio texts of *The Merry Wives*, without ever quite indicating what purpose such a history is intended to serve and without getting as far as G. R. Hibbard's substantial contribution to it in his New Penguin edition of the play. Klaus Bartenschlager[2] illustrates the difficulties imposed on German translators of Shakespeare by his wordplay and makes practical suggestions for overcoming them by a combination of freedom of rendering and amplitude of commentary. G. W. Williams[3] finds the common noun 'hamlet' with an initial capital and anomalously italicized in Thomas Creede's 1595 quarto of *The Pedlar's Prophecy*, in the phrase 'O most vnhappie *Hamlet*', and most ingeniously conjectures that the phrase triggered a memory of the old *Hamlet* play in the mind of the compositor. That the whole phrase, rather than the single word 'hamlet', occurred both in *The Pedlar's Prophecy*, written about 1561, and in the ur-*Hamlet*, probably dating from the mid-1580s, seems neither demonstrable nor especially likely.

1 '*The Merry Wives* Q and F: The Vagaries of Progress', *Shakespeare Studies*, VIII (1975), 143–75.

2 'Shakespeares Wortspiele als Problem einer deutschen Shakespeare-Edition', *Shakespeare Jahrbuch West* (1975), 93–108.

3 'Another Line from the Ur-"Hamlet"?', *Notes and Queries*, XXI (1976), 157–8.

INDEX

INDEX

INDEX

INDEX